KW-222-324

The Future of Test-Based Educational Accountability

The Future of Test-Based Educational Accountability

Edited by Katherine E. Ryan and Lorrie A. Shepard

NEW YORK AND LONDON

First published 2008
by Routledge
270 Madison Ave, New York, NY 10016

Simultaneously published in the UK
by Routledge
2 Park Square, Milton Park, Abingdon, Oxon OX14 4RN

Routledge is an imprint of the Taylor & Francis Group, an informa business

Transferred to Digital Printing 2009

Typeset in Minion by Wearset Ltd, Boldon, Tyne and Wear

Library of Congress Cataloging in Publication Data
Ryan, Katherine E.
The future of test-based educational accountability/Katherine E. Ryan, Lorrie A. Shepard.
p. cm.
Includes bibliographical references.
1. Educational tests and measurements–United States. 2. Educational accountability–United States. I. Shepard, Lorrie A. II. Title.
LB3051.R98 2008
379.1'58–dc22
2007051799

ISBN10: 0-8058-6470-9 (hbk)
ISBN10: 0-203-89509-6 (ebk)

ISBN13: 978-0-8058-6470-0 (hbk)
ISBN13: 978-0-203-89509-2 (ebk)

Contents

Figures

Tables

Notes on Contributors

1. Robert L. Linn,
   Center for Research on Evaluation, Standards, and Student Testing (CRESST), Distinguished Professor Emeritus, University of Colorado at Boulder.

2. Lorrie A. Shepard, Dean and Professor,
   School of Education,
   University of Colorado at Boulder.

3. Lorraine M. McDonnell,
   Department of Political Science,
   University of California.

4. Daniel Koretz,
   Professor, Harvard Graduate School of Education.

5. Vonda L. Kiplinger, President,
   WindWalker Consulting.

6. Vonda L. Kiplinger, President,
   WindWalker Consulting.
   Laura S. Hamilton (co-author),
   Senior Behavioral Scientist,
   RAND Corporation.

7. Edward H. Haertel,
   Professor of Education, Stanford University.

8. Damian Betebenner,
   Center for Assessment,
   Dover, NH.

9. Derek C. Briggs,
   University of Colorado at Boulder.
   Edward W. Wiley (co-author),
   University of Colorado at Boulder.

10. Katherine E. Ryan,
University of Illinois,
Department of Educational Psychology.

11. Joan L. Herman,
Director,
CRESST/UCLA.

12. Bella Rosenberg,
Independent Consultant.

13. M. David Miller,
University of Florida.

14. Stephen B. Dunbar,
Iowa Testing Programs,
College of Education,
University of Iowa.

15. Eva L. Baker,
UCLA/CRESST.

16. Michael J. Feuer,
National Research Council, The National Academies.

Preface

The Future of Test-Based Educational Accountability began as a tribute to Distinguished Professor Robert Lee Linn upon the occasion of his nominal retirement. A group of his former students and colleagues convened to consider an appropriate project to memorialize the career contributions of this remarkable scholar. A Festschrift conference was planned, to be hosted by the National Center for Research on Evaluation, Standards, and Student Testing (CRESST) at UCLA in January 2007. Unlike most commemorative writings, however, this book is not a retrospective account of past accomplishments. Rather, it examines the most pressing current issues to be faced by policymakers and technical experts as they consider the future of testing systems designed to hold schools accountable for student achievement.

Robert Lee Linn

Professor Linn is the single most eminent scholar in the field of educational measurement today. He has published more than 200 scholarly articles on technical and applied topics, but more significantly he has consistently brought his deep statistical and psychometric knowledge to bear in addressing knotty practical problems. His earliest work with Charles Werts and Karl Joreskog led to a Social Science Research Council project that brought together ideas from sociology, statistics, econometrics, and psychology, and in time made "structural equation modeling" a basic research method. He was similarly a pioneer in questioning common uses of analysis of covariance when comparing effects of educational programs.

Throughout his career, Professor Linn has made significant contributions to validity theory and has conducted numerous empirical investigations evaluating specific testing applications such as the use of standardized tests in national Title I evaluations, curricular validity of minimum competency tests, licensure examinations, college admissions tests, computer-administered tests, and performance assessments. He is also well known for a long line of work contributing to an understanding of test bias. His copious and often sophisticated technical work is connected with his public service in extraordinarily effective ways because he always tackles burning public issues faced by the field, including test bias, the validity of performance assessments, confusion about standards, and implications of the federal concept of adequate yearly progress (AYP).

Professor Linn's service to the profession includes the presidency of the American Educational Research Association, chair of the 1985 revision of the

Test Standards, co-chair of the National Academy of Education panel investigating the validity of the state-by-state National Assessment of Educational Progress (NAEP), and for two decades a member of nearly every National Academy of Sciences panel addressing issues of testing and assessment. Because of his expertise in both assessment policy and psychometrics, Robert Linn has consulted and communicated with state and national legislators and served on myriad state and national advisory committees. Moreover, his ideas are widely circulated in the national press. His advice is sought because of his expert knowledge but more importantly because of his integrity and wisdom.

Overview of the Book

In recent decades, testing has become a visible and high-stakes accountability mechanism. No longer a passive and neutral data-gathering activity, test-based accountability is seen as a powerful policy lever that can be used to drive school improvement. "The No Child Left Behind Act" (NCLB) of 2001 further intensified both the extent and impacts of testing. Although the impending reauthorization of NCLB will surely bring much needed improvements to the law, it is unlikely that core elements—mandated achievement testing and sanctions attached to test results—will be removed.

The purpose of this book is to identify and analyze the key issues associated with test-based educational accountability independent of the particular provisions of NCLB. We take up issues such as validity, test equating, growth modeling, fairness, causal inferences, and misuses of accountability data at the level at which they need to be understood by policymakers. Too often, legislation laying out the features of assessment systems is drafted and enacted presuming that the methodological details will be worked out later. Increasingly, however, methodological topics such as the glaring discrepancies between state standards and standards on the National Assessment of Educational Progress have become quite visible to policymakers. State lawmakers decide that measuring growth instead of status will solve the fairness problem of students starting school with widely different abilities. But what new problems arise when gain scores become the accountability metric?

The volume is written in non-technical language, intended for an audience of legislative aides conceptualizing policy or journalists following an educational assessment story. Other key audiences are state department of education assessment staff, test publishers and assessment contractors, and advanced graduate students in both educational policy and statistics and measurement. The book is organized into four sections.

Part I, "The context of educational accountability," begins with an overview chapter authored by Robert L. Linn. To set the stage for the rest of the volume, the Linn chapter frames several issues: the meaning of content and performance standards, rules for evaluating growth in achievement, the validity of causal inferences and problems of test score inflation, and suggestions for a more cautious descriptive use of accountability results. Lorrie A. Shepard provides a history of testing and accountability, dating from the time of the first Title I legislation in the 1960s; and Lorraine M. McDonnell uses political science theory to explain why test-based accountability is likely to remain the dominant policy paradigm.

Part II, "Educational accountability: technical and substantive issues," includes various technical topics typically found in measurement textbooks. However, each of these chapters is focused on how these issues play out in the context of large-scale assessment systems with the onus of supporting high-stakes decisions. In his chapter on the development of an accountability-oriented science of measurement, Daniel Koretz explains how both test design and test validation must take account of testing effects. In Chapter 5, Vonda L. Kiplinger describes the meaning of reliability or consistency of school-level results used to make judgments about schools and to hold schools accountable. Next, Kiplinger and Laura S. Hamilton consider critical issues of equating and linking including: equating of tests from year to year to ensure comparability, vertical scaling of tests across grades for purposes of measuring growth, and linking to NAEP as a way to provide common metrics.

In Chapter 7, Edward H. Haertel examines standard setting, the process by which performance standards, such as "proficient," are set on tests to determine if students are reaching a desired level of achievement. In his chapter, Damian W. Betebenner proposes a normative way of evaluating the adequacy of student growth comparable to pediatricians' growth charts for height and weight. Derek C. Briggs and Edward W. Wiley focus their chapter on the adequacy of statistical controls and value-added models for determining the effect of teachers and schools on student growth. In Chapter 10, Katherine E. Ryan summarizes the research literature on test bias but then specifically addresses the claims and counter-claims concerning the use of tests to ensure educational equity.

Part III, "Educational accountability effects," focuses on the more practical aspects of test development and the use of test data for school improvement as well as the resulting impacts of test-based accountability on teachers and students. In Chapter 11, Joan L. Herman reviews the extensive literature on the effects of accountability and offers a model for considering whether accountability serves the public interest. In Chapter 12, Bella Rosenberg speaks from her experience with the American Federation of Teachers about the initial promises of the standards movement and why current accountability policies can be seen as a betrayal of that vision. In his chapter, M. David Miller explains the limitations of trying to use one test for both school accountability and individual student diagnosis. In Chapter 14, Stephen B. Dunbar recounts, from the perspective of a test developer, the demands that constrain test development and considers what enhancements for accountability assessments might be feasible.

Part IV, "Future directions for educational accountability," comprises two forward-looking, theoretically based arguments for reconsidering both the design of assessments and of accountability systems. In Chapter 15, Eva L. Baker examines the ways that learning research can be brought into the development of assessments and provides examples of what she calls model-based assessment design. In the concluding chapter, Michael J. Feuer uses theory and examples from political economy to consider how reasonably good accountability policies could be developed to address consciously and manage "externalities," i.e., the unintended consequences of accountability testing.

We thank Andrea Solarz for her knowledgeable and thoughtful assistance with the editing process, and especially we wish to express our heartfelt gratitude to the authors of this volume—who have themselves contributed so much to educational measurement and policy. Concerns about the negative impacts of accountability tests recur throughout the book, but none of the authors imagines that accountability testing is likely to disappear. We expect that greater knowledge can lead to better policies, making it more likely that intended benefits from accountability will occur and that obviously foreseeable negative consequences will be forestalled. In this we are following Bob Linn's example, warning of the pitfalls in using fallible measures to make significant decisions, but always working to make existing systems more sensible.

Lorrie A. Shepard
Katherine E. Ryan

Part I
The Context of Educational Accountability

1
Educational Accountability Systems

Robert L. Linn

When President Bush made accountability the centerpiece of the education agenda announced at his January 23, 2001, press conference (White House, 2001), he reinforced what was already a central theme of state policies aimed at improving education. Many of the accountability features of President Bush's education agenda were incorporated into the "No Child Left Behind Act" of 2001 (NCLB) that President Bush signed into law on January 8, 2002. The law was enacted with strong bipartisan support in both houses of Congress.

NCLB amends the Elementary and Secondary Education Act of 1965 and provides significant financial support to schools and districts serving students from low-income families. NCLB's testing and accountability provisions are consistent with the broad outline provided in President Bush's January 23, 2001, press conference, including the requirement that students be tested every year in reading and mathematics in grades 3 through 8 (White House, 2001).

The NCLB accountability system, like accountability systems that were put in place by a substantial number of states in the 1990s, reflects the beliefs of politicians, policymakers, and the business community that educational achievement was inadequate and unequal and that educational reforms were needed (McDonnell, 2005). But, as Rouse (2005) has noted, many policymakers also believe "that traditional forms of school improvement, such as class-size reduction and professional development, are expensive and ineffective" (p. 275; see also McDonnell, 2004, pp. 9–10). And, they believe that a lack of school accountability has contributed to the poor performance of schools. Hence, they have turned to test-based school accountability as a major component of educational reform, reasoning that sanctions and rewards to schools will prod teachers and school administrators to be more effective (McDonnell, 2005; Rouse, 2005). President Bush's call for frequent testing of students in reading and mathematics is consistent with this set of beliefs, but that position did not originate with President Bush nor with the enactment of NCLB.

Rationales for Testing

There is nothing novel about the idea of using student achievement test results as a major component of an educational accountability system. As recently documented by Haertel and Herman (2005), a large number of accountability testing programs have been introduced over the past century. The uses of test results and rationales for testing have varied, but there are several common and recurring themes. Among other things, tests have been expected to:

- help clarify expectations for teaching and learning;
- monitor educational progress of schools and students;
- monitor the progress of demographic subgroups of students and the gaps in achievement of those subgroups;
- encourage the closing of the gaps in the performance among racial/ethnic subgroups and between economically disadvantaged students and their more affluent peers;
- motivate greater effort on the part of students, teachers, and school administrators;
- contribute to the evaluation of educational programs and schools;
- identify schools and programs that need to be improved; and,
- provide a basis for the distribution of rewards and sanctions to schools and students.

Tests are used as policy tools to hold teachers and school administrators accountable for student learning and as levers to change instruction in the classroom. As McDonnell (2004) has noted, "elected officials and policymakers have few tools at their disposal [to change classroom instruction]. Standardized tests are one of the most effective levers they have for influencing what happens in local schools and classrooms" (p. 9).

Assessment of Student Achievement

Achievement tests have been at the center of outcome-based accountability systems of school districts, states, and the federal government since the 1970s. However, the nature of achievement tests and the uses that are made of test results have undergone several changes over the years. There have been periods when multiple-choice, norm-referenced achievement tests dominated the educational testing and accountability scene. Basic skills were stressed during the minimum competency testing period of the late 1970s and early 1980s (Hamilton, 2003; Linn, 2000). And, worries that an exclusive emphasis on basic skills could make the minimum become the maximum led to calls for giving greater attention to more complex comprehension and problem-solving skills. The publication of *A Nation at Risk* (National Commission on Excellence in Education, 1983) is particularly notable in this regard.

A Nation at Risk marked the beginning of a turning point in educational testing and accountability. It planted the seeds for the standards and performance assessment movements (Haertel & Herman, 2005). The use of performance assessments, which required students to write extended responses and solve real-world mathematics problems and defend their solutions, was introduced in the late 1980s and early 1990s. Performance assessments stressed depth of understanding and complex problem-solving skills and were expected to have a major impact on education by providing models for teaching and learning.

Although there was a widely held belief in the early 1990s that the use of performance assessments would have instructional advantages over more traditional multiple-choice and short-answer test items, the heavy use of performance assessments faded fairly rapidly due to technical quality issues such as reliability and cost. The standards movement spawned by *A Nation at Risk*—and originally closely associated with performance-based assessments—continued, however, playing an increasingly central role in testing and accountability.

The standards movement of the 1990s was championed at the federal level by the Clinton administration's education initiative articulated in the "Goals 2000: Educate America Act." Content standards, student performance standards, and standards-based assessments were key ideas in this initiative. The standards-based approach to assessment and accountability was reinforced by the requirements for Title I evaluations mandated in the 1994 reauthorization of the Elementary and Secondary Education Act (ESEA), entitled the "Improving America's Schools Act" of 1994 (the predecessor to NCLB). Because of this earlier push for standards, a majority of the states had adopted or were working toward a standards-based approach prior to the enactment of NCLB. Although only nine states were reported to have standards-based tests in both reading/English language arts and mathematics at grades 3 through 8 in 2002 (Olson, 2002), most states had adopted content standards in those subjects and had tests that were arguably aligned with those standards at some grade levels.

Content and Performance Standards

By the 2004–2005 school year, every state except Iowa had adopted content standards in core subjects (*Education Week*, 2005, p. 86). With few exceptions, the core subjects for which content standards had been adopted included mathematics and reading or English language arts as required by NCLB. Forty-four states reported that they had developed tests that were customized to be aligned with their content standards and an additional five states reported that they had augmented or hybrid tests that were aligned with their content standards (*Education Week*, 2005). The adequacy of the alignment can, of course, be questioned; evaluation of the alignment of tests with content standards is discussed in the following section.

NCLB requires states to adopt "challenging academic content standards." Those standards are supposed to "specify what children are expected to know and be able to do; contain coherent and rigorous content; [and] encourage the teaching of advanced skills" (NCLB, 2001, part A, subpart 1, Sec. 1111, a [D]). The required academic content standards are expected to provide the basis for developing challenging assessments that are well aligned with the content standards. They also are expected to provide the framework for specifying "challenging student academic achievement standards" that are set at a minimum of three levels—usually called "advanced," "proficient," and "basic"—and divide the students into four categories: advanced, proficient, basic, and below basic. NCLB requires that the same set of student academic achievement standards be applied to all students.

Student academic achievement standards are more commonly referred to as performance standards. Although performance standards are dependent upon academic content standards, the two types of standards are distinct. The content standards specify the substantive "what" that should be learned, while performance standards specify "how much"; that is, the level of achievement that is expected of students. According to NCLB, students must demonstrate high levels of achievement to meet the proficient or advanced performance standard. In addition, all students are expected to perform at or above this high level of proficiency by 2013–2014.

Performance standards were identified in "Goals 2000" as an alternative way of reporting test results, and became popular as a way of reporting prior to the enactment of NCLB (Hamilton, 2003). Reporting percentages of students meeting or exceeding performance standards was seen as preferable to reporting mean scores or normative information because standards were supposed to specify a level of performance that was judged to be good enough or exemplary without referring to the performance of other students.

Performance standards have at least five critical characteristics. First, they are intended to be absolute rather than normative; that is, they are supposed to establish a fixed criterion of performance. Second, they are supposed to be challenging; that is, to be set to correspond to high levels of achievement. Third, a relatively small number of levels (e.g., advanced, proficient, and basic) are typically identified. Fourth, they are expected to apply to *all*, or essentially all, students rather than a selected subset such as college-bound students seeking advanced placement. Finally, they depend on judgments made by standard setters who review statements about expected levels of achievement and translate those statements into cut scores on assessments (Linn, 2005b).

It is easy enough to talk about basic, proficient, and advanced levels of performance in terms of the knowledge and skills specified in the content standards. Performance levels must be mapped onto scores on an assessment to have meaning, however, in terms of actual student achievement. Mapping performance levels onto an assessment has a great deal of uncertainty associated with it. Where the standards are set depends on characteristics of the judges who set the standards and on the method used to set the standards (Linn, 2003). The stringency of the standards also depends on the context in which the standards are set. States that set standards before NCLB, when there were no stakes attached to falling below the proficient cut, often set the standards at quite ambitious levels. The judges setting standards in states since NCLB became law, on the other hand, were aware of the consequences of students failing to reach the proficient level and generally set more lenient standards.

Currently, the variability in the stringency of the state standards defining proficient performance is so great that the concept of proficient achievement lacks meaning (Linn, 2003). Although state National Assessment of Educational Progress (NAEP) results do not perfectly track results on the assessments used by different states, NAEP does provide a reasonable benchmark for comparing the standards set by different states. Olson (2005) reported the percentages of students who were at the proficient level or above on the 2005 state grade 8 mathematics assessments for 33 states that administered mathematics assessments at that grade and for which results were available in time for her report. She also listed the percentage of students who scored at the proficient level or above on the 2005 grade 8 NAEP mathematics assessment for those same states. A plot of the differences in the percentages of students who were proficient or above on the state assessments, minus the corresponding percentages on the NAEP assessment, is displayed in Figure 1.1. The mean difference in percentage was 33%; that is, 33% more students scored at the proficient level or above according to the state assessment than did so according to NAEP. The difference ranged from 10% *fewer* students in Missouri being scored at the proficient level to 66% *more* students in Tennessee being scored as proficient, suggesting that the Missouri proficient standard is somewhat more stringent than the NAEP standard and that the Tennessee standard is much more lenient than NAEP.

The relationship between the percentages of students who were proficient or above in 2005 according to the state grade 8 mathematics assessments and the corresponding NAEP assessment is illustrated by the scatterplot shown in Figure 1.2. As can be seen, the relationship between the percentage of students who are proficient or above according to state assessments and NAEP is relatively weak ($r = 0.34$). It is also apparent that the variability in percentages is much greater on the state assessments (standard deviation = 18.4) than on NAEP (standard deviation = 6.7).

Alignment of Assessments with Content Standards

Academic content standards are supposed to specify what teachers should teach and students should learn. To accomplish these ends, the "[s]tandards must be specific enough to enable everyone (students, parents, educators,

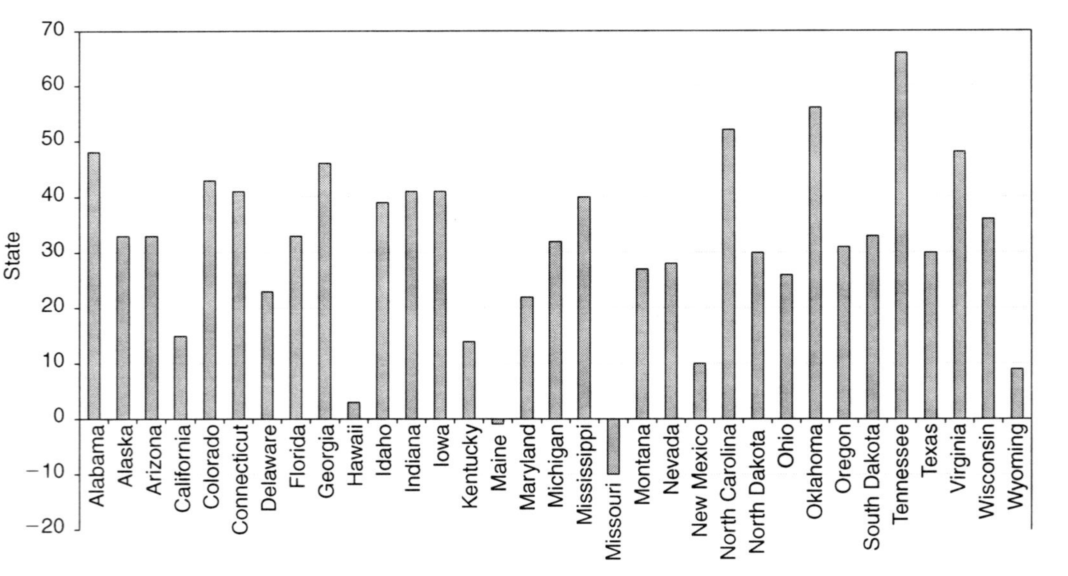

Figure 1.1 Differences Between Percentage of Students Proficient or Above on State Grade 8, and Grade 8 NAEP Mathematics Assessments (33 states) (source: Olson, 2005).

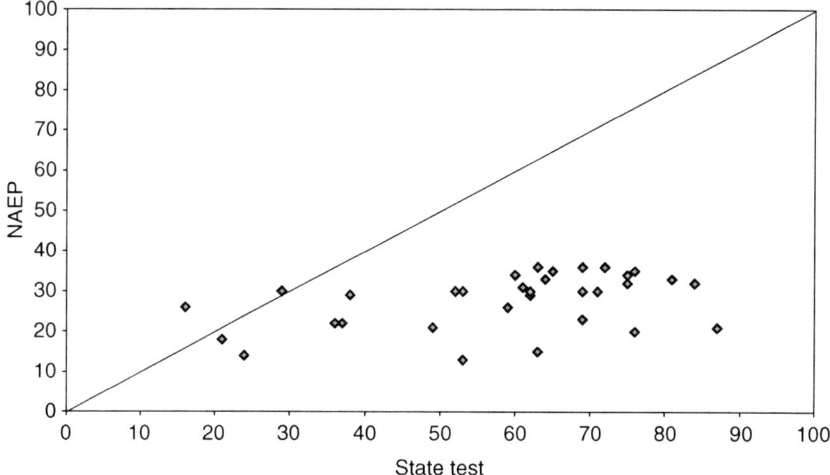

Figure 1.2 Scatterplot of Percent Proficient or Above on Grade 8 State Mathematics Assessments and Grade 8 NAEP in 2005 (33 states) (r=0.34) (source: Olson, 2005).

policymakers, the public) to understand what students need to learn" (Linn & Herman, 1997, p. 1). Specificity is also required if the academic content standards are to serve as the basis for developing the specifications for assessments. Alignment of assessments with the content standards is critically important. Although the content standards are supposed to provide the targets for instruction, in practice, it is often the assessments that drive instruction. Thus, at the very least, assessments should reinforce the content standards, rather than divert attention away from them, and that requires a high degree of alignment.

Alignment has received considerable attention in the last few years, in part because alignment of assessments and content standards is considered critical to the development of an effective standards-based accountability system, and in part because NCLB requires states to provide evidence that their assessments are aligned with their academic content standards. Several different methods have been developed for evaluating alignment. Bhola, Impara, and Buckendahl (2003) have reviewed several of the more widely used methods. Although the methods vary in complexity and specific details, the more widely used methods (e.g., Porter, 2002; Webb, 1999) evaluate the match of the test's content to the standard, the match of the test to the range of knowledge and skills specified in the standards, whether there is a match in the balance of coverage, the match of the test to the level of cognitive demand called for in the standards, and whether the test includes material not found in the standards.

According to the NCLB peer review guidance (U.S. Department of Education, 2004), ensuring alignment involves considering whether the assessments:

> Cover the full range of content specified in the State's academic content standards, meaning that all the standards are represented legitimately in the assessments; *and*
>
> Measure both the content (what students know) and the process (what students can do) aspects of the academic content standards; *and*
>
> Reflect the same degree and pattern of emphasis apparent in the academic content standards (e.g., if academic content standards place a lot of emphasis on operations then so should the assessments); *and*
>
> Reflect the full range of cognitive complexity and level of difficulty of the concepts and processes described, and depth represented, in the State's academic content standards; *and*
>
> Yield results that represent all achievement levels specified in the State's academic achievement standards.
>
> (p. 41, emphasis in original)

The peer review guidance clearly sets the bar at a high level with regard to the evidence that states need to provide to support the claim that their assessments are aligned with their academic content and achievement standards.

Test-Based Accountability Systems

Standards and tests may be the core of an accountability system, but accountability systems also require rules for the use of test results and usually specify a set of conditions for sanctions and, in some cases, rewards. There are two major approaches to the use of test results in accountability systems. The first is to compare test results at a given point in time to performance targets. Schools that meet or exceed the targets are considered to be successful, while schools where the test results fall short of the target are considered to be unsuccessful and may be subject to sanctions. This approach is sometimes referred to as a current-status model. It has also has been called a school-mean performance approach (Raudenbush, 2004a). The NCLB accountability system uses this current-status approach. Schools meet adequate yearly progress (AYP) requirements if the percentage of students for the school as a whole and for each of several subgroups meet or exceed the annual performance targets in both reading/English language arts and mathematics.[1]

The second general approach to using test results in accountability systems is to evaluate growth in achievement. In the simplest form, the performance of successive cohorts of students in a school (e.g., fifth grade students in the current year versus fifth graders the previous year) is compared. Kentucky's accountability system and California's Academic Performance Index (API) are examples of the successive-cohorts approach to measuring improvement in student achievement. A more sophisticated approach uses growth in achievement of individual students from one year to the next. Growth models based on tracking score changes of individual students are much more demanding than the successive-cohort approach to measuring improvement because they require the longitudinal tracking of individual students from year to year. Florida and Tennessee are examples of states that use this longitudinal-tracking approach.

The matched longitudinal analysis of growth has substantial conceptual and practical advantages over the estimation of gains based on successive cohorts of students. There is a great deal of uncertainty associated with the observed differences in scores of successive cohorts of students due to sampling error (Hill & DePascale, 2003; Linn & Haug, 2002; Linn, Baker, & Betebenner, 2002; Zvoch & Stevens, 2006). In addition, interpretating results from the successive-cohorts approach requires an assumption that the students attending the school are comparable from year to year in terms of background characteristics and prior learning. Changes in the composition of the student body due to student mobility call into question the basic assumption of comparability of the successive cohorts of students (Rouse, 2005). A growth-model approach based on longitudinal tracking of individual students does not require the assumption that cohorts are comparable, but mobility can still cause problems if it leads to students being omitted from the accountability system (Rouse, 2005).

At a rhetorical level, the current-status approach is appealing because it sets the same performance expectations for all students and schools regardless of where students start. Thus, it avoids the pitfall of having higher standards for some students (e.g., affluent white students) than other students (e.g., poor minority students). On the other hand, current-status approaches, such as that used to determine AYP, "pose the greatest challenges to high-poverty schools, which enroll a large percentage of students who have traditionally scored poorly on standardized achievement tests" (Kim & Sunderman, 2005, p. 4). As Kim and Sunderman go on to note, high-poverty schools also enroll a disproportionate number of African American or Latino students. Not surprisingly, they found that in each of the six states they studied, schools that according to NCLB were in need of improvement on average had larger percentages of African American or Latino students and smaller percentages of Asian American or white students than schools that made AYP (Kim & Sunderman, Table 1). Such differential impact on schools with larger numbers of African American and Latino students is consistent with the policy goal of closing the achievement gap, but still may be considered unfair to those schools where gains in achievement are being made, albeit not fast enough to meet the fixed performance targets for a given year.

A system based on growth in performance attends to student learning and thereby may be seen as fairer to students and schools because it takes into account previous performance. However, some advocates for poor and minority children worry that a growth model will result in lower expectations for "the nation's most disadvantaged young people" (Olson & Hoff, 2005, p. 16). By taking into account poor past achievement, such systems necessarily set lower current achievement targets for those students.

Because both current-status and growth-model approaches have distinct strengths and weaknesses, it is not surprising that several state accountability systems (e.g., Florida, Kentucky, Massachusetts) rely on a combination of status and growth to distinguish schools that are identified as successful from those that are considered to be less successful.

The current-status and growth approaches, whether using successive cohorts of students or longitudinal tracking of students to compute gains, yield different, often conflicting, results (Linn, 2005a; Raudenbush, 2004b; Zvoch & Stevens, 2006). A school that meets the targets of a current-status accountability system may not show the gains required to be considered successful under a growth-model accountability system and vice versa. Hence, schools in states with either a successive-cohorts improvement or a longitudinal-growth-model approach to school accountability may receive mixed messages from the state accountability system and NCLB (Linn, 2005a). A school may be considered to be successful or effective according to one accountability system but unsuccessful or in need of improvement by another system. Mixed messages of this kind are confusing to educators, parents, and the general public.

In response to interest expressed by several states in being able to use a growth-model approach for purposes of NCLB, the U.S. Department of Education convened groups of experts in the summer of 2005 to consider ways growth models might be used to calculate AYP. On November 21, 2005, Education Secretary Spellings announced a pilot program to allow states to submit proposals to use a growth model to make AYP determinations. In her letter to Chief State School Officers, Secretary Spellings listed seven "core principles" that a growth model must meet in order to be approved. The first core principle specifies that the growth model "must ensure that all students are proficient by 2013–2014 and set annual goals to ensure that the achievement gap is closing for all groups of students" (Spellings, 2005). Thus, the NCLB fixed achievement target of 100% proficient or above in 2013–2014 is maintained. Other core principles include the requirement of setting "high expectations for low achieving students, while not setting [them on] student demographic or school characteristics" and the requirement to make separate accountability decisions for reading/language arts and mathematics (Spellings, 2005).

It remains to be seen how many states will submit successful proposals to participate in the growth-model pilot program, which allows a maximum of ten states. The pilot program option, however, opens the door for states with longitudinal tracking systems to propose models that may make their state accountability systems more compatible with the NCLB system. On the other hand, the pilot program does not provide a similar option for states using a successive-cohorts approach to measuring improvement. Although as is discussed below, one of the enclosures to Secretary Spellings' letter describes index systems, currently approved for use in nine states, for calculating AYP that it might be argued could be used to track improvement in achievement for successive cohorts of students.

Illustrative Features of Accountability Systems

Compensatory and Multiple-Hurdle Approaches

The distinctions among accountability systems that focus on current status, those that focus on growth, and those that use some combination of current status and growth are central considerations in determining what is valued in a given system. There are several other features, however, that are also important in distinguishing accountability systems. Some systems allow for high performance in one subject area to compensate for lower performance in another area, while others treat each subject as a separate hurdle. The Kentucky accountability system, which has been in use for over a decade, uses the compensatory approach. An academic index is calculated based on test results at selected grades in seven content areas (reading, writing, mathematics, science, social studies, arts and humanities, and practical living/vocational studies) (http://www.kde.state.ky.us/). High student achievement in mathematics, for example, can compensate for somewhat lower performance in reading, or vice versa in the school's overall academic index score. California's API also uses a compensatory approach to combine student achievement on tests in different subjects.

NCLB, on the other hand, uses a multiple-hurdle approach. Students must meet targets in both mathematics and reading/English language arts in order for the school to meet its AYP requirements. The school must also have at least 95% of the eligible students included in each assessment and must meet another academic indicator defined by the state. Thus, even if there are no subgroups of students in the school with a sufficient number of students for disaggregated reporting, the school must clear all five hurdles to make AYP.

Although, as is discussed below, the U.S. Department of Education has shown a willingness to be flexible regarding some aspects of AYP calculations, the multiple-hurdle approach is not one of those areas of flexibility. Indeed, in the announcement of the growth-model pilot program, the Department explicitly indicated that states using assessments in other content areas in their model "should demonstrate that achievement on those other assessments does not compensate for low achievement in reading/language arts and mathematics" (Spellings, 2005). Nor can high achievement in reading compensate for lower achievement in mathematics.

Disaggregation

Systems differ in requirements for disaggregated reporting of results for subgroups of students and what the requirements are for subgroup performance on tests. California's API is a weighted combination of performance on tests in different content areas that is scaled to have a range of scores from 200 to 1,000. The statewide API target has been established as 800. California sets a schoolwide growth target for a school that is equal to 5% of the difference between the schools API in the base year and the statewide target of 800. For example, a school with a base year API of 700 would have a growth target of five points (5% of 800 minus 700), while a school with a base year API of 600 would have a growth target of ten points. In addition to calculations of growth for the school as a whole, a school must show "comparable improvement" for numerically significant ethnic and economically disadvantaged subgroups of students. "Comparable improvement" is defined as 80% of the schoolwide annual growth target (California Department of Education, 2005).

The NCLB requires that reporting be disaggregated for economically disadvantaged students from major racial and ethnic groups, students with disabilities, and students with limited English proficiency. Each subgroup with a sufficient number of students is used to define additional hurdles for making AYP using the same rules as are used for all students in a school.

For large schools with diverse student bodies, the disaggregated reporting requirements can greatly increase the number of hurdles a school must clear to make AYP. A school with a large enough number of students in, say, three racial/ethnic groups, students with limited English proficiency, economically disadvantaged students, and students with disabilities, would have a total of 29 hurdles to clear, four for each of the six subgroups plus the five that all schools have for the total student body.

Disaggregated reporting is essential for monitoring the degree to which achievement gaps are closing. It is clear, however, that when combined with NCLB's multiple-hurdles approach, disaggregation rules make it considerably more difficult for large schools with diverse student bodies to meet AYP requirements than it is for schools with homogeneous student bodies (Kim & Sunderman, 2005; Linn, 2005a). As was previously noted, however, the greater challenge for schools with diverse student bodies is consistent with the policy goal of NCLB; that is, to close the gaps in achievement among racial/ethnic groups and between economically disadvantaged students and students coming from more affluent backgrounds.

The Department of Education has allowed states to introduce a number of refinements in their AYP determinations that mitigate to some extent the difficulties caused for schools with multiple subgroups of students (Center on Education Policy, 2005). Several of the allowed changes that make it easier for schools to meet AYP requirements help schools that have multiple subgroups. For example, more states are now using confidence intervals, not only for comparing results to annual targets, but in safe harbor determinations. Confidence intervals lower the effective percent proficient target and the stringency of the safe harbor requirement, particularly for smaller subgroups, thereby making it easier for a school to make AYP (CEP, 2005; Porter, Linn, & Trimble, 2005).

Some states have been allowed to use performance indexes (see below) that give partial credit to students scoring below the proficient level. Retesting students with an alternate version of the test is also allowed in some instances, which permits use of a student's best scores. Finally, the minimum subgroup sizes have been increased, which means that fewer subgroups have to meet AYP targets (CEP, 2005; Porter et al., 2005). Each of these changes makes it somewhat easier to meet AYP requirements.

Performance Indexes

Focusing only on the percentage of students who score at the proficient level or above has several potential shortcomings. For example, it does not give credit for moving students from the lowest performance levels to higher levels of achievement that fall short of the minimum score required to be categorized as proficient. It has sometimes been suggested that this encourages teachers to focus their attention on "bubble students," who are performing near the proficient level, at the expense both of more needy students (who are performing so far below the proficient cut that there is little hope of raising their achievement enough to surpass the proficient cut score) and high achieving students (for whom there is little doubt that they will score at the proficient level or above). By giving partial credit to students who are performing below the proficient cut point, index scores avoid the disadvantages of only giving credit for students who are proficient or above.

Nine states (Massachusetts, Minnesota, Mississippi, New Mexico, New York, Oklahoma, Pennsylvania, South Carolina, and Vermont) have been approved to use index score in their AYP determinations (Spellings, 2005). For example, Massachusetts defines six levels of performance, with index scores being computed by awarding different numbers of points for students scoring at each level: advanced (100 points), proficient (100 points), needs improvement—high (75 points), needs improvement—low (50 points), warning/failing—high (25 points), and warning/failing—low (zero points) (http://www.doe.mass.edu).

In the baseline year, generally 2002, there was no advantage for Massachusetts to use index scores rather than percentage of students at the proficient level or above; this is because the latter is used to define the starting level and the 2013–2014 target of 100% proficiency, which are then translated into the index score scale. In subsequent years, however, index scores may show increases where the percent proficient or above remains unchanged. This difference is illustrated for a hypothetical school in Table 1.1 using the Massachusetts index score system. As can be seen in Table 1.1, the number and the percentage (because the total number of students is unchanged) of students who are at the proficient level or above is the same in 2006 and 2007. Therefore, without an index score the school's rating in terms of percent proficient or above would be the same in 2007 as it was in 2006. Because more students score in the higher achievement levels below the proficient cut in 2007 than in 2006, however, the index score shows a substantial improvement in 2007. This school clearly would benefit from the gains made in the percentage of students in the three higher categories below the proficient cut and would not be penalized for failing to increase the number of students in the proficient or advanced categories of performance.

Validity of Inferences from Accountability Systems

The simple claim that school A has met its AYP target requires only a modest inference that can be fairly easily validated. If the proportion of students in school A who perform at the proficient level or above exceeds the performance targets in both reading/English language arts and mathematics for the school as a whole and for each relevant subgroup of students, and the school has met other requirements such as assessing at least 95% of the eligible students in each subgroup, then the validity of the AYP claim is supported. To complete the validity argument (Kane, 2006), one would need to provide evidence that the tests are measuring what they are supposed to measure—that they are adequately aligned with the content standards, for example. In addition, assurance would be needed that the tests were appropriately administered and that scores were not inflated due to cheating. Overall, however, validation of the claim is rather straightforward.

Table 1.1 Illustration of MA Index Scores for a Hypothetical School in 2006 and 2007

Performance level	*Points*	*N: 2006*	*N: 2007*	*2006 index points*	*2007 index points*
Prof. or adv.	100	50	50	5,000	5,000
NI—high	75	75	100	5,625	7,500
NI—low	50	100	125	5,000	6,250
W/F—high	25	100	125	2,500	3,125
W/F—low	0	75	50	0	0
Total		400	400	18,125	21,875

Notes
Prof. = proficient, Adv. = Advanced, NI = needs improvement, W/F = warning/failing, N = number of students.
2006 index score = 18,125/400 = 45.31.
2007 index score = 21,875/400 = 54.69.

Causal Interpretations

Now consider the claim that school A is successful or that it is more effective than school B, where the proportion of students scoring at the proficient level or above was less than the AYP target. These claims are much more difficult to justify from the information provided by the NCLB accountability system. Indeed, Raudenbush (2004a) has made a convincing case that such claims are "scientifically indefensible" (p. 35).

As Raudenbush has argued, the claim that school A is more effective than school B requires an inference that it is the schools and their instructional programs that have caused the better achievement in school A versus school B. Such a causal inference, however, requires that many other competing hypotheses be eliminated as alternative explanations for the differences in achievement between the two schools. The alternate explanation, that students in school A were better readers and knew more mathematics than students in school B before the start of the school year, for example, provides an alternative explanation that needs to be eliminated before concluding that school A is more effective than school B.

Many other alternate explanations, such as differences in educational support from home for students in schools A and B or differences in composition effects created by the peer groups in the two schools, would also have to be ruled out. School characteristics are confounded with many factors (e.g., socioeconomic status and prior achievement of students). According to Meyer (2000), for example, current-status school accountability measures are

> contaminated by factors other than school performance, in particular, the average level of achievement prior to entering first grade—average effects of student, family, and community characteristics on student achievement growth from first grade through the grade in which students are tested.
>
> (p. 2)

Consequently, differences in achievement at a fixed point in time simply do not provide a defensible justification for the causal inference that school A is more effective than school B.

Accountability systems that focus on year-to-year change can rule out, or at least make less plausible, some of the alternative explanations that make causal inferences impossible to defend in a current-status approach to accountability. The longitudinal tracking of individual students, for example, makes it possible to eliminate the explanation that greater gains in school A than in school B are due to differences in the achievement of students in the two schools at the beginning of the year. Correcting for prior achievement is not so straightforward when using the successive-cohorts approach to measuring gains because, as was noted above, the students in a given grade the previous year may not be comparable to their counterparts in the current year.

Average gains in achievement based on longitudinal tracking of individual students provide a stronger basis for eliminating competing explanations for differences in school performance. Sophisticated value-added statistical models (e.g., Sanders & Horn, 1998; Ballou, Sanders, & Wright, 2004; McCaffrey, Lockwood, Koretz, Louis, & Hamilton, 2004) help to rule out the possibility that initial differences in student achievement rather than differences in school instructional programs explain the better gains in one school compared to another. The "value-added" terminology implies a causal interpretation. When teacher or school value-added results are reported it is assumed that it is the teacher or the school that is having an effect rather than some other factor such as students' families, student background, or student peers in the school.

Most applications of value-added models estimate gains based on a span of grades, the earliest of which is likely to be grade 2 or 3. In this way the value-added models control for differences in student achievement at the time of the earliest grade included in the analysis, but they do not rule out the possibility that achievement differences in kindergarten and grade 1 confound the value-added estimates. As Raudenbush (2004a) has noted, "measured cognitive status prior to school entry is the most important confounder in studying school effects" (p. 13).

Value-added models that use prior student achievement but do not include other student background characteristics are also subject to the criticism that the excluded variables might bias the estimates. In this regard, Raudenbush has argued that,

> the estimation of gains does not necessarily eliminate all confounding. A critic might argue that unmeasured student characteristics predict gains students can expect and the schools they attend. This criticism is impossible to refute, though Ballou, Sanders, and Wright (2004) provide evidence that use of longitudinal data in multiple subject areas virtually eliminates the need to control for the usual confounders (ethnicity, gender, and poverty).
>
> (p. 13)

The composition of the student body may influence both achievement status and growth. Hanushek, Kain, Markman, and Rivkin (2003), for example, found that peer average achievement had a significant effect on the gains in achievement throughout the achievement distribution. The peer group is a characteristic of a school, but as Rouse (2005) has noted, it is not a characteristic that is under the control of public schools. Peer group effects, like school effects, are difficult to isolate, but peer group composition provides an alternative explanation that is not easily dismissed when attempting to attribute absolute performance or gains in achievement to school quality. Thus, although value-added or other types of growth models provide substantial improvements over the current-status and successive-cohorts approaches to accountability, they still fall short of providing definitive evidence that school differences in student gains in achievement are attributable solely to differences in school quality.

Causal claims are best supported when random assignment can be used to place students in groups because random assignment makes it possible to eliminate many alternative explanations of results. Because neither school practices nor students are assigned to schools at random, it is much harder to support causal claims based on test results obtained as part of accountability systems. Recognizing the difficulties in supporting causal claims, Rubin, Stuart, and Zanutto (2004) have argued that value-added analyses "should not be seen as estimating causal effects of teachers or schools, but rather as descriptive measures" (p. 113).

Similarly, Raudenbush (2004b) has concluded that value-added results "should not be taken as direct evidence of the effects of instructional practice" (p. 128). In his rejoinder, Ballou (2004) stressed the superiority of value-added models over status accountability models such as the one used by NCLB where schools are held accountable by comparisons of student performance "against the same absolute yardstick" (p. 133). As has already been indicated, the value-added approach has substantial advantages over a current-status approach, but it is still found wanting when it comes to making causal claims that are required to reach conclusions about school quality. Determination of school quality is not the only goal, but is a logical requirement for accountability systems that provide sanctions to "failing" schools or rewards to successful or exemplary schools if the systems are to be considered fair and valid.

Score Inflation

After a test-based accountability system has been implemented, whether the system emphasizes current status or growth, it is common to see annual increases in student achievement test results for the state as a whole. In Colorado, for example, the percentage of fourth grade students scoring at the proficient level or above on the reading assessments increased from 60% in 2000 to 64% in 2005, and in mathematics the percentage for eighth grade students increased from 35% in 2000 to 44% in 2005. Similar increases have been experienced with a number of other state testing programs.

It is common to infer that increases in test scores reflect real improvement in student achievement, not just gains in test scores. The validity of this inference that score gains reflect real improvement has been called into question, however, by a number of authors (e.g., Hamilton, 2003; Koretz, 2005). *Score inflation*, which Koretz (2005) defines "as a gain in scores that substantially overstates the improvement in learning it implies" (p. 99), is a major threat to valid interpretations of test score gains. A number of studies have found that gains in scores on high-stakes tests often fail to generalize to other indicators of student achievement such as results on the NAEP or the ACT test (Klein, Hamilton, McCaffrey, & Stecher, 2000; Koretz & Barron, 1998).

Koretz, Linn, Dunbar, and Shepard (1991) studied a district where sharp gains in test scores were reported for the first several years that a particular test was in place, followed by a large drop in scores when a new test was introduced, after which steady gains were once again observed. This pattern of gains and losses associated with test familiarity had been frequently observed in similar circumstances (Linn, Graue, & Sanders, 1990), and was not unique to the district in the Koretz et al. (1991) study. When Koretz et al. (1991) re-administered the earlier test to students in the district with dramatic test score gains, they found that the students scored at about the same level as students had the first year the test was introduced—well below the level that was achieved the last year the original test was administered and also well below the level achieved on the district's current test in the year of the study (see Koretz, 2005, for a more complete description of the study and a graphical presentation of the results).

School Characteristics and Instructional Practices

A major shortcoming of current accountability systems that significantly restricts their usefulness for making valid inferences about school quality is that they include only a limited number of key variables. Accountability systems now being used to meet state and federal requirements throughout the country usually lack information about instructional practices, teacher characteristics, and student characteristics other than student test scores and selected student demographic data such as gender, race/ethnicity, indicators of economic disadvantage, disability status, and English language proficiency.

Student outcomes, even when prior achievement and student demographic information is included in the accountability analyses, do not provide a sufficient basis for making the type of causal inferences that are implied when accountability system results are used to identify successful and unsuccessful schools and to impose sanctions on failing schools. As Raudenbush (2004a) has argued, "to be successful, accountability must be informed by other sources of information, and, in particular, information on organizational and instructional practice" (p. 37). Even with such additional information, causal interpretations will be difficult to justify and subject to challenge, but they would be on much firmer ground than is possible without information about school organization and instructional practice.

In an earlier era, school resources (e.g., funding levels) and process information were used in school accreditation visits to draw conclusions about school quality. The current emphasis on outcomes is clearly preferable to a system that uses resources as the primary basis of judging school quality. It would be better still to base judgments about school quality on a combination of information about student outcomes, prior achievement and backgrounds of students, and school organizational and instructional processes.

Descriptive Uses of Accountability System Results

Accountability system results can have value without making causal inferences about school quality, solely from the results of student achievement measures and demographic characteristics. Treating the results as descriptive information and for identification of schools that require more intensive investigation of organizational and instructional process characteristics are potentially of considerable value. Rather than using the results of the accountability system as the sole determiner of sanctions for schools, they could be used to flag schools that need more intensive investigation to reach sound conclusions about needed improvements or judgments about quality.

Such a use of accountability system results would represent a profound change and would require revisions of state and federal laws. It is unlikely that such a change in perspective would be politically acceptable at the present time. The change, however, would make the use of accountability results more consistent with the tenets of scientific reasoning and research. In this sense, it would make accountability requirements more consistent with the major emphasis on the importance of using "scientifically based research" that is found throughout the NCLB Act (Feuer, Towne, & Shovelson, 2002).

Conclusion

There are many reasons for the longstanding emphasis on test-based accountability in the United States. Accountability is a politically attractive means of trying to reform education. Compared to other reforms, it is relatively inexpensive and represents one of the few ways in which politicians and policymakers can have an effect on classroom practice (Linn, 2000). Test results are used to monitor changes in student achievement and the closing of gaps in the achievement of different subgroups. Test-based accountability is also seen as an engine of educational reform that can induce changes in practice that will lead to improvements in student achievement, and the closing of gaps in achievement among racial/ethnic groups and between economically disadvantaged students and their more affluent counterparts.

For at least the last decade, test-based accountability systems have been based on state-adopted content standards and results have generally been reported in terms of a small number of performance standards. The content standards specify what students are supposed to learn, and they provide the basis for developing tests that are consistent with and reinforce those standards. Performance standards specify the levels of achievement that are expected for a student to be considered proficient or advanced. The passage of NCLB has given increased importance to a single performance standard in each state with a great emphasis on the proficiency level that all students are expected to achieve by 2013–2014.

There are a variety of approaches to test-based accountability. Systems can be distinguished in terms of their reliance on measures of current status in relationship to fixed targets or growth in achievement. NCLB uses a current-status approach while a number of state systems give greater priority to growth or use a combination of current-status and growth targets. Although accountability systems are used to make causal interpretations about school quality, such interpretations cannot be defended on scientific grounds. There are too many plausible alternate explanations of results to conclude that observed differences in the achievement of students in different schools are solely attributable to variations in school quality. Growth-model approaches are helpful in eliminating some, but not all plausible alternative explanations.

Accountability results are best viewed as a source of descriptive information about schools that can be a source of hypotheses that need to be checked by gathering additional information about school organizational characteristics, teacher characteristics, and instructional practice.

Acknowledgments

The work herein was partially supported under the Educational Research and Development Center Program PR/Award R305B960002, as administered by the Institute of Education Sciences, U.S. Department of Education. The findings and opinions expressed in this chapter are those of the author and do not necessarily reflect the positions or polices of the National Center for Education Research, the Institute of Education Sciences (IES), or the U.S. Department of Education.

Note

1. The one exception in NCLB to the comparison of current status to annual targets is the "safe harbor" provision. The safe harbor provision allows a school that would not otherwise make AYP to do so if the percentage of students in the school as a whole and for each relevant subgroup scoring below proficient has decreased by at least 10% from the previous year in both reading/English language arts and mathematics and if there is improvement on another performance indicator.

References

Ballou, D. (2004). Rejoinder. *Journal of Educational and Behavioral Statistics*, 29 (1), 131–134.

Ballou, D., Sanders, W., & Wright, P. (2004). Controlling for student background in value-added assessment of teachers. *Journal of Educational and Behavioral Statistics*, 29 (1), 37–65.

Bhola, D. S., Impara, J. C., & Buckendahl, W. (2003). Aligning tests with states' content standards: Methods and issues. *Educational Measurement: Issues and Practice*, 22 (3), 21–29.

California Department of Education. (2005). *2004–05 academic performance index growth report: Information guide*, October. Sacramento, CA: California Department of Education.

Online, available at: http://www.cde.ca.gov/ta/ac/ap/documents/infoguide05g.pdf (accessed August 29, 2007).

Center on Education Policy. (2005). States test limits of federal AYP flexibility. Washington, DC: Center on Education Policy. Online, available at: http://www.ctredpol.org/ (accessed August 29, 2007).

Education Week. (2005, January 6). Quality Counts 2005: No small change: Targeting money toward student performance, 24 (17).

Feuer, M. J., Towne, L., & Shavelson, R. J. (2002). Scientific culture and educational research. *Educational Researcher,* 31 (8), 4–14.

Goals 2000: Educate America Act of 1994, Public Law 103–227.

Haertel, E. H. & Herman, J. L. (2005). A historical perspective on validity arguments for accountability testing. In J. L. Herman & E. H. Haertel (Eds.), *Uses and misuses of data in accountability testing. Yearbook of the National Society for the Study of Education* (pp. 1–34), Vol. 104, Part I. Malden, MA: Blackwell Publishing.

Hamilton, L. (2003). Assessment as a policy tool. In R. L. Floden (Ed.), *Review of Research in Education,* 27, 25–68.

Hanushek, E. A., Kain, J. F., Markman, J. M., & Rivkin, S. G. (2003). Does peer ability affect student achievement? *Journal of Applied Economics,* 18 (5), 527–544.

Hill, R. K. & DePascale, C. A. (2003). Reliability of No Child Left Behind accountability designs. *Educational Measurement: Issues and Practice,* 22 (3), 12–20.

Improving America's Schools Act of 1994, Public Law 103–382.

Kane, M. (2006). Validation. In R. L. Brennan (Ed.), *Educational measurement* (4th ed., pp. 17–64). Westport, CT: American Council on Education/Praeger.

Kim, J. S. & Sunderman, G. L. (2005). Measuring academic proficiency under the No Child Left Behind Act: Implications for educational equity. *Educational Researcher,* 34 (8), 3–13.

Klein, S. P., Hamilton, L. S., McCaffrey, D. F., & Stecher, B. M. (2000). *What do test scores in Texas tell us?* Santa Monica, CA: RAND.

Koretz, D. (2005). Alignment, high stakes, and the inflation of test scores. In J. L. Herman & E. H. Haertel (Eds.), *Uses and misuses of data in accountability testing. Yearbook of the National Society for the Study of Education* (pp. 99–118), Vol. 104, Part I. Malden, MA: Blackwell Publishing.

Koretz, D. & Barron, S. I. (1998). *The validity of gains on the Kentucky Instructional Results Information System (KIRIS).* Santa Monica, CA: RAND.

Koretz, D., Linn, R. L., Dunbar, S. B., & Shepard, L. A. (1991). The effects of high-stakes testing on achievement: Preliminary findings about the generalization of findings across tests. Paper presented at the annual meeting of the American Educational Research Association, Chicago.

Linn, R. L. (2000). Assessments and accountability. *Educational Researcher,* 29 (2), 4–14.

Linn, R. L. (2003). Performance standards: Utility for different uses of assessments. *Education Policy Analysis Archives,* 11 (31). Online, available at: http://epaa.asu.edu/epaa/v11n31/ (accessed September 1, 2003).

Linn, R. L. (2005a). Conflicting demands of No Child Left Behind and state systems: Mixed messages about school performance. *Educational Policy Analysis Archives,* 13 (33). Online, available at: http://epaa.asu.edu/epaa/v13n33/ (accessed June 30, 2005).

Linn, R. L. (2005b). Issues in the design of accountability systems. In J. L. Herman & E. H. Haertel (Eds.), *Uses and misuses of data in accountability testing. Yearbook of the National Society for the Study of Education* (pp. 78–98), Vol. 104, Part I. Malden, MA: Blackwell Publishing.

Linn, R. L. & Haug, C. (2002). The stability of school building scores and gains. *Educational Evaluation and Policy Analysis,* 24 (1), 27–36.

Linn, R. L. & Herman, J. L. (1997). *A policymaker's guide to standards and assessment.* Denver, CO: Education Commission of the States. Online, available at: http://www.ecs.org/ecsmain.asp?page=/html/publications/home_publications.asp (accessed December 12, 2006).

Linn, R. L., Graue, M. E., & Sanders, N. M (1990). Comparing state and district test results to national norms: The validity of claims that "everyone is above average." *Educational Measurement: Issues and Practice,* 9 (3), 5–14.

Linn, R. L., Baker, E. L., & Betebenner, D. W. (2002). Accountability systems: Implications of requirements of the No Child Left Behind Act of 2001. *Educational Researcher,* 31 (6), 3–16.

McCaffrey, D. F., Lockwood, J. R., Koretz, D., Louis, T. A., & Hamilton, L. (2004). Models for value-added modeling of teacher effects. *Journal of Educational Statistics*, 29, 67–101.

McDonnell, L. M. (2004). *Politics, persuasion, and educational testing.* Cambridge, MA: Harvard University Press.

McDonnell, L. M. (2005). Assessment and accountability from the policymaker's perspective. In J. L. Herman & E. H. Haertel (Eds.), *Uses and misuses of data in accountability testing. Yearbook of the National Society for the Study of Education* (pp. 35–54), Vol. 104, Part I. Malden, MA: Blackwell Publishing.

Meyer, R. H. (2000). Value-added indicators: A powerful tool for evaluating science and mathematics programs and policies. *NISE Brief, 3*, No. 3. Madison, WI: National Center for Improving Science Education, University of Wisconsin-Madison.

National Commission on Excellence in Education. (1983). *A nation at risk: The imperative for educational reform.* Washington, DC: U.S. Government Printing Office.

No Child Left Behind Act of 2001, Pub. L. No. 107–110, 115 Stat. 1425 (2002).

Olson, L. (2002, January 9). Testing systems in most states not ESEA-ready. *Education Week*, 21 (16), 1, 26–27.

Olson, L. (2005, September 2). Defying predictions, state trends prove mixed on schools making NCLB targets. *Education Week*, 25 (2), 1, 26–27.

Olson, L. & Hoff, D. J. (2005, November 16). U.S. to pilot new gauge of "growth": Education Department to permit shifts in how states track gains. *Education Week*, 25 (13), 1, 16.

Porter, A. C. (2002). Measuring the content of instruction: Uses in research and practice. *Educational Researcher*, 31 (7), 3–14.

Porter, A. C., Linn, R. L., & Trimble, S. (2005). The effects of state decisions about NCLB Adequate Yearly Progress targets. *Educational Measurement: Issues and Practice*, 24 (4), 32–39.

Raudenbush, S. W. (2004a). Schooling, statistics, and poverty: Can we measure school improvement? The ninth annual William H. Angoff Memorial Lecture. Princeton, NJ: Educational Testing Service.

Raudenbush, S. W. (2004b). What are value-added models estimating and what does this imply for statistical practice? *Journal of Educational and Behavioral Statistics*, 29 (1), 121–129.

Rouse, C. E. (2005). Accounting for schools: Economic issues in measuring school quality. In C. A. Dwyer (Ed.), *Measurement and research in the accountability era* (pp. 275–298). Mahwah, NJ: Lawrence Erlbaum Associates.

Rubin, D. B., Stuart, E. A., & Zanutto, E. L. (2004). A potential outcomes view of value-added assessment. *Journal of Educational and Behavioral Statistics*, 29 (1), 103–116.

Sanders, W. & Horn, S. (1998). Research findings from the Tennessee value added assessment system (TVAAS) database: Implications for educational evaluation and research. *Journal of Personnel Evaluation in Education*, 12 (3), 247–256.

Spellings, M. (2005, November 21). Letter to Chief State School Officers, announcing growth model pilot program, with enclosures. Online, available at: http://www.ed.gov/nclb/landing.jhtm (accessed December 10, 2006).

U.S. Department of Education. (2004). *Standards and assessments peer review guidance: Information and examples for meeting the requirements of the No Child Left Behind Act of 2001.* Washington, DC: U.S. Department of Education. Online, available at: http://www.ed.gov/policy/elsec/guid/saaprguidance.doc (accessed December 10, 2006).

Webb, N. L. (1999). Research Monograph No. 18: *Alignment of science and mathematics standards and assessments in four states.* Madison, WI: National Institute for Science Education.

White House. (2001, January 23). Press conference with President George W. Bush and Education Secretary Rod Paige to introduce the President's Education Program, Office of the Press Secretary. Online, available at: http://www.whitehouse.gov/news/releases/2001/01/20010123–2.html (accessed August 29, 2007).

Zvoch, K. & Stevens, J. J. (2006, January 20). Successive student cohorts and longitudinal growth models: An investigation of elementary school mathematics performance. *Education Policy Analysis Archives*, 14 (2). Online, available at: http://epaa.asu.edu/epaa/v14n2/ (accessed January 20, 2006).

2
A Brief History of Accountability Testing, 1965–2007

Lorrie A. Shepard

Standardized testing has a long history in the United States, and testing is more salient in the U.S. education system than it is in any other country (Resnick, 1982). Predominantly, tests have been used to make decisions about individual students, especially to place students in special programs and to select students for college (Goslin, 1963). Accountability testing—focused on judging the quality of schools—is a more recent phenomenon, but it has its roots in the technology of IQ testing and the ardent belief among Americans that tests can scientifically determine merit and worth.

A hundred years ago, Goddard and Terman brought IQ tests to America in a climate of Social Darwinism and survival of the fittest. They were strict hereditarians who believed that mental tests could be used to measure innate ability and thereby assign students to education levels and even to their jobs later in life (Terman, 1916). Although beliefs about fixed, innate intelligence lost favor with scientists many decades ago, these ideas continued to have great sway with the public and with educators. Indeed, educational reformers at the end of the twentieth century specifically sought to challenge these endemic attitudes and practices by announcing that "*all* students can learn" and calling for "high standards for *all* students."

A less visible strand of educational testing, with an even longer history, focuses on the use of tests to evaluate the quality of schooling—though without voicing the notion of accountability. In 1845, Massachusetts State Superintendent of Instruction, Horace Mann, pressured Boston school trustees to adopt written examinations because large increases in enrollments made oral exams unfeasible. Long before IQ tests, these examinations were used to classify pupils (Tyack, 1974) and to put comparative information about how schools were doing in the hands of a state-level authority (Resnick, 1982). In the 1890s, in hopes of spending more time on richer subject matter (Cronbach et al., 1980), Joseph Rice administered spelling tests to 30,000 students and found no difference between students taught spelling for 15 minutes per day versus those taught for 30 minutes. Beginning in 1908, Thorndike and his students developed hundreds of achievement tests that then were implemented on a wide scale through university-based bureaus of cooperative research established to conduct school surveys (Cook, 1941).

Three general points are worth noting about these precursors to today's school accountability. First, achievement testing programs grew up alongside IQ testing, relied on the same statistical techniques for test construction and for evaluating test quality, and suffered from the same limitations. Second, both Mann and Thorndike instituted testing programs because they had already concluded that schools were failing (U.S. Congress Office of Technology Assessment, 1992); gathering data would help them promote school reform. Third, focusing attention on standardized tests often produces perverse results, as Rice discovered when educators spent *more time* on spelling after his study, despite his finding that more time made no difference (Cronbach et al., 1980).

Before 1970, testing programs were mostly local but relied on standardized test batteries available from commercial test publishers. Results from individual aptitude and achievement tests were used to make high-stakes decisions about individual children that could have crushing self-fulfilling consequences (Heller, Holtzman, & Messick, 1982), but test scores were rarely used to make judgments about individual schools. All of that changed relatively abruptly 40 years ago with the emergence of large-scale assessment systems and their use for school accountability. In this chapter, I trace the history of state and national assessments and the origins of educational accountability with its cycles of revision from minimum competency testing, to basic skills testing, to standards-based reform.

It All Started With Title I

Title I of the Elementary and Secondary Education Act (ESEA) of 1965 launched the development of the field of educational evaluation and the school accountability movement. The 1960s are remembered as a time of social unrest, when issues of equality were paramount. It was also a time when the federal government shifted its management practices to focus on cost–benefit analysis and production outcomes (Resnick, 1980), and when in many sectors of government and social services, evaluation research became the handmaiden to public policy (Cronbach et al., 1980). In education, evaluation of post-Sputnik curriculum projects predated Title I, but it was the ESEA mandate for evaluation of every Title I and Title III project that literally created the field of educational evaluation (Worthen & Sanders, 1973). The American Educational Research Association began a monograph series in 1967 to disseminate the latest thinking in evaluation theory, and several educational evaluation organizations and journals date from this period. The most important aspect of Title I evaluation, however, was the new implied contract with local districts whereby federal dollars would be spent on education in exchange for evidence of program effectiveness. It was this bargain—

which tied funding to measured outcomes—that created the accountability movement.

The evaluation provisions in Title I came about because Senator Robert Kennedy doubted whether school administrators understood the problems of or knew how to provide effective programs for disadvantaged children. He expected that evaluation data could be used by parents as a "whip" or a "spur" to leverage changes in ineffective schools (Halperin, 1975; McLaughlin, 1975). Kennedy's intention was almost identical to present-day accountability rhetoric. For example, in Colorado, Governor Bill Owens pushed for the development of school report cards because he believed that giving low grades to low performing schools would cause the school community to rally. Parents and business leaders would become involved and make sure that school performance improved (Owens, 1999).

Evaluations of the early 1970s, however, were quite benign with low stakes compared to today's context. The Colorado Accountability Act of 1971, for example, required only that districts conduct evaluations of their programs and report to their constituencies, causing one evaluation expert to grouse that requiring educators to conduct their own evaluations was like "asking banks to conduct their own audits" (Worthen, 1974, p. 26). Similarly, because of the need to mitigate the threat of federal intrusion, early Title I evaluations were "chaotically diverse" and could not be aggregated so as to inform policy decisions (Cronbach et al., 1980, p. 33). A few years later, when it was recognized that little could be learned from a multitude of different tests, score metrics, and research designs, a more uniform system of reporting was imposed, which led to a huge burgeoning in the amount of standardized testing (Tallmadge & Wood, 1978).

The National Assessment of Educational Progress: From Achievement Census to Policy Instrument

The National Assessment of Educational Progress (NAEP), begun in 1969, was part of the same general trend toward large-scale data gathering, but NAEP was intended to be an information source and neutral monitor, not an accountability device. Over time, however, as accountability pressures and political interest in test scores intensified, the independence and neutrality of NAEP would be increasingly challenged.

NAEP Beginnings

Ralph Tyler, NAEP's primary architect, called it a census-like data system and likened its purpose to the collection of health statistics on the incidence of heart disease and cancer for different age and occupational groups. Tyler (1966) specifically distinguished this large-scale use of evaluation data—"to help in the understanding of educational problems and needs and to guide in efforts to develop sound public policy regarding education"—from the kinds of information needed for individual pupil appraisal, teaching decisions, and even curriculum evaluation.

The independence of the National Assessment from specific educational programs or political jurisdictions was further assured by both its data collection methods and administrative structure. Matrix sampling of test items within a content domain would help to ensure that the assessment provided a much broader representation of subject matter fields than was possible on traditional standardized tests (but see Stake's (2007) perspective on the limitations of an assessment conceived by measurement specialists rather than curriculum scholars). At the same time, students were sampled to represent regions of the country and urban, suburban, or rural districts rather than specific states or districts. The contract for overseeing the National Assessment was given to the Education Commission of the States (ECS), a nonprofit organization of governors, chief state school officers, and legislators, again to buffer NAEP from the specter of federal control of education. Interestingly in the beginning, the one political purpose intended for NAEP—again using the disease analogy—was to obtain more generous appropriations for education (Cronbach et al., 1980) because it was expected that the identification of problems would naturally bring more resources to bear in solving them.

Over time, the purpose (and correspondingly the characteristics) of NAEP have become increasingly more politicized, although still relatively immune from politics compared to state assessments. The very features of the assessment that had been designed to shelter it from politics were later blamed for the lack of public interest in the assessment's results and systematically targeted for correction. In 1983, the Educational Testing Service won the contract for NAEP away from ECS by proposing a significant redesign that would be more responsive to policymakers' needs (Messick, Beaton, & Lord, 1983). The frequency of assessments was increased, reporting by grade level rather than age was begun, background and program variables were added to help in interpreting results, and sophisticated scaling methods were introduced to produce a single summary score that could be more readily understood by the public.

NAEP and Comparative State Data

Efforts to increase the visibility and usefulness of NAEP occurred in the context of concerns about education that led at that same time to *A Nation at Risk: The Imperative of Educational Reform* (National Commission on Excellence in Education, 1983). In addition to appointing the Commission to study the quality of American education, Secretary of Education Terrel Bell and his successor, William Bennett, stimulated interest in comparative state education data by publishing their famous "Wall Charts." Annual Wall Charts provided data on student characteristics and education resources, such as per pupil expenditure, but most heatedly they compared states on average ACT and SAT scores. Obviously, tests administered to non-representative samples of students could not be used to say anything about the quality of education in any state. But the flurry over Bennett's press conferences certainly generated enthusiasm for gathering state-by-state data using more legitimate means.

In 1987, a study group chaired by Lamar Alexander, former Governor of Tennessee, and directed by the Spencer Foundation's President, H. Thomas James, recommended that the NAEP assessment design be expanded to include state-by-state comparisons and possibly even district and school-level data (Alexander & James, 1987). When called upon to review the Alexander–James report, a National Academy of Education committee chaired by Robert Glaser expressed a few concerns but basically endorsed the idea that NAEP could be expanded and used as a "catalyst for school improvement." Specifically, the Glaser (1987) commentary cautioned (a) that future assessments, limited in the competencies they measure, might come "to exercise an influence on our schools that exceeds their scope and true merit" (p. 51) and (b) that "simple comparisons are ripe for abuse and are unlikely to inform meaningful school improvement efforts" (p. 59). Glaser's committee was optimistic, however, that by using more extended-response assessment formats, NAEP could serve "as a model of what students should know and how it should be assessed" (p. 47). Following from these recommendations, voluntary participation of states in the national assessment, called the NAEP Trial State Assessment project, was formally authorized by Congress in 1988. As anticipated, the availability of state comparisons greatly heightened the interest of policymakers and the media in assessment results.

NAEP as a Policy Instrument

In its 1988 reauthorization of NAEP, Congress implemented another recommendation of the Alexander–James and Glaser reports, creating a National Assessment Governing Board (NAGB) for the purpose of making NAEP more responsive to the concerns of various constituencies. One of the most visible and controversial acts of NAGB was to change the way that assessment results were reported. Instead of average scores and descriptive anchors showing what American students "could do," achievement levels were developed on the NAEP scales to show what students "should be able to do." The achievement levels, set through a judgmental process involving educators and lay citizens, were criticized in several evaluation reports (Shepard, Glaser, Linn, & Bohrnstedt, 1993; Stufflebeam, Jaeger, & Scriven, 1991; U.S. General Accounting Office, 1993). Beyond technical and validity problems, one of the main concerns was that judgmentally set standards—that varied dramatically from grade-to-grade and across subject areas and that departed dramatically from normative expectations of grade-level proficiency—would cause confusion and seriously mislead the public as to the meaning of assessment results.

Each time efforts have been made to increase the uses of NAEP results, debates have ensued about whether expansion would harm the integrity of assessment data. At issue are two chief concerns: (1) testing more often or in more jurisdictions increases costs, which if not adequately funded will likely reduce the substantive quality of the assessments; and (2) political attention to results could lead to the same kind of teach-the-test distortions that have affected state testing programs. In 1992, as standards-based assessments were being developed, the National Council on Education Standards and Testing called for a system of assessments that reserved for NAEP the role of program/system monitor while encouraging states, national professional associations, or consortiums of states to develop assessments that could be used for individual students. A key idea was to maintain the independence of NAEP so that it could be used to evaluate whether reported gains on assessments used locally for accountability purposes were accurate and thereby determine whether standards-based reforms were effective or ineffective in improving education. Checking on the validity of reported test score gains may have been what President George W. Bush had in mind when he proposed as part of the "No Child Left Behind" (NCLB) legislation that NAEP be used to confirm progress on state assessments. However, many feared that tying funding to outcomes on NAEP would undermine its independence, and as a result of this controversy, the language of the No Child Left Behind legislation was softened, requiring that states participate in NAEP but leaving unspecified how NAEP results would be used to check on the authenticity of achievement gains reported by state assessments.

The history of NAEP over several decades reflects a gradual shift from mere data collection, like the U.S. Census, to an increasingly powerful policy instrument used to garner attention and mobilize educational reform efforts. In this chapter, I pursue this theme of politicization of large-scale assessments, especially of state assessments, which have been much more dramatically affected. Before doing so, however, it is important to consider a larger change in the policy context, a change that shifted the reporting of assessment results from good news to bad news about public education.

The SAT Test Score Decline: Bad News About Public Education

During the 1960s and the nation's war on poverty, public education was viewed with approbation. The only criticism of education was that its benefits had not been extended to poor and minority children. The willingness of policymakers to invest in the Elementary and Secondary Education Act of 1965 was, in fact, a sign of their faith in the power of education to redress many of society's ills. Within a few years, however, the minimum competency testing movement was born in a political climate that had become hypercritical of education. Messick et al. (1983) offered several explanations for this change, including the Vietnam War and the disillusionment of the late 1960s. A very central cause of the decline in public opinion about education, however, was the famous SAT score decline.

In 1963, after two decades of steady or rising scores, SAT averages took a downward turn and continued downhill for the next 14 years. The loss over the entire period was dramatic: 49 points in verbal scores (one-half standard deviation) and 32 points in mathematics. A Blue Ribbon Panel commissioned by the College Board (1977) later found that two-thirds to three-quarters of the score decline was attributable to changes in the composition of the test-taking population during this period, that is, more women and minority group members were going to selective colleges and thus needed to take the test. Nevertheless, what the public remembered was the precipitous decline and the gist of the Panel's speculations about the causes of the smaller but real decline—too many electives instead of required courses, too much TV, and a decline in family participation in the learning process. In his analysis of the factors leading to the Minimum Competency Testing movement, Resnick (1980) cited as well public fears about rising unemployment and the tendency to blame the schools for lack of preparation.

Minimum Competency Testing

When the National Assessment first began, several states created their own state assessment programs modeled after NAEP with its emphasis on system evaluation rather than the performance of individual students. For example, in 1974 California stopped administering an off-the-shelf standardized test and developed the California Assessment Program using matrix sampling for the new purpose of "broad program evaluation rather than diagnostic assessment of individual students" (California State Department of Education, 1973, p. 1). Rhetoric surrounding the SAT test score decline, however, and concerns about an economic downturn quickly overtook the system-level data collection purpose of large-scale assessment and redirected efforts toward enforcement of minimum academic standards. By 1978, 33 states had taken action to mandate minimum competency standards for grade-to-grade promotion or high school graduation (Pipho, 1978). By 1980, all states had a minimum competency testing program or a state testing program of some kind (Baratz, 1980). By mandating state-administered tests and standards, legislators intended to improve the quality of schooling and "put meaning back into the high school diploma."

The minimum competency movement of the 1970s, like the accountability movement today, was driven by a business model. Wise (1978) identified the following management concepts adopted from business into the education sphere: accountability planning, programming, budgeting systems (PPBS); management by objectives (MBO); operations analysis; systems analysis; program evaluation and review technique (PERT); management information systems; and several additional planning and budgeting terms. A simplistic, bottom-line mentality made it easy to rely on single test scores, like the Gross National Product, as sufficient indicators of system health. Policymakers in both periods gave relatively little attention to the intervening variables needed to achieve mandated ends. In 1978, Wise argued that minimum competency testing programs would fail to improve education because they lacked a “theory of education”; what today would be called a “theory of action.” That is, legislators were mandating desired outcomes of schooling without having an understanding of how the mandate might or might not cause changes in curriculum and instruction that would in turn produce the desired outcomes.

The problem of setting performance standards—that is, determining the passing score for the test—also began with minimum competency testing and has continued unabated (Brickell, 1978; Glass, 1978). Because the testing program was intended to be the reform, not just measure its outcomes, minimum competency testing also marked the beginning of serious consequences attached to test results. The only differences between accountability testing then and now—and these differences are striking—were the levels of the standards (minimum standards then, world class standards now) and the content of the test. Figure 2.1 provides an illustration of the extremely low level of content included in minimum competency tests. For example, the mathematics items in this example are roughly at the third grade level according to present day curriculum standards.

Minimum competency graduation tests are still in place in some states, but the movement lasted less than a decade. By the time some slow moving states had developed and implemented a competency program, the movement was already judged by many to have failed in its efforts to improve the quality of education. The authors of *A Nation at Risk* (National Commission on Excellence in Education, 1983), which began the next wave of educational reform, specifically faulted minimum competency examinations as part of the problem, not part of the solution: “‘competency’ examinations (now required in 37 States) fall short of what is needed, as the ‘minimum’ tends to become the ‘maximum,’ thus lowering educational standards for all” (p. 2).

A Nation at Risk, Basic Skills, and the Excellence Movement

Among countless reports on education, *A Nation at Risk* (National Commission On Excellence in Education 1983) is perhaps the single most visible education policy report of the century. It blamed the mediocre performance of U.S. students and U.S. schools on neglect, low standards, and a dilute curriculum. Within two years of its publication, 30 national reports and 250 state reports had been issued on educational reform (Pipho, 1985), and nearly every state had introduced reform legislation. The excellence movement, launched by *A Nation at Risk*, sought to ratchet up expectations by reinstating course-based graduation requirements, extending time in the school day and school year, requiring more homework, and—most importantly—requiring more testing.

Consumerism

1. Group health insurance, offered by an employer, will cost you less than a health policy you purchase by yourself.

2. One must use credit to have a good credit rating. A good way to keep a satisfactory rating is:

   a. borrow money from friends
   b. make a budget to avoid using credit
   c. pay your bills promptly
   d. pay cash for everything you buy
   e. none of the above

3. Steve borrowed $200 from his bank. He repaid it in six monthly installments of $37.50 each. What was the "cost" in dollars?

   a. $15 b. $25 c. $37.50 d. $237.50

4. Match the letter of the consumer protection agency with the function it performs:

   a. Federal Trade Commission
   b. Better Business Bureau
   c. City Health Department
   d. Food and Drug Administration

   _____ investigates false claims in advertisements of nationally sold products

   _____ provides information regarding the reputation of local business firms

   _____ inspects public eating places and hospitals

   _____ analyzes foods, drugs and cosmetics suspected of being harmful for human use

5. A brand of cola is available in four bottle sizes. Which of the following bottles has the lowest price per ounce?

   a. 6 oz. at 36 cents
   b. 8 oz. at 42 cents
   c. 12 oz. at 56 cents
   d. 24 oz at $1.20

Mathematics

1. Which digit represents hundredths in: 1234.567?

2. 21 5/7
   +2 3/7

   a. 24 1/7 b. 23 1/2 c. 19 2/7 d. 16 1/7 e. 168/7

3. Chain-link fencing costs 59 cents a foot. Approximately how much will it cost for 50 feet of fencing?

   a. $10 b. $25 c. $30 d. $ 40 e. $2,950

4. How long should a roast cook if it weighs 5 pounds and must cook 20 minutes for each pound?

   a. 2 hours
   b. 1 hour and 20 minutes
   c. 2 hours and 40 minutes
   d. 1 hour and 40 minutes
   e none of the above

5. Express 15% as a decimal

   a. 15 b. 15 c. 1.5 d. 150 e. 0.15

Democratic process

Which of the following would you expect to find in a democratic society?

	Would	Would not
1. Joe Smith gives $5 each to vote for him	_____	_____
2. Citizens legally picket and protest a court decision	_____	_____
3. A group of people go to the city council to ask for an investigation of the mayor	_____	_____
4. Congress overrides a Presidential veto	_____	_____
5. A citizen is arrested for breaking a law that is not written down	_____	_____

Answers:

Consumerism: 1. True 2. c 3. b 4. a, b, c, d 5. c
Mathematics: 1. 6 2. a 3. c 4. d 5. b
Democratic process: 1. Would 2. Would 3. Would 4. Would 5. Would not

Figure 2.1 Examples of Low-Level Questions Typical of Minimum Competency Graduation Tests in the 1970s.

Although the rhetoric of the excellence movement called for "new basics" and a rigorous academic curriculum for all students, critics even at the time warned that reliance on quantitative rather than qualitative factors was more likely to ensure educational adequacy rather than excellence (Duke, 1985).

In retrospect, it may seem odd that the excellence movement, with its aversion for low standards, did not provoke a more thorough reexamination of the kinds of tests used to lead as well as measure the reform. Some states did forego their minimum competency tests, but even the new tests adopted in the mid 1980s were predominantly multiple-choice basic skills tests. It was not until the effects of high-stakes tests began to be evaluated that any doubt arose about whether rising test scores on limited tests could be trusted as evidence that achievement was improving. Initially, gains on these tests, mostly in reading, math, and writing (measured by multiple-choice questions) were applauded as evidence of the success of reforms. Popham (1987), for example, used the gains in percent passing the tests in five different states to show the effectiveness of "measurement-driven instruction."

Ultimately, however, there were several validity challenges to the rosy picture painted by steadily rising test scores. John Cannell (1987), a West Virginia physician, frustrated at discovering above average test scores reported for a patient with grave school difficulties, conducted a survey and found that all 50 states claimed to be performing above average on nationally normed tests. More systematic evidence from the National Assessment for the 1980s showed gains in basic skills, but the gains were not so great as those reported on state assessments. Moreover, trends on higher-order skills were either flat or declining (U.S. Congress, Office of Technology Assessment, 1992).

Prompted by complaints that "high-stakes" accountability tests were narrowing the curriculum and producing inflated test score gains, numerous studies were undertaken to examine the effects of testing on teaching and learning. Several large-scale surveys of teachers showed essentially the same patterns. Because of pressure to improve test scores, teachers reduced or eliminated time for non-tested subjects, spent considerable amounts of time practicing test-taking skills, and changed their instructional materials and activities to imitate test formats as closely as possible (Darling-Hammond & Wise, 1985; Rottenberg & Smith, 1990; Shepard & Dougherty, 1991). These practices, which reduced the curriculum to drill and practice for the test, were the most pronounced in schools and districts serving large numbers of poor and minority children (Madaus, West, Harmon, Lomax, & Viator, 1992). Other studies, designed to investigate the effect of such practices on learning, used independent measures to evaluate whether apparent learning gains were real (Koretz, Linn, Dunbar, & Shephard, 1991). Unfortunately, high levels of student performance on accountability tests could not be replicated on independent measures of the same content, suggesting that students drilled constantly in preparation for the test lacked understanding of underlying concepts.

By the end of the 1980s, concerns about the huge increase in the amount of testing, as well as concerns about potential negative effects, prompted Congress to commission a comprehensive report on educational testing (U.S. Congress Office of Technology Assessment, 1992). Evidence of negative effects from high-stakes testing was sufficient to cause framers of the 1994 reauthorization of Title I to redirect substantially evaluation requirements that had theretofore driven the mandate for norm-referenced assessments. It would be a mistake to conclude, however, that policymakers, educators, and researchers all shared a common understanding of what had gone wrong with previous reforms. Researchers and teachers in subject matter fields were the most likely to be knowledgeable about research on the distorting effects of test-driven instructional decisions. Cognitive researchers, new to the assessment game, were aware of severe distortions caused by teaching to the test, but were inclined to believe that this problem could be solved by making better tests (Frederiksen & Collins, 1989; Resnick & Resnick, 1992). Policymakers, with little time for academic quibbles, were willing in many states to invest in the development of new forms of assessment, but at the same time continued to interpret the results from all different sorts of tests as if they were equally trustworthy.

Using Standards to Correct Previous Reforms

Just as *A Nation at Risk* was both a rejection and extension of minimum competency testing, so too were standards-based reforms of the 1990s both a rejection and extension of the recent basic skills reforms. Unlike the prior reform, which reaffirmed traditional curricula, the standards movement called for the development of much more challenging curricula: focused on reasoning and processes of inquiry, as well as content knowledge, and directed toward engaging students in using their knowledge in real-world contexts. Leading the way, the National Council of Teachers of Mathematics report on *Curriculum and Evaluation Standards for School Mathematics* (1989) expanded the purview of elementary school mathematics to include geometry and spatial sense, measurement, statistics and probability, and patterns and relationships, and at the same time emphasized problem solving, communication, mathematical reasoning, and mathematical connections rather than computation and rote activities.

As an extension of previous reforms, the standards movement continued to rely heavily on large-scale accountability assessments to leverage changes in instruction. In contrast to previous reforms, however, standards-based reformers explicitly called for a radical transformation of the substance of those assessments as a corrective for the distorting effects of existing high-stakes testing programs. Various terms such as *authentic*, *direct*, and *performance-based* assessments were used in standards parlance to convey the idea that assessments themselves had to be reformed to reflect more faithfully how learning would be used in non-test situations.

A great many standards documents provided sample assessment tasks both to exemplify and to enact curricular reforms. For example, the Mathematics Sciences Education Board of the National Research Council developed a set of prototypes for mathematics assessment. Intended for fourth graders, the tasks illustrated how different education would have to be to build students' confidence as well as provide them with the proficiencies needed to do well. Consistent with the reform's intentions, the tasks called for connections with other academic areas, and promoted higher-order thinking by asking students to justify their answers, draw a picture to explain their solution, make predictions, and draw generalizations from their problem solutions. Similarly in science, assessment tasks devised to mirror the new standards required students to formulate a question, design and conduct scientific investigations, use tools for data collection, formulate and defend a scientific argument, evaluate alternative explanations on the basis of evidence, and communicate the results of a scientific study.

The standards movement also differs from earlier reforms in that it has been informed and guided by an underlying theory of teaching and learning drawn from the cognitive sciences. Learning is no longer thought to be a mechanical process of memorization and accumulation of information but is rather an active process that requires reasoning and sense making on the part of the learner. Correspondingly then, effective teaching involves creating the necessary social supports (activities and patterns of interaction) so that students become accustomed to working on interesting problems, reasoning aloud or explaining their thinking, and monitoring and reflecting on their own learning. These substantially more challenging curricular goals place heavy demands on both the content knowledge and pedagogical skills of teachers.

Given the ambitious and unprecedented aims of the reform, nearly every report involved in the creation of the standards movement said something about the need for capacity building. For example, Smith and O'Day (1990), who were among the early architects of standards-based reform, envisioned a reform that was systemic, affecting all aspects of the educational system. They emphasized the need for professional development for both pre-service and in-service teachers and for conditions that would enhance teacher professionalism. Similarly, the National Council on Education Standards and Testing (NCEST) called for the development of school and system "delivery standards," acknowledging that ambitious goals would not be met without shared responsibility for improvement at both the state and local levels (NCEST, 1992). The National Academy of Education Panel on Standards-Based Educational Reform verified that compelling research evidence existed to support much higher expectations for students under fundamentally different conditions of teaching and learning; but the Panel cautioned that the knowledge base was fragmentary. Considerably more development would be needed before these ambitious ideas could be implemented on a wide scale (McLaughlin & Shepard, 1995).

No Child Left Behind and the Standards Movement: Contradictions and Controversies

Standards-based reform, begun in the early 1990s, is the most enduring of test-based accountability reforms, yet the version of reform instantiated in No Child Left Behind contradicts core principles of the standards movement. Understanding the current accountability scene requires greater awareness of the competing versions of reform, wildly different performance standards, and conflicting findings about accountability's beneficial and harmful effects.

Competing Models

Although the standards movement, in principle, has a theory of action—what it would take to get from here to there—in fact, the reform cannot be said to rest on a sound theory if most of the participants do not have access either to the theory or to its enabling conditions. An honest look at the current scene suggests that there are at least two fundamentally different models, and perhaps many, underlying standards-based reforms, though all are dressed up in the same rhetoric.

We might label the original vision of systemic change put forth by Smith and O'Day (1990), Resnick and Resnick (1992), and Frederiksen and Collins (1989) as examples of the *teaching and learning* or *cognitive science* version of standards-based reform. In contrast, in a 1999 NRC report aimed at helping states develop new Title I assessment and accountability systems, Elmore and Rothman (1999) retrospectively describe a simplified, *basic* standards-based reform model:

> The centerpiece of the system is a set of challenging standards for student performance. By setting these standards for all students, states would hold high expectations for performance; these expectations would be the same regardless of students' backgrounds or where they attended school. Aligning assessments to the standards would allow students, parents, and teachers to monitor student performance against the standards. Providing flexibility to schools would permit them to make the instructional and structural changes needed for their students to reach the standards. And holding schools accountable for meeting the standards would create incentives to redesign instruction toward the standards and provide appropriate assistance to schools that need extra help.
>
> (pp. 2–3)

Elmore and Rothman concluded that such a model has failed to improve the system significantly because it omits direct efforts to "build the capacity of teachers and administrators to improve instruction" (p. 3).

Most politicians are unaware of the original learning theory and research-based arguments as to why it should be possible to hold all students to high "world class" standards. To the extent that policymakers subscribe to a theory of action, they are more likely to hold with Elmore and Rothman's basic model or to adopt a *high-stakes incentives* version of standards-based reform. For example, Hess (2002) argues for "minimum standards" and for what he calls "the coercive force of self-interest":

> High-stakes accountability systems link rewards and punishments to demonstrated student performance in an effort to transform the quality of schooling. Such systems press students to master specified content and force educators to effectively teach that content. In such a regime, school improvement no longer rests upon individual volition or intrinsic motivation. Instead, students and teachers are compelled to cooperate by threatening a student's ability to graduate or a teacher's job security. Such transformative systems seek to harness the self-interest of students and educators to refocus schools and redefine the expectations of teachers and learners.
>
> (p. 70)

These competing views of both ends and means surely hinder the ability of states and school districts to implement the kind of coherent and mutually supportive system envisioned by the teaching and learning model advocates. Although NCLB includes teacher quality provisions and mandates for scientifically-based reading instruction, its testing and accountability requirements were modeled after proclaimed successes in Texas and Florida and rely primarily on the threat of sanctions to induce greater effort and improved achievement.

Cacophonous Standards

Hess's comments also point to another source of confusion underlying the standards movement despite its seemingly monolithic form. Hess calls the Virginia reforms ambitious, but then says that the standards represent—at a minimum—the knowledge and skills that should be taught. This rhetorical slight of hand—labeling rigorous standards minimal—has become commonplace. When the standards movement began, the phrase "world class standards for all students" was used to indicate that new expectations would be created that required all children to attain a level of proficiency theretofore achieved by only an elite group of students. World-class language was used with teachers involved in setting standards, and they were encouraged to eschew normative expectations and to dream about what might be. The result has been very high standards, in many cases set at the seventieth or even ninetieth percentile, as well as great variety in the level of standards from state to state. In 1990, the baseline year for the new NAEP Mathematics Assessment, for example, the standard for proficiency was set at a score level corresponding to the eightieth percentile for eighth graders and at the eighty-seventh percentile for fourth and twelfth graders.

No Child Left Behind increased the amount of testing and the potential negative consequences attached to test results. As a result, some states adjusted their proficiency standards, thus increasing the variability in state standards. Linn (in this volume) documents the tremendous differences between the percent proficient reported on NAEP for each state versus the percent proficient determined by the states' own tests. For example, in 2005 only 18% of fourth graders in Mississippi met the proficiency standard in reading on NAEP, but 87% of fourth graders were reported to be proficient on Mississippi's own test. Differences among states and between states and NAEP could be due to differences in content standards, differences in tests, differences in the stringency of the passing score, or to real differences in student achievement. A recent report by the National Center for Education Statistics (2007), however, reveals that the greatest source of the variability in state results is the differences in the stringency of proficiency standards.

Figure 2.2 is a simplified graphic intended to illustrate that proficiency standards might be set anywhere from the top to the bottom of the test score distribution. These different levels correspond roughly to different eras in the history of test-based accountability. However, these trends are not pervasive, so although there has been a general ratcheting up of standards over time, current practice includes a hodgepodge of leftover minimum competency standards, world-class standards, and "adjusted" proficiency standards adopted by some states for purposes of NCLB.

Unfortunately, most policymakers are not aware of how high some standards have been set and are inclined to treat all standards as if they refer to the same level of accomplishment. Policymakers and journalists also use pass–fail language without realizing that standards are no longer set at a minimum level. In Colorado, for example, there are four reporting categories: unsatisfactory, partially proficient, proficient, and advanced. The unsatisfactory level more closely corresponds to what traditionally would be thought of as inadequate or failing performance. The partially proficient category includes students who are both below average and above average in comparison to national norms; but partially proficient students are now identified in newspaper headlines as "failing" grade-level standards. A striking consequence of reporting assessment results in relation to world-class proficiency levels is that failure rates are alarmingly high and media stories constantly report bad news about public education.

Good and Ill Effects

If the purpose of large-scale assessments is now not to monitor change but to lead it, then how effective have standards-based assessments been in directing positive changes in curriculum and teaching? Studies after a decade of standards-based reform still show the strong influence of high-stakes tests on what gets taught (McNeil & Valenzuela, 2000; Stecher & Chun, 2001; Taylor, Shepard, Kinner, & Rosenthal, 2001). To the extent that the content of assessments has improved, there have been corresponding improvements in instruction and curriculum. In Washington state, for example, teachers reported spending more time during writing instruction on the genres to be

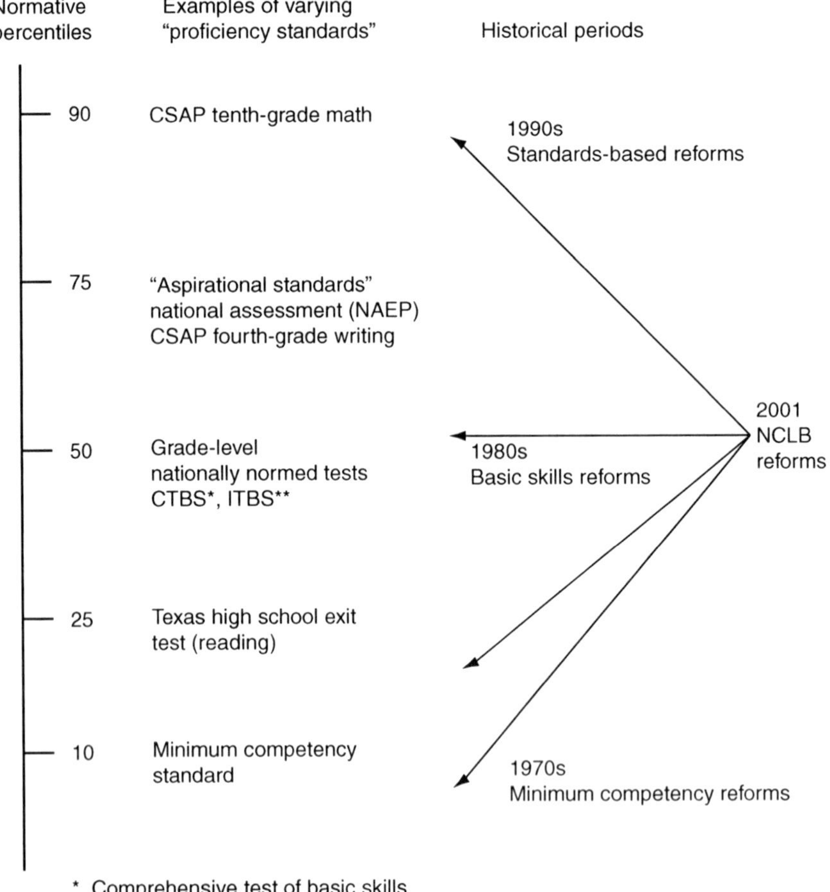

Figure 2.2 "Proficiency Standards" from Different Historical Periods Shown in Comparison to National Norms.

tested and attending to rubric-based writing strategies such as topic, audience, and purpose. In mathematics, the state learning goals and assessments prompted increased instructional time devoted to topics such as probability and statistics and to sense-making activities such as representing and sharing information, relating concepts, and formulating questions (Stecher & Chun, 2001). In Colorado, districts invested in professional development and new writing curricula, which teachers said had genuinely improved instruction (Taylor, et al., 2001).

Unfortunately, recent studies on the effects of standards-based reforms also confirm many of the old negative effects of high-stakes testing. The same surveys that found positive effects in Washington and Colorado also found that time for teaching social studies and science was eliminated or reduced because the state tests focused only on reading, writing, and mathematics. These patterns appear to have intensified under NCLB (Dillon, 2006; Manzo, 2005) with the greatest effects being felt in low performing schools.

Ultimately, an evaluation of the effectiveness of NCLB's high-stakes incentives version of standards-based reform will depend on how well it meets its primary goals of raising student achievement and closing the achievement gap. Nearly three decades of experience with accountability and test-driven reforms has at least provided some wisdom about how these questions should be addressed. In contrast with previous analysts who used score gains on accountability tests themselves as evidence of effectiveness, it is now widely understood by researchers and policymakers that some independent confirmation is needed to establish the validity of achievement gains. For example, two contrasting studies by researchers at the RAND Corporation used NAEP as an independent measure of achievement gains and documented both real and spurious aspects of test score gains in Texas. The study by Grissmer, Flanagan, Kawata, & Williamson (2000) found that Texas students performed better than expected based on family characteristics and socioeconomic factors. However, the study by Klein, Hamilton, McCaffrey, & Stecher (2000) found that gains on NAEP were nothing like the dramatic gains reported on the Texas Assessment of Academic Skills (TAAS). Klein et al. also found that the gap in achievement between majority and minority groups had widened for Texas students on NAEP whereas the gap had appeared to be closing on the TAAS. Both the Grissmer and Klein studies could be true, of course. Texas students could be learning more in recent years, but not as much as claimed by the TAAS.

A 2007 report from the Center on Education Policy (CEP) used state assessment data to evaluate the impact of NCLB on student achievement nationally. They found that most states with three years of data saw increases in reading and math scores, and that there was more evidence of gaps closing than gaps increasing (although gaps remained substantial). CEP attempted to analyze data from all 50 states, but only 13 states had adequate data for analyzing even short-term trends. Lee (2006), using NAEP data through 2005, found quite a different picture. Lee found that NAEP reading trends were flat before and after NCLB; and that the rate of gain in math was the same before and after the new law. Similarly, when CEP looked at NAEP results they noted low correlations between gains on state tests and gains on NAEP. Many states showing rising scores on their own tests have shown declines or flat results on NAEP. In the period from 1990 to 2005, few states reduced gaps significantly, and Lee found no systematic differences between strong accountability states and weak accountability states in the closing of achievement gaps for blacks, Hispanics, or poor students. Still, the longer-term positive trend on NAEP mathematics might be a sign of general improvements attributable to standards-based reforms more generally rather than NCLB specifically.

Accountability Testing: Lessons Learned

McDonnell (this volume) provides a political science analysis explaining why the core policy ideas of test-based accountability are well entrenched. In addition to the political ideal of democratic accountability, accountability mandates tap into powerful belief systems underpinning Americans' love affair with testing.

Accountability testing and its impacts are not new. Policymakers in successive decades seem to discover, each time for the first time, that U.S. economic competitiveness is threatened by poor achievement, especially in math and science. In response, test-based accountability is seen as an effective top-down means to ensure that schools work harder to improve student learning. Each time, well documented consequences of high-stakes testing have been the narrowing of curriculum and instruction to focus only on tested subjects using test-like formats. In many cases, teaching the test hurt learning rather than helped it. Indeed, the standards and assessment reforms of the 1990s were intended to correct the teaching-the-test consequences of 1980s reforms, which before that had been intended to correct the severe limitations of minimum competency testing in the 1970s. Not remembering any of this, the framers of NCLB took a backward step, imposing more testing, which made it more likely that cost constraints would limit the substantive quality of tests.

Over time, there has been a general ratcheting up of standards but also a proliferation of different standards without any transparency for the public about what has changed and what has stayed the same. Schools look worse and worse if students are said to "fail" when they don't meet high "world class standards" or when "adequate" yearly progress (which seems to imply "normal" progress) is defined in terms of 100% proficiency.

In thinking about how to reform the reforms, the following lessons are the most critical: (1) better quality, substantively challenging assessments are less likely to cause curriculum distortion than limited, multiple-choice-only tests; (2) when tests are used to drive reform, they can't be used as the sole measures of the reform's effects; (3) when an incentives-based coercive model of standards-based reform is adopted instead of one based on capacity building (including more challenging curricular resources, improved assessments, and teacher professional development), there is little evidence that accountability systems will achieve their desired ends; and, (4) test scores may go up—but in cases without real improvements in teaching and learning—apparent gains have not been confirmed by independent tests.

The claims about the benefits of test-based accountability for improving education should themselves be subjected to audit and evaluation. Given several decades of high-stakes, test-based accountability, it is conceivable that such programs are sometimes the *cause* of poor instruction and limited learning rather than being a guaranteed cure. The most recent study using NAEP fails to find improved achievement or closing of achievement gaps associated with NCLB. Nonetheless, steadily rising gains in mathematics since 1990, especially at fourth grade, suggests that reforms have had beneficial effects. Although it is impossible to isolate the specific causes of large-scale trends, teacher survey data and smaller-scale studies of innovations tell us that content standards and improved curriculum have made more of a difference in effecting these changes than test scores and pressure alone.

Acknowledgments

The author wishes to thank Carl Kaestle, Katherine Ryan, and Nancy Cole for thoughtful comments and critique in response to earlier versions of the manuscript. Portions of this chapter were originally presented at the Spencer Foundation's 30th Anniversary Conference, "Traditions of Scholarship in Education," Chicago, January 24–25, 2002.

References

Alexander, L. & James, H. T. (1987). *The nation's report card: Improving the assessment of student achievement.* Washington, DC: National Academy of Education.

Baratz, J. C. (1980). Policy implications of minimum competency testing. In R. Jaeger & C. Tittle (Eds.), *Minimum competency achievement testing: Motives, models, measures, consequences* (pp. 529–539). Berkeley, CA: McCutchan.

Brickell, H. M. (1978). Seven key notes on minimum competency testing. *Phi Delta Kappan*, 59 (9), 589–592.

California State Department of Education. (1973, January). *Feedback, 1.* Sacramento, CA: California State Department of Education.

Cannell, J. (1987). *Nationally normed elementary achievement testing in America's public schools: How all 50 states are above the national average.* Daniels, WV: Friends for Education.

Center on Education Policy. (2007). *Answering the question that matters most: Has student achievement increased since No Child Left Behind?* Washington, DC: Center on Education Policy.

College Board. (1977). *On further examination: Report of the advisory panel on the Scholastic Aptitude Test score decline.* New York: College Board.

Cook, W. W. (1941). Achievement tests. In W. S. Monroe (Ed.), *Encyclopedia of educational research* (pp. 1283–1301). New York: Macmillan.

Cronbach, L. J., Ambron, S. R., Dornbusch, S. M., Hess, R. D., Hornik, R. C., Phillips, D. C., et al. (1980). *Toward reform of program evaluation: Aims, methods, and institutional arrangements.* San Francisco: Jossey Bass.

Darling-Hammond, L. & Wise, A. E. (1985). Beyond standardization: State standards and school improvement. *Elementary School Journal*, 85 (3), 315–336.

Dillon, S. (2006, March 26). Schools cut back subjects to push reading and math. *New York Times*. Online, available at: http://www.nytimes.com/2006/03/26/education/26child.html (accessed February 21, 2008).

Duke, D. L. (1985). What is the nature of educational excellence and should we try to measure it? *Phi Delta Kappan*, 66 (10), 671–674.

Elmore, R. F. & Rothman, R. (Eds.) (1999). *Testing, teaching, and learning: A guide for states and school districts*. Washington, DC: National Academy Press.

Findley, J. (1978). Westside's minimum competency graduation requirements: A program that works. *Phi Delta Kappan*, 59 (9), 614–618.

Frederiksen, J. R. & Collins, A. (1989). A systems approach to educational testing. *Educational Researcher*, 18 (9), 27–32.

Glaser, R. (1987). Commentary by the National Academy of Education. In L. Alexander & H. T. James (Eds.), *The nation's report card: Improving the assessment of student achievement* (pp. 43–76). Washington, DC: National Academy of Education.

Glass, G. V (1978). Standards and criteria. *Journal of Educational Measurement*, 15 (4), 237–261.

Goslin, D. A. (1963). *The search for ability: Standardized testing in social perspective*. New York: Russell Sage Foundation.

Grissmer, D., Flanagan, A., Kawata, J., & Williamson, S. (2000). *Improving student achievement: What state NAEP test scores tell us*. Santa Monica, CA: RAND.

Halperin, S. (1975). ESEA ten years later. *Educational Researcher*, 4 (8), 5–9.

Heller, K. A., Holtzman, W. H., & Messick, S. (Eds.). (1982). *Placing children in special education: A strategy for equity*. Washington, DC: National Academy Press.

Hess, F. M. (2002). *Reform, resistance,... retreat? The predictable politics of accountability in Virginia*. In D. Ravitch (Ed.), *Brookings Papers on Educational Policy: 2002* (pp. 69–122). Washington, DC: Brookings Institution Press.

Klein, S. P., Hamilton, L. S., McCaffrey, D. F., & Stecher, B. M. (2000). *What do test scores in Texas tell us?* Santa Monica, CA: RAND.

Koretz, D., Linn, R. L., Dunbar, S. B., & Shepard, L. A. (1991, April). The effects of high-stakes testing on achievement: Preliminary findings about generalization across tests. Paper presented at the annual meeting of the American Educational Research Association, Chicago.

Lee, J. (2006). *Tracking achievement gaps and assessing the impact of NCLB on the gaps: An in-depth look into national and state reading and math outcome trends*. Cambridge, MA: Civil Rights Project at Harvard University.

McLaughlin, M. W. (1975). *Evaluation and reform: The Elementary and Secondary Education Act of 1965*. Cambridge, MA: Ballinger.

McLaughlin, M. W. & Shepard, L. A. (1995). *Improving education through standards-based reform. A report of the National Academy of Education Panel on standards-based reform*. Stanford, CA: National Academy of Education.

McNeil, L. & Valenzuela, A. (2000). *The harmful impact of the TAAS system of testing in Texas: Beneath the accountability rhetoric*. Cambridge, MA: Harvard University Civil Rights Project.

Madaus, G. F., West, M. M., Harmon, M. C., Lomax, R. G., & Viator, K. A. (1992). *The influence of testing on teaching math and science in grades 4–12*. Boston, MA: Center for the Study of Testing, Evaluation, and Educational Policy, Boston College.

Manzo, K. K. (2005, March 15). Social studies losing out to reading, math, *Education Week*, 24 (1), 16–17.

Messick, S., Beaton, A., & Lord, F. (1983). *National Assessment of Educational Progress reconsidered: A new design for a new era*. Princeton, NJ: National Assessment of Educational Progress.

National Center for Education Statistics. (2007). *Mapping 2005 state proficiency standards onto the NAEP scales* (NCES 2007–482). U.S. Department of Education. Washington, DC: National Center for Education Statistics.

National Commission on Excellence in Education. (1983). *A nation at risk: The imperative for educational reform*. Washington, DC: U.S. Department of Education.

National Council of Teachers of Mathematics. (1989). *Curriculum and evaluation standards for school mathematics.* Reston, VA: National Council of Teachers of Mathematics.

National Council on Education Standards and Testing. (1992, January 24). *Raising standards for American education: A report to Congress, the Secretary of Education, the National Education Goals Panel, and the American people.* Washington, DC: U.S. Government Printing Office.

Owens, B. (1999, December 8). Announcement of "Putting Children First: A plan for safe and excellent public schools" [Remarks as prepared for delivery]. Online, available at: http://www.state.co.us/childrenfirst/ChildrenFirstRemarks.htm (accessed February 21, 2008).

Pipho, C. (1978). Minimum competency testing in 1978: A look at state standards. *Phi Delta Kappan,* 59 (9), 585–588.

Pipho, C. (1985). The excellence movement: On ice for the summer? *Phi Delta Kappan,* 66 (10), 669–670.

Popham, W. J. (1987). The merits of measurement-driven instruction. *Phi Delta Kappan,* 68 (9), 679–682.

Resnick, D. P. (1980). Minimum competency testing historically considered. *Review of Research in Education,* 8, 3–29.

Resnick, D. P. (1982). History of educational testing. In A. K. Wigdor & W. R. Garner (Eds.), *Ability testing: Uses, consequences, and controversies, Part II* (pp. 173–194). Washington, DC: National Academy Press.

Resnick, L. B. & Resnick, D. P. (1992). Assessing the thinking curriculum: New tools for educational reform. In B. R. Gifford & M. C. O'Connor (Eds.), *Changing assessments: Alternative views of aptitude, achievement, and instruction* (pp. 37–75). Boston, MA: Kluwer Academic Publishers.

Rottenberg, C. & Smith, M. L. (1990, April). Unintended effects of external testing in elementary schools. Paper presented at the annual meeting of the American Educational Research Association, Boston.

Shepard, L. A. & Dougherty, K. (1991, April). Effects of high stakes testing on instruction. Paper presented at the annual meeting of the American Educational Research Association, Chicago.

Shepard, L., Glaser, R., Linn, R., & Bohrnstedt, G. (1993). *Setting performance standards for student achievement.* Stanford, CA: National Academy of Education.

Smith, M. S. & O'Day, J. (1990). Systemic school reform. In S. H. Fuhrman & B. Malen (Eds.), *The politics of curriculum and testing: The 1990 yearbook of the Politics of Education Association* (pp. 233–267). London: Taylor & Francis.

Stake, R. E. (2007). NAEP, report cards and education: A review essay. *Education Review,* 10 (1). Online, available at: http://edrev.asu.edu/essays/v10n1index.html (accessed September 28, 2007).

Stecher, B. & Chun, T. (2001, November). *School and classroom practices during two years of educational reform in Washington state.* Los Angeles: Center for Research on Evaluation, Standards, and Student Testing, University of California, Los Angeles.

Stufflebeam, D. L., Jaeger, R. M., & Scriven, M. (1991, August). *Summative evaluation of the National Assessment Governing Board's inaugural 1990–91 effort to set achievement levels on the National Assessment of Educational Progress.* Washington, DC: National Assessment Governing Board.

Tallmadge, G. K. & Wood, C. T. (1978). *The user's guide: ESEA Title I evaluation and reporting system.* Mountain View, CA: RMC Research Corporation.

Taylor, G., Shepard, L., Kinner, F., & Rosenthal, J. (2001). *A survey of teachers' perspectives on high-stakes testing in Colorado: What gets taught, what gets lost.* Boulder, CO: Center for Research on Evaluation, Standards, and Student Testing, University of Colorado.

Terman, L. M. (1916). *The measurement of intelligence.* Boston, MA: Houghton Mifflin.

Tyack, D. (1974). *The one best system: A history of American urban education.* Cambridge, MA: Harvard University Press.

Tyler, R. W. (1966). The objectives and plans for a national assessment of educational progress. *Journal of Educational Measurement,* 3 (1), 1–4.

U.S. Congress Office of Technology Assessment. (1992, February). *Testing in American schools: Asking the right questions* (OTA-SET-519). Washington, DC: U.S. Government Printing Office.

U.S. General Accounting Office. (1993, June). *Educational achievement standards: NAGB's approach yields misleading interpretations* (Report No. GAO/PEMD-93-12). Washington, DC: U.S. General Accounting Office.

Wise, A. E. (1978). Minimum competency testing: Another case of hyper-rationalization. *Phi Delta Kappan*, 59 (9), 596–598.

Worthen, B. R. (1974). *A look at the mosaic of educational evaluation and accountability.* Portland, OR: Northwest Regional Educational Laboratory.

Worthen, B. R. & Sanders, J. R. (1973). *Educational evaluation: Theory and practice.* Belmont, CA: Wadsworth Publishing.

3

The Politics of Educational Accountability
Can the Clock be Turned Back?

Lorraine M. McDonnell

Since its passage, No Child Left Behind (NCLB) has dominated discussions of educational accountability and testing. Yet, NCLB is just one part of a larger controversy surrounding test-based accountability in public education that predates the federal legislation. The issue is how standardized test results should be used. Should they serve as one among several indicators of school quality or as the sole or dominant measure? Should they be part of a low-stakes accountability system providing data about public school performance under the assumption that information alone will lead people to act? Or, should the system be high stakes with tangible rewards and sanctions attached to test data as a goad to action. Although NCLB represents a major milestone in the move to a high-stakes system, the trend began a decade earlier with state policies that rewarded and sanctioned local districts and individual schools on the basis of their students' test scores.

In his chapter in this volume, "Educational accountability systems," Robert Linn discusses the possibility of using accountability system results "descriptively":

> Accountability system results can have value without making causal inferences about school quality, solely from the results of student achievement measures and demographic characteristics. Treating the results as *descriptive information and for identification of schools that require more intensive investigation of organizational and instructional process characteristics are potentially of considerable value. Rather than using the results of the accountability system as the sole determiner of sanctions for schools, they could be used to flag schools that need more intensive investigation to reach sound conclusions about needed improvements or judgments about quality.*
>
> Such a use of accountability system results would represent a profound change and would require revisions of state and federal laws. It is unlikely that such a change in perspective would be politically acceptable at the present time. The change, however, would make the use of

> accountability results more consistent with the tenets of scientific reasoning and research.
>
> (p. 21, emphasis added)

Linn does not provide additional detail in his chapter about how such a system might work. However, there appear to be two dimensions. The first is the basis on which a school is judged. A descriptive accountability system would require that indicators in addition to standardized test scores be used. Linn suggests that a low test score would serve as a trigger, leading to an analysis of other indicators measuring a school's organizational and instructional processes. The assumption is that including these indicators in determining a school's performance would produce more valid judgments and would also provide information useful in diagnosing the reasons for a school's low quality. An unanswered question is how these other factors would be weighted. Would a system be considered descriptive if, for example, standardized test scores were still the primary determinant of a school's status even if other indicators were used in assessing it and analyzing the reasons for its low performance?

Linn's conception of descriptive accountability does directly address a second dimension: whether a school's status, once determined, would then be used as part of a low- or high-stakes system. If the main purpose of having a descriptive accountability system is to improve the basis on which a school's status is determined, then that information might be used in either low- or high-stakes accountability regimes. Even if a descriptive system were conceived primarily as a mechanism for school improvement, remedial actions by schools might be voluntary or mandatory as part of a high-stakes system that imposed consequences (albeit ones assumed to be constructive) on low performing schools.

In this chapter, I analyze the likelihood that a widespread shift to a descriptive accountability system could occur. My assessment is grounded in the political science research literature on the determinants of public policy and on what is known about the politics of student testing. Most theories of policy change tend to be *ex post*—explaining cycles of stability and change after they occur—rather than predictive of future shifts. However, these theories can provide a basis for what might be called grounded speculation in considering two questions:

- How well-institutionalized is the prevailing system of test-based accountability?
- What conditions are necessary for major changes in accountability and testing policies, and are they likely to develop in the near future?

I conclude that although incremental changes are likely to expand the basis on which school performance is judged, the current high-stakes system with standardized assessments as the primary basis for evaluating schools is sufficiently well-institutionalized to persist over the next five to ten years.

The Current Testing Regime: How Well Entrenched Are its Ideas, Institutions, and Interests?

The Ideas

Although their theoretical models and research methods vary, most social policy analysts focus not just on the societal interests that shape policy, but also on the ideational and institutional processes through which those interests compete and resolve their differences. The literature on policy ideas defines the concept in several different ways. At its most basic, the term *policy ideas* refers to specific policy alternatives (e.g., test-based accountability) as well as to the organized principles and causal beliefs in which policy proposals are embedded (e.g., notions of democratic representation) (Beland, 2005, p. 2). Ideas capture normative and instrumental dimensions of policy. In the case of test-based accountability—whether low or high stakes—three ideas serve to rationalize the policy approach:

- As public institutions, schools should be held accountable to citizens and their elected representatives for their effective operation and especially for student learning (Gruber, 1987).
- However, because educators know a lot more about what occurs in schools than do either politicians or the public, this serious information asymmetry has often hindered efforts to hold schools accountable (Gormley & Weimer, 1999; McDonnell, 2004).
- Consequently, some kind of externally imposed, standardized instrument is needed to provide comparable data on schools and students, so as to equalize the information available to everyone with a stake in the educational system (U.S. Congress, 1992; Heubert & Hauser, 1999).

Four factors stand out as likely to be the most significant in explaining why test-based accountability developed as the dominant policy idea. The first is that testing is pervasive and widely accepted in modern society. Whether it is to help select candidates for employment, license barbers, lawyers, and those in other occupations, or to certify competency to drive a car, testing is viewed as a seemingly neutral way to make decisions and allocate societal benefits. Like most myths in public policy, the belief that standardized tests can provide sound information that eliminates the potential bias of individualized, case-by-case judgments is an influential one (De Neufville & Barton, 1987). A second related factor is that standardized testing was already widespread in education, and its uses had been growing over the past 30 years through various forms of diagnostic and admissions testing. The advent of minimum competency testing in the 1970s moved the concept from its diagnostic and allocational functions to an accountability purpose.

A third factor is the low cost of testing, particularly given its perceived effectiveness as an instrument of top-down policy and because in education, much of that cost is hidden and often shifted to the lowest levels of the system.[1] A final factor that helps explain how the idea of an externally imposed, standardized instrument evolved into the current test-based system was policymakers' desire to avoid excessive regulation and micromanagement. As Hess (2003, p. 59) notes, traditionally schools were judged on whether or not they complied with various regulations and directives, rather than on student performance or progress. The standards and accountability movement allowed policymakers to focus on specifying expected outcomes and then freeing educators to decide how to achieve them.

Ideas about accountability, transparency, and a reliance on standardized tests apply regardless of the consequences for those being held accountable. However, at a more specific level, high- and low-stakes testing make different assumptions about the incentives necessary to motivate policy targets to take action and change collective behavior. For policies based on low-stakes tests, the assumption is that a standardized test can reliably and validly measure student achievement; that politicians, educators, parents, and the public will then act on the information generated by the test; and that their actions will improve educational quality and student achievement. High stakes uses of tests, in contrast, are based on the assumption that information alone is insufficient to motivate educators to teach well and students to learn to high standards. Instead, the promise of rewards or the threat of sanctions is needed to ensure change. Rewards in the form of monetary bonuses may be given to schools or teachers; sanctions may be imposed through external oversight or takeover by higher-level officials. For individual students, high stakes include the use of tests in decisions about their promotion and graduation (Heubert & Hauser, 1999). The policy trajectory for test-based accountability has been away from low to high stakes largely because policymakers and other elites came to believe that their early reliance on information disclosure alone had proven inadequate to change school and classroom behavior.

Ideas do more than encapsulate a policy alternative or problem-solving approach. They also act as a persuasive device that advocates can use to convince others to support a particular policy proposal. The frames used to promote test-based accountability have varied over time. An early one focused on the need to enhance U.S. economic competitiveness by improving the skills and knowledge of young entrants into the workforce (e.g., G. H. W. Bush as quoted in McGuinn, 2006, p. 53). NCLB has been framed as a strategy to promote greater equity in schooling processes and outcomes, and as an efficiency measure to ensure more effective use of federal funds by states and school districts (Rudalevige, 2003). Through its link to content standards, test-based accountability has also been framed as a way to instill specific curricular values in schools and classrooms (McDonnell, 2004).

Like most major social policies, test-based accountability is grounded in normative and instrumental ideas with broad-based appeal. A strong belief in democratic accountability has been combined with a policy theory positing that the dissemination of information about school and student performance will change behavior. In their simplest form, the core elements of the policy idea include: the need for externally imposed political accountability; transparency as a way to equalize the information available to the public and professional educators; and assumptions about the sources of human motivation and the process of educational change. With the advent of high-stakes testing, policymakers have assumed that information as a policy tool needs to be joined with rewards and sanctions to augment its impact. Those espousing a descriptive form of accountability would have to challenge this belief in the power of testing and the usefulness of student score information decontextualized from school characteristics. Their success would depend on the appeal of the alternative idea, and on how well institutionalized test-based accountability has become.

The Institution of Test-Based Accountability

The education system's fragmentation is a critical institutional characteristic; not only do multiple levels of government share authority over and responsibility for public education and its funding, but power is also fragmented among institutions within each level. Historically, this fragmentation has made it more difficult for policy ideas to spread across jurisdictions. However, the emergence of national education interest groups, such as the National Governor's Association (NGA) and the Business Roundtable, has not only helped reduce the transaction costs associated with persuading policymakers state-by-state and community-by-community, but it has also accelerated the nationalization of policies such as high-stakes testing.

In his analysis of NCLB, Manna (2006) develops the concept of *borrowing strength* that "occurs when policy entrepreneurs[2] at one level of government attempt to push their agendas by leveraging the justification and capabilities that other governments elsewhere in the federal system possess" (p. 5). Like other authors (e.g., McDonnell, 2005a), Manna argues that the passage of NCLB was possible because state governments had earlier enacted reforms organized around standards and assessments. Policy entrepreneurs promoting NCLB could then mobilize around the *license*, or arguments, states had already made to justify the involvement of higher levels of government in classroom processes and outcomes, and around the *capacity* or resources and administrative structures that state reforms had created.

The opportunities and constraints stemming from a federalist policy system are clearly significant in estimating the likely success of various policy alternatives. However, equally or perhaps more important in predicting the likelihood of policy change is the extent to which a policy is institutionalized or embedded in political and administrative structures. Historical institutionalists have used the concept of *path dependence* to explain how and why social policies can become entrenched and difficult to alter. In its simplest form, path dependence refers to the process by which policy choices create institutional arrangements that make reversal or change costly.

Major social policies create networks of vested interests that benefit from a policy and that develop operational rules and structures to protect it from political attacks and attempts to alter it. These rules determine allocation procedures, performance standards, and the conditions under which the policy can be changed. Bureaucratic rules and structures often have political origins and reinforce the preferences of dominant political interests (Moe, 1990). But, once administrative structures and street-level practice are in place, they can take on a life of their own independent of the politics that created them. So, for example, teachers' tendency to focus their teaching on whatever academic content is being measured can become so embedded in their professional practice that it may not matter whether an accountability policy is based on high- or low-stakes rules and structures (McDonnell, 2004).

It is not possible to make a blanket assessment of the degree to which test-based accountability is institutionalized. Rather, one has to examine separate elements of the policy regime, as well as its design and implementation at different levels of the education system. At the federal level, standards and assessment as a strategy for increasing student achievement has been integrated into major categorical programs for over a decade. The effect has been to make federal education policy more coherent (Manna, 2006, p. 150), and thus more difficult to change than when there were more small, disparate categorical programs. However, it is too soon to judge how well institutionalized some elements of federal policy are. For example, it is reasonable to assume that adequate yearly progress (AYP) is still a tenuous concept that could be significantly modified or even eliminated, and it is not yet clear how far the federal government is willing to go in enforcing AYP and other provisions of NCLB if states, local districts, and schools fail to meet their requirements. So at the federal level, the core policy idea and some of its institutional arrangements are well established, while some newer elements are only weakly rooted in structure and practice.

At the state level, the same pattern of well-institutionalized elements operate side-by-side with newer, seemingly less stable ones. By the time NCLB was enacted, the overwhelming majority of states had experience with some form of statewide standardized testing of elementary and secondary students. However, only six states used standards-based assessments to test students in all the subjects and grade levels required by NCLB, although 20 were testing students in English/language arts and mathematics in grades 3–8 and once in grades 10, 11, or 12 (Center for Education Policy, 2003, p. 23). Not only was the expanded scope of standardized testing new to most states with the enactment of NCLB, but only about half had assessment systems aligned with specific content and performance standards, and about the same number had linked positive or negative incentives to schools' test scores by 2001 (Council of Chief State School Officers, 2001; Hess, 2003).

Judged by the short duration these particular features have been in place, the costs of switching to other alternatives may not yet be prohibitive, and could be sustained under the right conditions. However, two caveats are in order. First, the core policy idea of testing as an externally imposed accountability instrument seems well established, so the possibilities for change are likely to be in how a particular accountability system is structured, the relative importance of student testing results in that system, and the stakes attached to those results rather than in the abolition of standardized testing. Second, some of the elements of a descriptive accountability system have already been tried by states and either rejected or allowed to atrophy. For example, in the 1990s, a number of states intended to assist teachers in developing curriculum-embedded assessments that would be tied to state standards, but would be administered and scored by teachers at their discretion and used for instructional, rather than external accountability, purposes. However, faced with fiscal constraints, states abandoned this project, viewing it as a lower priority than developing and maintaining their external accountability systems. Similarly, earlier efforts to build statewide indicator systems that included more comprehensive and valid measures of school quality—particularly related to students' opportunity-to-learn—have stagnated as states have turned their attention to calculating AYP and other student demographic measures required by NCLB. Consequently, because forms of descriptive accountability have already been on the policy agendas of some states but have not flourished as viable alternatives, that past history may actually strengthen the staying power of the status quo.

At the local level, externally imposed testing systems have altered classroom practices. A variety of studies using different research methods have found that teachers modify their instruction in response to state assessments, with studies conducted prior to NCLB also reporting that changes occurred whether or not the state used its test to impose tangible consequences on schools (for a review of these studies, see McDonnell, 2004, pp. 169–174). At the same time, the extent of change has been largely confined to shifts in classroom activities (e.g., devoting more instructional time to tested subjects, aligning curricular content with state standards) rather than in how students are taught conceptual understandings of subject matter. The limited information available on the school- and classroom-level effects of NCLB point to similar, though intensified, changes. For example, several evaluations of

NCLB's implementation (Center for Education Policy, 2006a; Hamilton et al., 2007) have found increased efforts to align curriculum and instruction with state academic standards and assessments, expanded instructional time at the elementary level in reading and mathematics at the expense of other non-tested subjects, teacher reports of increased use of test data in adjusting their instruction to address student needs, and greater district regulation of what and how teachers teach.

Although they are significant and have produced a larger effect than top-down policy usually induces in education, these changes are not yet deeply embedded in school and classroom practice. Something like the amount of instructional time spent on a particular subject is relatively easy to modify. So, although it is clear that teachers change their behavior in response to externally imposed assessments, the degree of institutionalization depends on such factors as the length of time a policy is in place, the organizational routines developed to socialize teachers into new classroom practices, and the incentives—material and otherwise—to maintain or change behaviors expected by the policy.

The Interests

The successful enactment of legislation does not ensure that a policy will be implemented or that it will endure. Consequently, the interests supporting a policy need to establish administrative structures that will be difficult to dismantle if they no longer prevail in the legislative arena and opponents attempt to abolish or significantly alter the policy (Moe, 1990). In scanning the interest group terrain around test-based accountability, then, we need to consider not only which groups have the incentives and resources to maintain or change it, but also whether or not its administrative structures reinforce the interests of those with a stake in perpetuating the status quo.

Three features characterize the interest environment for test-based accountability. The first is the number and diversity of the groups involved. They range from well-organized national organizations such as the Business Roundtable and the National Education Association to small, grassroots parent groups. In between are organizations that represent elected officials, test publishers, school administrators, education researchers, students with special needs, and those pressing for equal learning opportunities for all students. These groups all subscribe to the same general goal of improving student learning, but disagree about the means to achieve it and the role of testing in education reform strategies.

A second feature is that these interests do not divide along traditional partisan or ideological lines. Standards and assessment has been a bipartisan issue at the state level since the policy's inception, with the active involvement of both Democratic and Republican governors who recognized its appeal for business elites interested in economic development and for voters concerned about the quality of public schools and the use of their tax dollars. At the national level, Republican support for test-based accountability has been a way to neutralize the Democrats' traditional advantage in public perceptions about the two parties' relative ability to handle education (Hess & McGuinn, 2002).

The relationship between the institutionalized elements of test-based accountability and the interests that benefit from them is a third feature. One group that benefits is state policymakers who have found that espousing education reform through standards and accountability has given them an electoral advantage with their constituents. In contrast, their opposition to parts of NCLB and to the general trend toward greater federal involvement in specifying the direction of state and local education policy strongly suggests that they would be supportive of changes in federal policy as long as they did not threaten the established core of state accountability policies.

The interest with the largest financial stake in the current system is the testing industry. The General Accountability Office (2003) estimates that from fiscal years 2002 through 2008, states will spend between $1.9 billion and $5.3 billion (depending on the mix of multiple-choice and open-response items) for tests mandated under NCLB. Although the increased demand has prompted some new entrants into the field, the testing market remains highly concentrated among a few firms who have moved to become full-service providers offering test development, administration, and scoring (Olson, 2004). Although little is known about the political activities of test publishers, and they have been relatively invisible as political actors, they do have an association working on their behalf and the major test publishers have at least a modest lobbying presence in Washington. However, their interest is in the requirement that standardized tests be administered on a regular basis, not necessarily in how test results are used. So, issues of high- versus low-stakes testing and whether test scores are the sole determinant in judging schools or one among several indicators is of considerably less importance to them.

Other major interests supporting test-based accountability do so largely because of its effectiveness in changing school and classroom behavior. Although critics argue that the downsides of the various manifestations of "teaching to the test" outweigh the benefits, organizations such as the national Business Roundtable see it as the most effective intervention currently available to improve student achievement. The extensive public relations and lobbying operations of the Business Roundtable and its state affiliates have been directed at maintaining NCLB and blocking attempts to weaken it. But, it is not clear whether the Roundtable and its member firms would abandon or diminish their strong support for standards and accountability if another educational alternative could be shown to promote their economic competitiveness and human capital formation goals equally well or better.

Similarly, some civil rights groups and advocates for students living in poverty, such as the Education Trust, the Citizens' Commission on Civil Rights, and the National Council of La Raza, support test-based accountability (and particularly NCLB) because right now it seems to be the most effective way to force schools to address the achievement gap. Although the evidence is largely anecdotal and unsystematic at this point, it does appear that the NCLB requirement to report test scores by subgroup has led districts and schools to pay greater attention to students who were often ignored when only grade- or school-level averages were reported. Like the Business Roundtable, these groups are committed to a particular educational goal, and it may be the case that their support of test-based accountability would diminish if other, equally effective strategies were available to promote greater equality of educational opportunity. In contrast, groups such as the NAACP, the Council for Exceptional Children, and the National Association for Bilingual Education, have called for shifting NCLB's emphasis and that of other testing and accountability policies from sanctioning schools to holding the federal government, states, and local communities accountable for providing the resources needed to improve student learning, and to basing evaluations of school performance on achievement measures beyond just multiple-choice tests (Forum on Educational Accountability, 2007). This split among groups sharing similar goals but differing on what the most effective strategies are will likely lead to expanded criteria for judging schools, increased resources, and greater flexibility in how schools are sanctioned, but it is unlikely to result in standardized tests being displaced as the dominant basis for high-stakes judgments as long as some public interest groups remain allied with influential economic-based ones such as the Business Roundtable.

Although ostensibly supporting the general concept, organized teachers have been the interest most critical of test-based accountability. The National Education Association (NEA) has traditionally voiced stronger criticisms and has been more active in its opposition than the American Federation of Teachers (AFT).[3] Although both unions announced during the deliberations over NCLB that they supported the concept of using standardized test scores to evaluate school performance, they differed on how the law should be operationalized. The NEA opposed the use of assessment scores as a single measure of school performance and pressed for requiring that states also consider student attendance, high school graduation rates, and the percentage of certified teachers in a school. In contrast, the AFT initially believed that standardized tests could be a sufficient indicator, but wanted Congress to ensure that the exams were of high quality and aligned with state curricular standards. Since the passage of NCLB, both unions have been publicly critical of the law's implementation, with the NEA filing lawsuits and the AFT working behind the scenes through the regulation drafting process to ease what it considers some of the law's more unworkable provisions.

The AFT and the NEA have both argued that accountability should be based on multiple measures of student progress and that school-level results should be reported in ways that provide

> a context for understanding test results by including data, such as class size, numbers of certified teachers, student attendance and mobility rates, that make the results intelligible to parents and the public and useful to teachers and other school personnel.
>
> (American Federation of Teachers, 2002)

In formulating their stances on test-based accountability, the AFT and the NEA face a major dilemma. Their members are feeling the brunt of what many believe is unfair scrutiny and they expect their unions to fix the problem. At the same time, although the teacher unions continue to be major political players through their lobbying and electoral activities, they are less influential than in the past and they can gain little for their members if they appear to oppose the dominant policy idea of test-based accountability.[4]

Summary

The answer to the first question about the degree to which test-based accountability is institutionalized is a mixed one. The core policy idea seems well entrenched. It is connected to a powerful normative belief in democratic accountability and, more recently, to notions of equality of educational opportunity. It has instrumental value in that it appears to be more effective than past top-down policies in shaping classroom practices, and except for the concept of school choice, no other ideas have emerged robust enough to challenge it in the policy arena.

But, a powerful policy idea does not necessarily mean that all policies reflecting its principles and assumptions are well institutionalized. In the case of test-based accountability, the institutionalized elements are those that states implemented over the past 20 years: the administration of standardized tests in several subjects and grade levels on a regular schedule, the public reporting of test scores, and more recently, the alignment of those tests with state-defined academic content standards. Less widespread and well established prior to NCLB were forms of high-stakes testing and administrative rules specific to NCLB such as universal testing in grades 3–8 and consequences based on calculations of AYP.

At this time, the balance of interest group influence favors the continuation of the well-institutionalized elements of test-based accountability. For most federal and state policymakers, the political and administrative costs of moving off this path would be very high. But incremental changes, such as modifications to NCLB, or the addition of other indicators to state accountability systems, would be less costly and could even enhance the political value of the core concept. For groups other than test publishers, support of the concept stems largely from its instrumental value in advancing their organizational goals. Consequently, they might be amenable to alternatives that promise similar pay-offs in furthering their group objectives. The history of the teacher unions and other groups opposed to test-based accountability over the past two decades suggests that they will continue to be able to block or modify parts of accountability programs that threaten their members' interests, but they are unlikely to be successful in promoting alternatives that seriously challenge the core policy idea of test-based accountability.

Shifting to a Descriptive Accountability System: What Would it Take?

Two models of agenda setting and policy change have withstood numerous empirical tests in a variety of policy domains, and they now dominate the political science and policy analysis research literature. The first, proposed by John Kingdon (1995), explains the process by which a proposal reaches the governmental agenda and is considered by policymakers, though not necessarily enacted into law. Kingdon hypothesized that policy emerges from the coupling of three independent process streams—problems, policy proposals, and politics.

> They are largely independent of one another, and each develops according to its own dynamics and rules. But at some critical junctures the three streams are joined, and the greatest policy changes grow out of that coupling of problems, policy proposals, and politics.
>
> (p. 19)

> A problem is recognized, a solution is developed and available to the policy community, a political change makes it the right time for policy change, and potential constraints are not severe.
>
> (p. 165)

Policy entrepreneurs are often critical to the process of bringing the three streams together—in effect, opening a policy window. They are willing to invest their resources in calling attention to problems and mobilizing support for pet proposals in the hope of obtaining future policies they favor.

In contrast to Kingdon's agenda-setting model, Baumgartner and Jones (1993, 2002) set out to explain a persistent condition in U.S. public policy: although most policymaking is incremental, dramatic and deep changes in policy do occur. Borrowing from the natural sciences, Baumgartner and Jones call this condition *punctuated equilibrium*—long periods of stability interrupted by major alterations to the system. Stability is maintained through the creation of policy monopolies that are structural arrangements supported by powerful policy ideas. These ideas or policy images are generally connected to core political values, combine empirical information and emotive appeals, can be easily understood, and are communicated directly and simply through image and rhetoric.

However, policy monopolies and the interests they represent can be disrupted, resulting in major policy changes. A primary reason such changes occur is that those opposed to the policy monopoly, or excluded from it, constitute slack resources policy entrepreneurs can mobilize. They do so through a redefinition of the dominant policy image using ideas that challenge it and thereby capture the imagination of the media, policymakers, and the public. They provide new understandings of policy problems and new ways of conceptualizing solutions. These ideas can fuel powerful changes as they are communicated through a variety of rhetorical mechanisms, including stories about decline or negative consequences resulting from the current policy monopoly and stories of hope about what can be accomplished with a new framing of the policy problem and solution (Stone, 2002, p. 138). Even when new ideas lead to policy changes, however, the old policy monopoly often continues until the institutional structures and norms through which new policies are implemented are also transformed.

These two models have four elements in common that can serve as the basis for speculation about the likelihood that more descriptive forms of educational accountability could augment or replace the existing system. They are: the extent of problems with the current policy monopoly, the power of the competing idea, political conditions, and the availability of policy entrepreneurs.

Problems with the Current Policy Monopoly

Problems can be instrumental, such as difficulties encountered during implementation, unintended consequences, or the policy's inability to produce its expected effects. For test-based accountability, the types of problems that might be identified could include the system's inability to make valid distinctions among schools, narrowing of the curriculum to focus on tested subjects, schools' inability to act on assessment data to improve student performance, or the policy's failure to produce sustained achievement for all or most student groups.[5] Consistent with Baumgartner and Jones' model, however, problems with a current policy monopoly can also be political and reinforce instrumental problems. Groups that are outside the policy monopoly because they were sidelined during the formulation process or because their interests are not reflected in a policy's goals and operational framework can present a serious political threat to its stability. Several groups fit that category for test-based accountability. The most significant are classroom teachers, but some parents of students attending schools designated as failing to improve and members of the education research community are also groups that feel their views and interests have been ignored in forms of test-based accountability. Their discontent is a resource that could be mobilized in opposition to existing policy.

Power of the Competing Idea

The second common element is Kingdon's policy proposal or Baumgartner and Jones' notion of an alternative policy image. Both models specify that for this alternative idea to change the dominant image, it has to provide a more compelling understanding of the policy problem and offer a potentially effective solution that is politically and administratively feasible. Advocates have to be able to communicate this alternative in simple language to engage a wide range of audiences. Based on what we know about the degree of institutionalization of test-based accountability, it appears that any alternative would have to embody the following characteristics: (1) demonstrate a direct link to improving and equalizing student achievement; (2) make schooling processes and outcomes transparent and publicly accountable; and (3) motivate the public and its agents (namely, policymakers and educators), as well as students, to work to raise the quality of schooling. In terms of feasibility, advocates would either have to demonstrate that an alternative would not cost significantly more than the status quo and would not disrupt existing institutional arrangements, or if it did, that it was superior to the current system with benefits significantly outweighing costs.

Although alternatives have been proposed that move the accountability system closer to a descriptive one, it is not evident that any are sufficiently comprehensive or compelling at this time to challenge the current policy monopoly successfully. However, some ideas have the potential to modify elements of test-based accountability while not threatening its core concept. For example, the National Research Council (NRC) Committee on the Foundations of Assessment proposed alternative approaches to the design and interpretation of student assessments that build on research-based models of cognition and learning, and thus provide more valid judgments about student achievement. The NRC committee's "vision for the future of assessment" includes the use of classroom-based and large-scale assessments, grounded in principles of how students think and learn and measuring achievement in a variety of ways (e.g., responding to teachers' questions, producing projects, working with computerized tutoring systems). Teachers would use this information to modify instruction, and large-scale assessments would provide more valid data about the characteristics of competent student performance as compared with that of less proficient achievement (Pellegrino, Chudowsky, & Glaser, 2001). Recently, state policymakers and commercial test publishers have drawn on ideas in the NRC report and similar analyses in promoting the use of formative assessments as a supplement to the NCLB-mandated ones. These assessments, embedded in teachers' instruction, are designed to help them modify their instruction in light of data about which content and skill domains students are mastering and where they are encountering difficulties (Olson, 2005, 2006a, 2006b). However, as formulated and discussed at this time, these classroom-based assessments will operate at the periphery of the current test-based accountability system, rather than replace it.

Another alternative that has been discussed is an adaptation of the British system in which schools are visited every three years for several days by a team of inspectors. The purpose is to judge the school's effectiveness and efficiency, with an emphasis on the quality of its leadership and the capacity of the school to make improvements. Although student performance data are one factor, the school's own self-evaluation is the starting point, and input from teachers, parents, and students is also considered along with the inspectors' on-site observations. The assumption is that the inspection team's report will provide a measure of accountability and help a school manage its improvement (Office for Standards in Education, 2005). New York City, with assistance from British consultants, has begun to adopt this model, and will make it a part of its own accountability system beginning in 2007–2008. The aim of the program is to balance outcome measures, such as test scores, with a more qualitative picture of how schools are functioning, particularly in how they use data to meet students' needs (Archer, 2006). This model embodies the use of organizational and instructional process measures as a complement to achievement results in the manner of a descriptive accountability system, and also includes publicly available ratings of school performance. In essence, it is designed to motivate schools to improve student performance and to give them the analytical tools to inform their efforts.

These are just two examples of alternative policy ideas now under discussion and being implemented in a number of localities though they are not yet on the national policy agenda.[6] Options such as these could, under the right conditions, become more widespread. However, they do not represent comprehensive approaches to education reform in the way that the standards and assessment and school choice movements do. Rather, they are partial remedies to the shortcomings of the dominant policy paradigm, and as such, can probably only be offered as enhancements to it. It is unlikely that ideas such as these will dislodge annual standardized assessments of students as the primary measure of school performance. Nor will they likely lead to a reversal of the current high-stakes system.

Political Conditions

The third element of Kingdon's and Baumgartner and Jones' models is the political conditions that can facilitate policy change. One might think of identified problems and the availability of possible solutions as necessary but not sufficient conditions for agenda setting and change. Focusing on shorter-term processes, Kingdon notes that some policy windows open on a predictable schedule and provide opportunities for agenda setting. These include elections, budgetary cycles, and legislative reauthorizations. But, policy windows may also open unpredictably through focusing events such as crises or disasters that call attention to problems or highlight ones already identified. Because Baumgartner and Jones are explaining the collapse and replacement of well-established policy monopolies, the political process they outline has a longer time frame, and involves mobilization of those outside the monopoly around an alternative policy image. That policy image, if effectively communicated, is picked up by the media and other opinion leaders, and it eventually becomes the subject of deliberations by relevant policymakers. Public opinion is also a factor, though changes in public support for a dominant policy image tend to lag media and elite shifts.

Predicting whether political conditions are conducive to a policy window opening for alternatives to test-based accountability is speculative at this point because most of the relevant factors are in flux. For example, even though the partisan balance in Congress shifted after the 2006 midterm elections, divisions within the political parties between the leadership and some newly elected and more junior members will likely affect not only the reauthorization of NCLB, but also what political incentives are created for state action. However, whether demands to remedy identified problems with the status quo will result in more than incremental legislative changes is difficult to gauge at this time. With regard to other factors, the media are certainly a potential resource that can be tapped by those offering critiques of test-based accountability and presenting alternative approaches. Coverage of student testing policies—especially NCLB—and problems encountered during implementation continue to be a regular feature in print and electronic media.[7]

Public opinion, in contrast, is more difficult to interpret and to discern its implications for changing the current policy monopoly. Until recently, a variety of poll data indicated strong support for standardized testing and its high-stakes uses, with the public also seeming to acknowledge its shortcomings and potential consequences (for a review of these data, see McDonnell, 2005b, pp. 41–43). The shape of public opinion has changed somewhat since the advent of NCLB, although even four years after its enactment, less than half of public school parents (49%) and only 42% of those without children in school reported that they knew a great deal or a fair amount about NCLB (Rose & Gallup, 2006). Of those who reported knowing anything about NCLB, only 26% thought it is helping schools in their community, with 21% viewing it as hurting the schools and 37% seeing it as making no difference. The overwhelming majority (69%) of those questioned in the 2006 *Phi Delta Kappan* (PDK)/Gallup survey also believed that the performance of students on a single statewide test does not provide a fair picture of whether or not the school needs improvement (Rose & Gallup, 2006).[8]

Despite this seemingly negative assessment of NCLB and an acknowledgment of the limits of standardized testing, the majority of parents with public school students indicate that the emphasis on achievement testing in their community is either about right (37%) or not enough (17%) (Rose & Gallup,

2006). In addition, over 60% of parents and those without school-age children favor requiring that all students pass an exam in order to graduate from high school, and support for that particular use of high-stakes tests has been quite stable for close to 30 years (Hochschild & Scott, 1998). Consistent with earlier surveys, recent public opinion about standardized testing suggests ambivalence, with the public recognizing its limits while also supporting its high-stakes uses. Nevertheless, although core attitudes about testing remain relatively stable, public opinion has become more negative since the advent of NCLB. However, there is no evidence of a strong backlash, so both those supporting the status quo and those challenging it could potentially exploit public opinion.

Policy Entrepreneurs

The fourth element common to both models is the critical role of policy entrepreneurs who can create the conditions that bring problem, proposal, and political streams together, and who can mobilize those opposed to or disenchanted with the current policy monopoly around an alternative. Major changes in education policy in the recent past, such as school finance reform, standards and assessment, and school choice, resulted from the combined efforts of policy entrepreneurs who came from academia, foundations, public interest law firms, interest groups, and elected officials. Entrepreneurs promoting these past reforms took advantage of education policy's multiple institutional venues, and "borrowed strength" using the license and capacity afforded by different governmental levels.

But, the most important resource at the heart of all these entrepreneurial efforts was an idea that embodied both normative principles and an instrumental theory about how those principles could be advanced. One need only recall "fiscal neutrality," "systemic reform," and "market competition" to recognize how central a powerful, but easily conveyed, idea is to the process of policy change. Policy entrepreneurs, like those in business, need something to sell. Even if the problem and political streams are conducive to change and even if there are groups motivated to challenge a policy monopoly, there has to be a compelling and feasible option in the proposal stream that skilled policy entrepreneurs believe in and can promote.

As the preceding analysis suggests, there do not appear to be any ideas currently under discussion in academic or policy circles equivalent in potential appeal to those that framed major education reforms over the past 30 years. Policy entrepreneurs, concerned about test-based accountability, could promote one or more of the available options most akin to a descriptive accountability system, but they will likely have to sell them as improvements or modifications of the dominant policy monopoly, not as alternatives to it.

Conclusions

At first glance, it appears that test-based accountability is ripe for major change. The reauthorization of NCLB opened a policy window: there are identified problems with the existing policy monopoly and those problems are most evident in the least institutionalized elements associated with NCLB; and classroom teachers, a group with political resources, are bearing a disproportionate share of the policy's costs. All these conditions have been widely reported in the media, and public opinion seems to recognize the shortcomings of test-based accountability, and is growing increasingly skeptical of its promised benefits.

Nevertheless, the analysis presented in this chapter suggests that test-based accountability is likely to remain the dominant policy paradigm for the near future. Incremental changes seem quite likely, and some of them may introduce enhancements that will make judgments about student and school performance more valid and give educators, policymakers, and the public better diagnostic tools to use in improving educational quality. However, educational accountability does not appear to be poised for the kind of fundamental changes that define a punctuated equilibrium in policy analysis. Rather, its core elements—large-scale state assessments as the dominant element and the consequences attached to test results—are well institutionalized. Test-based accountability has become path dependent with institutional arrangements well embedded in states and local school districts.

Still, although these administrative structures and the policies they represent are costly to change, they could be altered. But, they cannot be changed without a powerful idea that offers a feasible alternative to the status quo. Although it should reflect an understanding of and offer a solution to problems with current policy, that idea must be more than a critique of the existing system. It must embody normative ideals and instrumental tools that provide an alternative vision of how educational quality can be improved and that can persuade policymakers and the interests they represent to incur the costs of change. Furthermore, as Kingdon's and Baumgartner and Jones' models indicate, the process of major policy change is complex, strategic, and often serendipitous. Consequently, ideas need champions—skilled policy entrepreneurs invested in those ideas and able to use them to mobilize supporters and to maneuver their alternative vision through the multiple venues of educational policymaking. Descriptive accountability currently lacks sufficiently compelling ideas and champions influential enough to challenge test-based accountability, but it may be a source for incremental improvements to the reigning policy monopoly.

Acknowledgments

The author thanks William Firestone and Margaret Goertz for constructive reviews that were most useful in clarifying the chapter's main arguments, and is grateful to the editors for their extraordinary efforts in sharpening and condensing the text.

Notes

1. Clearly, the effects of mandated assessments have not always been beneficial for students or what policymakers intended. Nevertheless, given the limited array of strategies available to them, politicians have viewed standardized testing as too powerful a lever not to use it. From their perspective, assessment policies also produce results quickly because test scores typically rise during the first few years after a new test is introduced. The validity of such score gains has long been questioned by researchers (Koretz, McCaffrey, & Hamilton, 2001; Linn, 2000), but most policymakers remain convinced that something real occurs if only because the tests shine a public spotlight on educators who must then respond.
2. Policy entrepreneurs are "advocates who are willing to invest their resources—time, energy, reputation, money—to promote a position in return for anticipated future gain in the form of material, purposive, or solidary benefits" (Kingdon, 1995, p. 179). Policy entrepreneurs can occupy a variety of formal and informal policymaking roles, but the more effective ones typically have a claim to a public hearing, are known for their political connections or negotiating skills, and are persistent (pp. 180–181). The potential role of policy entrepreneurs in moving to a descriptive accountability regime is discussed in subsequent section.
3. For example, both unions have argued strongly in favor of using other indicators in addition to a single test score in high-stakes decisions about individual students. However, the AFT has been more supportive of the high-stakes use of tests in making promotion and graduation decisions than the NEA, which voted to support any legislation that allows parents to opt their children out of standardized testing requirements (Heubert & Hauser, 1999; Associated Press, 2001).
4. Grassroots groups, largely consisting of suburban, middle-class parents, have also periodically opposed test-based accountability. Reasons for parental opposition vary, but the most common stem from concerns that extensive test preparation is hindering classroom innovation; that the standards being tested are vague or inappropriate; that reliance on tests disadvantages children who either have not had the opportunity to learn the material being tested or are poor test takers; and that tests consume too much time and are a source of stress, especially for younger students (Schrag, 2000). However, these so-called "testing backlash" groups have only arisen in a few states, and have not been institutionalized. Groups that were operating several years ago are not currently active, though they could be mobilized again if there is a catalytic event or issue.
5. Some of these problems have already been identified with regard to NCLB—e.g., the shortcomings of AYP as compared with a growth model of student achievement (Peterson & West, 2006); the narrowing of the curriculum (Center for Education Policy, 2006a); and limits on states' ability to work with large numbers of schools requiring restructuring (Center for Education Policy, 2006b).
6. In seeking policy options based on descriptive accountability, advocates might also look to other policy domains that have used mandatory information disclosure as a policy instrument. For example, in their review of such policies, Weil, Fung, Graham, and Fagotto (2006) evaluated eight systems ranging from corporate financial disclosure to restaurant hygiene cards and toxics release reporting. They found that transparency policies are effective only when the information they produce is embedded in the routine decision-making of both information users and disclosers. Consequently, such policies need to be designed with careful attention to both parties' decisionmaking routines and cognitive processes, and to their incentive systems and capacity.
7. For example, a Lexus-Nexus search of the *New York Times* between 2003 and 2006 found that an article mentioning NCLB appeared on average about once a week.
8. Supporters of NCLB have questioned the item wording in the *PDK*/Gallup poll and have noted that other surveys with different item wordings have found more positive public and parental attitudes toward testing (e.g., Susan Traiman's commentary in Rose & Gallup, 2004, p. 43; Greifner, 2006, p. 7).

It also appears that some of the negative assessment of NCLB stems from public opposition to reporting test scores by subgroups (54%) and a belief that students enrolled in special education should not be required to meet the same academic standards as all other students in a school (75%) (Rose & Gallup, 2006).

Another survey focused on attitudes toward standardized testing also suggests that there may be significant differences among ethnic groups. The Pew Hispanic Center/Kaiser Family Foundation (2004) *National Survey of Latinos* on education found that Latinos were significantly more supportive than either whites or African Americans of using standardized tests to ensure that all students meet national academic standards (81 versus 68%); to determine whether students are promoted or can graduate (75 versus 52%); and to rank or rate schools (69 versus 51%).

References

American Federation of Teachers. (2002, July). Convention resolution on standards-based assessment and accountability. Washington, DC: American Federation of Teachers.

Archer, J. (2006, May 17). British inspectors bring instructional focus to NYC. *Education Week*, 25 (37), 10.

Associated Press. (2001, July 8). Teachers vote to let parents decide on tests. *New York Times*, p. A15.

Baumgartner, F. & Jones, B. (1993). *Agendas and instability in American politics.* Chicago, IL: University of Chicago Press.

Baumgartner, F. & Jones, B. (2002). *Policy dynamics.* Chicago, IL: University of Chicago Press.

Beland, D. (2005). Ideas and social policy: An institutionalist perspective. *Social Policy and Administration*, 39 (1), 1–18.

Center for Education Policy. (2003). *From the capital to the classroom: State and federal efforts to implement the No Child Left Behind Act.* Washington, DC: Center for Education Policy.

Center for Education Policy. (2006a). *From the capital to the classroom: Year 4 of the No Child Left Behind Act.* Washington, DC: Center for Education Policy.

Center for Education Policy. (2006b). *Wrestling the devil in the details: An early look at restructuring in California.* Washington, DC: Center for Education Policy.

Council of Chief State School Officers. (2001). *State student assessment programs: Annual survey: Summary report.* Washington, DC: Council of Chief State School Officers.

De Neufville, J. & Barton, S. (1987). Myths and the definition of policy problems. *Policy Sciences*, 20, 181–206.

Forum on Educational Accountability. (2007). Online, available at: www.edaccountability.org (accessed February 15, 2007).

General Accountability Office. (2003). *Title I: Characteristics of tests will influence expenses* (GAO-03–389). Washington, DC: General Accountability Office.

Gormley, W., Jr. & Weimer, D. (1999). *Organizational report cards.* Cambridge, MA: Harvard University Press.

Greifner, L. (2006, August 30). NCLB seen as largely ineffective, PDK-Gallup poll finds. *Education Week*, 26 (1), 7.

Gruber, J. (1987). *Controlling bureaucracies: Dilemmas in democratic governance.* Berkeley, CA: University of California Press.

Hamilton, L., Stecher, B., Marsh, J., McCombs, J., Robyn, A., Russell, J., et al. (2007). *Standards-based accountability under No Child Left Behind: Experiences of teachers and administrators in three states.* Santa Monica, CA: RAND.

Hess, F. (2003). Refining or retreating: High-stakes accountability in the states. In Martin R. West & Paul E. Peterson (Eds.), *No Child Left Behind? The politics and practice of school accountability* (pp. 55–79). Washington, DC: Brookings Institution Press.

Hess, F. & McGuinn, P. (2002). Seeking the mantle of "opportunity": Presidential politics and the educational metaphor, 1964–2000. *Educational Policy*, 16 (1), 75–95.

Heubert, J. & Hauser, R. (Eds.). (1999). *High stakes: Testing for tracking, promotion, and graduation.* Washington, DC: National Academy Press.

Hochschild, J. & Scott, B. (1998). Trends: Governance and reform of public education in the United States. *Public Opinion Quarterly*, 62 (1), 79–120.
Kingdon, J. (1995). *Agendas, alternatives, and public policies* (2nd ed.). New York: Harper Collins College Publisher.
Koretz, D., McCaffrey, D., & Hamilton, L. (2001, April). Toward a framework for validating gains under high-stakes conditions. Paper presented at the annual meeting of the National Council on Measurement in Education, Seattle, WA.
Linn, R. (2000). Assessments and accountability. *Educational Researcher*, 29 (2), 4–16.
McDonnell, L. (2004). *Politics, persuasion, and educational testing.* Cambridge, MA: Harvard University Press.
McDonnell, L. (2005a). No Child Left Behind and the federal role in education: Evolution or revolution? *Peabody Journal of Education*, 80 (2), 19–38.
McDonnell, L. (2005b). Assessment and accountability from the policymaker's perspective. In J. L. Herman & E. H. Haertel (Eds.), *Uses and misuses of data for educational accountability and improvement. Yearbook of the National Society for the Study of Education* (pp. 35–54), Vol. 104, Part II. Malden, MA: Blackwell Publishing.
McGuinn, P. (2006). *No Child Left Behind and the transformation of federal education policy, 1965–2005.* Lawrence, KS: University Press of Kansas.
Manna, P. (2006). *School's in: Federalism and the national education agenda.* Washington, DC: Georgetown University Press.
Moe, T. (1990). Political institutions: The neglected side of the story. *Journal of Law, Economics, and Organizations*, 6, 213–253.
Office for Standards in Education. (2005). *Every child matters: Framework for the inspection of schools in England from September 2005.* London: Office for Standards in Education.
Olson, L. (2004, December 1). NCLB Law bestows bounty on test industry. *Education Week*, 24 (14), 1, 18–19.
Olson, L. (2005, October 19). Purpose of testing needs to shift, experts say. *Education Week*, 25 (8), 7.
Olson, L. (2006a, July 12). Chiefs to focus on formative assessments. *Education Week*, 25 (42), 12.
Olson, L. (2006b, July 12). Center to study student progress. *Education Week*, 25 (42), 12.
Pellegrino, J., Chudowsky, N., & Glaser, R. (2001). *Knowing what students know.* Washington, DC: National Academy Press.
Peterson, P. & West, M. (2006). Is your child's school effective? *Education Next*, 6 (4), 76–80.
Pew Hispanic Center/Kaiser Family Foundation. (2004, January). *National survey of Latinos: Education. summary and chartpack* (Report No. 3301). Washington, DC: Pew Hispanic Center/Kaiser Family Foundation.
Rose, L. & Gallup, A. (2004). The 36th annual Phi Delta Kappa/Gallup poll of the public's attitudes toward the public schools. *Phi Delta Kappan*, 86 (1), 41–52.
Rose, L. & Gallup, A. (2006). The 38th annual Phi Delta Kappa/Gallup poll of the public's attitudes toward the public schools. *Phi Delta Kappan*, 88 (1), 41–53.
Rudalevige, A. (2003). No Child Left Behind: Forging a congressional compromise. In M. R. West and P. E. Peterson (Eds.), *No Child Left Behind? The politics and practice of school accountability* (pp. 23–54). Washington, DC: Brookings Institution Press.
Schrag, P. (2000, August). High stakes are for tomatoes. *Atlantic Monthly*, 286 (2), 19–21.
Stone, D. (2002). *Policy paradox* (rev. ed.). New York: W.W. Norton.
U.S. Congress, Office of Technology Assessment. (1992). *Testing in American schools: Asking the right questions.* Washington, DC: U.S. Government Printing Office.
Weil, D., Fung, A., Graham, M., & Fagotto, E. (2006). The effectiveness of regulatory disclosure policies. *Journal of Policy Analysis and Management*, 25 (1), 155–181.

Part II
Educational Accountability
Technical and Substantive Issues

4

Further Steps Toward the Development of an Accountability-Oriented Science of Measurement

Daniel Koretz

Large-scale educational assessment has gone through many changes in recent decades, but none has implications for the practice of measurement so great as the shift to using tests as a means of holding educators and educational systems accountable. Achievement testing has never been entirely free of this purpose, but the balance of goals has shifted greatly, and accountability has become the most important function of many large-scale testing programs in the United States (Koretz & Hamilton, 2006) and increasingly in other nations as well.

Research has brought to light many serious concerns about the functioning and effects of test-based accountability systems. Yet the science and practice of measurement have been slow to respond, continuing in key respects much as they had before the shift to accountability-oriented testing. The consequences of this inertia are serious, including biased measurement and distorted incentives for educators.

To clarify the issues raised by test-based accountability, one can think of the evolution of modern measurement as having three stages. This is an oversimplification; the dividing lines among the stages are fuzzy, and one can find in each stage early examples of the types of work that characterize the later ones. Nonetheless, the distinctions are useful in that they highlight both recent developments related to accountability-oriented testing and challenges that remain.

The entire history of modern measurement up to the 1980s constitutes the first stage, which could be called "traditional psychometrics." High-stakes testing was not uncommon during this era. (The term "high stakes" is often used to refer only to tests that have tangible consequences for students or teachers. However, the term is used here to refer to tests on which teachers or students feel pressured to raise scores, even if the mechanism of pressure is not concrete sanctions or rewards.) Indeed, high-stakes testing existed long before the science of measurement began. Nonetheless, traditional psychometrics was in two critical respects tacitly premised on low stakes. The first is that it gave relatively little attention to the consequences of testing. The second is a special case of the first: traditional psychometrics focused little on behavioral responses to testing, other than the behavior of the student while taking the test and of proctors administering it. Most important for present purposes, traditional psychometrics gave little attention to behavioral responses to testing that might threaten the validity of score-based inferences about student achievement.

In the traditional view, changes in behavior in response to testing were expected, and indeed one of the functions of testing has long been to foster them. For instance, a common rationale for the norm-referenced tests that dominated achievement testing in the United States until the end of the period of traditional psychometrics was the expectation that teachers would use the information the test provided about the relative strengths and weaknesses of students' performance to refine their instruction. But a key, if sometimes tacit, assumption was that if students' performance on a test improved because of such responses to testing, this change represented real improvements in achievement, not test-specific gains in scores. For this reason, these behavioral responses were of little concern to psychometrics and did not greatly complicate decisions about design, methods, or validation.

Of course, warnings that this assumption was unrealistic were voiced long ago. For example, Lindquist offered this caution in a standard reference in 1951:

> The widespread and continued use of a test [that is a proxy for an unattainable measure of criterion behaviors] will, in itself, tend to reduce the correlation between the test series and the criterion series for the population involved. Because of the nature and potency of the rewards and penalties associated in actual practice with high and low achievement test scores of students, the behavior measured by a widely used test tends in itself to become the real objective of instruction, to the neglect of the (different) behavior with which the ultimate objective is concerned.
>
> (Lindquist, 1951, pp. 152–153)

Nonetheless it is fair to say that most of the psychometric enterprise—what people in the field did when developing methods or operating testing programs—proceeded without much attention to these concerns.

The labeling of this period as "traditional" is unrelated to the theoretical and mathematical models used in the construction of tests and the analysis of scores. It is not related to the conventional distinction between "classical" and "modern" approaches to measurement, that is, between classical test theory and both generalizability theory and item response theory (IRT). Although generalizability theory could be extended to address issues raised by accountability-oriented testing (e.g., to evaluate the generalizability of performance from tests used for accountability to other tests), it is not typically used in this way. Similarly, while it may be feasible to employ IRT as a tool for evaluating the results of accountability-oriented testing (e.g., Koretz & McCaffrey, 2005), IRT models are usually applied in a manner that assumes no general behavioral responses to testing that would undermine validity. Specifically, IRT retains the traditional assumption that changes in item-level performance most often reflect true changes in proficiency. Thus, the shift to modern test theory has not taken the field beyond traditional psychometrics in the sense that the latter term is used here.

During the 1970s and 1980s, the field of measurement entered a "traditional psychometrics plus" period that continues to the present. This stage was marked by important developments in both theory and empirical research relevant to the growing use of large-scale assessments for monitoring aggregate performance and for accountability. However, the actual practice of educational measurement, from test design through validation, has changed far less.

During this stage, the most important theoretical development bearing on the evolving uses of achievement tests was the growing attention to the effects of testing. The notion that validity encompasses consequences of testing as well as the reasonableness of the inferences based on scores dates back at least to the middle of the last century (Kane, 2006; Shepard, 1997), but it became much more central to the theory of validity over the past several decades (e.g., Linn, 1997; Messick, 1989; Shepard, 1997). Argument continues about whether it is useful to group both the impact of testing and the appropriateness of score-based inferences under the single term "validity" (e.g., compare Shepard, 1997 and Popham, 1997). For present purposes, however, these arguments are not critical, and the term validity is used below only to refer to the reasonableness of score-based inferences.

At the risk of oversimplification, one could say that most of the discussion of consequences in writings about validity has focused on the effects of testing as outcomes in their own right. For example, Shepard (1997, p. 8) notes concerns about medical students taking fewer courses in the humanities and social sciences because of the content of the MCAT exam and comments that "these consequences could hardly be brought under the tent of validity for judging the test battery as a measure of science knowledge."

However, a few writers began to focus on the risk that some behavioral responses to testing could bias inferences about achievement by creating larger gains in scores than real gains in achievement warrant, influencing the validity of the test. This bias is typically called "score inflation" or "score corruption." For example, Linn, Baker, and Dunbar (1991) wrote that

> considering validity in terms of consequences forces our attention on aspects of the assessment process that may not be intended or anticipated by the designers of the instruments. We know from experience

> that results from standardized tests can be corrupted [i.e., inflated], and we have clear examples of some of the factors that lead to that corruption.
>
> (p. 17)

The past several decades have also witnessed a growth in empirical research exploring the effects of accountability-oriented testing programs. A limited amount of work has investigated the validity of gains obtained under high-stakes conditions (e.g., Jacob, 2005, 2007; Koretz, Linn, Dunbar, & Shepard, 1991; Koretz & Barron, 1998). A somewhat larger body of research has used surveys and case study methods to explore the responses of teachers and principals to accountability-oriented testing programs (e.g., Stecher, 2002). Research has also explored numerous other components of test-based accountability systems, such as problems in the establishment and the use of performance standards (e.g., Burstein et al., 1995/1996; Linn, 2003; Shepard, 1994) and inconsistencies among alternative aggregate measures of performance (e.g., Linn, 2000).

This new theoretical and empirical work, discussed in more detail in the next part of the chapter, has profound implications both for the practice of measurement and for the design of test-based accountability systems. For example, research has shown that the responses of teachers and principals to these systems include not only some desired effects, but also a variety of undesirable behaviors (e.g., excessive narrowing of instruction). These findings call into question the simple model of incentives that motivates this form of assessment. And more important for the science of measurement is the finding that scores can become seriously inflated, introducing a bias that is sometimes very large and that undermines the key inferences based on scores. That is, the traditional working assumption that behavioral responses to testing do not seriously threaten validity, only somewhat problematic in Lindquist's day, appears to have become untenable.

Yet, the main body of the measurement enterprise has been largely impervious to the implications of these theoretical and empirical developments and has continued largely as before—hence the label traditional psychometrics plus, which is intended to imply a veneer of accountability-related work alongside a much larger body of traditional psychometric work. This is true of the whole span of measurement activities, starting with test design, continuing through many of the nuts and bolts of the psychometric enterprise, such as linking methods, and ending with validation. If this seems to be an overstatement, search recent technical reports of operational assessments or the texts used to train students in measurement to see how much discussion is devoted to the issues raised here.

The theoretical and empirical work on accountability-oriented testing conducted over the past two decades suggests the need to move to a third stage, which might be called "accountability-oriented measurement." It is time to take more seriously the warning Lindquist offered more than half a century ago and to begin to adapt the core work of the measurement enterprise to the widespread use of tests for accountability. Of course, other uses of testing will continue, and even for accountability testing, all of the concerns of traditional psychometrics will remain critically important. Therefore, this third stage requires additions to current work, not its replacement. Which aspects of the practice of measurement will need modification remains arguable; the argument has barely been joined, and a great deal of research remains to be done. But, we already have enough evidence to suggest that changes should span the entire process, starting with test design and continuing through validation.

Issues Arising From the Use of Tests for Accountability

There is not sufficient space here to review all of the research exploring the implications of accountability-oriented testing. However, it is necessary to sketch a number of issues in order to explore their possible implications for measurement practice.

The issues raised to date can be categorized as behavioral and non-behavioral, with behavioral issues being those that arise when behavioral responses to testing affect test validity. The distinction is not always clean because some issues—for example, the reliance on standards-based reporting—have both behavioral and non-behavioral aspects, but it is conceptually important. Consistent with its history, the field of measurement has been more responsive to the non-behavioral issues, but the behavioral issues may have even more profound implications for measurement practice.

Non-Behavioral Issues

ERROR

Accountability-oriented testing has altered the problem of error. The discussion of error in traditional psychometrics focuses primarily on measurement error that is, inconsistencies across repeated measuremeants of a single individual, such as variations arising from the sampling of test items (e.g., individual differences from one form of the SAT to another) or from fluctuations in a given student's performance over time (e.g., from having more sleep before retaking an exam). In classical test theory, measurement error takes the form of simple random inconsistencies, while generalizability theory considers both random and systematic sources of measurement error. Sampling error—that is, inconsistencies arising from sampling of units of analysis, whether these are individual students or groups—received only limited attention because the science of measurement focused primarily on the precision of estimates of attributes of individuals. For the most part, sampling error remained the province of statisticians and analysts employing test scores for other purposes.

But because of accountability-oriented testing, sampling error has become more important, and the field has responded quickly to this change. Many of the most important results of current large-scale testing programs are aggregate scores, and the inferences based on these aggregate scores are often about classrooms, schools, or systems, not about the particular cohorts of students who produced them. Thus, one element of traditional psychometrics plus has been a growing attention to sampling error. For example, Kane and Brennan (1977) extended the use of generalizability analysis to evaluating the reliability of class means. They argued that this extension was important because of large-scale program evaluations that used classes as the unit of analysis and "studies of school effectiveness and accountability" (p. 267).

Development of generalizability analysis to address aggregate statistics that include sampling error continues. For example, Cronbach, Linn, Brennan, & Haertel (1997) explored the application of generalizability analysis to performance assessments as indicators of school effectiveness. Brennan, Yin, & Kane (2003) investigated its application to both norm-referenced and criterion-referenced inferences about group means and explored the application of multivariate generalizability analysis to data from adjacent grades.

In addition to developments of generalizability theory, recent work on sampling error has included research on error estimates for the percent of students scoring above a cut score, on the instability of aggregate results over time, and on sources of aggregate instability apart from simple sampling error. No Child Left Behind requires that performance be reported for aggregates smaller than entire schools (e.g., for each school's population of students with disabilities, if there are enough of them to produce reliable estimates) and this has led to considerable debate about the instability of the results of this disaggregated reporting (e.g., Kane & Staiger, 2002).

STANDARDS-BASED REPORTING

The shift to accountability-oriented testing need not have been accompanied by a change to standards-based reporting, but in practice it was, perhaps because both accountability testing and standards-based reporting reflect a focus on expectations for performance rather than on descriptions of the current distribution of performance. Research investigating this change in reporting has raised concerns about the adequacy of the standards themselves (e.g., their robustness, their reasonableness given normative data, the appropriateness of and justification of the verbal labels they are given), the adequacy of standards-based statistics as a summary of performance, and the behavioral incentives created by reporting results only when they reflect a move from one performance category to another (e.g., from basic to proficient).

Despite often sharing similar or identical verbal labels, performance standards are highly inconsistent from state to state (Braun & Qian, 2007; Linn,

2003). And, they are often set at levels that appear unreasonable given normative data (Linn, 2000). Perhaps more troubling than these problems, which in theory can be remedied, is evidence that the results of standard setting are not robust and that variations among standard-setting results can be large. This has been clear at least since Jaeger's review of the literature through the 1980s. For example, Jaeger examined the percentages labeled as failing by different methods in 32 published comparisons and found that the median ratio of the largest to the smallest was 1.5 and the mean 5.3 (Jaeger, 1989). Shepard (1994) showed that the results of item-based and holistic methods are inconsistent, and in the case of the Angoff methods used with NAEP, are not robust across item formats or levels of difficulty. Linn (2003) noted that the composition of panels of judges also introduces inconsistencies, although he warned that the data on this point remain limited. In a recent article, Linn summarized empirical evidence about performance standards and argued against using this form of reporting. He maintained that "the variability [in state standards] is so great that characterizing achievement is meaningless" and argued that "There are a number of reasons to question the wisdom of setting a performance standard for a test if the standard is not essential to the use of the test results" (Linn, 2003).

The weaknesses of standards-based statistics as summaries of performance have also been made clear. The loss of information inherent in using a coarse ordinal scale is obvious: information about changes in performance within the large bands between adjacent standards, no matter how large, go unnoted. Conversely, even very small changes in performance register as important if they happen to push students into another performance category. However, standards-based reporting has a less obvious cost as well: it can bias comparisons of trends among groups that have substantially different initial levels of performance (Koretz & Hamilton, 2006). Linn (2007) illustrated how substantial this distortion can be by examining NAEP data on the achievement gaps between minority and majority students. In grades 4 and 8, the gaps in mean scores between whites and both Hispanics and blacks narrowed between 1996 and 2005. Using the "percent above basic" and "percent above proficient" statistics, however, showed conflicting results: some comparisons showed the gap between groups decreasing, while others appeared to show an increase. This kind of distortion is a mathematical certainty: even if one constructs a hypothetical case in which all students in all groups show identical gains, standards-based measures will necessarily show the gap changing.

The response of the field to the negative evidence about performance standards fits the model of traditional psychometrics plus all too well. The operation of most large-scale testing programs has proceeded without much regard for these myriad negative findings. To be fair, the field cannot entirely resist the strong external pressure for standards-based reporting, which now currently include the statutory requirements of No Child Left Behind. There is, however, ample room for more vigorous debate about these problems and for efforts to design ways of mitigating them.

CHOICE OF AGGREGATE PERFORMANCE METRICS

When applied to aggregates, accountability-oriented testing requires choosing a metric to summarize performance and improvement. The measures commonly in contention often categorize schools very differently (e.g., Linn, 2000). A recent and well-publicized example is the major inconsistencies in the ratings of Florida schools between the metrics mandated by No Child Left Behind and the state's A-Plus Plan (Dillon, 2006; Peterson & West, 2006).

One aspect of this issue is the choice between value-added measures (measures that reflect the gains that students make over time) and measures that compare one cohort's performance in a given grade to the previous cohort's. The cohort-to-cohort model has dominated accountability-oriented testing in the U.S. up to the present.[1] However, interest in value-added approaches has recently become widespread, and numerous states and localities are implementing or are planning some form of value-added analysis (VAA).

Measurement issues have received short shrift in the recent debates about VAA. Some of the most salient trials of VAA have used happenstance measures of performance—whatever tests happened to be in place for other reasons, scaled however they were for those other purposes. And, the scholarly literature has focused less on measurement than on issues of statistical analysis, such as the choice of statistical model (e.g., covariate adjustment models, simple gains models, and a variety of multivariate models), problems of omitted variables, the specification of fixed versus random effects, and the impact of missing data (e.g., McCaffrey, Lockwood, Koretz, Louis, & Hamilton, 2004; Raudenbush, 2004).

Although critically important, these statistical concerns should not obscure the complex measurement issues VAA raises. The challenges are not so much new issues as extensions of traditional concerns. One example is test content. Many of the VAA approaches require tracking students over several years (e.g., for three years before a given year of evaluation). A traditional concern raised by this is that vertical linking becomes less and less tenable as the grade span increases because of content differences across the grades. However, there are additional reasons to be concerned about test content with some value-added approaches. If VAA is to be used to compare or evaluate teachers or schools, curricular differentiation becomes a serious issue, particularly in the secondary grades. For instance, in middle-school mathematics, a test that is designed for general use is likely to offer relatively weak coverage of the content that is the focus of teachers of high-track students (McCaffrey, Lockwood, Koretz, & Hamilton 2003) and therefore may incorrectly identify these teachers as "ineffective."

A less obvious but formidable concern is posed by the problem of indeterminacy of scale. Indeterminacy refers to the fact that there is no single clearly correct way to place performance on a test onto a numerical scale, and alternative scales can provide different views of the relative performance of students or schools. The general problem of indeterminacy and its potential to undermine the robustness of inferences is well established (e.g., Spencer, 1983). Many common inferences are reasonably robust across the range of commonly used scales (Hoover, 1984), but some of the inferences entailed by VAA may be far more problematic in this respect. For example, it has been well established in the literature for more than two decades that longitudinal achievement test batteries show inconsistent trends in variance across grades. Some show the variation in student achievement increasing with grade, while others show little change, and yet others show students becoming more homogeneous. Although these disparities are often considered to be a result of the mathematical procedures used to construct the scales, the literature suggests that they result not simply from scaling, but from some unknown mix of test content, linking method, and scaling method. This indeterminacy of scale poses a serious threat to some inferences based on VAA, such as comparisons of teachers in high- and low-scoring schools (see McCaffrey et al., 2003, for discussion of these issues). Discussions of how best to address this uncertainty have barely begun.

Behavioral Issues

The behavioral issues raised by accountability-oriented testing have been explored less than non-behavioral ones, and the field has changed its practices much less in response to them. But the behavioral issues are at least as important, and they may suggest even more fundamental changes in the practice of measurement.

Discussions of behavioral responses to testing and their impact have begun to appear in theoretical discussions of the validity of inferences. In Kane's (2006) recent overview of validity theory, he provides a framework for conceptualizing these problems. In this framework, an interpretation based on performance on a test involves several stages of inference. Measurement theorists have long noted that tests are usually limited and non-random samples from the domain they are intended to represent, in part because some important aspects of performance are very difficult or impossible to assess and are therefore not included in the test design (e.g., Lindquist, 1951). In keeping with this tradition, Kane distinguishes between the target domain that the test is intended to represent and the more circumscribed subset of behaviors from which one samples in constructing a test, which he labels the universe of generalization. He calls the inference from a test score to this smaller universe of generalization "generalization" and the inference from the universe of generalization to the larger target "extrapolation" (Kane, 2006, pp. 30–33). He then cautions:

> The extent to which extrapolation remains plausible over time can depend, in part, on the stakes associated with the test. In a low-stakes context, performance in various subsets of the target domain may represent performance in the target domain fairly well. In a high-stakes context, standardization to a subset of the target domain may lead to instruction and test-preparation activities aimed specifically at the test, thus making test performance less representative of performance in the target domain as a whole.
>
> (p. 38)

With one important exception, Kane's discussion is consistent with a framework for evaluating validity under high stakes conditions suggested earlier by Koretz, McCaffrey, and Hamilton (2001). Koretz et al. note that the construction of a test entails not only deliberate selection of substantive elements from the domain, but also choices, some unintentional, among substantively unimportant elements, such as minor details of content, item format, style of presentation, and so forth. They note that test preparation can focus on these non-substantive elements as well as the substantively important ones, and this can substantially affect scores. This implies that behavioral responses to high stakes can threaten not only inferences from the subset of the domain eligible for testing to the larger target, but also from the specific items employed in the test to the smaller intended subdomain.

Recent empirical research has confirmed the importance of behavioral responses to accountability-oriented testing. Three outcomes bear particular note.

DISTORTING THE TEST-TAKING POOL

Research in a variety of fields has demonstrated that outcomes-based accountability systems can lead practitioners to game the system by altering the pool of people from whom outcome measurements are obtained. For example, a recent study of the effects of health care report cards in New York found that they induced many cardiologists to shift certain types of care to healthier patients (Dranove, Kessler, McClellan, & Satterthwaite, 2003). Similarly, gaming of this sort has been shown in evaluations of job training programs (Heckman, Heinrich, & Smith, 2002). Numerous studies have found examples of responses of this type to accountability-oriented testing, such as increasing special education placements and retaining students in grades prior to those in which the most important tests are given (e.g., Figlio & Getzler, 2002; Jacob, 2005). Note that although these actions may bias aggregate scores by removing potentially lower-scoring students from the test-taking pool, they do not bias score-based inferences for students who are tested.

BEHAVIORAL RESPONSES TO STANDARDS-BASED REPORTING

Standards-based reporting also raises behavioral issues. Educators often discuss the resulting incentives to focus disproportionate effort on the "bubble kids" thought to be near the cut scores used for accountability. In a study of the responses of educators in three states to No Child Left Behind, Hamilton et al. (2007) found that teachers reported focusing more on bubble kids. Educators express concern about this because of potentially negative effects on the students not thought to be near the cut score, but it can also bias inferences about overall school performance based on aggregate scores. Whether it biases inferences about individual students will depend on how the bubble kids are prepared for the tests.

INAPPROPRIATE TEST PREPARATION AND SCORE INFLATION

For the science and practice of measurement, the most serious behavioral responses to testing—other than those that actually improve student learning—are those that cause score inflation, the deterioration of the relationship between the criterion and scores noted by Lindquist in the quotation above. The construction of the test requires not only sampling from the domain of knowledge and skills, but also sampling from various item formats, styles of presentation, task demands, scoring rubrics, and so forth (Koretz & Hamilton, 2006). Excessive focus on the specifics of a given test will undermine the ability of the test to represent the domain, and scores will therefore increase more than the proficiency they are intended to represent. Given the direction of the resulting bias, the term "inflation" is more descriptive than the vaguer "corruption."

Studies of validity under high-stakes conditions have compared trends in scores on a high-stakes test to trends on a lower-stakes test designed to support similar inferences about achievement (the "focal" and "audit" tests, respectively). The logic of this approach is simple: if performance on the test generalizes to the domain about which inferences are drawn, it should also generalize to scores on other tests designed to support similar inferences. As Audrey Qualls put it, to be a valid indicator of mastery of the domain, performance on the focal test must generalize to other tests with "unfamiliar particulars" (personal communication, 2004). For example, in what appears to be the first systematic study of this phenomenon, Koretz et al. (1991) wrote that:

> We expected that good performance on high-stakes tests would be caused in part by focusing undue attention on the specific content of the tests and therefore would not generalize very well when alternative measures of the same content and skills were used.
>
> (p. 2)

This is the sampling notion of validity (Kane, 1982) applied to trends over time. One would not expect the generalization to be perfect, but the more similar the targets of inference, the greater the generalization should be, and if the focal and audit tests are similar enough in terms of intended inferences, gains on the former should be substantially echoed by gains on the latter.

The few systematic studies of the validity of gains under high-stakes conditions show striking failures of generalization (Fuller, Gesicki, Kang, & Wright, 2006; Ho & Haertel, 2006; Jacob, 2005, 2007; Klein, Hamilton, McCaffrey, & Stecher, 2000; Koretz et al., 1991; Koretz & Barron, 1998; Lee, 2006; Linn & Dunbar, 1990; Schemo & Fessenden, 2003). When gains have been found on the audit test (e.g., NAEP), these have typically been one-fifth to one-third the size of gains on the focal test, and in numerous cases, rapid gains on the focal test have been accompanied by no gain on an audit test (e.g., Klein et al., 2000; Koretz et al., 1991; Koretz & Barron, 1998). Disparities this large clearly indicate that scores are inflated.

However, some discrepancy in trends may be reasonable because the focal and audit tests may not be designed to support precisely the same conclusions about achievement (Koretz & Barron, 1998; Koretz & Hamilton, 2006). For example, Reys and Lappan (2007) found variation among states in the grade-level timing of certain content standards in mathematics. Suppose that a given state's standards call for introducing a certain topic in the fifth grade, so the focal test in fourth grade does not include this topic, but the audit test does. In the absence of any score inflation, it would be reasonable to expect modestly smaller gains on the fourth-grade audit test because it includes content not taught in that grade in that state (to the extent that teachers are in fact following the timing established by the standards). Therefore, evaluating whether scores are inflated would be more difficult when the disparity in trends is smaller than in the studies cited. For the same reason, a simple difference in trends is in many cases insufficient to ascertain precisely the amount of inflation. More precise estimation of inflation would require greater specificity of inferences than one typically finds and a careful analysis of changes in performance on items tapping various aspects of content (Koretz & Hamilton, 2006).

Although differences in intended inferences may suggest that comparisons between focal and audit tests may overstate the degree of inflation, they may also understate inflation because of similarities among tests. These similarities are of two types. First, as Lindquist (1951), Kane (2006), and many others have noted, some important outcomes of education either cannot be tested with standardized achievement tests or can be tested only poorly. Therefore, to use Kane's (2006) terminology, the universe of generalization from which the tested sample is drawn is only a subset of the target about which inferences are made. Students can be inappropriately prepared for a high-stakes test in ways that make performance on the specific test, and also across the entire universe of generalization, unrepresentative of the broader target about which inferences are drawn. Because these limitations are largely unavoidable, they are shared among tests, and a comparison across tests will fail to reveal this type of inflation. Second, even within the subset of a domain that can be measured well by standardized assessments, tests are likely to show substantial similarities in content and format because of practical constraints. Therefore, the unfamiliar particulars of an audit test—to use Quall's phrase—may not be as unfamiliar as one would ideally want. These limitations would be acceptable if tests did not bear high stakes and were not used as summary judgments of entire educational programs and systems. However, when stakes are high—encouraging educators and students to focus on the particulars of the focal test—and scores from a single test are considered a summary evaluation, these limitations are serious and can lead to a substantial understatement of score inflation.

The practical importance of score inflation is exacerbated by its inconsistency. Studies have shown that inflation is highly variable across schools and over time, but they have not yet provided any information on factors that predict its severity. Furthermore, analytical methods are still insufficient to disentangle inflation from meaningful gains in scores at the level of schools or classrooms (e.g., Koretz & McCaffrey, 2005). The variability and unpredictability of inflation render comparisons among schools and classrooms suspect at best and potentially seriously misleading.

Studies of teachers' and administrators' responses to high-stakes testing, which have been an element of traditional psychometrics plus, may help explain the inflation of scores. Although the dividing line between actions that improve achievement and those that inflate scores is often hard to determine, the principle is straightforward: actions inflate scores to the extent that they boost performance on the particular test without producing generalizable gains in achievement (i.e., gains that will appear in other contexts). At one extreme, suppose that a teacher learns from the results of a large-scale assessment that his students are relatively weak in the area of ratios and proportions. If the teacher "teaches to the test" by strengthening instruction of this content, the accountability system is functioning as it should, and both scores and achievement should rise. But if the teacher's response is to look for shortcuts that take advantage of the particulars of that one test to boost scores, such as by taking time from other important aspects of the curriculum to focus on material emphasized in the accountability test, there is a risk that scores will increase more than achievement. Alternatively, some responses to testing may improve both achievement and scores. For example, some test-based accountability systems have led to a greater emphasis on writing across the curriculum (e.g., Stecher, 2002), which one would expect to improve students' writing. However, studies have also shown "rubric-driven instruction" (Stecher & Mitchell, 1995), an instructional focus on the particulars of the rubric used to score the accountability test at the expense of other important aspects of writing. This tends to inflate scores, in that improvements on the test using that one rubric will be larger than the improvement students would manifest under any other circumstances. The actions of administrators—such as establishing policies about curricula, test preparation activities, student retention, exclusion from testing, or assignment to alternate assessments; instituting "benchmark" testing; or imposing policies about the allocation of instructional time—can also boost achievement, inflate scores, or both.

We have suggested a taxonomy of test-preparation activities that helps to clarify the link between behavioral responses to testing responses and the validity of gains under high-stakes conditions (Koretz et al., 2001; Koretz & Hamilton, 2006). We use the term "test preparation" in an entirely descriptive sense to denote all activities, desirable or not, intended to improve students' performance on the test. Three types of responses to testing can be expected to produce meaningful gains in scores: teaching more, working harder, and working more effectively. These are the responses that many advocates of test-based accountability anticipate. The more interesting and difficult categories are "reallocation," "alignment," and "coaching," all of which can produce true gains in achievement, score inflation, or both.

Reallocation refers simply to the shifting of instructional resources (primarily instructional time, but other resources as well) among substantive parts of the curriculum to target better the particulars of the test. To some degree, reallocation is desirable, in that accountability tests are designed in part to signal what is important. Reallocation poses a risk, however, because tests are small and necessarily incomplete samples from the domains of achievement they are intended to represent. Allocating more time to one set of topics requires taking time away from others, and if the material that is dropped or de-emphasized is also important for the intended inferences about achievement, then scores can rise more than gains in achievement warrant. The more predictable a test is over time, the easier it is to reallocate instruction in response. Numerous surveys have found that teachers report reallocating in response to testing, including in many cases de-emphasizing important material (Stecher, 2002).

At present, alignment between tests and standards is a cornerstone of education policy. Performance standards establish what is deemed most important; tests are aligned with these to signal to teachers what is desired and to hold them accountable for producing it, and instruction is expected to change to that end. Although some degree of alignment is clearly desirable—there is nothing to be gained by testing unimportant material or by imposing tests inconsistent with the intended curriculum—alignment in itself does not protect against score inflation. Alignment is merely reallocation, but with the constraint that the material gaining emphasis in response to testing should be consistent with content standards. But score inflation depends both on what is emphasized and what is de-emphasized in response to testing and does not require a focus on unimportant material. Standards are not exhaustive, but typically focus on a subset of content goals; tests must then sample from those content areas. Therefore, alignment can entail de-emphasizing material important for inferences about achievement, thus leading to score inflation.

The final type of test preparation is coaching. This term has been used in many different ways, but we use it to denote several things: focusing on minor, unimportant details of test content; focusing on non-substantive aspects of the test, such as item format; and teaching test-taking tricks. The first of these, which we label "substantive coaching," shades into reallocation at one extreme and into cheating at the other. For example, teachers may focus on a particular way in which a type of algebraic expression is likely to appear on the test. Teaching to the rubric is an example of non-substantive coaching. Test-taking tricks include, for example, instructing students to use process of elimination rather than trying to solve multiple-choice mathematics problems. These approaches inflate scores if they generate gains that are specific to that one test and therefore do not appear in other contexts. For example, if students raise their scores on a math test by relying on a process of elimination, those gains are unlikely to appear in other contexts in which problems are not presented in multiple-choice format—for example, on certain other tests or in later employment.

Although it is obvious that score inflation undermines many interpretations of scores, it may be less obvious that it also poses difficulties for the psychometric work undergirding ongoing operational testing programs. One example is IRT non-equivalent groups anchor test (NEAT) linking, one of the methods most commonly used to link scores on accountability-oriented tests across time. In these linking methods, some secure test items (the anchor test) are reused. These anchor items serve as the constraint that allows one to make the scale comparable from one year to the next, and they provide the basis for judging the amount of overall change in achievement. The key assumption underlying this method is that if comparably proficient students perform better on these linking items in the second year, that improvement represents true gains in learning. Under high-stakes conditions, however, this assumption is not warranted. If test preparation has inflated performance on the linking items—that is, if it has improved performance on these items more than it would have improved it on other items measuring the same constructs but not sharing the same particulars—then NEAT linking will build score inflation into the scale itself. Inflation on the linking items can occur if the anchor items are sufficiently memorable that teachers can adapt their instruction to them. This can also occur even in the absence of memorable anchor items if the anchors share enough particulars with other items.

In technical terms, this entails a misplacement of the equating line. IRT NEAT linking requires that the difficulty parameters of these items be held approximately constant across years, forcing the parameter estimates for new items onto the same scale as was used the year before. In one approach, one first calibrates the data separately for each year and plots these difficulty estimates against each other. Ideally, the item difficulties in the two samples should form a straight line; items that fall far from that line are not functioning the same in the two samples and are therefore not used in linking. The position of the equating line itself, however, is treated as immaterial, and it is removed later by adjusting the item difficulty parameters in the new data. In IRT terminology, the key assumption is that the relationship between the latent trait (achievement) and observed item difficulty is fixed and that differences in estimated parameters reflected in the placement of the equating line are a function of the indeterminacy of scale that linking is designed to overcome. This is the IRT variant of the classical test theory assumption that differences in item-level performance represent differences in mastery of the underlying construct.

Behavioral responses to high-stakes testing threaten the assumption underlying NEAT linking. If inappropriate test preparation has made the linking items easier than latent proficiency warrants, the equating line will shift, and score inflation will be built into the scale for the new year of testing (Koretz & Barron, 1998; Koretz, 2007). That various factors can make an item inappropriate for linking by undermining the relationship between latent proficiency and observed difficulty is well known. For example, in a recent comprehensive review of both common practice and recent innovations in linking, Holland and Dorans (2006) mention three factors that can have this effect and thereby undermine the utility of an anchor item: changes in general knowledge, security breaches, and context effects (i.e., from anchor items being embedded in different tests in each of the two years). However, the potential impact of behavioral responses on the functioning of anchor items has as yet gained much less attention.

Although it is clear that behavioral responses to high-stakes testing pose serious challenges to conventional practices in measurement, the field's responses to them have been meager. Little has been done to explore alternative practices—either in the design of tests or in the operation of testing programs—that would be more responsive to these challenges. Perhaps most striking, the problem of score inflation gets fleeting mention, if any at all, in most evaluations or discussions of validity, whether in technical reports of testing programs, the scholarly literature, or textbooks—even though the bias introduced by score inflation can dwarf that caused by some factors that receive more attention.

Toward an Accountability-Oriented Field of Measurement

Unless accountability-oriented testing becomes less important—seemingly an unlikely prospect—the model of traditional psychometrics plus will no longer be sufficient. The science and practice of measurement must begin to respond systematically to the challenges of aggregate accountability-oriented testing. Meeting this challenge will require several lines of work.

First, we need more empirical investigation of the effects of accountability-oriented testing and its implications for measurement. There is enough research to indicate that the problems are severe but not yet enough to chart adequately a future course. There are far too few studies of the validity of scores under high-stakes conditions, and we know very little about the distribution and correlates of score inflation (e.g., its variation across types of testing programs, types of schools, or types of students). Extant research on teachers' and principals' responses to testing, although somewhat more copious, is still insufficient, providing little systematic data on the use of test-preparation materials and other forms of coaching or on the relationships between test design and instructional responses. And there is too little research exploring the implications for the practice of measurement. For example, although the threat coaching poses for NEAT linking is clear, there are no empirical studies of its actual effects.

Second, we need to experiment with new approaches to test design. It is no longer sufficient to design tests with an eye to reliability and validity under low-stakes conditions. We need to design tests with an eye to improving validity under the high-stakes conditions that currently characterize much of large-scale testing. In one sense, this is not a new concern. For two decades, we have seen numerous efforts to confront this problem by creating "tests worth teaching to." In some cases, this has been taken to mean tests that comprise rich, cognitively demanding tasks; in others, it has been construed to mean tests that are aligned with standards. Both of these efforts are laudable, and both may improve the instructional effects of testing. However, neither addresses a core cause of score inflation: that is, that tests are small and incomplete samples from target domains, which in turn affords educators opportunities to take shortcuts and inflate scores.

We must work to design tests that provide less incentive to reallocate and coach inappropriately and that make those behavioral responses less damaging to validity. One particularly important question is whether tests can be designed to reduce unnecessary recurrences of details of content, styles of item presentation, construct-irrelevant task demands, and so on, and to lessen the opportunity to use test-taking tricks. In theory, introducing items with unfamiliar particulars—items that do not unnecessarily repeat details of content, that vary forms of presentation, and so on—could help provide less biased estimates of performance gains, better incentives to teachers, and perhaps even an inbuilt audit mechanism for differentiating between score inflation and meaningful gains. There is a cost to this strategy, however, as any reduction in consistency over time could threaten linking, even if only to increase random fluctuations in scores. Thus, efforts to reduce gratuitous consistency pose a tradeoff: the potential for better incentives and a reduction of bias in return for potential increases in other forms of linking error. The practicality of lessening unwanted recurrences while retaining the necessary ones remains untested, and the resource demands—in time as well as money—of attempting this could be large. Only experimentation and rigorous evaluation will clarify the degree to which innovations in test design such as this are practical and helpful.

Third, depending on the results of the evaluations noted above, the field may need to develop new methods for the procedures that maintain operational testing programs. Although the jury is still out, two of the most difficult of these may be linking and addressing the problem of scale in value-added assessments. In both cases, the problem is indeterminacy: we lack an unambiguous choice of scale, and the impact of alternative choices can be substantial. For example, most approaches to linking over time require either administering both of the tests to be linked to a single sample or holding items fixed (in the IRT context, holding their parameters constant). The former is not a realistic possibility in the case of most high-stakes testing programs, and the latter can introduce bias into the scale if the effects of coaching or other undesirable test preparation boost performance on the anchor items. This leaves us with little reason to be confident that scales are consistent and that comparisons over time are valid.

Fourth, major changes are needed in our approach to validation, that is, evaluating the degree to which score-based inferences are warranted. As long as the principal inferences based on test scores include conclusions about aggregate changes in performance achieved under high-stakes conditions, validation must include evaluating these particular inferences. This requires that we confront the problem of score inflation directly and routinely. Doing so will not be easy; it requires suitable audit measures that, in many contexts, are not available and will have to be constructed for this purpose. It will also require access to data, when it is not in the self-interest of some parties to provide it for this purpose. And, in some cases, it will require new analytical methods (e.g., Koretz & McCaffrey, 2005).

Fifth, we need routine attention to the effects of testing, regardless of whether we chose to subsume this under the label of validity. Traditional psychometrics often assumed an indirect link between testing and instruction: that the primary purpose of testing is to garner information, and that this information in turn might affect behavior. But we have long since made the transition to what Popham (1987) called "measurement-driven instruction." Tests are now intended to provide direct incentives for educators and students to change behavior, and users of scores generally assume that changes in scores on the accountability-oriented tests are themselves sufficient to determine whether those goals have been met. However, the sparse research to date has shown that this assumption is unwarranted. Therefore the quality of testing programs cannot be addressed fully without empirically evaluating impact.

This is a tremendously ambitious and as yet poorly delineated agenda. Nonetheless, the evolution of the uses of tests requires a parallel evolution in educational measurement. It is time to build on the innovative theoretical and empirical work that have characterized the current era in educational testing and to begin the development of a truly accountability-oriented science and practice of measurement.

Acknowledgments

I would like to thank Michael Kane, Laura Hamilton, and Lorrie Shepard for thoughtful and constructive comments on an earlier draft of this chapter. I bear sole responsibility for any remaining errors or omissions.

Note

1. The No Child Left Behind accountability system is not strictly speaking a cohort-to-cohort gain model in that each school's performance in a given year is compared to a statewide target rather than to its past performance, but it is in most respects similar to a cohort-to-cohort gain approach, and in most states, no measure of individual growth is used in the accountability system.

References

Braun, H. & Qian, J. (2007). An enhanced method for mapping state standards onto the NAEP scale. In N. J. Dorans, M. Pommerich, & P. W. Holland (Eds.), *Linking and aligning scores and scales.* New York: Springer-Verlag.

Brennan, R. L., Yin, P., & Kane, M. T. (2003). Methodology for examining the reliability of group mean difference scores. *Journal of Educational Measurement,* 40 (3), 207–230.

Burstein, L., Koretz, D., Linn, R., Baker, E., Sugrue, B., Novak, J., et al. (1995/1996). Describing performance standards: The validity of the 1992 NAEP achievement level descriptors as characterizations of mathematics performance. *Educational Assessment,* 3 (1), 9–51.

Cronbach, L. J., Linn, R. L., Brennan, R. L., & Haertel, E. H. (1997). Generalizability analysis for performance assessments of student achievement or school effectiveness. *Educational and Psychological Measurement,* 57 (3), 373–399.

Dillon, S. (2006, November 7). As 2 Bushes try to fix schools, the tools differ. *New York Times.* Online, available at: http://select.nytimes.com/search/restricted/article?res=F60C13FC3D540C7B8EDDA00894DE404482 (accessed November 7, 2006).

Dranove, D., Kessler, D., McClellan, M., & Satterthwaite, M. (2003). Is more information better? The effects of "report cards" on health care providers. *Journal of Political Economy,* 111 (3), 555–588.

Figlio, D. N. & Getzler, L. S. (2002) *Accountability, ability and disability: Gaming the system?* (Working Paper 9370). Cambridge, MA: National Bureau of Economic Research. Online, available at: http://www.nber.org/papers/w9307 (accessed November 7, 2006).

Fuller, B., Gesicki, K., Kang, E., & Wright, J. (2006). *Is the No Child Left Behind Act working? The reliability of how states track achievement.* University of California, Berkeley: Policy Analysis for California Education.

Hamilton, L. S., Stecher, B. M., Marsh, J. A., McCombs, J. S., Robyn, A., Russell, J. L., et al. (2007). *Standards-based accountability under No Child Left Behind* (MG589). Santa Monica: RAND. Online, available at: http://www.rand.org/pubs/monographs/2007/RAND_MG589.pdf (accessed June 26, 2007).

Heckman, J. J., Heinrich, C., & Smith, J. (2002). The performance of performance standards. *Journal of Human Resources,* 37 (4), 778–811.

Ho, A. D. & Haertel, E. H. (2006). *Metric-free measures of test score trends and gaps with policy-relevant examples.* CSE Technical Report 665. Los Angeles: Center for the Study of Evaluation, University of California.

Holland, P. W. & Dorans, N. J. (2006). Linking and equating. In R. L. Brennan (Ed.), *Educational measurement* (4th ed., pp. 187–220). Westport, CT: American Council on Education/ Praeger.

Hoover, H. D. (1984). The most appropriate scores for measuring educational development in the elementary schools: GEs. *Educational Measurement: Issues and Practice*, 3 (4), 8–14.

Jacob, B. A. (2005). Accountability, incentives and behavior: The impact of high-stakes testing in the Chicago public schools. *Journal of Public Economics*, 89 (5–6), 761–796.

Jacob, B. A. (2007). *Test-based accountability and student achievement: An investigation of differential performance on NAEP and state assessments* (Working Paper 12817). Cambridge, MA: National Bureau of Economic Research. Online, available at: http://www.nber.org/papers/w12817 (accessed November 7, 2006).

Jaeger, R. M. (1989). Certification of student competence. In R. L. Linn (Ed.), *Educational measurement* (3rd ed., pp. 485–514). New York: American Council on Education/MacMillan.

Kane, M. T. (1982). A sampling model for validity. *Applied Psychological Measurement*, 6 (2), 125–160.

Kane, M. T. (2006). Validation. In R. L. Brennan (Ed.), *Educational measurement* (4th ed., pp. 17–64). Westport, CT: American Council on Education/Praeger.

Kane, M. T. & Brennan, R. L. (1977). The generalizability of class means. *Review of Educational Research*, 47 (1), 267–292.

Kane, T. J. & Staiger, D. O. (2002). The promise and pitfalls of using imprecise school accountability measures. *Journal of Economic Perspectives*, 16 (4), 91–114.

Klein, S. P., Hamilton, L. S., McCaffrey, D. F., & Stecher, B. M. (2000). *What do test scores in Texas tell us?* (Issue Paper IP-202). Santa Monica, CA: RAND. Online, available at: http://www.rand.org/publications/IP/IP202/ (accessed January 12, 2004).

Koretz, D. (2007). Using aggregate-level linkages for estimation and validation: Comments on Thissen & Braun & Qian. In N. J. Dorans, M. Pommerich, & P. W. Holland (Eds.), *Linking and aligning scores and scales* (pp. 339–353). New York: Springer-Verlag.

Koretz, D. & Barron, S. I. (1998). *The validity of gains on the Kentucky Instructional Results Information System (KIRIS)* (MR-1014-EDU). Santa Monica: RAND.

Koretz, D. & Hamilton, L. S. (2006). Testing for accountability in K-12. In R. L. Brennan (Ed.), *Educational measurement* (4th ed., pp. 531–578). Westport, CT: American Council on Education/Praeger.

Koretz, D. & McCaffrey, D. (2005). *Using IRT DIF methods to evaluate the validity of score gain* (CSE Technical Report 660). Los Angeles: Center for the Study of Evaluation, University of California.

Koretz, D., McCaffrey, D., & Hamilton, L. (2001). *Toward a framework for validating gains under high-stakes conditions* (CSE Technical Report 551). Los Angeles: Center for the Study of Evaluation, University of California.

Koretz, D., Linn, R. L., Dunbar, S. B., & Shepard, L. A. (1991, April). The effects of high-stakes testing: Preliminary evidence about generalization across tests. In R. L. Linn (Chair), *The effects of high stakes testing.* Symposium conducted at the annual meetings of the American Educational Research Association and the National Council on Measurement in Education, Chicago.

Lee, J. (2006). *Tracking achievement gaps and assessing the impact of NCLB on the gaps: An in-depth look into national and state reading and math outcome trends.* Cambridge, MA: Civil Rights Project at Harvard University.

Lindquist, E. F. (1951). Preliminary considerations in objective test construction. In E. F. Linquist (Ed.), *Educational measurement* (2nd ed., pp. 119–158). Washington: American Council on Education.

Linn, R. L. (1997). Evaluating the validity of assessments: The consequences of test use. *Educational Measurement*, 16 (2), 14–16.

Linn, R. L. (2000). Assessments and accountability. *Educational Researcher*, 29 (2), 4–16.

Linn, R. L. (2003). Performance standards: Utility for different uses of assessments. *Education*

Policy Analysis Archives, 11 (31). Online, available at: http://epaa.asu.edu/epaa/v11n31/ (accessed October 20, 2003).

Linn, R. L. (2007, January). Educational accountability systems. Paper presented at the meeting of the National Center for Research on Evaluation, Standards, and Student Testing, Los Angeles.

Linn, R. L. & Dunbar, S. B. (1990). The nation's report card goes home: Good news and bad about trends in achievement. *Phi Delta Kappan*, 72 (2), October, 127–133.

Linn, R. L., Baker, E. L., & Dunbar, S. B. (1991). Complex, performance-based assessment: Expectations and validation criteria. *Educational Measurement: Issues and Practice*, 20 (8), 15–21.

McCaffrey, D. F., Lockwood, J. R., Koretz, D. M., & Hamilton, L. S. (2003). *Evaluating value-added models for teacher accountability* (MG-158-EDU). Santa Monica: RAND.

McCaffrey, D. F., Lockwood, J. R., Koretz, D., Louis, T. A., & Hamilton, L. (2004). Models for value-added modeling of teacher effects. *Journal of Educational and Behavioral Statistics*, 29 (1), 67–101.

Messick, S. (1989). Validity. In R. L. Linn (Ed.), *Educational measurement* (3rd ed., pp. 13–103). New York: American Council on Education/Macmillan.

Peterson, P. E. & West, M. R. (2006). Is your child's school effective? Don't rely on NCLB to tell you. *Education Next*, (6) 4, 76–80.

Popham, W. J. (1987). The merits of measurement-driven instruction. *Phi Delta Kappan*, 68 (9), 679–682.

Popham, W. J. (1997). Consequential validity: Right concern—wrong concept. *Educational Measurement: Issues and Practice*, 16 (2), 9–13.

Raudenbush, S. (2004). Schooling, statistics, and poverty: Can we measure school improvement? The ninth annual William H. Angoff Memorial Lecture. Princeton, NJ: Educational Testing Service.

Reys, B. & Lappan, G. (2007). Consensus or confusion: The intended math curriculum in state-level standards. *Phi Delta Kappan*, 88 (9), 676–680.

Schemo, D. J. & Fessenden, F. (2003, December 3). Gains in Houston schools: How real are they? *New York Times*, pp. A1, A27.

Shepard, L. A. (1994). Implications for standard setting of the National Academy of Education evaluation of the National Assessment of Educational Progress Achievement Levels. In *Proceeding of the joint conference on standard setting for large-scale assessments, Vol. II* (pp. 143–160). Washington, DC: National Assessment Governing Board and National Center for Education Statistics.

Shepard, L. A. (1997). The centrality of test use and consequences for test validity. *Educational Measurement: Issues and Practice*, 16 (2), 5–8, 13, 24.

Spencer, B. D. (1983). On interpreting test scores as social indicators: Statistical considerations. *Journal of Educational Measurement*, 20 (4), 317–333.

Stecher, B. M. (2002). Consequences of large-scale, high-stakes testing on school and classroom practices. In L. S. Hamilton, B. M. Stecher, & S. P. Klein (Eds.), *Making sense of test-based accountability in education* (pp. 79–100). Santa Monica, CA: RAND.

Stecher, B. M. & Mitchell, K. J. (1995). *Portfolio-driven reform: Vermont teachers' understanding of mathematical problem solving and related changes in classroom practice* (CSE Technical Report No. 400). Los Angeles: Center for the Study of Evaluation, University of California.

5
Reliability of Large-Scale Assessment and Accountability Systems

Vonda L. Kiplinger

Reliability is a core measurement issue that has taken on new meaning in this era of educational accountability and No Child Left Behind (NCLB). In this chapter, reliability is discussed in the context of NCLB requirements; in the context of measurement error, sampling error, and score volatility; and in the context of accountability systems and the probability of misclassifying schools. Following these discussions, several recent developments in evaluating the reliability of accountability systems, alternative approaches for better evaluating school effectiveness, and new models for gauging the success of *all* students are described.

Accountability Systems and Particular Challenges of NCLB's Adequate Yearly Progress

The No Child Left Behind Act of 2001 requires each state to create an accountability system that is "valid and reliable," establishes challenging academic content standards and challenging student academic achievement standards, annually assesses students in grades 3 to 8 and once in high school in English/language arts and mathematics, and establishes annual targets for "adequate yearly progress" (AYP) such that all students in every school will perform at or above the "proficient" achievement standard by 2014. The definition of proficient is left up to each state, and varies widely. AYP targets are specified as percentages of students classified as proficient or better annually. NCLB further requires that the AYP decisions be "statistically valid and reliable" for all students and for each of the following specific subgroups of students: students from major racial and ethnic groups, students who are economically disadvantaged, students with disabilities, and students with limited English proficiency.

The terms "valid" and "reliable" are often used interchangeably by policymakers in speaking about the technical adequacy of tests, but the two terms are not synonymous. Validity is a substantive issue. Does a test measure as intended, and is there both the necessary theoretical and evidentiary support for the inferences, uses, and actions that will be taken based on assessment results? Reliability refers to replicability or consistency of results. At the student level, that is, for individual test scores, the reliability coefficient is usually reported using a measure of internal consistency.

In the AYP context, reliability refers to the consistency and accuracy with which schools are classified as either meeting or failing to meet their AYP targets. The statistic of interest is not a measure of an assessment's internal consistency or test–retest reliability; it is not a reliability coefficient. Rather, under NCLB, the statistic of interest is *a measure of the probability of correctly classifying, or conversely, of misclassifying, a school as meeting AYP*. The likelihood of misclassifying a school is of primary concern because the consequences of misclassification can be substantial. Schools that are incorrectly classified as meeting their AYP targets may not receive the assistance they need or institute reforms that could improve the learning and achievement of their students. Schools that are incorrectly classified as failing their AYP targets may suffer serious consequences. For example, schools that fail to make AYP in two consecutive years are required to offer supplemental services and public school choice and to submit a school improvement plan. Schools that fail to make AYP in three consecutive years are required to offer choice and supplemental services, and must receive technical assistance from the school district. Schools that fail to make AYP for four years continue all of the previous interventions and must take at least one additional corrective action. Corrective actions can include replacing school staff, implementing a new curriculum, significantly decreasing management authority in the school, appointing outside experts to advise the school, extending the school year or school day, and restructuring the internal organization of the school. Schools that miss AYP for five or six years face the above consequences plus alternative governance (e.g., state takeover, reopening as a charter school, replacing all or most of the school staff, or contracting with another entity such as a private management company to operate the school). Thus, the consequences of school AYP misclassification can be severe, ranging from schools not receiving needed assistance to the imposition of unjust and costly sanctions, including possible alternative governance.

Requirements of the No Child Left Behind Act present two interrelated sets of challenges to reliability: challenges related to reliability of assessment results and challenges concerning design and adequacy of accountability systems. As Hill and DePascale (2003) aptly point out, "*assessment systems* are not *accountability systems*" (p. 12). Assessment systems are the mechanisms by which student achievement or performance data are collected. In addition, states typically have other information-gathering systems that provide information about schools beyond test scores. Accountability systems use assessment data as a component in making decisions about schools and applying consequences, either good or bad. This chapter addresses these two types of challenges to reliability: those relating to student- and school-level assessment and those related to accountability systems.

Challenges to Reliability: Student-Level Measurement Error

The assessment component of accountability systems is based on individual student test results that are aggregated to the school level. Current assessments are imperfect measures of student knowledge and skills. No assessment, no matter how well constructed, is perfectly reliable. For example, if a group of students takes alternate forms of the same mathematics test on the same day or if the students take an end-of-course test today and then retake the test a few days later—and no additional learning takes place between the testing periods—it is unlikely that they will obtain the same scores on the pairs of tests. Alternatively, suppose that two classmates of the same ability take their state assessment. One scores slightly above the proficient cut point while the other scores slightly below the proficient cut point when, in actuality, these two students are indistinguishable in terms of their true proficiency. These phenomena are termed *measurement error.* Measurement error does not mean that mistakes have been made. Rather, tests contain a limited sample of many possible items from the content domain, and conditions in the testing situation may vary from one administration to another. Measurement error simply means that factors other than student knowledge of the content domain can affect their responses.

Possible sources of measurement error include student-specific factors, test-specific factors, scoring-specific factors, and situational factors of the test setting.

- Student-specific factors include both examinee transient states (such as fatigue, mood, health, carelessness in marking answers, guessing) and stable characteristics (such as motivation, individual differences in exposure to tested content, individual differences in ability to generalize).
- Test-specific factors include the specific sample of questions on the test, item order effects, clarity of the test directions, ambiguity of the questions or response options, and so forth.
- Scoring-specific factors include scorer unreliability, incorrect or non-uniform scoring rubrics, scoring errors, and the like.
- Situational factors of the test setting include such variables as administration errors, distractions outside the testing room, disruptive students in the classroom, room temperature, crowding, and interactions between students and the test administrator or teacher.

Thus, measurement error is the variability associated with testing a particular group of students on a particular occasion.

Challenges to Reliability: School-Level Assessment

For the purposes of school accountability and AYP classification decisions, reliability is a measure of the consistency of school-level results used to make judgments and decisions about schools. Many states' accountability systems take the successive cohorts approach to comparing student achievement over time; this approach compares the performance of students in a particular grade in one year with the performance of students in that same grade in previous years. For example, the percentage of fourth grade students scoring proficient or above in reading on the 2006 state assessment could be compared with the percentage of fourth grade students scoring proficient or above on the 2005 state reading assessment. This approach is based on an implicit *stability assumption* that student cohorts within a school are very similar from year to year with respect to characteristics that are related to achievement. For example, it is assumed that the entering abilities, interests, level of parental support, and motivation of one year's group of fourth graders is the same as the next year's group of fourth graders, so that any change in performance can be attributed to an increase or decrease in the quality of instruction.

The major factors that affect the volatility and reliability of summary school scores used to determine AYP classifications are *measurement error* and *sampling error*. As described above, measurement error is the variability associated with testing a particular group of students on a particular occasion. *Sampling error* is the variability associated with testing a different group of students each year. It has been shown that sampling error is by far the larger contributor to volatility of school scores (Cronbach, Linn, Brennan, & Haertel, 1997; Hill & DePascale, 2003; Linn & Haug, 2002). For example, some cohorts of students are simply more able than others and will demonstrate greater achievement than other cohorts of students, even if the instructional program remains the same. If the assessment results from a more able cohort of fourth graders are compared to the assessment results from a less able prior cohort of fourth graders, a common inference under NCLB would be that the school has improved its instructional program. However, the "achievement gain" may be due to the same instruction being delivered to more able students. Regarding school-level AYP objectives, Linn, Baker, and Betebenner (2002) note, there

> seems to be little recognition that school-level results are often volatile from year to year because of differences in cohorts of students.... Unfortunately, changes in scores for students tested at a given grade from one year to the next can be *markedly unreliable.*
>
> (p. 12, emphasis added)

Other factors have been shown to affect the variability, or volatility, of school summary scores and change scores.[1] For example, Kane and Staiger

(2002) describe three sources of variability in such scores: sampling error, nonpersistent variation (due to situational factors such as a few disruptive students in a class or favorable chemistry between a teacher and the class), and change score unreliability. They estimated the fraction of total variation that is due to the nonpersistent factors and found, based on the test results of more than 133,000 students in North Carolina, that as much as 73% of the between-school variation in mean change scores[2] among "averaged-sized" schools[3] is due to sampling variability and other one-time, nonpersistent factors. In other words, these results indicate that for average-sized schools, only slightly more than one-quarter of the between-school variability in change scores is due to persistent factors associated with the school.

Kane and Staiger also demonstrate that the amount of sampling variability is inversely related to school size. That is, sampling variability accounts for a greater percentage of the between-school variance for small schools than for larger schools. They found that for both reading and mathematics test scores, the variance between schools is approximately 50% larger for the smallest quintile of schools than for the largest quintile.[4] For gain scores, the between-school variance is roughly two to three times larger for the smallest quintile of schools than for the largest quintile. Moreover, Kane and Staiger found that after subtracting estimates of sampling variation, the between-school variance is still greater for small schools than for large schools. These results are presented in Figure 5.1 (parts a and b). The solid line in each graph indicates the total between-school variance, while the dashed line represents the between-school variance after subtracting the authors' estimate of the sampling variation.[5]

Furthermore, Kane and Staiger (2002) demonstrate that test scores "fluctuate much more from year to year among small schools than among large schools" (p. 245). Figure 5.2, reproduced from their report, clearly demonstrates that the variance in the one-year change in fourth grade reading and math scores was three times as large for the smallest school quintile than for the largest school quintile (upper panel, 0.079 and 0.027, respectively). In addition, the variance in the change for fourth grade *gain scores* was five times larger for the smallest quintile schools than among the largest quintile schools (lower panel, 0.060 versus 0.13).

Similarly, in a study of about 1,000 Massachusetts schools over four years (1998 to 2001), Haney (2002) showed that smaller schools demonstrate much more volatility in average scores than larger schools. He found that schools with fewer than 100 tested students demonstrated changes in average scores on the Massachusetts Comprehensive Assessment System that were three to four times the magnitude of changes in average scores for schools with more than 150 tested students (year-to-year changes of 15 to 20 points for the smaller schools as opposed to typically fewer than five points for the larger schools).

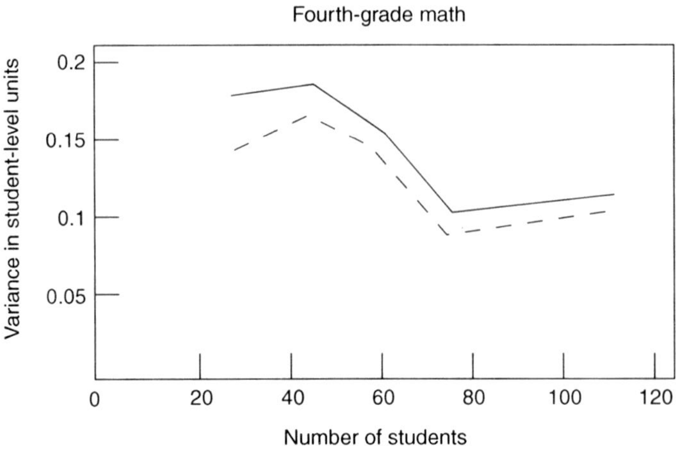

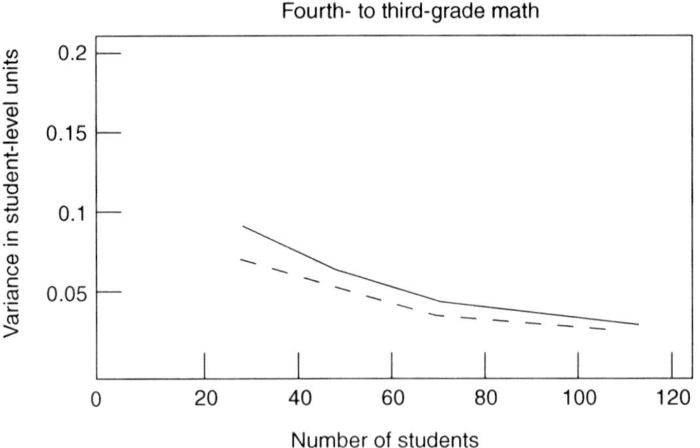

(part a)

Figure 5.1 Between-School Variances by School Size (source: Kane & Staiger, 2002. Copyright 2002 by Brookings Institution. Reprinted with permission.).

Linn and others (Cronbach & Furby, 1970; Hill & DePascale, 2003; Kane & Staiger, 2002; Linn & Haug, 2002) have noted that the change scores typically computed to indicate school progress tends to be less reliable than the baseline scores and the later scores from which the differences are computed. For example, Kane and Staiger (2002) point out that, in contrast to a school's average test performance, which can be measured reliably, mean change scores are "measured remarkably unreliably" (p. 252). This is due to the sampling and measurement errors and nonpersistent factors associated with the two scores.

Although NCLB does not use change scores and, therefore, is not as

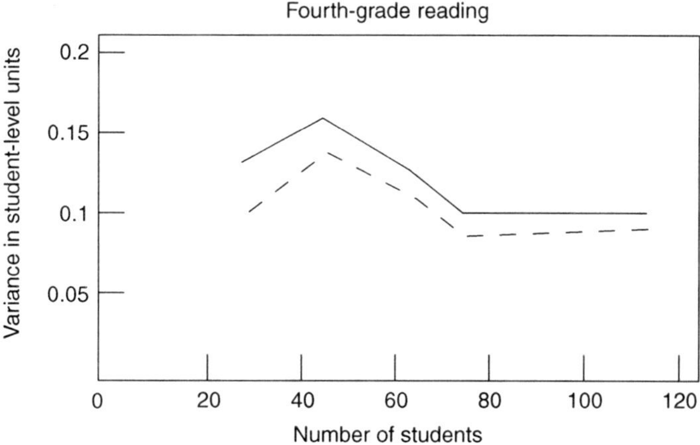

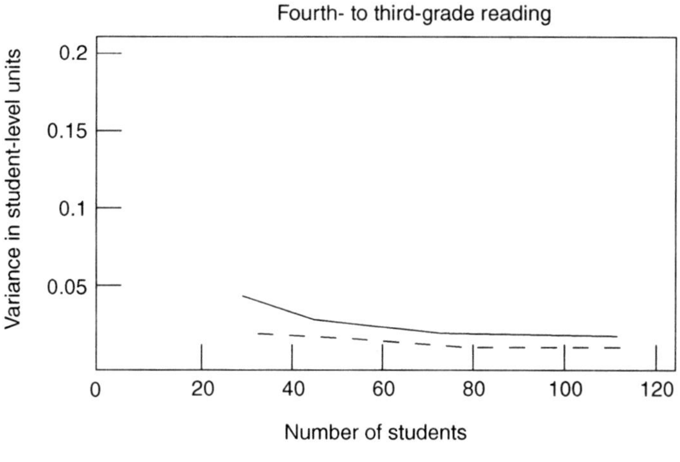

(part b)

Figure 5.1 continued

vulnerable to the particular concerns discussed above, the issue is very important for accountability assessments and systems in general. The volatility of change scores has been of concern in many state programs such as the ones cited by Kane and Staiger and by Haney (2002). Test score interpretations and consequences that are the most vulnerable to this problem of volatility of year-to-year change scores, and its direct relationship to school size, include ranking of schools based on average test scores, use of rankings to identify best practices, rewards for high performance or large

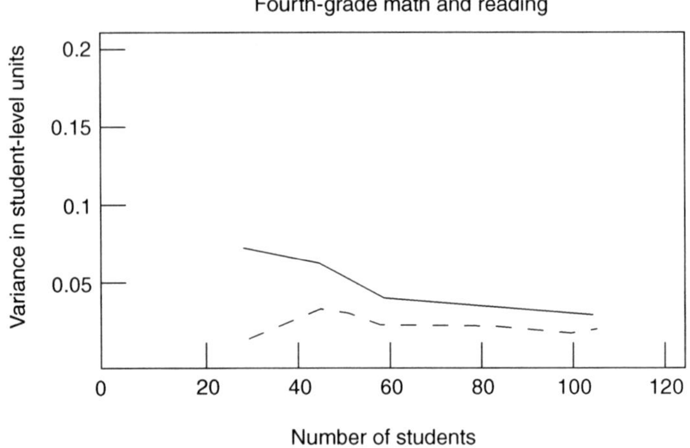

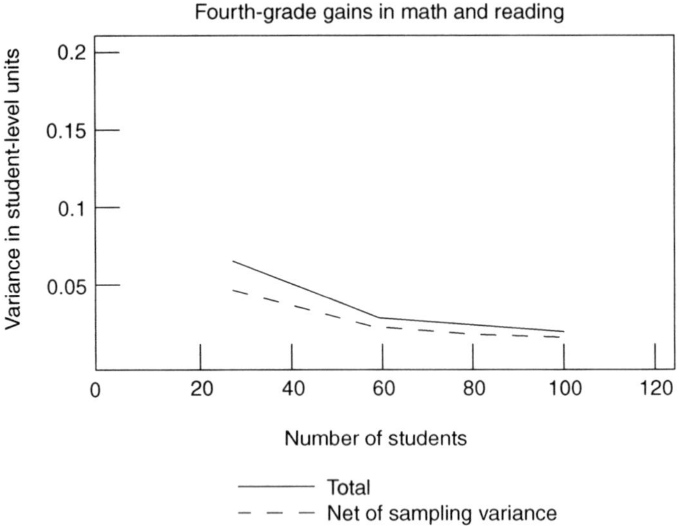

Figure 5.2 Between-School Variance in Annual Change (source: Kane & Staiger, 2002. Copyright 2002 by Brookings Institution. Reprinted with permission.).

"improvements," and sanctions for poor performance or "declining" performance. In addition, gap scores (i.e., measures of achievement gaps between student subgroups) are just as vulnerable to this problem as are change scores themselves. For this reason, changes in the size of achievement gaps should be evaluated over time.

Many studies have shown that the amount of average gain observed from one year to the next is negatively correlated with initial status, the average score on the first measurement occasion. This holds true whether a successive cohorts approach or a longitudinal approach to estimating change is used. For example, in a longitudinal study of factors affecting growth in reading and mathematics in 36 school districts in Colorado (over 113,000 students), Kiplinger (2003) found substantial negative relationships between initial status in reading, writing, and mathematics and average progress of students over a two year period (three measurement occasions). Results from the 2001, 2002, and 2003 Colorado Student Assessment Program (CSAP) assessments of reading, writing, and mathematics were analyzed for seven longitudinal cohorts of students. The purpose of this study was to model the effects of schools on student reading, writing, and mathematics achievement while controlling for the effects of student and school characteristics and estimating the cross-level effects. A multi-level, "value-added" approach was employed. Correlations of school average annual gain with school initial status for the seven cohorts are shown in Table 5.1. For the most part, the correlation coefficients are substantial, with five of the seven ranging from –0.56 to –0.91.[6] These results suggest that it may become increasingly difficult for initially high performing schools to make either their AYP status or growth targets.

Furthermore, Kiplinger (2003) found, as have Linn and Haug (2002), that schools that demonstrate large gains from year one to year two tend to show smaller gains from year two to year three, regardless of starting point. Linn and Haug's study found that schools that initially showed large gains in percentage proficient or advanced had large declines from year two to year three. Conversely, schools that declined in percentage proficient or advanced from year one to year two demonstrated increases from year two to year three. Kiplinger found similar results *within* cohorts of students. For example, schools whose seventh grade students showed large increases in their average scores over their average sixth grade results had smaller average gains from grade 7 to grade 8. Regardless of which approach is used, change scores can be volatile and unreliable measures. As discussed above, the magnitude of the

Table 5.1 Correlations of Average Initial Status and Average Gains in Reading, Writing, and Mathematics for Seven Longitudinal Cohorts of Students: Colorado Student Assessment Program, 2001–2003

Reading	r
Grade 3–5 cohort	–0.65
Grade 6–8 cohort	–0.56
Grade 8–10 cohort	–0.48
Writing	
Grade 4–6	–0.64
Grade 7–9	–0.91
Mathematics	
Grade 5–7 cohort	–0.39
Grade 8–10 cohort	–0.61

difference in year-to-year gains is related to initial status, as well as to the regression effect when the two gain scores are not perfectly correlated.

Implications for schools and AYP are numerous. Schools that initially make their AYP targets may fail to do so the next year. Conversely, schools that make small gains in one year are likely to show greater gains the next year. If a school was provided additional support after the first year and appeared to rebound during the second, the gains after the second year are likely to be attributed to the additional resources. However, an equally likely explanation may be the regression effect in combination with measurement error, sampling error, and nonpersistent factors unrelated to improved instruction.

Challenges to Reliability: Accountability Systems

The preceding discussion has focused on factors impacting the reliability of test scores and change scores. The remainder of this part of the chapter focuses on the effects on reliability of an accountability *system*, both in the general sense and as they pertain to the particular requirements of NCLB.

It is important to note here that accountability systems are more than test scores or testing systems. For example, NCLB requires high schools to meet graduation targets and elementary schools to meet a target on a state-chosen indicator, in addition to meeting their AYP targets for all students and for each reportable subgroup. Components of state accountability systems typically go beyond simple academic achievement or improvement goals. Missouri's educational accountability system (the Missouri School Improvement Program, MSIP), for example, evaluates public schools based on resource standards (basic requirements that all school districts must meet); process standards (instructional and administrative processes used in schools); and performance standards (multiple measures of student performance, including academic achievement on the state assessments, ACT achievement, career preparation, and educational persistence) (Council of Chief State School Officers, 2006).

Many factors impact the reliability of accountability systems. The most salient of these are discussed below.

NUMBER OF STUDENTS

As discussed earlier, sampling error tends to be a much larger contributor to volatility of school scores than is measurement error. The magnitude of the sampling error is a function of the number of individuals in the sample. The smaller the sample size, the larger the sampling error.[7] In fact, because of the square root in the formula (shown in Note 7), the standard error will be reduced by one-half if the sample size is quadrupled. For example, two schools with identical percentages proficient or above (e.g., 70%), but one with 100 students tested and the other with 400 students, will have sampling errors of 4.6% and 2.3%, respectively. Of course, this relationship holds for estimates regarding the total group or any subgroup of students.

NUMBER OF SUBGROUPS

Under NCLB, the reliability of an accountability system also depends on the number of subgroups for which decisions have to be made. NCLB requires school systems to set AYP targets for *each* subgroup for which there is a sufficient number of students to produce "statistically reliable" results. It is up to each state to determine what the "sufficient number" is. Currently, states' minimum number of students for AYP subgroup reporting typically ranges from ten to 60 in a subgroup. Clearly, the size of the "minimum n," or number needed, influences the number of subgroups for which reporting is required. It also affects the reliability of test scores for the subgroups specified by NCLB (i.e., students from major racial and ethnic groups, students who are economically disadvantaged, students with disabilities, and students with limited English proficiency). In general, the larger the school, the greater the number of subgroups, and the greater the number of ways that the school can fail to meet AYP. Thus, larger schools with their greater numbers of measurable subgroups are at a disadvantage.

TOTAL NUMBER OF INDEPENDENT JUDGMENTS REQUIRED

The NCLB requirements are *conjunctive.* That is, to meet AYP, schools must hit *all* targets in both reading and mathematics, both for students as a whole and for each reportable subgroup. Schools must also test at least 95% of students as a whole and in each subgroup, meet graduation targets for high schools, and meet a target on a state-chosen indicator for elementary schools. Larger schools and districts typically have more targets to meet than small schools and districts. High-poverty and racially diverse schools also have more AYP targets to meet than do more affluent and homogeneous schools. For example, a large, diverse high school that has sufficient numbers of students in three major racial and ethnic subgroups, who are English language learners, who are disadvantaged, and who have disabilities, would have 14 academic performance targets, plus 14 testing participation rates and the high school graduation target. Thus, such a school would have to meet a total of 29 AYP targets to "make AYP." The results for each target have associated error. The greater the number of targets, the greater the combined error, and the greater the likelihood of school misclassification—a significant unfairness to larger schools.

NUMBER OF GRADES TESTED

As discussed above, change scores are typically less reliable than either of the status scores used to compute the change score due to sampling and measurement errors and nonpersistent factors associated with the two scores. However, as Hill and DePascale (2003) have pointed out, testing in every grade level, three through eight, will reduce the standard error of change scores due to the interdependence (i.e., correlation) of the scores when many of the same students are tested from one year to the next. The example they provide shows that if one grade is tested in a school of 50 students per grade where 50% of students pass, the standard error of the change score across the two years of testing is: Standard Error of Measurement (SEM) = $\sqrt{(2*50*50)/50}$, or 10.0%. However, if three grades in this school are tested and the correlation of test scores across years is 0.7, the standard error of the change score is: SEM = $\sqrt{(2*50*50)-(2*0.7*0.5*50*50)/150}$, or 4.67%. In this situation, the effect of greater stability due to overlapping samples of students is equivalent to quadrupling the number of students tested.

NUMBER OF MEASUREMENTS

Cohort effects inherent in the successive cohorts approach lead to sampling error and score volatility for individual grade-level results. Increasing the amount of information on which decisions are based, by increasing the number of measurements across years or across grades and subjects, can be used to improve reliability. NCLB permits states to aggregate up to three years of data in making AYP determinations. Combining data over two or three years can reduce cohort effects of the successive cohorts approach and increase the effective sample size, thereby decreasing sampling error and score volatility. The use of rolling averages is an example of aggregating data that can increase the reliability of AYP determinations. The construction of composite index scores across subjects and grades also can reduce cohort effects and the likelihood of misclassification.

DISTANCE FROM THE GOAL

Distance from the goal, or the difference between the target and the observed performance results, also has a major impact on the reliability of an accountability system. As Hill and DePascale (2003) and others have pointed out, large differences between the goal and observed performance are easier to detect than small differences. For example, if a school's AYP target is 60% at or above proficient and the observed percentage is 45, then we may be fairly certain that the "true" percentage is below the required 60% and that the school did not meet this AYP target. If 58% of students tested at or above the proficient level, the AYP determination would be the same; however, the result for the next sample of students from the school might be above 60%. "The extent to which different decisions would be made about a school when the school has changed nothing to warrant the change in decision is the unreliability of the accountability system" (p. 3).

PERFORMANCE STANDARDS AND "PERCENT ABOVE CUT"

The use of performance standards and percents above a cut point, and especially where in the distribution the cut point is placed (e.g., to determine basic or proficient status), have tremendous implications for efforts to evaluate gaps between subgroups, which is a major component of NCLB. Holland (2002) has shown that measuring gaps using differences in percents above a cut point has an inherent sensitivity to the location of the cut point in the score distribution. For example, Holland shows that the black–white gap in percent at or above the basic cut point on the 2000 NAEP grade 8 mathematics assessment is approximately 44 percentage points. At the proficient cut point, however, the gap in the percent above that cut is about 28 points, and only about six points at the advanced cut point (about 6% for whites and less than 1% for blacks). Focusing on gaps at a selected cut point does not tell us anything about what is happening elsewhere in the distribution. Furthermore, this problem is exacerbated when one attempts to measure *changes* in achievement gaps. Although it is not usually thought of as a "reliability" issue, the inaccuracy in measurement of change at the cut score or of change in group differences at the cut score is an extremely important issue in a context where policymakers have forced us to interpret "progress" as a change in percent proficient.

New Developments: Evaluating the Reliability of Accountability Systems and Better Gauging School Effectiveness

Recent developments and proposals for ameliorating some of the more problematic issues with current AYP models and accountability systems include methodologies for evaluating the probability of misclassifying schools, alternative "percent-above-cut-score" approaches, alternative disaggregation approaches, and new models for tracking student progress over time and gauging the success of *all* students.

Estimating the Probability of Misclassifying Schools

Hill and DePascale (2002) have developed methodology and software to determine the probability of misclassifying schools for AYP determination under different accountability designs. They describe four different methods for computing the reliability of an accountability system: direct computation, split-half, random draws with replacement, and Monte Carlo methods. Only the two methods most recommended by Hill and DePascale—the Monte Carlo method and random draws with replacement—are discussed here (descriptions of the other two methods are found in Hill & DePascale, 2002).

The Monte Carlo method involves repeated sample draws of students for a school using a random number generator after all parameters for a school[8] are carefully estimated. Crucial to this method is the accuracy of the initial estimate of the variance of the school's students. The decision rules of the accountability system are applied to each draw, and the proportion of classification decisions for the school that are consistent with the original classification decision is computed. This result is the classification reliability of the accountability system. Hill and DePascale maintain that this approach is well suited to complex decision rules. The random draws with replacement method involves drawing repeated samples from a given sample for a school. This method has several disadvantages enumerated by Hill and DePascale (2002). However, they recommend it because it "has the advantage of simplicity and appears to provide generally accurate results" (p. 9).

Both the Monte Carlo and random draws with replacement methods generate sets of plausible results for every school that can be aggregated to estimate the accuracy of the classification system under hypothesized conditions of improvement or lack of improvement. Before drawing the sets of plausible results, true score means ($\bar{T}$) for each school are estimated. Once $\bar{T}$ and the plausible results are generated, potential or hypothetical changes in scores over time can be modeled. For example, if one wished to estimate what the decision (i.e., classification) accuracy of the accountability system would be if no schools made improvement, one would draw "data" for the number of years for which change is to be modeled under the assumption that $\bar{T}$ remained constant over time. The system's decision rules are then applied to each replication of the data (i.e., the sets of plausible results referred to above), and the number of times a school is correctly and incorrectly classified is counted. If one wished to estimate what the decision accuracy of the system would be if all schools made some amount of improvement, the researcher would specify the amount of improvement each year, add that amount to $\bar{T}$ for each school, and generate a distribution of "observed" student scores around that estimate. The number of times a school is correctly and incorrectly classified is then counted. The classification accuracy for each school is the number of correct classifications divided by the number of replications (Hill & DePascale, 2002).

Alternative Percent-Above-Cut-Score Approaches

The use of performance standards and percents above a cut point to indicate achievement status or growth is pervasive in state systems and central to AYP and NCLB accountability. Holland demonstrates that estimates of subgroup gaps in scores are affected by where in the distribution the cut score is set. Although this issue is not typically seen as a reliability issue, inaccuracy in measurement of change at the cut score or of change in group differences at the cut score is an extremely important issue in the NCLB context of "progress" measured as increases in percents proficient and narrowing subgroup achievement gaps.

Linn (2004) offers two alternatives to the current percentage above cut-score approach based on state-established performance standards. States have had considerable leeway in the performance standard cut score that they can use as proficient for AYP purposes. Because the rigor of those standards varies greatly from state to state, there also is great state-to-state variability in the percentages of students scoring above the proficient cut score.

Linn suggests that if the percentage scoring above a cut score is to be used, then that cut score should be more meaningful and comparable across states than the extremely variable placement of their current proficient cut scores. A simple approach would be to set a constant cut score, such as the *median* score on each state's assessment in a base year. The percentage of students scoring above that cut score could be used to monitor improvement. Reasonable increases in that percentage, for example 3% per year, could be set as the improvement targets. If the base year is 2002 and the targets are increases of three percentage points annually, the percentage of students scoring above the cut score would increase from 50% in 2002 to 86% in 2014, a huge improvement and more realistic than 100% proficient on widely variable definitions of proficient. An alternative suggestion is use of an effect size measure to monitor change over time. Using 2002 and 2003 as the base years for change, the effect size for 2003 would be computed by subtracting the mean achievement score in 2002 from the mean achievement score in 2003 and dividing by the standard deviation in 2002. The average effect size for the 10% of best performing schools could be used to set the annual target increase in effect size. For example, if the average effect size increase from 2002 to 2003 for the top 10% of schools was 0.05, then the target *annual* increase in effect size would be 0.05. This would escalate to a target of 0.6 in 2014 compared to the base year of 2002 (i.e., 0.05×12 years $= 0.6$). An effect size of 0.6 would indicate that the average student in 2014 would be performing at a level comparable to the seventy-third percentile on the 2002 assessment. Again, this would represent a huge improvement in student performance, greater than has been observed in any similar time period in the last 50 years, according to Linn.

Disaggregation

Although disaggregation of results is necessary for monitoring the progress of traditionally lower performing subgroups such as the disadvantaged, special needs students, racial and ethnic minorities, and students with limited English proficiency, and should be continued, the requirement has caused a major problem. The greater a school's number of subgroups for which reporting is required, the greater the likelihood that the school will miss AYP. Diverse schools with several reportable subgroups will have more targets, and more ways to fail AYP, than more homogeneous schools of similar size and performance.

Because a large part of the problem is due to year-to-year volatility of scores for small groups, Linn suggests allowing schools to aggregate results for subgroups over two or three years in order to reduce that score volatility.

Tracking Student Academic Progress Over Time

NCLB focuses more on status than on change. In the early years of the system, initially high scoring schools might show a decline in average performance, but still meet the AYP status targets. On the other hand, initially low performing schools are required to make disproportionately large annual gains to meet AYP status targets; many such schools will not make AYP even though they may be making commendable gains. A recommendation for incorporating change that has many supporters is the use of longitudinal models to track the academic progress of individual students over time. For example, value-added models are suggested as a way to provide evidence of increased achievement and school improvement. Because value-added models track individual student performance over time, analyze trends over multiple years, and reduce standard errors through the interdependence (i.e., correlation) of scores when many of the same students are tested from year to year, their estimates of growth are more reliable than those from status models common in the successive cohorts approach. In addition, value-added and other growth models typically include the results for *all* students in their estimates, rather than considering only students in the proficient and above categories.

Value-added models can be used to estimate the unique school effect on student growth, and thus are sometimes used to make causal inferences (for a more in-depth treatment of causal inferences and educational accountability, please see the Briggs and Wiley chapter in this volume).

A Catch-Up-Keep-Up-Move-Up (CUKUMU) Model for Gauging the Success of All Students

Betebenner (2005, 2006) has argued that growth models based on ordinal outcomes (i.e., performance-level categories) of states' standards-based accountability measures are more consistent with current NCLB and state accountability mandates than are the current value-added models of longitudinal growth.[9] As an alternative to current value-added models, Betebenner developed a "transition probabilities" model based on empirical longitudinal data, performance-level outcomes and, most significantly, the probability of *transitions* between the performance levels. A transition matrix for performance-level outcomes describes the probabilities that students will move (transition) between performance levels or remain in the same performance level from one grade to the next.[10]

Building on Betebenner's work, Academy School District Twenty (ASD20) in Colorado Springs, Colorado, has extended the transitions probability approach with growth models that incorporate expectations for cohorts of students as they progress through school, as well as setting increasingly higher expectations for successive cohorts of students entering the system. The ASD20 methodology incorporates a growth model based on ordinal outcomes on the statewide assessment, the probability of transitions between performance levels, and a new approach that sets targets for *all* students maintaining or increasing their performance levels. The ASD20 methodology has multiple components. The first component is an extension of Betebenner's approach. For each school in the district, growth is modeled as the empirical "transitions" within or between performance levels for cohorts of students as they move from one grade level to the next.

Although Betebenner's techniques work well for cohorts across an entire district, the small numbers of students encountered in cells of the transition matrices for individual schools can steer growth models down unrealistic paths. For example, the empirical transition matrix for one school showed unusually high proportions of students moving from proficient to advanced or remaining advanced from 2004 to 2005, resulting in 16% of students in the "advanced" performance category in 2005. Carrying the mathematical projection out further resulted in a target of 54% advanced in 2010, which is unreasonable.

Accordingly, the performance-level matrices for each ASD20 school were averaged across grades. This not only provided much better stability in the growth models, but the more reliable approach also reflects the overall performances of students in the school as a whole, given that each student eventually progresses through all of the grade transitions. This averaging process is a crucial departure from the methodology developed by Betebenner (2005, 2006).

A centerpiece of ASD20's work to include *all* students in the accountability system is the conceptualization and operationalization of the concepts of "catch-up, keep-up and move-up" (see Elrod, Krebs, Vedra, & Turner 2005). This "Catch-Up-Keep-Up-Move-Up" model is referred to as the CUKUMU model. Although NCLB focuses on moving students from the "below proficient" achievement category to proficient, ASD20 focuses on (a) catching students up to proficient *and*, equally importantly, (b) maintaining or (c) advancing the achievement of students who are already proficient. The goal is to specify targets that lead schools to the district's goals of 0% unsatisfactory *and* no students falling into a lower performance level than they were in the previous year.

For AYP purposes, the primary objective is decreasing the percentage of students in the lowest performance level until no students are in this category by the end date (2014 for NCLB and 2010 in ASD20's accountability system). These annual *catch-up* targets are determined using the modified transitions probabilities approach described above. Targets are specified in terms of maximum annual percentages in the lowest performance level and are based on the school's starting place. "*Keep-up*" students are those performing above the lowest performance category and who should at least maintain their performance level. Targets are based on the school's starting place. "*Move-up*" students are those who move up at least one performance level.

Thus, *all* students are included in ADS20's calculations of improvement. The CUKUMU "growth targets" are based on changes in the performance in reading and math on the statewide assessment during the preceding two years. The overall judgment about a school's improvement in terms of longitudinal growth is determined by combining the results by subject[11] and cohort.[12] The combination by subject and cohort can be implemented in either a conjoint or compensatory fashion. Currently, this process operates as an early warning system to help direct resources to schools and is not used for accountability or accreditation purposes.

Another model for gauging school effectiveness that includes *all* students is the "Hybrid Success Model" (HSM) model proposed by Kingsbury, Olson, McCahon, and McColl (2004). This model is a "hybrid" because it combines information on both growth and proficiency levels of individual students. Unlike the current AYP model, which focuses attention on students who are near or below the proficient cut point and ignores students who are already proficient, the HSM identifies a growth target for each student reaching or surpassing the proficient level in a prescribed time, regardless of current performance level. The model calculates the school effect on an individual student as the proportion of the student's target growth that was obtained. The success of the school is gauged by the extent to which each student reaches the individual growth target. Thus, measuring school success in this way should

> prompt schools to work with all of their students. Talented and gifted students who do not grow in their capabilities are as clear an indicator of poor performance by the school as are low performing students who do not reach the performance standards.
>
> (p. 3)

Conclusions

The reliability of educational assessments and educational accountability systems are core issues that have taken on new meaning in this era of educational accountability and No Child Left Behind. In addition to the general NCLB requirement that each state create an accountability system that is "valid and reliable," states must establish adequate yearly progress (AYP) targets that will lead to the goal of 100% of students proficient by 2014. In school accountability and AYP contexts, reliability refers to the consistency and accuracy with which schools are classified as either meeting or missing their AYP targets. Severe sanctions are imposed on schools that consistently miss their AYP targets. Thus, it is *crucial* that schools be accurately classified with regard to AYP targets.

Recent developments and alternative approaches described above hold great promise for mitigating some of the more problematic areas of current (i.e., 2006 to 2007) AYP models and NCLB accountability requirements. Hill and DePascale's methodology and software are important steps in estimating the probability of misclassifying schools for AYP determination under different accountability designs. Linn's proposals for improving the accountability provisions of NCLB merit serious consideration in the upcoming reauthorization of NCLB. Likewise, the alternative models for estimating school improvement and effectiveness proposed by Betebenner (2005, 2006) and Kingsbury et al. (2004), are all attractive and viable alternatives. Although these methods vary in their approaches to estimating school effectiveness, each is concerned with the progress of *all* students—higher performing students and the most challenged students, as well those who are just below the proficient level and could likely clear that hurdle.

There now are clear signs (Walsh, 2007) that NCLB is slated for revisions intended to remove the most obvious defects in its accountability requirements. The proposed alternatives and new developments examined in this chapter should provide new focus on the importance of accurate and reliable classification of schools in any educational accountability system, as well as on continued improvement of NCLB's accountability requirements.

Acknowledgment

The author is indebted to Lorrie Shepard, Laura Hamilton, Brian Gong, Neil Dorans, and Katherine Ryan for providing careful reviews, constructive suggestions for improving the technical quality and readability of the chapter, and for their helpful comments on earlier drafts. The author also thanks Bob Linn for reviewing the original outline of the chapter. The author hopes that she has done justice to their excellent suggestions. Responsibility for the final product, of course, remains with the author.

Notes

1. Change scores are the difference between scores from two time periods, obtained by subtracting the score obtained in Time 1 from the scores obtained in Time 2. Change scores can be computed for students, schools, districts, etc.
2. The change scores are computed as the annual change in fourth grade combined reading and math scores.
3. Schools in the middle quintile in terms of number of students assessed.
4. Quintiles are defined in terms of the number of students assessed.
5. The gaps between the solid and dashed lines represent Kane and Staiger's estimates of sampling variation by school size. Because the dashed lines represent between-school variance after the sampling variance has been subtracted out, the gaps between the solid and dashed lines indicate the amount of sampling variance. Thus, the larger gaps for small schools indicate greater sampling variance.
6. The correlation of school growth rates with school initial status is termed an "ecological correlation" because it is based on a correlation between variables that are group means, in contrast to a correlation between variables for individuals. It is not surprising that the ecological correlations reported are "substantial," indicating tighter clustering than might be found at the individual level because variability in the underlying individual data is lost in the averaging. Examination of correlations between the individual-level variables confirms that the correlations are indeed lower than the group correlations, but all are negative, as in the ecological correlations. Correlations between individual-level initial status and average annual raw gain scores for five of the seven cohorts reported above ranged from –0.2 to –0.6.

7. The formula for estimating the sampling error (or standard error) of a percentage, such as the percentage "proficient or above" on a state assessment is: $s = \sqrt{\frac{pq}{n}} \times 100$, where p = the proportion proficient or above, q = the proportion below proficient (i.e., q = 1 − p), and n is the sample size (or number of students tested).
8. Parameters are the mean and standard deviation of student scores, standard deviation of school mean scores, reliability of the test, and the shape of the student score distribution.
9. Current value-added models rely on scale scores as their analysis metric. Consistent with NCLB and state mandates, Betebenner's growth models are based on ordinal (i.e., performance-level) outcomes, and the probability of transitions, or movement, among the performance levels.
10. A transition matrix of performance-level outcomes describes the probabilities that students will move, or "transition," between performance levels or remain in the same performance from one grade to the next.

		Grade 4			
		A	P	PP	U
Grade 3	A	A,A			
	P	P,A			
	PP				
	U			U,PP	

Performance levels:
A = Advanced
P = Proficient
PP = Partially Proficient
U = Unsatisfactory

The probabilities are expressed as proportions of students who move among the performance levels. Thus, Cell A,A (upper left hand corner of the matrix) is the proportion of Advanced students in grade 3 who remain Advanced in grade 4. Cell P,A (immediately below Cell A,A) is the proportion of Proficient students in grade 3 who moved up to Advanced in grade 4. Cell U,PP (bottom right quadrant of the matrix) represents the proportion of students who moved from Unsatisfactory in grade 3 to Partially Proficient in grade 4. The remaining cells of the transition matrix are interpreted similarly.
11. Reading and mathematics.
12. The Colorado Student Assessment Program assesses all students in grades 3 through 10. There are two elementary cohorts (those who advance from grade 3 to grade 4 and those who advance from grade 4 to grade 5); three middle school cohorts (grade 5 to grade 6, grade 6 to grade 7, and grade 7 to grade 8); and two high school cohorts (grade 8 to grade 9 and grade 9 to grade 10).

References

Betebenner, D. W. (2005, June). Performance standards in measures of educational effectiveness. Paper presented at the Council of Chief State School Officers National Conference on Large-Scale Assessment, San Antonio, TX.

Betebenner, D. W. (2006, June). The data doesn't speak for itself. Paper presented at the Council of Chief State School Officers National Conference on Large-Scale Assessment, San Francisco, CA.

Council of Chief State School Officers. (2006). *State accountability systems beyond NCLB.* Washington, DC: Council of Chief State School Officers.

Cronbach, L. J. & Furby, L. (1970). How we should measure change—or should we? *Psychological Bulletin,* 74 (1), 66–80.

Cronbach, L. J., Linn, R. L., Brennan, R. L., & Haertel, E. H. (1997). Generalizability analysis for performance assessments of student achievement or school effectiveness. *Educational and Psychological Measurement,* 57 (3), 373–399.

Elrod, A., Krebs, S., Vedra, K., & Turner, K. (2005, April). Measuring student achievement over time. Paper presented at the North Central Association Commission on Accreditation and School Improvement Conference, Chicago, IL.

Haney, W. (2002, May 6). Lake woebeguaranteed: Misuse of test scores in Massachusetts, part I. *Education Policy Analysis Archives*, 10 (24). Online, available at: http://epaa.asu.edu/epaa/v10n24/ (accessed July 30, 2007).

Hill, R. K. & DePascale, C. A. (2002). *Determining the reliability of school scores.* Washington, DC: Council of Chief State School Officers.

Hill, R. K. & DePascale, C. A. (2003, April). Adequate yearly progress under NCLB: Reliability considerations. Paper presented at the annual meeting of the National Council on Measurement in Education, Chicago, IL.

Holland, P. W. (2002). Two measures of change in the gaps between the CDFs of test-score distributions. *Journal of Educational and Behavioral Statistics*, 27 (1), 3–17.

Kane, T. J. & Staiger, D. O. (2002). Volatility in school test scores: Implications for test-based accountability systems. In D. Ravitch (Ed.), *Brookings Papers on Education Policy: 2002* (pp. 235–283). Washington, DC: Brookings Institution.

Kingsbury, G. G., Olson, A., McCahon, D., & McCall, M. S. (2004, July). Adequate yearly progress using the hybrid success model: A suggested improvement to No Child Left Behind. Paper presented at a forum on No Child Left Behind sponsored by the Center for Education Policy, Washington, DC.

Kiplinger, V. L. (2003). *Longitudinal study of student growth in reading, writing and mathematics achievement in thirty-six Colorado public school districts: Phase II final report.* Colorado Springs, CO: Academy School District Twenty.

Linn, R. L. (2003). Accountability: Responsibility and reasonable expectations. *Educational Researcher*, 32 (7), 3–13.

Linn, R. L. (2004, July 28). Rethinking the No Child Left Behind accountability system. Paper presented at a forum on No Child Left Behind sponsored by the Center for Education Policy, Washington, DC.

Linn, R. L. (2005). *Issues in the design of accountability systems* (CSE Technical Report 650). Los Angeles, CA: Center for Research on Evaluation Standards.

Linn, R. L. & Haug, C. (2002). Stability of school-building accountability scores and gains. *Educational Evaluation and Policy Analysis*, 24 (1), 29–36.

Linn, R. L., Baker, E. L., & Betebenner, D. W. (2002). Accountability systems: Implications of requirements of the No Child Left Behind Act of 2001. *Educational Researcher*, 31 (6), 3–16.

No Child Left Behind Act of 2001, Pub. L. No. 107–110, 115 Stat. 1425 (2002).

Walsh, M. (2007, July 30). Miller outlines proposed changes for NCLB [online exclusive]. *Education Week.* Online, available at: http://www.edweek.org/ew/articles/2007/07/30/44nclb_web.h26.html?print=1 (accessed August 1, 2007).

6
Equating and Linking of Educational Assessments in High-Stakes Accountability Systems

Vonda L. Kiplinger and Laura S. Hamilton

To ensure comparability of tests from one test administration to the next, large-scale assessment programs use a process of test score equating. Without such methods for building equivalent tests, it would be impossible to measure changes in achievement over time. Traditionally, equated tests have been used to measure year-to-year changes for different students in the same grade. Have this year's third graders performed better in reading than last year's third graders? Increasingly, however, there is interest in measuring growth in achievement, which requires linking different tests across grades. How much growth did fourth graders show compared to their achievement last year in third grade? Linking is the term used to refer to several types of statistical methods used to establish a relationship between the score scales from two tests so that results from one test can be compared to results on another test.

In recent years, there has also been growing pressure from policymakers, educators, and some in the media to compare directly results of different states' assessments. Certainly, No Child Left Behind (NCLB) has provided a new impetus to the call. NCLB requires that each state develop challenging academic content, challenging student achievement (i.e., performance) standards, and annual yearly progress (AYP) goals that lead to the 2014 goal of all students performing at or above the proficient standard. These requirements, together with questions concerning the relative rigor or stringency of different state assessments and their student performance standards, have given new urgency to the desire to link results from different assessments. There has always been the need within a single assessment program to link results from different forms or levels of a test, but NCLB and other test-based accountability policies have increased the need to link scores from tests that were never intended to be part of the same testing program. This chapter addresses both applications of test linking and also describes the diversity in state testing programs, challenges to linking tests in accountability systems, factors that affect the validity of a test linking, and the particular challenges in linking results from state assessments with results from the National Assessment of Educational Progress.

Types of Test Linkages

Before proceeding further, the most common types of linking methods should be discussed. Because equating is the most stringent form, we use "linking" or "linkage" as the generic terms for the statistical procedures by which scores on two different tests are related. There are several levels of these methodologies where each type of method requires different degrees of alignment of test content, difficulty, reliability, purpose, format, populations, and administration practices (see, e.g., Linn, 1993; Mislevy, 1992). Five types of linking methodologies are discussed here: equating, calibration, projection, moderation, and concordance.

Equating is the most stringent form of linking. It is a process used to adjust statistically scores from two test forms so that they can be used interchangeably (see, e.g., Kolen & Brennan, 2004; Linn, 1993; Mislevy, 1992). Most often, equating is used to adjust scores on alternate forms of the same test, such as different forms of the SAT. Equating is possible only when test forms are built to the same specifications and test content, difficulty, reliability, format, purpose, administration, and populations are equivalent. Dorans and Holland (2000, pp. 282–283) identify five "requirements" widely considered "basic" for test equating:

a. *The Same Construct Requirement.* Tests that measure different constructs should not be equated.
b. *The Equal Reliability Requirement.* Tests that measure the same construct but differ in reliability should not be equated.
c. *The Symmetry Requirement.* The equating function for equating the scores of Y to those of X should be the *inverse* of the equating function for equating the scores of X to Y.
d. *The Equity Requirement.* It should not make any difference for an examinee to be tested by either one of the two tests that have been equated.
e. *Population Invariance Requirement.* The choice of (sub)population used to compute the equating function between the scores of tests X and Y should not matter. In other words, the equating function used to link the scores of X and Y should be the same regardless of whether it was derived using a sample of only boys or only girls or a national or local sample.

Calibration is a type of linking with somewhat less stringent requirements than equating. This method assumes that two tests measure the same construct and is typically used to link a shorter, less reliable, test form to a longer, more reliable form. As Linn (1993) has shown, calibration cannot satisfy the equity criterion. Examinees whose proficiency levels are below the standard are more likely to pass the shorter form of a test due to luck. However, calibration can support useful types of comparisons such as estimating the likely score on the longer form for examinees who only take the shorter version. Calibration is also used to link scores from tests that are designed for different development levels (e.g., scores on a state's third grade and fourth grade reading assessments). This type of calibration is often called vertical equating, but Linn (1993) argues that calibration is a better descriptor because

> tests designed for different developmental levels generally do not satisfy the requirements for a true equating. Indeed, the calibration requirement that two tests measure the same thing is generally only crudely approximated with tests designed to measure achievement at different developmental levels.
>
> (p. 91)

Projection (also termed "prediction" by Linn, 1993) is a much weaker form of linkage. Projection is a unidirectional form of linking in which scores on one test are predicted, or projected, from scores on another test, usually via regression. These methods require a single group data collection; that is, one group of examinees is administered both tests in order to develop the projection equations. There is no expectation that the same construct is being measured by the two tests, and the prediction equations are asymmetric. That is, projecting test X on test Y and projecting test Y on test X yields different results. Also, the projection may or may not hold true across different populations.

Moderation is the weakest form of linkage. Like projection, scores on one test are predicted from scores on another. Unlike projection, however, the two tests are given to different, nonequivalent groups. Uncommon Measures (Feuer, Holland, Green, Bertenthal, & Hemphill, 1999) lists two types of moderation: statistical moderation and social moderation. In statistical moderation, score distributions are matched; for example, the percentile ranks of one test are matched to the percentile ranks of the other. An example of a statistical moderation to link scores on two different tests is use of an external examination to serve as an anchor test. The scores on the local tests are adjusted to match the mean and standard deviation of the anchor test. As noted by Linn (1993): "The utility of such an approach depends heavily on the relevance of the anchor test and its comparability to the locally defined tests" (p. 93). Social moderation matches distributions using direct human judgments concerning examinee performance. Two examples are the grading of written essays by test scorers and comparing performance levels on different assessments.

Concordance is another type of linking that has less stringent requirements than equating, and is sometimes placed in the "moderation" category (Kolen & Brennan, 2004). Scores on two tests that measure a similar construct, but are written to different specifications, can be linked by the same statistical procedures used for equating in order to establish a "concordance" relationship between the scores. An example of this type of linking is the linkage between the ACT and SAT I college entrance examinations. Although these two tests are strongly correlated, they are developed independently to different sets of test specifications, and measure different, although similar, constructs (Linn, 1993). Concordance functions are used to establish concordance tables that allow one to obtain SAT I equivalent scores from ACT scores and ACT equivalent scores from SAT I scores. Thus, concordance linkages typically do not meet the symmetry and equity requirements. In addition, concordances may be sensitive to the populations used to estimate the concordance relationships.

What constitutes a satisfactory linkage? As summarized by Cizek, Kennedy, Kolen, Peters, and van der Linden (1999),

> a satisfactory linkage is one that would permit the same inferences about student achievement from comparable scores on the two assessments.... The key question that must be answered when selecting a linking method is: "Do the two assessments measure the same construct?"
>
> (p. iii)

In the context of educational accountability assessments, the two most common linking applications are year-to-year equating (also known as horizontal equating) and vertical scaling (also known as vertical equating). The purpose of year-to-year equating is to link the scores from different tests given to different students in different years in the *same* grade level. The purpose of vertical equating, on the other hand, is to link assessments of the same construct across grade levels, usually adjacent grades, in order to track student progress over time on a common scale. These two types of equating applications are now discussed.

Year-to-Year Equating

The use of tests for school accountability requires an assessment system that supports valid inferences about changes in students' performance over time. Any gain in scores on a test in the same subject and at the same grade level is likely to be interpreted by users as an indication of a gain in the knowledge and skills the test was designed to measure. In other words, scores from tests administered in different years are generally treated as if they came from the same test. Because it is not feasible to use an identical test year after year, particularly when high stakes are attached to scores, accountability testing requires the application of equating methods to establish equivalent scores for two or more different test forms.

Even in contexts in which each year's test is carefully built to align to a stable set of content standards or test specifications, as is typical in statewide accountability testing programs, small differences in the content and difficulty of the test items will render the raw scores non-interchangeable. Equating methods are applied to produce scores that can reasonably be treated as interchangeable. As discussed above, there are several conditions that should be met to ensure successful test equating, and these need to be kept in mind from the early stages of test development. Failure to meet these requirements is likely to lead to inappropriate inferences about the meanings of test score changes and, in the context of high-stakes accountability systems, to inappropriate decisions about school or student performance.

Methods for equating tests used in accountability systems should be designed to accommodate the practical constraints inherent in those systems. In particular, examinees and educators must not be exposed to the test before it is administered, so designs that involve having a common set of examinees complete both test forms, or having equivalent groups of examinees complete alternate forms at the same time, are not likely to be acceptable. In addition, educators and administrators are often reluctant to require more testing than is mandated by state or federal accountability policies, which limits the feasibility of some equating approaches. As a result of these constraints, a commonly used strategy is the use of anchor items. This approach is sometimes referred to as the nonequivalent groups with anchor test (NEAT) design (von Davier, Holland, & Thayer 2004; Holland & Dorans, 2006). The anchor-items method accommodates situations in which two different examinee populations (e.g., third graders in 2007 and third graders in 2008) take two different test forms (e.g., the 2007 and 2008 versions of the third grade mathematics test in a particular state). It requires that administrations include a common set of items, either embedded in the test forms ("internal anchor test") or administered as a separate section ("external anchor test"). Scores on this common set of anchor items are then used to link the total scores on the two tests. This method addresses some of the practical constraints discussed above by requiring only a subset of the items to be re-administered and therefore decreasing the likelihood that examinees or educators will be able to predict which items will be included in a future administration.

It is critical that users of this method understand the importance of carefully designing the anchor test. As Holland and Dorans (2006) note, "[The anchor test] is the only means for separating the *differences between the abilities* of the two groups of examinees from the *differences between the two tests* that are being equated" (p. 201, emphasis in original). In the case of year-to-year equating, therefore, the anchor test is the only way to determine whether changes in scores over time reflect increases or decreases in the underlying proficiency or differences in the content or difficulty of the tests used each year. Two primary requirements are that the anchor test function in a stable manner over time and that the correlations between the anchor test and the other tests be as high as possible. The need for high correlations can be addressed in several ways, including ensuring that the anchor items are broadly representative of the standards or specifications on which the larger tests are based, using a similar distribution of item formats (e.g., percentage of items that are multiple choice) on the anchor test and the full tests, making the anchor test as long as possible given practical constraints, and using internal rather than external anchor tests (Holland & Dorans, 2006).

A variety of methods exists for equating using anchor items. Some commonly used methods rely on a simple linear regression model in which scores on the separate tests are regressed on the anchor tests to create the equivalent scores. More recently, the use of item response theory (IRT) for equating has become widespread. IRT enables the estimation of a "latent trait" or ability that is presumed to underlie performance on all of the items, including the anchor items. IRT-based equating methods involve estimating item parameters for the anchor items for each test form and adjusting for the differences in the anchor item parameters across forms to create equivalent scores on the full test forms. Kolen and Brennan (1995) provide a thorough discussion of equating methods and their strengths and limitations.

Issues in Year-to-Year Equating of Accountability Tests

The validity and usefulness of any equating are influenced by a variety of factors. Several thorough discussions of these issues have been published (see, e.g., Holland & Dorans, 2006). Here, we focus on a few issues that are particularly relevant to year-to-year equating in accountability systems.

First, it is critical that the inferences and decisions made on the basis of test score changes from one year to the next reflect an appropriate degree of caution. Users must understand that there is some error inherent in any equating function, and must be given information to help them determine how large this error is likely to be. The standard error of equating, or SEE, is a commonly used measure of this error. There are several variations on this index, and a number of ways of estimating it. Regardless of which approach is used, it is important for information about the magnitude of the error to be provided to users, along with clear guidance about how to interpret this information. Moreover, as noted by Koretz (this volume), the notion of error in test scores has become more complicated as a result of accountability testing and, in particular, the reporting of scores in the aggregate. Inferences about change in a school's performance, for example, depend on a number of factors that include but are not limited to the error inherent in the test equating and the sampling error that arises from the inclusion of different students from one year to the next. To the extent possible, users need to understand these sources of error and how they hinder inferences about change.

Second, steps must be taken to ensure that the anchor items function equivalently across test administrations, which typically occur a year apart.

Some steps can be taken during test design, such as placing the anchor items at roughly equivalent positions in the test at each administration (e.g., avoiding having most of them appear at the beginning of the test one year and at the end of the test the next year). Of particular relevance to high-stakes accountability is the need to prevent breaches of test security and minimize the likelihood that scores on the anchor items will become inflated. Even when strong security is in place, factors that contribute to score inflation can create particular problems for equating designs that reuse items over time. As discussed by Koretz (this volume), if teachers or other educators engage in test preparation activities that lead to artificially large gains on the anchor items, the year-to-year equating will be distorted by score inflation (see Koretz & Barron, 1998, for an illustrative example).

Third, as noted earlier, the tests administered on each occasion must measure the same constructs. Behavioral responses and score inflation may affect the anchor items or the entire test in ways that change what is measured, such as when items originally intended to assess complex problem-solving skills become routine recall items as a result of teaching the specific solution strategy. Moreover, the construct being measured may change by design, such as when states refine their standards or attempt to improve the alignment between tests and standards. Even when such changes are minor, they are important for users to be aware of because they can affect the validity of inferences about score changes.

Vertical Scaling

The previous part of the chapter focused on inferences about changes in performance across time for the same subject and grade level. Because most accountability systems involve testing in multiple grades, there is also frequently a need for creating links between scores for tests administered in different grades. This type of linking, which is typically called *vertical equating* or *vertical scaling*, is intended to place scores from the various grades on a single scale, which could facilitate inferences about growth in learning in a subject area as students move from grade to grade. The resulting scale is typically called a vertical or developmental scale.

The most straightforward approach to measuring growth from one grade to the next would be to administer the same test each time and use the difference in scores as the growth measure. This approach might be feasible when only two consecutive grades are of interest, though for most subjects and grade pairs some of the tested content will be inappropriate for one grade or the other. The use of a single test becomes less appropriate as more grades are added because the content of the curriculum tends to differ fairly dramatically for grades that are farther apart. As a result, testing systems typically use different tests for different grades, and vertical equating is used to create a common scale across these different tests. As noted earlier, this form of linking may be best described as an example of calibration rather than equating, because the assumptions required for true equating are violated by the need to measure different content at different grade levels.

The increasing prevalence of growth-based and value-added models (Betebenner, this volume; McCaffrey, Lockwood, Koretz, & Hamilton, 2003) has led to a growing interest in creating vertically equated scores for tests used in accountability systems. Although some applications of growth or value-added modeling do not use vertically scaled test scores, most of these models are designed to quantify the achievement gains attained by students in a particular classroom or school, and they rely on vertically scaled scores to enable the calculation of these gains across several grade levels. Most commercially available standardized achievement testing programs provide vertically scaled scores, as do many state-developed tests, and the demand for this type of scale is likely to continue to grow as states and districts develop the capacity to gather the longitudinally linked student achievement test scores that are necessary for complex growth models.

The primary assumption underlying vertical scaling, as with other equating contexts, is that the tests that are to be linked measure the same construct. The commonly used methods for creating vertically scaled scores are similar to those used for other equating applications, including the year-to-year equating discussed earlier. Common sets of items are included on the test forms administered to different grade levels; typically, the greatest overlap in items (and sometimes the only overlap) is between adjacent grades. The scores on the common items are used to create the between-grade link, typically through the application of item response theory methods. Successful vertical equating also involves careful design of the tests for each grade so that overlap of the tests for adjacent grades are systematic and attempt to capture content (although not necessarily difficulty level) common to both grades.

Issues in Vertical Scaling

Many of the equating issues discussed earlier also apply to vertical scaling, but the attempts to link tests administered to students in multiple grade levels creates additional challenges. The assumption that the tests measure a common construct is critical to the validity of the information provided by vertically scaled test scores but is enormously difficult to satisfy in practice. Moreover, valid use of these scales for evaluating the effects of teachers or schools also requires that the focus of instruction at each grade be aligned with the content of the test in a consistent way (Huynh & Schneider, 2005; Lissitz & Huynh, 2003). Vertical scales are more commonly used in reading and mathematics than in other subjects, a difference that reflects not only the greater prevalence of testing in those subjects but also the greater likelihood that these assumptions will be satisfied. Teaching and learning in these subjects is reasonably continuous and cumulative, in contrast to subjects like science or social studies in which the curriculum provided to students in one grade level may focus on completely different topics or skills than the curriculum provided at an adjacent grade level.

Math and reading, however, are not immune to problems stemming from differences in what is taught and learned across grade levels. The assumption of a common dimensional mix and a consistent degree of alignment between what is taught and what is tested is typically violated to some degree. Lissitz and Huynh (2003) note that

> a vertical scale captures the common dimension(s) across the grades; it does not capture grade-specific dimensions that may be of considerable importance. The instructional expectations for teaching and learning reading/language arts and mathematics may not really be summarized by one (or even a few) common dimensions across grades.
>
> (Major problems with vertical equating section, para. 1)

A study by Schmidt, Houang, and McKnight (2005) illustrates the magnitude of the problem through an analysis of mathematics curricular offerings in the United States. The topics taught, along with the relative emphasis placed on each topic, varied widely across schools, both across grades and within the same grade. Cross-grade variation is a natural consequence of the sequential way in which mathematics topics are usually taught. Schmidt et al.'s analysis shows, for example, that first grade curricula are dominated by topics related to numbers and measurement, whereas eighth grade tends to emphasize algebra and geometry. Even within the same grade, Schmidt et al. found substantial variation in what was taught, in part because different students take different courses (algebra and general math at the middle school level, for example), but also because of the local autonomy that characterizes decisions about curriculum and instruction in the U.S. The analysis made it clear that mathematics achievement is a multidimensional construct and that the weights assigned to each dimension are not constant across and within grades. These differences demonstrate how assumptions about a single underlying construct are typically violated in vertical equating contexts, particularly when a wide grade span is used.

Martineau (2006) used the term "construct shift" to refer to the changes from one year to the next in the constructs measured and the extent to which each contributes to the total test score. He found that this construct shift led to distorted inferences about student learning and about school and teacher effectiveness (see also Reckase, 2004). For a simple example of how estimates of individual teacher effectiveness can be affected by content differences, consider a pair of eighth grade mathematics teachers, one of whom teaches algebra and the other general math. An eighth grade test that consists of only a few algebra items might result in a higher effectiveness ranking for the general mathematics teacher because the test will not be sensitive to the algebra teacher's curriculum. Another test that is heavily weighted with algebra items, by contrast, might favor the algebra teacher (see McCaffrey et al., 2003, and Hamilton, McCaffrey, & Koretz, 2006, for additional discussion of this example). The problem is exacerbated when combining information across a large number of grade levels with changing content emphasis.

There are a few additional threats to the valid interpretation of vertically scaled scores that should be mentioned. First, by providing users with a single scale that is intended to describe performance across a large number of grade levels, there is a risk that they will make inappropriate inferences about the meanings of those scores. For example, the use of grade equivalent scores, a type of vertically scaled score, has been common in commercial testing programs. Test publishers have been careful to warn against inappropriate interpretation; for example, a fifth grade student who scores two years above his grade level would not necessarily perform well on the test given to seventh graders because of differences in test content. In fact, the fifth grade test might include very little seventh grade content. The same interpretation issue pertains to other vertically scaled scores. One cannot conclude that a fifth grade student who scores in the seventh grade score range is performing at the seventh grade level on content that is not taught or tested at the fifth grade level. In addition, the scores do not always satisfy the equal-interval property (e.g., the difference between the average scores on the third and fourth grade test may not represent the same amount of "growth" as the difference between average scores on the seventh and eighth grade tests). Similarly, vertical scales constructed from different tests sometimes show different variance trends, with scores on some tests becoming more variable as grade level increases, and others remaining constant or becoming less variable. If variability increases across grades, students scoring at the ninetieth percentile will show greater growth than students scoring at the tenth percentile; but the reverse will be true if variances shrink across grades. These apparent differences in growth patterns are most likely an artifact of the scaling methodology and do not necessarily reflect real differences in rates of growth. Together, all of these issues raise questions about the extent to which the inferences most users would like to make based on vertical scales are warranted.

One approach that has been recently proposed as a way of addressing the shortcomings of vertical scales, while simultaneously accommodating the requirements of some accountability systems for reporting according to proficiency levels, is the use of vertically moderated standards (Lissitz and Huynh, 2003). This approach is intended to create performance categories such as "proficient" or "basic" that have the same meaning across grade levels, and its advocates argue that it can accommodate situations in which the assumptions of vertical scaling are not met, such as a science curriculum that emphasizes biology in one grade and earth science in the next. The emphasis of this approach is on the ability to predict a student's achievement in subsequent grades based on his or her current achievement (Lissitz & Huynh, 2003). The process for setting vertically moderated standards usually involves creating agreed upon definitions for each proficiency level for all grades, setting cut scores for some grades, and using a growth curve applied across all grades to set the cut scores for the remaining grades (see Huynh, Meyet, & Barton, 2000, for a specific example using a state testing system). These techniques are relatively new and have not yet been subjected to extensive research or validation, but they are likely to grow in popularity as a result of the growing emphasis on reporting according to proficiency levels.

Diversity in State Testing Programs and the History of Linking

The current call by policymakers for a system that would allow the direct comparison of results on different educational tests is not new. Over 40 years ago, in 1964, the lead articles in the first issue of the *Journal of Educational Measurement* were from the 1964 annual meeting of the National Council on Measurement in Education's symposium, "Equating Non-Parallel Tests Scores." The symposium participants and authors were four measurement giants, William Angoff, John Flanagan, Roger Lennon, and E. F. Lindquist. All four concluded that results from non-parallel tests could not be equated in the strict measurement sense of the word. They believed that misinterpretations of results were likely, that development of conversion tables was problematic, and that conversions would be group-specific (i.e., applicable only to the groups used to compute the conversion equation; Angoff, 1964; Flanagan, 1964; Lennon, 1964; Lindquist, 1964). It appears that little heed was paid to these leaders in educational measurement. Congress passed the Elementary and Secondary Education Act (ESEA) in 1965, which included requirements for test-based evaluation and accountability for programs supported by the ESEA. At that time, states administered standardized, norm-referenced tests provided by commercial test publishers. The score scales were not equivalent across the different tests; thus, results from different tests were not comparable, and not much could be learned in aggregate about the effectiveness of Title I or other programs.

Fast-forward to the 1990s. During this decade some states began developing academic content standards, revising curriculum goals, and developing customized assessments aligned with the new content standards and curricula. These assessments often contained constructed response and performance-based items. Diversity in state programs increased rapidly from dependence on a few (perhaps six or eight) commonly used commercial norm-referenced tests to different state-developed or customized tests aligned to state content standards. The content and format of these state tests were much more variable than in the commercial norm-referenced tests. According to Feuer et al. (1999),

> Reforms in Title I of the Improving America's Schools Act, passed in 1994, reflected and reinforced the trend toward greater state and local innovation in standard-setting, testing, and accountability. Similar patterns were articulated in the Goals 2000-Educate America Act, also passed in 1994, and the Individuals with Disabilities Education Act, passed in 1997.
>
> (p. 9)

The diversity in educational testing and lack of comparability of assessments in the United States fueled President Clinton's 1997 proposal to create the Voluntary National Test (VNT). Strong negative reaction to the proposed VNT and debate over whether a new test was needed or whether an equivalency scale could be established to link results on existing tests led Congress in November of 1997 to request the National Academy of Sciences (NAS) to conduct a feasibility study (Feuer et al., 1999). In addition to the question of whether commercially available standardized tests and state assessments could be compared to each other, there was also the desire to link these various tests to the National Assessment of Educational Progress (NAEP). The conclusions of the NAS National Research Council (NRC) panel and the feasibility of linking to NAEP will be discussed after first considering the important differences among testing programs that will affect the validity and reliability of desired linkages.

Testing and Accountability: Challenges to Linking

Many factors affect the validity of linkages among different tests, including content domain coverage, test reliability, test formats, and test characteristics, test uses, and consequences. These factors are briefly discussed below.

Test content. Tests vary significantly in their most fundamental aspect—the knowledge and skills they ask students to demonstrate. A test is a sample of a much larger body of content. For example, one fourth grade reading test might consist of short passages and simple recall and comprehension questions, while another test might consist of more complex texts and questions that require examinees to draw inferences. When content differs significantly, scores from one test provide poor estimates of scores on the other and inferences dependent on the linkage could be misleading.

Test reliability and measurement error. Measurement error plays a large role in the interpretation of scores on linked tests. For example, if test X has a large measurement error and is linked to test Y, which is more precise and reliable, the scores predicted on test Y will still have the measurement error of test X. Test X would then appear more reliable than it actually is. If two tests differ in reliability, a strict equating is not possible, and the scores cannot be used interchangeably.

Test format. Tests can be quite varied in format. Some tests are composed solely of multiple-choice questions, others entirely of constructed response items, and many contain a mix of both item formats. In addition, constructed response items can be short, requiring a single phrase or sentence type of answer, or long, such as a written essay. Research shows that item format can make a significant difference in student performance. The effects of format differences on linkages are not always predictable, but they can be substantial.

Test characteristics, uses, and consequences. In evaluating linkages one also must consider the different characteristics of tests, how the results are used, and consequences attached to scores. In addition to differences in content, format, and reliability, tests also differ in their inclusion rules (i.e., who is tested and who is excluded), administrative practices (e.g., group or individual, time of year), and reasons for testing. Variation in how tests are used, especially their consequences, can affect the stability of linkages over time. The degree to which tests differ will affect the validity of any links between them. All of these factors point to the difficulty of establishing trustworthy links among different tests.

Particularly challenging is the type of linking discussed next, where the results from the various and diverse state assessments are linked to the results from the NAEP.

Linking to NAEP: the Voluntary National Tests and No Child Left Behind

When President Clinton first proposed creating voluntary national tests in 1997, Congress, much to their credit, recognized that science could play an important role in sorting through the claims and heated discussions in the testing debate. They asked the National Academy of Sciences National Research Council (NRC), through its Board on Testing and Assessment, to study the feasibility of developing a scale to compare—or link—scores from existing tests to each other and to the NAEP. The Board-appointed Committee on Equivalency and Linkage of Educational Tests then reviewed research on statistical and technical aspects of creating links between tests and the "landscape" of the testing environment in the states at that time, and examined how the content, format, purposes, and use of educational tests influence the quality and meaning of those links. The Committee was disposed to seeking a technological solution to the problem: how can we bring greater coherence to the reporting of student achievement data and still maintain the innovative "tapestry" of tests currently in use? Despite this intention, this group of statisticians reached the following conclusions, described in their 1999 report, *Uncommon Measures* (Feuer et al., 1999, pp. 4–5):

1. Comparing the full array of currently administered commercial and state achievement tests to one another, through the development of a single equivalency or linking scale, is not feasible.
2. Reporting individual student scores from the full array of state and commercial achievement tests on the NAEP scale and transforming

individual scores on these various tests and assessments into the NAEP achievement levels are not feasible.

3. Under limited conditions it may be possible to calculate a linkage between two tests, but multiple factors affect the validity of inferences drawn from the linked scores. These factors include the content, format, and margins of error of the tests; the intended and actual uses of the tests; and the consequences attached to the results of the tests. When tests differ on any of these factors, some limited interpretations of the linked results may be defensible while others would not.
4. Links between most existing tests and NAEP, for the purpose of reporting individual student's scores on the NAEP scale and in terms of the NAEP achievement levels, will be problematic. Unless the test to be linked to NAEP is very similar to NAEP in context, format, and uses, the resulting linkage is likely to be unstable and potentially misleading.

No Child Left Behind 2001

Two years after the release of *Uncommon Measures*, NCLB was enacted. The emphasis on assessing all students and setting AYP targets in terms of percentages "proficient" according to each state's different (and widely varying) definition of proficient again focused demands for comparing results on different assessments and comparing the rigor, or stringency, of states' performance-level standards. In particular, NAEP is the obvious and most often cited benchmark assessment for comparing state performance and assessing the stringency of state definitions of proficient (cf., Hoxby, 2005; Peterson & Hess, 2005), despite the cautions voiced by the NRC panels.

NAEP and the Challenge of Linkage

NAEP's distinctive characteristics present special challenges to any attempts to develop an equivalency scale to allow direct comparison of results from state tests with NAEP. These characteristics include content coverage, item format distribution, test administration conditions, use of results, achievement levels, and individual-level scoring. However, these special challenges do not preclude the use of NAEP as a rough benchmark in examining the results of state assessments.

Content coverage. The content representation in NAEP is very broad, and the assessment covers a much larger array of test items than is possible on most state or commercial assessments. NAEP achieves this by using matrix sampling and a balanced incomplete block design. All the test items in a given assessment are divided into sets, or blocks. Test booklets contain a few short blocks of test items, and no test booklet is completely representative of the entire NAEP assessment of that grade and subject area. Thus, each student answers only a portion of the total items in the assessment. By carefully balancing the blocks and distribution of the test booklets, NAEP is able to keep student testing time to a minimum (approximately 50 minutes) and include a greater number of items and broader range of subject area content. Because each test item is administered to an equal number of students, the data from the administration of each test book can be pooled across test takers and the distribution of students' scores estimated. However, these assessments do not collect enough data from individual students to produce valid individual scores (Beaton & Gonzalez, 1995; Mislevy, Beaton, Kaplan, & Sheehan, 1992).

Item format distribution. Because a limited number of items is administered to each individual student, the NAEP assessments can contain a larger percentage of constructed response items than is possible on a typical statewide assessment. Approximately 50% of items in NAEP assessments are constructed response items, compared to something in the neighborhood of 0 to 25% in a typical state assessment.

Test administration conditions. The administration of NAEP assessments is more highly standardized and controlled than is typical in most state and commercial tests. Differences in test administration can affect test results, and subsequently, the results from a linkage of NAEP and state tests.

Use of results and individual-level scoring (or lack thereof). NAEP is designed to estimate distributions of scores by state, region, or the nation and for subgroups of students. It is not designed to report individual student scores. Furthermore, NAEP is a very low-stakes test. Because results for individuals, classes, and schools are not reported, teachers have little incentive to prepare students for the test (indeed, NAEP is designed to be independent of any particular curriculum) and students have little motivation to perform well (cf., Kiplinger & Linn, 1996; O'Neil, Sugrue, Abedi, Baker, & Golen, 1992; O'Neil, Sugrue, & Baker, 1996).

Achievement levels. NAEP's reporting of results in terms of achievement (i.e., performance) levels[1] creates additional challenges to linking to other assessments. The standard setting process by which the NAEP achievement levels were set; the levels at which the cut scores for basic, proficient, and advanced were set; and discrepancies between the achievement-level descriptors and the actual competencies demonstrated by examinees (as indicated by item content) have long come under fire (Linn, 1998; Linn, Koretz, Baker, & Burstein, 1991; Pellegrino, Jones, & Mitchell, 1999; Shepard, Glaser, Linn, & Bohrnstedt, 1993). Linn et al. and Shepard et al., for example, found through external validity comparisons that NAEP's performance levels are set unrealistically high. Comparison with state performance results are consistent with that conclusion. In addition, states have different numbers of performance levels in their assessment systems; NAEP has four, and the number of performance levels in state tests typically range from two to five. States use a variety of standard-setting methods, and the levels descriptors can differ greatly.

In early conversations about linking to NAEP, the thought was that mapping student performance on state assessments onto the NAEP achievement levels could provide evidence of the validity of NAEP achievement levels and achievement level descriptors (cf. Feuer et al., 1999). In the context of NCLB, these roles have completely reversed so that NAEP is now discussed as an external check on the validity of the *state* assessment performance standards.

NAEP as an External Check

The NRC Committee on Equivalency and Linkage of Educational Tests (Feuer et al., 1999), the NRC Committee on Embedding Common Test Items in State and District Assessments (Koretz, Bertenthal, & Green, 1999), and others have concluded that it is not feasible to link state assessments to NAEP for the purpose of reporting individual student scores in terms of the NAEP scale or NAEP achievement levels. Attempts to link student achievement levels would be problematic and results possibly misleading and unstable over time. However, for some limited purposes, comparing state assessment results to NAEP results can be useful:

> Although there is no requirement that state assessments be linked to NAEP or any specification of how state NAEP results should be used in considering state NCLB results, NAEP is clearly intended to provide some kind of rough benchmark against which state results can be judged.
>
> (Linn, 2005, p. 12)

It is well known that state-established performance standards, particularly the definition of proficient, vary greatly from state to state (Haertel, this volume; Linn, this volume). If state NAEP results are to be considered as the benchmark, or external check, of state assessment results, then one must consider how states differ in the rigor of their performance standards. One simple way to examine the variability in the stringency of state performance standards is to report side-by-side, for each state, the percentages of students performing at the proficient or above level on both the state assessment and state NAEP (see, for example, Olson, 2005). Because NAEP has very stringent performance standards, one could assume that states that score similarly on both assessments have very high performance standards for their state tests. Conversely, one could assume that states that have much greater percentages of students scoring at or above the proficient level on their state assessments than on NAEP have less rigorous performance standards. However, these simple side-by-side comparisons do not allow us to separate the differences in the stringency of standards from differences in state performance.

Developments in Linking State Tests to NAEP: Linking State Performance Standards to the NAEP Scale

McLaughlin and Bandeira de Mello (2002, 2003) have developed a procedure to create a scale for comparing mathematics and reading achievement standards in different states by statistically linking them to NAEP. The procedure does not meet the stringent requirements of equating or even calibration, but can be considered a type of statistical moderation. The analyses utilize data from the School-Level State Assessment Scores Database (SSASD) collected by the American Institutes of Research and funded by the U.S. Department of Education. This database contains student test scores for over 80,000 public schools in 49 states, the District of Columbia, and Puerto Rico.

For their linking analyses, McLaughlin and Bandeira de Mello identified schools in the database that had participated in the 2000 and 2002 state NAEP assessments of mathematics and reading, respectively. They used data from matched schools to create a scale for comparing the mathematics and reading achievement standards in different states by linking to the NAEP scale. For each school in a state, they determined the percentage of students scoring above each performance level on the state assessment; they then determined the corresponding locations on the NAEP scale for each level. Using this method, if 60% of students in a school score above the proficient cut point on the state assessment, for example, the NAEP scale score above which 60% of students in the school perform is considered the NAEP score[2] that corresponds to the state standard. This procedure is repeated for each NAEP school in the state. The location of the state proficient performance standard on the NAEP equivalency scale can serve as a more direct indicator of the stringency or rigor of the state's achievement standards.

McLaughlin and Bandeira de Mello calculated standard errors and concluded that average standard errors are approximately 11 points on the NAEP scale for the higher state test performance ranges (e.g., proficient and advanced); however, reliability is lower (i.e., higher standard errors) in lower performance ranges. They concluded that the lack of reliability is primarily a function of limitations of the database, although it is also a function of the reliability and comparability of the tests being compared, particularly at the lower performance ranges. They also concluded that (a) NAEP can provide a reasonable link between state achievement standards at the proficient and advanced levels; (b) most of the links for the "below proficient" performance levels are weak; (c) there is substantial variation in performance standards among the states as indicated by linked NAEP equivalency scores; and, (d) percentages of students "meeting state standards" (i.e., proficient or above) are lower in states in which the state proficiency standards are set high relative to NAEP scale (McLaughlin & Bandeira de Mello, 2002, 2003). Averaged across schools, this procedure appears to produce reasonable linkages that are consistent with other comparisons.

As reported in Linn (2005), Braun and Qian also have developed a procedure to create a scale for comparing mathematics and reading achievement standards in different states by statistically linking them to NAEP. The techniques of the two groups of researchers vary in the manner in which standard errors and confidence intervals are computed. Linkages of the 2000 NAEP and state mathematics assessments and 2002 NAEP and state reading assessments by Braun and Qian resulted in patterns of score mapping that are similar to the results reported by McLaughlin and Bandeira de Mello. In addition, Braun and Qian found that differences between proficiency rates reported on NAEP and on state tests were more affected by differences in the stringency of the standards than by other possible factors such as state standards, test content, or sampling error. Further, they found that there was only a weak correlation between the stringency of the standard and the state's performance on NAEP. In other words, it is not the case that high performing states necessarily tend to set more rigorous standards on their state tests.

New Developments in Measuring the "Equatability" of Tests

Although the NRC Committee on Equivalence and Linkage (Feuer et al., 1999) concluded that a single equivalency or linking scale to compare currently administered commercial and state achievement tests to each other or to NAEP is not feasible, they also recommended that future research be conducted: (1) on the criteria for evaluating the quality of linkages; (2) to determine the level of precision needed to make valid inferences from linked tests; and (3) on the reporting of linked assessment information. Research conducted by Neil Dorans and Paul Holland (the Chair of the Equivalency and Linkage Committee) (2000) address the first two of the committee's recommendations. In their research, they focus on the most stringent form of linking, test equating, which statistically adjusts scores from two test forms so that they can be used interchangeably. They identified the five requirements for test equating discussed earlier in this chapter (i.e., equal constructs, equal reliability, symmetry, equity, and population invariance). Holland (2005) further reported that they found that:

> Population invariance provided the most direct method … for evaluating the "validity of a link." … [I]f you got different equating functions depending on which subpopulation of examinees supplied the data for the computation then that was a sign of a problem. If the difference was small then it was a small problem, but if it were large then that was one measurable sense in which a link could be "invalid."
>
> (p. 189)

Stated rather simplistically, their reasoning was that if a substantially different equating function results when based on data from boys as opposed to girls, for example, then the link is unsatisfactory.

The goal of the Dorans and Holland study (2000) was not merely to determine whether there is disparity in equating functions, but to quantify the magnitude of the disparity. They introduce three methods for quantifying the degree to which the equating functions computed on different subpopulations differ from the equating function computed on the population as a whole (Holland, 2005). For example, the simplest method provides a single-number index of dissimilarity. Suppose Test X is being equated to Test Y. A system of equating functions is produced; that is, an overall equating function based on all examinees and separate functions for each subpopulation. Differences between the overall population equating function and the equating functions for the separate subpopulations for a given score on Test Y are computed, summed into the root mean square and divided by the standard deviation of Test Y over the population to give the measure, RMSD(x) for each score on Test Y. If the index is reported as 100(RMSD(x)), the measure represents a percentage of a standard deviation of Test Y over the equating population and is a type of "effect size." This procedure can be applied to any system of equating functions regardless of how they are computed (e.g., equipercentile or linear equating).

The work by Neil Dorans and Paul Holland represents a milestone in research on the criteria for evaluating the quality of linkages and research to determine the level of precision needed to make valid inferences from linked tests. However, as Holland (2005) notes, "Much more can and should be done on these topics to give us a quantitative assessment of what goes wrong and by how much it goes wrong when we try to link the scores on tests that were never meant to be linked" (p. 195).

Conclusions

This chapter addresses issues related to various types of test linkages. Test-based state accountability systems require assessment results that can be compared over time. Factors discussed in this chapter that affect the validity and stability of linkages must be addressed in accountability systems in order to provide valid and useful information about changes in student performance over time, particularly if consequences are attached to changes in test scores. This is true whether changes in student performance are measured as year-to-year differences between successive cohorts in the same grade level or as changes over time within longitudinal cohorts of students. Vertical scaling across grade levels is more problematic, however, than equating multiple forms of the same test because of shifts in test content. A few potential solutions have been explored; these include Martineau's suggestion (2005) to supplement traditional annual grade-level testing with the administration of additional items or tests to increase overlap across grades, and Schultz et al.'s (2005) recommendation for creating separate measures of student growth for domains within a test.

No Child Left Behind has given new significance to the possibility of linking results from different assessments and comparing the stringency of states' performance standards. Concerns today about the lack of comparability of assessments are quite similar to the concerns that prompted President Clinton to propose Voluntary National Tests in 1997. Strong negative reaction to the VNT then led to the convening of several National Research Council panels to investigate the feasibility of developing equivalency scales to allow comparisons among state tests and to link those tests to NAEP. These panels generally concluded that developing a single equivalency scale to compare state achievement tests was not feasible and that reporting individual student scores from state and commercial achievements on the NAEP scale or in terms of performance levels was not feasible. However, the panels noted that under some limited conditions it might be possible to calculate a linkage (not an equating), but that multiple factors could affect the validity of inferences and interpretations that could be drawn from linkages.

McLaughlin and Bandeira de Mello and Braun and Qian were able to develop equipercentile linking procedures to create a common metric for comparing mathematics and reading achievement standards in different states by statistically linking them to NAEP. However, both groups of researchers concluded that there is a considerable amount of uncertainty around the NAEP equivalency scores, particularly at the "below proficient" achievement levels.

Recent developments and research in test equating and linking are quite promising. Holland and Dorans' research on criteria for evaluating the quality of test linkages and research to determine the level of precision needed to make valid inferences from linked tests are milestones in measuring the "equitability" of tests. Nonetheless, more research is needed to explore alternative approaches to the various types of test linking and to measuring the validity and precision of test linkages.

Acknowledgments

The authors are indebted to Lorrie Shepard and Katherine Ryan for providing careful reviews, constructive suggestions for improving the technical quality and readability of the chapter, and for their helpful comments on earlier drafts. The authors also thank Bob Linn for reviewing the original outline of the chapter. We hope that we have done justice to the reviewers' excellent suggestions. Responsibility for the final product, of course, remains with the authors.

Notes

1. NAEP's achievement levels are "below basic," "basic," "proficient," and "advanced."
2. Because of its matrix sampling, NAEP cannot produce scores for individual students. Instead, NAEP estimates conditional distributions of possible scores, called "plausible values," for examinees. Five plausible values for each examinee are provided in the NAEP data files. In the McLaughlin and Bandeira de Mello method, the score correspondence procedure is repeated for each of the five plausible values, and the mean of the values is computed as the equivalent NAEP "score."

References

Angoff, W. H. (1964). Technical problems of obtaining equivalent scores on tests. *Journal of Educational Measurement*, 1 (1), 11–13.

Beaton, A. E. & Gonzalez, E. J. (1995). *The NAEP primer*. Chestnut Hill, MA: Boston College, Center for the Study of Testing, Evaluation, and Educational Policy.

Cizek, G. J., Kennedy, P. A., Kolen, M. J., Peters, C. W., & van der Linden, W. J. (1999). *An investigation of the feasibility of linking scores on the proposed Voluntary National Tests and the National Assessment of Educational Progress*. Washington, DC: National Assessment Governing Board.

Dorans, N. J. & Holland, P. W. (2000). Population invariance and the equitability of tests: Basic theory and the linear case. *Journal of Educational Measurement*, 37 (4), 281–306.

Feuer, M. J., Holland, P. W., Green, B. F., Bertenthal, M. W., & Hemphill, F. C. (1999). *Uncommon measures: Equivalence and linkage among educational tests*. Washington, DC: National Academy Press.

Flanagan, J. C. (1964). Obtaining useful comparable scores for non-parallel tests and test batteries. *Journal of Educational Measurement*, 1 (1), 1–4.

Hamilton, L. S., McCaffrey, D. F., & Koretz, D. M. (2006). Validating achievement gains in cohort-to-cohort and individual growth-based modeling contexts. In R. Lissitz (Ed.), *Longitudinal and value-added models of student performance* (pp. 407–435). Maple Grove, MN: JAM Press.

Holland, P. W. (2005). Assessing the validity of test linking: What has happened since Uncommon Measures? In C. A. Dywer (Ed.), *Measurement and research in the accountability era* (pp. 185–195). Mahwah, NJ: Lawrence Erlbaum Associates, Inc.

Holland, P. W. & Dorans, N. J. (2006). Linking and equating. In R. L. Brennan (Ed.), *Educational measurement* (4th ed., pp. 187–220). Westport, CT: American Council on Education/ Praeger.

Hoxby, C. M. (2005). Inadequate yearly progress: Unlocking the secrets of NCLB. *Education Next*, 5 (3), 46–51.

Huynh, H. & Schneider, C. (2005). Vertically moderated standards: Background, assumptions, and practices. *Applied Measurement in Education*, 18 (1), 99–113.

Huynh, H., Meyer, P., & Barton, K. (2000). *Technical documentation for the South Carolina 1999 Palmetto Achievement Challenge Tests of English language arts and M = mathematics, grades three through eight*. Columbia, SC: South Carolina Department of Education.

Kiplinger, V. L. & Linn, R. L. (1996). Raising the stakes of test administration: The impact on student performance on the National Assessment of Educational Progress. *Educational Assessment*, 3 (2), 111–134.

Kolen, M. J. & Brennan, R. L. (1995). *Test equating: Methods and practices*. New York: Springer-Verlag.

Kolen, M. J. & Brennan, R. L. (2004). *Test equating, scaling, and linking: Methods and practices*. New York: Springer Science and Business Media, Inc.

Koretz, D. M. & Barron, S. I. (1998). *The validity of gains on the Kentucky Instructional Results Information System (KIRIS)*. Santa Monica, CA: RAND.

Koretz, D. M., Bertenthal, M. W., & Green, B. F. (1999). *Embedding questions: The pursuit of a common measure in uncommon tests*. Washington, DC: National Academy Press.

Lennon, R. T. (1964). Equating non-parallel tests. *Journal of Educational Measurement*, 1 (2), 15–18.

Lindquist, E. F. (1964). Equating scores on non-parallel tests. *Journal of Educational Measurement*, 1 (2), 5–9.

Linn, R. L. (1993). Linking results of distinct assessments. *Applied Measurement in Education*, 6 (1), 83–102.

Linn, R. L. (1998). Validating inferences from National Assessment of Educational Progress achievement-level setting. *Applied Measurement in Education*, 11 (1), 53–81.

Linn, R. L. (2005, December 9). Adjusting for differences in tests. Paper presented at a Symposium on the Use of School-Based Data for Evaluating Education Programs. Washington, DC: Board on Testing and Assessment, The National Academies.

Linn, R. L., Koretz, D. M., Baker, E. L., & Burstein, L. (1991). *The validity and credibility of the achievement levels for the 1990 National Assessment of Educational Progress in mathematics.* Los Angeles, CA: Center for Research on Evaluation Standards.

Lissitz, R. W. & Huynh, H. (2003). Vertical equating for state assessments: Issues and solutions in determination of Adequate Yearly Progress and school accountability. *Practical Assessment, Research, and Evaluation*, 8 (10). Online, available at: http://PAREonline.net/getvn.asp?v=8&n=10 (accessed November 18, 2005).

McCaffrey, D. F., Lockwood, J. R., Koretz, D. M., & Hamilton, L. S. (2003). *Evaluating value-added models for teacher accountability.* Santa Monica, CA: RAND.

McLaughlin, D. & Bandeira de Mello, V. (2002, April). Comparison of state elementary school mathematics achievement standards, using NAEP 2000. Paper presented at the Annual Meeting of the American Educational Research Association, New Orleans, LA.

McLaughlin, D. & Bandeira de Mello, V. (2003, June). Comparing state reading and math performance standards using NAEP. Paper presented at the Council of Chief State School Officers National Conference on Large-Scale Assessment, San Antonio, TX.

Martineau, J. A. (2005, June). Un-distorting measures of growth: Alternatives to traditional vertical scales. Paper presented at the Council of Chief State School Officers Annual National Conference on Large-Scale Assessment, San Antonio, TX.

Martineau, J. (2006). Distorting value added: The use of longitudinal, vertically scaled student achievement data for growth-based, value-added accountability. *Journal of Educational and Behavioral Statistics*, 31 (1), 35–62.

Mislevy, R. J. (1992). *Linking educational assessments: Concepts, issues, methods, and prospects.* Princeton, NJ: Educational Testing Service.

Mislevy, R. J., Beaton, A. E., Kaplan, B., & Sheehan, K. M. (1992). Estimating population characteristics from sparse matrix sample of item responses. *Journal of Educational Measurement*, 29 (2), 131–154.

No Child Left Behind Act of 2001, Pub. L.107–110, 115 Stat.1425 (2002).

Olson, L. (2005, September 7). Defying predictions, state trends prove mixed on schools making NCLB targets. *Education Week*, 27 (2), 1, 26–27.

O'Neil, H. F., Sugrue, B., Abedi, J., Baker, E., & Golen, S. (1992). *Final report of experimental studies on motivation and NAEP test performance.* Los Angeles, CA: Center for Research on Evaluation, Standards, and Student Testing.

O'Neil, H. F., Sugrue, B., & Baker, E. (1996). Effects of motivational interventions on the National Assessment of Educational Progress mathematics performance. *Educational Assessment*, 3 (2), 135–158.

Pellegrino, J. W., Jones, L. R., & Mitchell, K. J. (1999). *Grading the nation's report card: Evaluating NAEP and transforming the assessment of educational progress.* Washington, DC: National Academy Press.

Peterson, P. E. & Hess, F. M. (2005). Johnny can read … assessing the rigor of state assessment systems. *Education Next*, 5 (3), 52–53.

Reckase, M. D. (2004). The real world is more complicated than we would like. *Journal of Educational and Behavioral Statistics*, 29 (1), 117–120.

Schmidt, W. H., Houang, R. T., & McKnight, C. C. (2005). Value-added research: Right idea but wrong solution? In R. Lissitz (Ed.), *Value-added models in education: Theory and applications* (pp. 145–164). Maple Grove, MN: JAM Press.

Schulz, E. M., Lee, W. C., & Mullen, K. (2005). A domain-level approach to describing growth in achievement. *Journal of Educational Measurement*, 42 (1), 1–26.

Shepard, L. A., Glaser, R., Linn, R. L., & Bohrnstedt, G. (1993). *Setting performance standards for student achievement: A Report of the National Academy of Education panel on the evaluation of the NAEP trial state assessment: An evaluation of the 1992 achievement levels.* Stanford, CA: National Academy of Education.

von Davier, A. A., Holland, P. W., & Thayer, D. T. (2004). *The Kernel method of test equating.* New York: Springer-Verlag.

7
Standard Setting

Edward H. Haertel

It is commonplace to see information about student achievement presented by comparing test scores to a defined performance standard. We read, for example, that only 31% of fourth graders performed at or above a "proficient" level in reading on the National Assessment of Educational Progress (NAEP), that 86% of school children tested in Nebraska are at the "proficient" level in writing, that more than half of all twelfth graders lack even a "basic" understanding of United States history, or that 42% of California students scored at or above "proficient" on the California Standards Tests in English Language Arts. Few stop to ask what labels like basic or proficient actually mean, or how the lines dividing one performance level from another are drawn. Moreover, standards are used not only to describe educational achievement, but also to set requirements and expectations. State-level school accountability systems mandated under the No Child Left Behind Act of 2001 (NCLB) require that annual measurable objectives in both reading and mathematics be formulated as the percentage of all students required to reach the state's "proficient" level for each school as well as for specified subgroups within a school.[1]

Using standards to interpret test scores appears to be more satisfying than interpreting raw or scale scores. When told that the mean SAT math score for college-bound seniors in 2006 was 518, many people will be unsure if that is good, bad, or indifferent. Being told in addition that 518 was two points lower than the mean in 2005 may help a little, but not a lot. It might seem appealing to be able, instead, to say what proportion of SAT test takers were doing "well enough," or "as well as should be expected," or even "at the level required to succeed in college." For accountability, too, it seems helpful to have clear rules for deciding which test scores are good enough, and by extension, which students are performing well enough. As Linn (this volume) observes, standards-based interpretations are also regarded as less invidious than norm-referenced interpretations. By definition, the scores of half the children in any norming sample fall below the fiftieth percentile. In principle, though, all students can be proficient.

Unfortunately, the seeming clarity and simplicity of standards, of standards-based reporting, and of standards-based accountability mask serious technical and conceptual problems. It is well documented that the same label (e.g., proficient) may designate wildly different levels of achievement on different tests of the same subject matter (Braun & Qian, 2007; Hoover, 2003; Linn, 2003a, 2003b; McLaughlin & Bandeira de Mello, 2002; Musick, 1997; National Center for Education Statistics, 2007; Rosenberg, 2004). Such inconsistencies may be explained in part by the different purposes for which standards are established (Linn, 2003b, and this volume). A minimum expectation required of all students for graduation ought to differ from a challenging, aspirational standard for a test with no high stakes attached. Furthermore, inconsistencies were almost guaranteed when NCLB gave states the freedom to establish their own standards on their own respective tests, aligned to their own curriculum frameworks, but using the same labels, basic, proficient, and advanced, for their performance levels.

Moreover, the problems with interpreting test scores against standards go well beyond differences attributable to the range of purposes for which standards are used, or overuse of the labels basic, proficient, and advanced. Contemporary standard-setting methods have been strenuously criticized by individual scholars and by prestigious review panels of both the National Academy of Education (NAEd) and the National Research Council (e.g., Berk, 1995; Glass, 1978; Haertel, 2001; Haertel & Lorié, 2004; Pellegrino, Jones, & Mitchell, 1999; Shepard, Glaser, Linn, & Bohrnstedt, 1993). The National Assessment Governing Board, which oversees NAEP, has invested heavily in developing state-of-the-art standard-setting procedures, but both an evaluation by the National Academy of Education (Shepard et al., 1993) and a second congressionally mandated evaluation by the National Research Council (Pellegrino et al., 1999) found the NAEP standard setting to be "fundamentally flawed." The latter evaluation found that "the judgment tasks are difficult and confusing; raters' judgments of different item types are internally inconsistent; appropriate validity evidence for the cut scores is lacking; and the process has produced unreasonable results" (p. 182).

After defining some key terms, this chapter briefly describes three categories of standard-setting approaches, which together include all of the methods commonly used with educational achievement tests. It then discusses the validation of these methods, presenting an interpretive argument (Kane, 1992, 1994) to support a standards-based score interpretation. The three categories of methods are considered in light of that argument. The chapter concludes with short-term recommendations for more enlightened use and interpretation of present-day standards, as well as new directions for standard-setting research and future practice.

Content Standards, Performance Standards, and Cut Scores: The Logic of Standards-Based Interpretations

The term *standards* is used in many different ways. Two usages important in the context of test-based accountability are *content standards* and *performance standards.*[2] Content standards (what NCLB refers to as academic content standards) describe the subject matter students are expected to cover at each grade level. They may take the form of a curriculum framework or a scope-and-sequence chart. The requirement that tests be aligned with standards means in part that the content covered on the test must be representative of the content standards, or an explicitly defined subset of the content standards.

If content standards describe what is to be learned, performance standards (called academic achievement standards in NCLB) describe how well that content is to be learned. The term "performance standard" is often used to refer simply to a cut score on a test—the minimum number correct required to reach the "proficient" standard, for example. In this chapter, however, following Kane (1994), the performance standard is defined as distinct from and usually prior to the cut score and refers to "a description of what 'meeting the standard' is supposed to mean. It is typically set forth in ... a paragraph, saying what 'basic,' 'proficient,' 'master,' or some such designation is intended to signify" (Haertel & Lorié, 2004, p. 63). Stated differently, content standards describe the contents of instruction, whereas a performance standard describes the capabilities of students who have mastered the material taught to some specified degree. Note that, just as the test score stands for achievement in a domain that goes beyond the specific items on the test itself, so too the performance standard describes proficiency with respect to that broader domain beyond the test itself.

As an example of a performance standard, a fourth grader able to do mathematics at the "basic" level as defined for the NAEP is described as follows:

> Fourth-grade students performing at the *Basic* level should show some evidence of understanding the mathematical concepts and procedures in the five NAEP content areas.... Fourth-graders performing at the *Basic* level should be able to estimate and use basic facts to perform simple computations with whole numbers; show some understanding of fractions and decimals; and solve some simple real-world problems in all NAEP content areas. Students at this level should be able to use—though not always accurately—four-function calculators, rulers, and geometric shapes. Their written responses will often be minimal and presented without supporting information.
>
> (National Assessment Governing Board, 2004, p. 57)

The *cut score* is a score on a test that serves as an operational definition of the performance standard.[3] Students scoring at or above the cut score are considered to have met the standard; those with lower scores are not. This formulation suggests two basic requirements for a valid standards-based score interpretation.[4] First, the performance standard must describe a set of capabilities that is accurately measured (or predicted) by the test. Second, the cut score must be chosen in such a way that, by and large, students scoring at or above the cut can do what the performance standard says they can, and students scoring below the cut cannot. The first of these requirements may seem obvious. As Thorndike (1918, p. 22) said long ago, "A pupil's score on a test signifies first, such and such a particular achievement, and second, *only whatever has been demonstrated by actual correlations to be implied by it*" (emphasis in original). The performance standard should likewise be limited to describing a level of proficiency with respect to the particular achievements directly sampled by the test itself (i.e., performance on a domain of items of which the test is a sample) unless there is some empirical basis for asserting that the test predicts more than what it directly measures. Obvious or not, this longstanding requirement is often neglected or imperfectly satisfied (Haertel, 2002; Haertel & Lorié, 2004). Problems arise in practice when it is assumed that the test and the performance standard are in alignment simply because both are derived from the same content standards. Unfortunately, achievement tests used in large-scale assessment programs rarely reflect the full range of intellectual processes or contexts of application set forth in the content standards—alignment typically means that everything on the test can be found in the content standards, but not conversely. For that reason, a performance standard derived from the content standards may reach far beyond what a test directly measures or has been shown to predict.

The second requirement for valid standards-based score interpretations is that the cut score must accurately distinguish between students who do or do not possess the capabilities the performance standard describes.[5] The degree of accuracy required will depend on the stakes and intended test uses. Greater accuracy should be demanded if there are significant consequences for individual learners, or if significant rewards or sanctions are attached to a school's measured percent proficient.

Three Kinds of Standard-Setting Methods

Virtually all standard-setting approaches used for educational tests may be classified as test-centered (sometimes referred to as item-centered, item-judgment methods, or judgmental; e.g., Berk, 1986; Hambleton, 1980), person-centered (sometimes referred to as examinee-centered or empirical; e.g., Berk, 1986; Hambleton, 1980), or performance-centered. Given that performance standards describe what examinees are supposed to be able to do, perhaps the most obvious approach is the *person-centered* approach. Examples of this approach include Livingston and Zieky's (1982) "borderline group" and "contrasting groups" methods. The defining feature of these approaches is that the locus of judgment (Haertel & Lorié, 2004) is the proficiency demonstrated by examinees in non-test settings. In the contrasting groups method, for example, teachers or other qualified judges might determine—from students' classroom performance, written work, grades, and so forth—which of them met some agreed upon performance standard that defines minimum proficiency. Then, after students had been classified into groups based on their non-test performance, they would take the examination for which the cut score was to be determined. A statistical procedure (logistic regression) would then be used to find the cut score that best distinguished between the two groups. If the costs of passing a below-minimum examinee versus failing an above-minimum examinee were judged equal, then the optimum cut score would be that score at which the predicted probability of membership in the proficient group was one-half.

The defining feature of *performance-centered* approaches is their focus on specific student work samples. Among them, the "body of work" method (Kingston, Kahl, Sweeney, & Bay, 2001) is perhaps the best known. Judges might examine entire booklets of students' constructed responses, for example, to determine which students had demonstrated proficiency as defined by the performance standard. Independent of these judgments, all items would also be scored according to their established scoring rubrics, and item scores would be combined to obtain an overall scale score for each student. In an initial round, judges would be given booklets with scores at widely spaced points along the overall score scale. Once they had narrowed their focus to a limited range of booklets, they would be given additional student work samples within that narrow range. The proportions of booklets at different scale scores judged to demonstrate proficiency would then be used to determine the cut score most congruent with the performance standard.

Although *test-centered* approaches are most commonly used, they are the least defensible either logically or empirically (Haertel & Lorié, 2004). Unlike the person-centered or performance-centered methods, which directly consider examinees or samples of their work, test-centered methods focus on the test items themselves. The widely used "modified Angoff" (Angoff, 1971) and "Bookmark" (Mitzel, Lewis, Patz, & Green, 2001) approaches will serve as examples. Modified Angoff methods vary from one application to another, but in all cases judges examine test items one at a time and record a judgment indicating whether a minimally proficient or borderline examinee would be able to answer that item correctly, or what proportion of such borderline examinees would be able to answer it correctly. In some variations, panelists are given a fixed set of proportions to choose from (e.g., 1%, 5%, 10%, 25%, 50%, 75%, 90%, 95%, 99%). A scientific-sounding name for this judgment task is "knowledge estimation" (e.g., Wheeler, 1991). In the Bookmark method, rather than examining items individually, judges are given a set of items ordered according to their empirically determined difficulty, and are asked to locate a bookmark at a point in the series that divides those items that borderline examinees should be expected to answer correctly (with some specified probability) from the items they should not be expected to answer.

Angoff methods in particular have been strenuously criticized for requiring a judgmental task that some writers believe is virtually impossible. A panel convened by the National Academy of Education critiqued one of the first standard-setting exercises of the National Assessment Governing Board in the following terms:

> The Panel recommends that use of the Angoff method or any other item-judgment method to set achievement levels be discontinued. As the Panel's studies demonstrate, the Angoff method approach and other item-judgment methods are fundamentally flawed. Minor improvements, such as allowing more discussion time or providing instructions about guessing, cannot overcome the nearly impossible cognitive task of estimating the probability that a hypothetical student at the boundary of a given achievement level will get a particular item correct. Furthermore, the Angoff method does not allow for an integrated conception of subject-matter proficiency.
>
> (Shepard et al., 1993, p. xxiv)

The cognitive task referred to in the NAEd report requires estimating a conditional probability—that is, the probability of a correct response to an item conditional upon the examinee's having an overall level of proficiency right at the borderline between not satisfying versus satisfying the performance standard. Experts and lay judges alike are reasonably able to make distinctions between clearly proficient and clearly not proficient students, but the Angoff method requires that experts hold in mind the concept of a hypothetical borderline "proficient" examinee and judge the probability of that hypothetical examinee correctly answering each item. Human judgments of conditional probabilities are subject to well-known biases (e.g., Tversky & Kahneman, 1993). Moreover, judgments of item difficulties show a characteristic pattern in which easy items are judged to be more difficult than they actually are and difficult items are judged to be easier (Schulz, 2006).

The Angoff method was first proposed for situations where no external criteria are available. It was conceived as a common-sense method of arriving at "minimum raw scores for passing and honors" on course examinations (Angoff, 1971, p. 514). Such applications are far smaller in scale than the NAEP testing program, for example, and entail a much more limited range of score interpretations and testing consequences than do high-stakes accountability testing programs. As the limitations of judgmental procedures came to be better understood and as new statistical methods based on item response theory were developed, new strategies such as the Bookmark method were developed to minimize certain kinds of errors and inconsistencies that arise with the Angoff method (Mitzel et al., 2001).

The Bookmark method offers somewhat more support for the complex item judgment task by providing the judge with a prespecified item difficulty order so that the items before and after each given item can provide some additional context. The nature of the Bookmark task also makes it impossible for judges to register internally inconsistent patterns of judgments (e.g., with borderline examinees judged more able to answer a harder item than an easier item), which is common with the Angoff method.[6] In addition, the Bookmark task may resolve a potential problem with cumulative errors under the Angoff method (see Linn & Shepard, 1997, for a discussion). However, the fundamental difficulty of the task, judging the conditional probability of a correct response by a hypothetical borderline examinee, remains the same.

An Interpretive Argument for Standard Setting

It is generally accepted by measurement experts that what is subject to validation is a use or interpretation of test scores, not the test itself. Because performance standards and cut scores constitute the rules by which test scores are used and interpreted, it is necessary and appropriate to consider the argument for their validity. In test validity, an *interpretive argument* (Kane, 1992, 1994) is a set of propositions that together form a rationale for an intended score use or interpretation. It sets forth the chain of reasoning from an observed test performance to some inference or action based on that performance. The accompanying *validity argument* offers evidence in support of the propositions included in the interpretive argument. For example, an interpretive argument might include a proposition stating that an achievement test is aligned with a state's content standards. The accompanying validity argument might support that proposition with documentation of the test design process or an alignment study (e.g., Webb, 1997, 2002). The interpretive argument represents a case to be made for an intended interpretation. In addition to highlighting possible weaknesses in the case (e.g., plausible rival interpretations), it can guide test validation efforts. Haertel and Lorié (2004) have framed a general interpretive argument for the validity of a standards-based score interpretation, consisting of five propositions. That argument is summarized here as it would apply to an achievement test.

The *content standards* proposition holds that there is a well-defined content domain that the test is intended to measure, and that this content domain is appropriate to the intended application. In accountability testing (e.g., under NCLB), the material the test is intended to cover is defined by a state's academic content standards or some similar framework.

The *alignment* proposition requires that the test faithfully reflect the intended content—in earlier terminology, that it possesses content validity. Taken together, these first two propositions establish that the test is designed to measure an appropriate domain of content for the intended application.

The *accuracy and precision* proposition encompasses a variety of concerns that arise with any high-stakes testing program. Accuracy implies an absence of construct-irrelevant biases for or against any subgroups of examinees, appropriate standardization of testing conditions, accurate scoring, and adherence to additional principles of sound test design and use. Precision implies adequate test reliability. Taken together, these first three propositions establish that the test scores (prior to any standards-based interpretation) are sound measurements of an appropriate construct. Given that these first three propositions are satisfied, the last two address the standards-based interpretation itself. One concerns the performance standard and the other the cut score.

The *performance standard* proposition addresses two aspects of the performance standard. The *procedural* aspect requires the performance standard to have been formulated through an appropriate process, representing a legitimate exercise of authority by an appropriate policy body. The *substantive* aspect requires that the performance standard does in fact describe what examinees at or above some point along the score scale know or are able to do. This second aspect of the performance standard requires that there be a criterion-referenced score interpretation; in other words, the test score must in fact indicate directly what an examinee knows or is able to do, not just how that examinee is ranked in comparison with others.

The *cut score* proposition holds that the cut score has been set so that the great majority of students who score above the cut score meet the performance standard, and those who score below the cut score do not. If the first four propositions are satisfied, then determining an appropriate cut score should be an essentially technical process, simply implementing the value judgments embodied in the performance standard (see, for example, Kane, 1994). The only additional value consideration in determining the cut score concerns the relative costs of the two possible kinds of classification errors—placing examinees who do not truly meet the performance standard above the threshold versus placing examinees who truly meet the standard below the threshold. There are standard statistical methods for incorporating relative costs of misclassifications in creating such decision rules (e.g., Hambleton & Novick, 1973).

Validating Standard-Setting Applications

The interpretive framework highlights the importance of sound test design and use as a prerequisite to sound standards-based score interpretation. It also highlights several additional requirements. A standards-based score interpretation is a form of criterion-referenced interpretation. Unlike a norm-referenced interpretation, which brings meaning to a score by relating it to some score distribution, a criterion-referenced interpretation draws implications about what the examinee knows or is able to do, irrespective of the performance of any other examinees. As a general rule, criterion-referenced interpretations require stronger assumptions than norm-referenced interpretations.

The performance standard offers a description of something an examinee knows or is able to do. Applied to any individual, the accuracy of that description may be a matter of degree. If the first four propositions of the interpretive argument are satisfied, then the performance standard should describe the capabilities of higher-scoring examinees better than it describes those of lower-scoring examinees. There is no argument that the cut score is somewhat arbitrary, but it does not follow that any cut score will do. If a cut score is placed outside some (ill-defined but nonetheless real) range of score values, it will provide a misleading characterization of examinees' capabilities relative to the performance standard.

Intended inferences from standards-based descriptions (e.g., "Sarah is proficient") generally pertain to students' capabilities in a range of non-test situations. Thus, person-based standard-setting methods are easiest to justify. Indeed, the same methods used to set standards based on groups distinguished by performance on a criterion have also been used to evaluate the adequacy of standards established using test-centered methods (e.g., McLaughlin et al., 1993). Person-based standard-setting methods also have the virtue of quantifying the empirical relationship between test scores and expert judgments of proficiency. If test scores are only weakly related to experts' judgments of test takers, then users of standards-based descriptions can exercise appropriate caution. If the performance standard is narrowly written to refer to academic tasks resembling those the test requires, then performance-centered standard-setting methods can also be justified. The student work examined by judges is (more or less) a direct sample of the kind of work to which such a performance standard refers. By comparison, the case for test-centered standard-setting methods appears to require heroic assumptions. It must be assumed that judges are able to bring their knowledge and experience to bear in a principled way to determine the level of item or test performance that predicts that an examinee has attained the performance standard. Such methods sometimes produce results that appear reasonable, and sometimes not. In fact, empirical studies have often found serious problems with cut scores established in this way (e.g., Chang, 1999; Goodwin, 1999; Impara & Plake, 1998; Shepard et al., 1993).

Recommendations for Practice and Directions for Further Research

Standards-based interpretations employing existing standards and present-day standard-setting methods are not going away anytime soon. States are understandably loath to modify their definitions of "proficient," lest they be accused of playing games with accountability or lowering expectations. The Angoff method has been found to be legally defensible in various court cases (e.g., *U.S.* v. *South Carolina, 1977/1978*); it is also inexpensive to implement and there has been an enormous investment over the years in refinements to make it work better. It is still a contentious issue within the field whether the method in fact remains fundamentally flawed. Both the 1993 National Academy of Education critique (Shepard et al., 1993) and the National Research Council critique (Pellegrino et al., 1999) of the NAEP standard-setting were countered with strenuous rebuttals (Cizek, 1993; Hambleton et al., 2000).

Regardless of how they were developed, there is often a strong argument for leaving standards alone once they have been established. As experience with a fixed score scale accumulates, it acquires additional meaning. The origin of the Fahrenheit temperature scale is of little more than historical interest, but persons who have lived with the scale know how to dress when the predicted high for the day is 72 degrees. Likewise, a standard like "proficient" on a given test may acquire meaning as teachers or employers gain experience over time with proficient versus non-proficient students so-defined. (Caution is required, of course, when the same label, e.g., proficient, has different meanings for different examinations.) Holding scales fixed over time also facilitates the analysis of trends. Even if absolute levels are suspect, it is meaningful to ask whether over time performance is worsening or improving.

Professionals who make extensive use of standards-based score interpretations should become thoroughly familiar with performance standards as well as the method by which cut scores were determined; however, regardless of the methods used, absolute interpretations of standards should be approached with great caution. Labels like proficient carry surplus meanings that are probably not warranted given current practices. Where standards are set independently for successive grade levels on state tests, for example, it is not uncommon for the percent "proficient" to vary from grade to grade in a way that defies common sense. Standards may be adjusted to smooth out such anomalies. Otherwise, a student's transitions between "proficient" one year and "not proficient" another year may reflect variation in cut scores as opposed to meaningful changes in the student's performance or progress.

Further research is needed on the problem of establishing meaningful and realistic performance standards. One promising approach was discussed by Linn and Baker (1995), who developed an argument for using *achievement benchmarks* as a source of performance standards to define levels of student achievement regarded as acceptable or outstanding. Such performance standards would provide substantive descriptions of what examinees know and can do at specified performance levels, but would differ from most contemporary performance standards in that those levels would be chosen based on normative considerations. As with any standards-based score interpretation, performance standards based on achievement benchmarks are criterion-referenced; they describe what the examinees meeting the standard know and are able to do. These standards are justified, however, by empirical evidence of the proportion of students in some reference population who have actually met that standard.

A variation of the Linn and Baker proposal was implemented in the Trends in International Mathematics and Science Study (TIMSS). Benchmarks were chosen at the twenty-fifth, fiftieth, seventy-fifth, and ninetieth percentiles of the international distribution of science and mathematics achievement (Kelly, Mullis, & Martin, 2000). To make these levels more meaningful, an *item anchoring* procedure was used. Item anchoring involves empirically determining those items that students at a given anchor (benchmark) level can generally answer correctly but those at the next lower benchmark cannot. Narrative descriptions of proficiency at each level are then derived from an expert review of the items at each level (Beaton & Allen, 1992). This is an important conceptual innovation: one begins with a cut score and derives a substantive description of what that cut score means or signifies, as opposed to beginning with a performance standard and then looking for a cut score that reflects that standard.

Cut scores representing such benchmarks provide norm-referenced as well as criterion-referenced interpretations of student achievement. For example, in 1999, an estimated 61% of U.S. eighth grade students scored above the international median performance level. Descriptions of items that students at this level can typically answer include such specifics as, "Solves a one-step addition word problem involving numbers with differing numbers of decimal places" or "Estimates the value, to one decimal place, of a point on a number line marked at whole number intervals" (Kelly et al., 2000, p. 106). Benchmarking procedures like this hold great promise for providing the criterion-referencing benefits of purely judgmental standards, while avoiding unsupportable claims about the meaning of particular score levels.

A second possible approach to establishing meaningful and realistic performance standards is the briefing book method proposed by Haertel (2002). With this method, a range of possible cut scores is considered, and an appropriate performance standard is then written to match each one. Relevant additional information is assembled and organized so as to enable a coherent deliberation by the appropriate policy body, ideally informed by public comment. As described by Haertel, a series of perhaps five to ten possible cut scores would be chosen for consideration. These would be more or less equally spaced along the score scale, and would be chosen such that the resulting percentages of students passing if any were adopted would fall within some acceptable range, however defined. A briefing book would then be prepared presenting information about each successive cut score. This information would include the overall proportion correct at that cut score, and members of the policy body would be invited to examine or even to take the actual test to get a sense of its difficulty. Performance standards would be constructed using scale anchoring methods like those used early on in NAEP and later in TIMSS and other international assessments. The content, format, and cognitive demands of items likely versus not likely to be answered correctly by examinees at a specified cut score would serve as the basis for an empirically grounded characterization of the capabilities signified by that cut score. Along with these performance standards, the briefing book would also provide projected passing rates overall and for major demographic groups, as well as the school-level distribution of percent proficient. If intended interpretations included predictions of performance in non-test settings, studies would be carried out in advance of the standard-setting exercise to determine the empirical relationship between test scores and performance on some illustrative real-world tasks of interest. The briefing book could then include estimated probabilities of successful completion of each such task at each possible cut score.

The briefing book method would be more expensive and time consuming than current methods, but given the scale of application and the consequences attached to accountability test score interpretations, the required expenditure seems justified. In addition to helping to assure a sensible standard-setting outcome, the briefing book approach would also help to assure that there was an explicit performance standard well aligned with the cut score.

Both the achievement benchmarks and briefing book approaches make use of norm-referenced information in the form of actual distributions of student test performance, and both make use of scale anchoring methods to provide criterion-referenced descriptions of what students at different performance levels can do. Which method is most suitable will depend on the purpose and context of the testing application.

Conclusion

Despite the popular appeal of standards-based score interpretations, they are deeply problematic. Labels like basic, proficient, and advanced invite surplus meanings that cannot be supported by present-day standard-setting practices. Common test-centered standard-setting methods lead judges through seemingly scientific procedures, but these procedures do not ensure internal consistency; nor do they offer any empirical mechanism for linking the resulting standard to external validity criteria. The weight of empirical evidence suggests that test-centered methods in particular are deeply flawed. Nonetheless, there is value in stability. If score scales and performance levels can be held steady for a period of years, then as education professionals and other test users gain familiarity with them, they will accrue additional meaning.

Consumers of test score reports should be cautioned about what classifications like proficient do or do not signify, and should focus on trends over time or differences among subgroups instead of on absolute levels when interpreting scores. Publishers of test results should explain more clearly that standards on different tests are created for different purposes, and that labels like proficient may carry very different meanings in different contexts (Linn, 2003b, and this volume). Even for purposes of examining gaps and trends, standards-based interpretations are a poor choice (Ho & Haertel, 2006; Holland, 2002). Because standards-based interpretations focus on the percent above a particular point along the score scale, they can offer misleading and inconsistent characterizations of group differences and of trends over time.

More research is needed on methods of bringing external validity evidence into the standard-setting process, including norm-referenced information on actual distributions of student test performance. Two such methods are the use of achievement benchmarks, as illustrated with TIMSS, and the briefing book method.

Acknowledgments

I wish to thank Scott Marion, Barbara Plake, Katherine Ryan, Lorrie Shepard, and Laurie Wise for helpful and constructive comments on drafts of this chapter. Any remaining errors and omissions are my own.

Notes

1. Some states have obtained waivers permitting the use of indexes or value-added models that do not conform precisely to the mandates of the original legislation. Also, the NCLB Act includes a safe harbor provision based on change in performance rather than absolute level of performance. For the most part, however, these alternatives are still cast in terms of percentages of students at or above successive achievement levels, or year-to-year changes in these percentages, rather than raw scores, scale scores, or norm-referenced derived scores.
2. Other kinds of standards include "Opportunity to Learn" (or educational delivery) standards for the quality and availability of education, as well as professional standards like those set forth in the *Standards for Educational and Psychological Testing* (American Educational Research Association, American Psychological Association, and National Council on Measurement in Education, 1999).
3. The cut score may be defined as a number correct (raw score) or as some kind of scaled score. Regardless of how the cut score is defined initially, it is likely to be expressed as a scale score if two or more alternative test forms are created.
4. Kane (1994) might add that the performance standard must represent an accepted policy decision, perhaps reached through a complex social/political process. Our concern here is with the more narrow, technical problem of setting a cut score.
5. Note that the critical requirement is that the cut score and the performance standard must be congruent. It is not strictly necessary that the performance standard come first. A cut score, or a series of cut scores, might be established first, and performance standards might then be derived from a study of those test items examinees at each performance level tend to get correct versus incorrect (e.g., see Beaton & Allen, 1992).
6. Mislevy (1998) notes that such an inconsistency might in principle reflect no more than a judge's belief that the content measured by an easier item is less critical for a minimally

competent examinee to master than the content measured by some more difficult item. Empirical and substantive orderings are conceptually distinct and need not agree.

References

American Educational Research Association, American Psychological Association, and National Council on Measurement in Education. (1999). *Standards for educational and psychological testing*. Washington, DC: American Educational Research Association.

Angoff, W. H. (1971). Scales, norms, and equivalent scores. In R. L. Thorndike (Ed.), *Educational measurement* (2nd ed., pp. 508–600). Washington, DC: American Council on Education.

Beaton, A. E. & Allen, N. (1992). Interpreting scales through scale anchoring. *Journal of Educational Statistics*, 17 (2), 191–204.

Berk, R. A. (1986). A consumer's guide to setting performance standards on criterion-referenced tests. *Review of Educational Research*, 56 (1), 137–172.

Berk, R. A. (1995). Standard setting—the next generation. *Proceedings of the Joint Conference on Standard Setting for Large-Scale Assessments*, Vol. II (pp. 161–181). Washington, DC: National Assessment Governing Board, National Center for Education Statistics.

Braun, H. I. & Qian, J. (2007). An enhanced method for mapping state standards onto the NAEP scale. In N. J. Dorans, M. Pommerich, & P. W. Holland (Eds.), *Linking and aligning scores and scales* (pp. 313–338). New York: Springer.

Chang, L. (1999). Judgmental item analysis of the Nedelsky and Angoff standard-setting methods. *Applied Measurement in Education*, 12 (2), 151–165.

Cizek, G. J. (1993). Reactions to National Academy of Education report, "Setting Performance Standards for Student Achievement." Paper commissioned by the National Assessment Governing Board (ERIC Document Reproduction Service No. ED360397).

Glass, G. V. (1978). Standards and criteria. *Journal of Educational Measurement*, 15 (4), 237–261.

Goodwin, L. D. (1999). Relations between observed item difficulty levels and Angoff minimum passing levels for a group of borderline examinees. *Applied Measurement in Education*, 12 (1), 13–28.

Haertel, E. H. (2001). Comment by Edward Haertel [Discussion of "The controversy over the National Assessment Governing Board Standards" by Mark D. Reckase]. In D. Ravitch (Ed.), *Brookings Papers on Education Policy: 2001* (pp. 255–262). Washington, DC: Brookings Institute Press.

Haertel, E. H. (2002). Standard setting as a participatory process: Implications for validation of standards-based accountability programs. *Educational Measurement: Issues and Practice*, 21 (1), 16–22.

Haertel, E. H. & Lorié, W. A. (2004). Validating standards-based test score interpretations. *Measurement: Interdisciplinary Research and Perspectives*, 2 (12), 61–103.

Hambleton, R. K. (1980). Test score validity and standard-setting methods. In R. A. Berk (Ed.), *Criterion-referenced measurement: The state of the art* (pp. 80–123). Baltimore: The Johns Hopkins University Press.

Hambleton, R. K. & Novick, M. R. (1973). Toward an integration of theory and method for criterion-referenced tests. *Journal of Educational Measurement*, 10 (3), 159–170.

Hambleton, R. K., Brennan, R. L., Brown, W., Dodd, B., Forsyth, R. A., Mehrens, W. A., et al. (2000). A response to "Setting reasonable and useful performance standards" in the National Academy of Sciences' *Grading the Nation's Report Card. Educational Measurement: Issues and Practice*, 19 (2), 5–14.

Ho, A. D. & Haertel, E. H. (2006). *Metric-free measures of test score trends and gaps with policy-relevant examples* (CSE Report No. 665). Los Angeles: University of California, National Center for Research on Evaluation, Standards and Student Testing (CRESST).

Holland, P. (2002). Two measures of change in the gaps between the CDFs of test-score distributions. *Journal of Educational and Behavioral Statistics*, 27 (1), 3–17.

Hoover, H. D. (2003). Some common misconceptions about tests and testing. *Educational Measurement: Issues and Practice*, 22 (1), 5–14.

Impara, J. C. & Plake, B. S. (1998). Teachers' ability to estimate item difficulty: A test of the assumptions in the Angoff standard setting method. *Journal of Educational Measurement*, 35 (1), 69–81.

Kane, M. (1992). An argument-based approach to validation. *Psychological Bulletin*, 112 (3), 527–535.

Kane, M. (1994). Validating the performance standards associated with passing scores. *Review of Educational Research*, 64 (3), 425–461.

Kelly, D. L., Mullis, I. V. S., & Martin, M. O. (2000). *Profiles of student achievement in mathematics at the TIMSS international benchmarks: U.S. performance and standards in an international context.* Chestnut Hill, MA: Boston College.

Kingston, N. M., Kahl, S. R., Sweeney, K. P., & Bay, L. (2001). Setting performance standards using the Body of Work method. In G. J. Cizek (Ed.), *Setting performance standards: Concepts, methods, and perspectives* (pp. 219–248). Mahwah, NJ: Erlbaum.

Linn, R. L. (2003a). *Accountability: Responsibility and reasonable expectations* (CSE Report No. 601). Los Angeles: University of California, National Center for Research on Evaluation, Standards and Student Testing (CRESST).

Linn, R. L. (2003b). Performance standards: Utility for different uses of assessments. *Education Policy Analysis Archives*, 11 (31). Online, available at: http://epaa.asu.edu/epaa/v11n31/ (accessed August 2, 2007).

Linn, R. L. & Baker, E. L. (1995). What do international assessments imply for world-class standards? *Educational Evaluation and Policy Analysis*, 17 (4), 405–418.

Linn, R. L. & Shepard, L. A. (1997). Item-by-item standard setting: Misinterpretations of judges' intentions due to less than perfect item inter-correlations. Unpublished manuscript, University of Colorado at Boulder.

Livingston, S. A. & Zieky, M. J. (1982). *Passing scores: A manual for setting standards of performance on educational and occupational tests.* Princeton, NJ: Educational Testing Service.

McLaughlin, D. & Bandeira de Mello, V. (2002, April). Comparison of state elementary school mathematics achievement standards using NAEP 2000. Paper presented at the meeting of the American Educational Research Association, New Orleans, LA.

McLaughlin, D. H., DuBois, P. A., Eaton, M. S., Ehrlich, D. E., Stancavage, F. B., O'Donnell, C. A., et al. (1993). Comparison of teachers' and researchers' ratings for students' performance in mathematics and reading with NAEP measurement of achievement levels. In R. Glaser, R. Linn, and G. Bohrnstedt (Eds.), *Setting performance standards for student achievement: Background studies* (pp. 283–364). Stanford, CA: National Academy of Education.

Mislevy, R. J. (1998). Implications of market-basket reporting for achievement-level setting. *Applied Measurement in Education*, 11 (1), 49–63.

Mitzel, H. C., Lewis, D. M., Patz, R. J., & Green, D. R. (2001). The Bookmark procedure: Psychological perspectives. In G. J. Cizek (Ed.), *Setting performance standards: Concepts, methods, and perspectives* (pp. 249–281). Mahwah, NJ: Erlbaum.

Musick, M. (1997, June). Setting standards high enough. Paper presented at the CCSSO Annual Assessment Conference, Colorado Springs, CO. (ERIC Document Reproduction Service No. ED414309).

National Assessment Governing Board. (2004). Mathematics framework for the 2005 National Assessment of Educational Progress. Washington, DC: U.S. Government Printing Office. Online, available at: http://www.nagb.org/pubs/m_framework_05/761607-Math%20 Framework.pdf (accessed January 12, 2007).

National Center for Education Statistics (2007). *Mapping 2005 State Proficiency Standards Onto the NAEP Scales* (NCES 2007–482). U.S. Department of Education. Washington, DC: National Center for Education Statistics. Online, available at: http://nces.ed.gov/nationsreportcard/pdf/studies/2007482.pdf (accessed August 2, 2007).

Pellegrino, J. W., Jones, L. R., & Mitchell, K. J. (Eds.). Committee on the Evaluation of National and State Assessments of Educational Progress, Board on Testing and Assessment, Commission on Behavioral and Social Sciences and Education, National Research Council. (1999). *Grading the nation's report card: Evaluating NAEP and transforming the assessment of educational progress.* Washington, DC: National Academy Press.

Rosenberg, B. (2004). *What's proficient? The No Child Left Behind Act and the many meanings of proficiency.* Washington, DC: American Federation of Teachers. Online, available at: http://www.aft.org/pubs-reports/downloads/teachers/WhatsProficient.pdf (accessed January 12, 2007).

Schulz, E. M. (2006). Commentary: A response to Reckase's conceptual framework and examples for evaluating standard setting methods. *Educational Measurement: Issues and Practice,* 25 (3), 4–13.

Shepard, L. A., Glaser, R., Linn, R., & Bohrnstedt, G. (1993). *Setting performance standards for student achievement* (Report of the NAE Panel on the Evaluation of the NAEP Trial State Assessment: An Evaluation of the 1992 Achievement Levels). Stanford, CA: National Academy of Education.

Thorndike, E. L. (1918). Specific uses of measurement in the solution of school problems. In G. M. Whipple (Ed.), *The seventeenth yearbook of the National Society for the Study of Education, Part II: The measurement of educational products.* Bloomington, IL: Public School Publishing.

Tversky, A. & Kahneman, D. (1993). Probabilistic reasoning. In A. I. Goldman (Ed.), *Readings in philosophy and cognitive science* (pp. 43–68). Cambridge, MA: MIT Press.

U.S. v. *South Carolina,* 445 F. Supp. 1094 (D.S.C. 1977), aff'd, 434 U.S. 1026 (1978).

Webb, N. L. (1997). *Criteria for alignment of expectations and assessments in mathematics and science education* (Research Monograph No. 6). Madison, WI: University of Wisconsin-Madison, National Institute for Science Education.

Webb, N. L. (2002). *Alignment study in language arts, mathematics, science, and social studies of state standards and assessments for four states.* Washington, DC: Council of Chief State School Officers.

Wheeler, P. (1991, November). The relationship between modified Angoff knowledge estimation judgments and item difficulty values for seven NTE specialty area tests. Paper presented at the meeting of the California Educational Research Association, San Diego, CA (available from the ERIC Document Reproduction Service, No. ED340745).

8
Toward a Normative Understanding of Student Growth

Damian W. Betebenner

The availability of annual student achievement data and the dissatisfaction with status reporting of assessment results have led to widespread enthusiasm for statistical models suitable for longitudinal analysis. In response, the United States Department of Education recently solicited growth model proposals from states as a means of satisfying No Child Left Behind (NCLB) adequate yearly progress requirements. It is not surprising, given the intense focus on schools and their impact on student achievement, that most of the proposed growth models are formulated and implemented primarily as school accountability models. In this chapter, I suggest that the use of such models has led to a blind spot concerning other uses of longitudinal test data, especially for descriptive or diagnostic ends. The purpose of the chapter is twofold: (1) to situate growth analyses within a larger search for measures of school quality, and (2) to introduce student growth percentiles as a means of understanding student growth normatively. I demonstrate how student growth percentiles, analogous to pediatric growth charts, can help various stakeholders understand change in student assessment outcomes and its relationship to accountability systems designed to monitor educational quality.

Background

Accountability systems built upon federal adequate yearly progress (AYP) requirements currently rely upon annual measurement of student achievement to render judgments about school quality. Since their adoption and incorporation into accountability systems, such status measures have been the focus of persistent criticism (Linn, 2003; Linn, Baker, & Betebenner, 2002). Status measures, though appropriate for making judgments about the achievement level of students at a given school in a given year, are inappropriate for judgments about the educational effectiveness of a school. In particular, status measures are blind to the possibility of low-achieving students attending effective schools. It is this possibility that has led some critics of NCLB to label its achievement mandates as unfair and misguided and to demand the use of growth analyses as a better means of auditing the quality of schools.

The primary purpose of growth analyses over the last decade has been to use prior student achievement to disentangle status from effectiveness (Ballou, Sanders, & Wright, 2004). The Tennessee Value-Added Assessment System (TVAAS) and Educational Value-Added Assessment System (EVAAS), value-added analyses developed by William Sanders, represent the most sophisticated attempt to use prior student achievement to quantify effectiveness at the teacher and school levels (Sanders, Saxton, & Horn, 1997). These models have gained tremendous notoriety, so much so that the entire Spring 2004 issue of the *Journal of Educational and Behavioral Statistic* was devoted to the topic. If the assumption of value-added analysis is true, that student background characteristics can be completely accounted for, the benefit to measures of school or teacher quality is obvious: effectiveness can be distinguished from achievement so that effective schools serving low, average, and high performing students can be identified.

There is a growing body of literature that scrutinizes the validity of the value-added procedures and the estimates they produce (Braun, 2005; Rubin, Stuart, & Zanutto, 2004). At issue is whether observational data can be used to infer the effectiveness of a given teacher or school and, more fundamentally, what the terms "teacher effect" or "school effect" actually mean (Raudenbush, 2004). Rubin et al. (2004) suggest that such effects might be useful as "descriptive measures" in that they potentially provide actionable data that can be used by stakeholders to improve the quality of education. Expanding on this, Linn (this volume) outlines the possibility of a more descriptive use of accountability system results, diminishing their current deterministic role. Such a descriptive use of assessment outcomes coincides with Christopher Edley's (2006) vision for a regulatory approach to understanding achievement disparities: "This is the difference between a retrospective question of identifying fault as opposed to a prospective strategy [of engineering] some corrective measure—almost independent of considering whether there was blame-worthiness."

In line with this vision, this chapter presents a third way between the status-based accountability measures employed by states and the deterministic growth models that currently find favor. Borrowing concepts from pediatrics used to describe infant and child weight and height progressions, this chapter introduces student growth percentiles. These individual reference percentiles augment individual status measures and sidestep many of the thorny questions of causal attribution. Instead, they provide descriptions of student growth that can inform discussions about assessment outcomes and their relation to education quality. Student growth percentiles can be used to understand growth in student achievement relative to both population patterns of growth and state performance standards. Student growth percentiles can also be aggregated to summarize transparently differences in student growth among schools, districts, or any aggregation unit of interest. To situate growth percentiles within the spectrum of currently used school quality measures, I begin with a general discussion of measures of school quality.

A Taxonomy of Different Measures

Before introducing student growth percentiles and their relationship to measures of educational quality, it is necessary to clarify terminology. A great deal of confusion currently exists regarding growth, even among experts; much of this confusion is because of sloppy nomenclature. In particular, the term "growth" is employed in an imprecise manner. Most often, the word growth is used to connote change in student achievement over time; however, growth is also associated with school performance over time (i.e., "school growth" or AYP). The NCLB accountability system, for example, mandates that levels of achievement at the school level (i.e., school-level growth) increase between now and 2014. Growth or change associated with students and the schools in which they reside are related, but are not synonymous. A useful semantic distinction is to restrict use of the term growth to discussions of student change and to employ the term improvement when discussing change at the institutional level.

Dale Carlson (2001) introduced a four-cell table (reproduced in Table 8.1) that summarizes the different measures and associated questions currently used to assess school quality. All measures of school quality (as quantified by assessment outcomes) currently in use today fall into one of these cells (or in some cases, into a combination of cells).[1] The rows of the table denote two distinct qualities associated with judging the merit of schools: achievement (i.e., status) and effectiveness. Neither quality is a necessary nor a sufficient condition for the other. That is, it is possible to conceive of a highly effective school that is not outstanding in terms of achievement and vice versa.

The columns of Table 8.1 indicate the time frame within which the school is examined. Column 1 addresses school quality in the present while Column

Table 8.1 Carlson's Taxonomy (2001) Represents the Four Facets Associated with Measures of School Quality

	How good is this school?	*Is it getting better?*
Achievement	**A1:** What is the achievement level of students in this school? **Examples:** Percent proficient students, mean scale score, composite performance index.	**A2:** Is the achievement level of this school increasing? **Example:** Percent NCLP proficient over time.
Effectiveness	**E1:** Is this an effective school? That is, given the achievement level of students when they enter, how much do they learn or develop while they are in the school? **Examples:** Value-added residuals, transition matrices.	**E2:** Is this school *more* effective? How much more, or less, are the students learning this year than they did the year before? **Examples:** None in widespread use (to my knowledge)

2 concerns changes in school quality over time. Generally, the qualities addressed in Column 1 represent likely concerns of parents—what is the school's achievement or effectiveness level today? Whereas, issues associated with Column 2 are of most interest to administrators, policymakers, and researchers—how are the school's achievement or effectiveness levels changing over time? Each of the four qualities depicted in Table 8.1 provides information relevant to stakeholders interested in assessing school quality:

- cell A1 represents the achievement level (i.e., status) of a school at a given time;
- cell A2 represents change in achievement level over time (this is the concern of NCLB related to meeting the goal of universal proficiency by 2014: is the percent of children who meet the proficient standard increasing over time?);
- cell E1 is where much current attention is focused in terms of measuring student growth—a school is deemed effective if the students attending the school, no matter where they start, show significant growth; and,
- cell E2 represents one of the primary goals of education reform: increase in efficacy over time.

Most current growth analyses attempt to assess effectiveness (depicted by cell E1). These growth analyses utilize prior student information in an attempt to assess the effectiveness of the education process to which students were exposed.[2] Improvement in student achievement vis-à-vis increasing percentages of proficient students for a school, as mandated by current NCLB accountability guidelines, is depicted in cell A2. These two qualities—cell A2, achievement across time and cell E1, current effectiveness—are conceptually distinct. However, current attempts to incorporate student growth into accountability systems obscure this distinction, which leads to confusion regarding determination of school quality. Measures of greatest relevance to education reform, which quantify whether effectiveness is increasing over time, are situated in cell E2. Current NCLB year-to-year percent proficient statistics, represented in cell A2, are consistent with a call to increase educational *effectiveness* levels (represented in cell E2), which NCLB attempts to capture by imposing AYP targets on the proficiency data.

A central argument of this chapter is that it is possible to relate the qualities depicted in Table 8.1 through an appropriate, descriptively rich, analysis of student growth (Rubin et al., 2004, p. 113). To do so requires the introduction of a normative dimension to growth. Using ideas and methods from pediatrics, I begin with the familiar normative understanding of achievement, and show how familiar pediatric reference growth charts can be used to understand the relationship between normative and standards-based achievement across the entire assessment system. Passing from achievement to growth, I extend these ideas and present student growth percentiles as a quantification of student growth. These normative growth descriptions are interpretable and easily adapted for use within criterion-referenced systems like those found in state assessment programs.

Reference Charts for Assessment Outcomes

To motivate discussions of individual achievement and growth and its relation to education quality, it is worthwhile to borrow ideas and methods from other contexts where longitudinal data are frequently examined. The time-dependent examination of human height, weight, and other body measurements, broadly referred to as anthropometry (Quetelet, 1871), is well suited for this purpose. Throughout most of the developed world today, pediatric height and weight charts are used to monitor infant health and are familiar to almost every parent. Such charts are frequently used by physicians to assist parents in understanding their child's height and weight in relation to a population of children of the same age. The charts are valuable for both educational and diagnostic purposes. In what follows, I introduce methods and representations of achievement and growth derived from pediatric reference growth chart literature (Cole, 1988, 1994; Cole & Green, 1992; Wei & He, 2006; Wei, Pere, Koenker, & He, 2006) and propose their use with assessment outcomes. These well-understood methods are ideally suited to provide information that is diagnostically useful for each student as well as to inform current accountability-focused educational policy with regard to aggregate assessment outcomes.

In any given year, states assess tens of thousands of students across numerous grades, resulting in cross-sectional data commonly used to determine percentages of students in a school at or above proficient for AYP purposes. Rarely are data examined across grades within a given year as a means of understanding the normative dimension of achievement change across grades. By contrast, such examinations are common with weight and height and form the basis of the unconditional reference growth charts most familiar to parents. These charts allow parents and doctors quickly to make normative statements or comparisons about a variety of child physical characteristics and, in turn, to identify children whose measurements lie in the tails of the distribution for further examination. When applied to student assessment data, unconditional growth charts can be combined with information about performance levels to provide a simple to understand summary of the distribution of achievement across all grades and performance levels.

Achievement Reference Charts

Reference growth charts are a widely employed graphical representation that assists in the identification of children demonstrating (ab)normal measurements, usually as the result of poor physical growth, called failure to thrive in medical discourse. The charts, produced from cross-sectional data based upon a reference sample of interest, depict the distribution of some measurement (e.g., height or weight) that typically varies with age. The reference chart displays the time dependent distributions via smoothed curves representing relevant percentiles of the distribution. Typically, the charts depict smoothed curves for the third, fifth, tenth, twenty-fifth, fiftieth, seventy-fifth, ninetieth, ninety-fifth, and ninety-seventh percentiles associated with the weight distributions for girls and boys by age.

Following Wei and He (2006), I parameterize the percentile functions of reference growth charts associated with educational outcomes as a linear combination of polynomial spline basis functions. Using polynomial splines enables smooth curves to be fit to data associated with assessment outcomes. The result mimics the feel of reference growth charts associated with weight and height. Figures 8.1 and 8.2 are reference achievement charts associated with grade 3 through 10 math and reading scores, respectively, based on the population of students in Colorado (approximately 50,000 students per grade). The figures provide various percentiles across grades 3 through 10 in addition to four shaded regions representing the performance levels that the state uses to qualify performance.

Close examination of the reference percentiles for math achievement shown in Figure 8.1 reveals interesting characteristics of student achievement across grades. The reference percentiles, moving from Grade 3 to 10, do not increase at a rate comparable to the rate of increase for the performance-level cut points over time. That is, the boundaries between shaded regions, which represent boundaries between performance levels, increase faster than do the smoothed percentile curves. This indicates that a student who maintains his or her relative position in the distribution over time will nonetheless tend to move down in terms of performance-level classification. Figure 8.2 for reading indicates that the reference percentiles increase at a rate on par with the performance-level expectations for students. In reading, in contrast to the math results, students who maintain their relative position (i.e., achievement percentile) over time will tend to maintain their performance level.

Treating performance standards as absolute criteria, Figure 8.1 suggests that, particularly in the latter grades, the math education system is not effective enough—students are declining relative to the performance standards against which students and the system are judged. The reading results suggest that enough is being done with already proficient students, but that more needs to be accomplished with those students not yet at the proficient level. However, if the performance standards are not taken as absolute and become subject to evaluation and revision, then these results provide a normative basis against which the performance-level boundaries might be set based on conscious deliberation about the relationship of desired attainment levels to

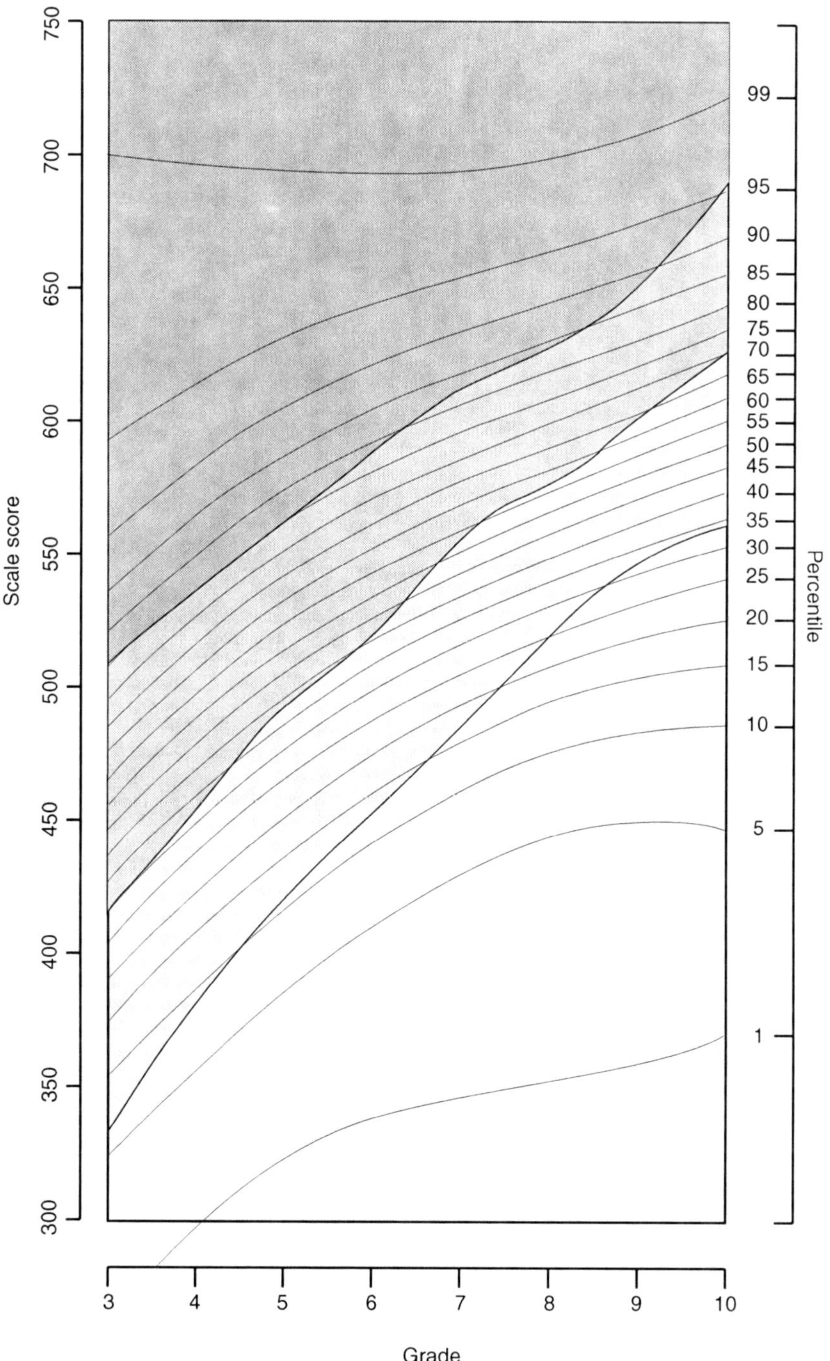

Figure 8.1 Unconditional Reference Growth Chart for Cross-Sectional State Math Scores, Grades 3 to 10, 2005.

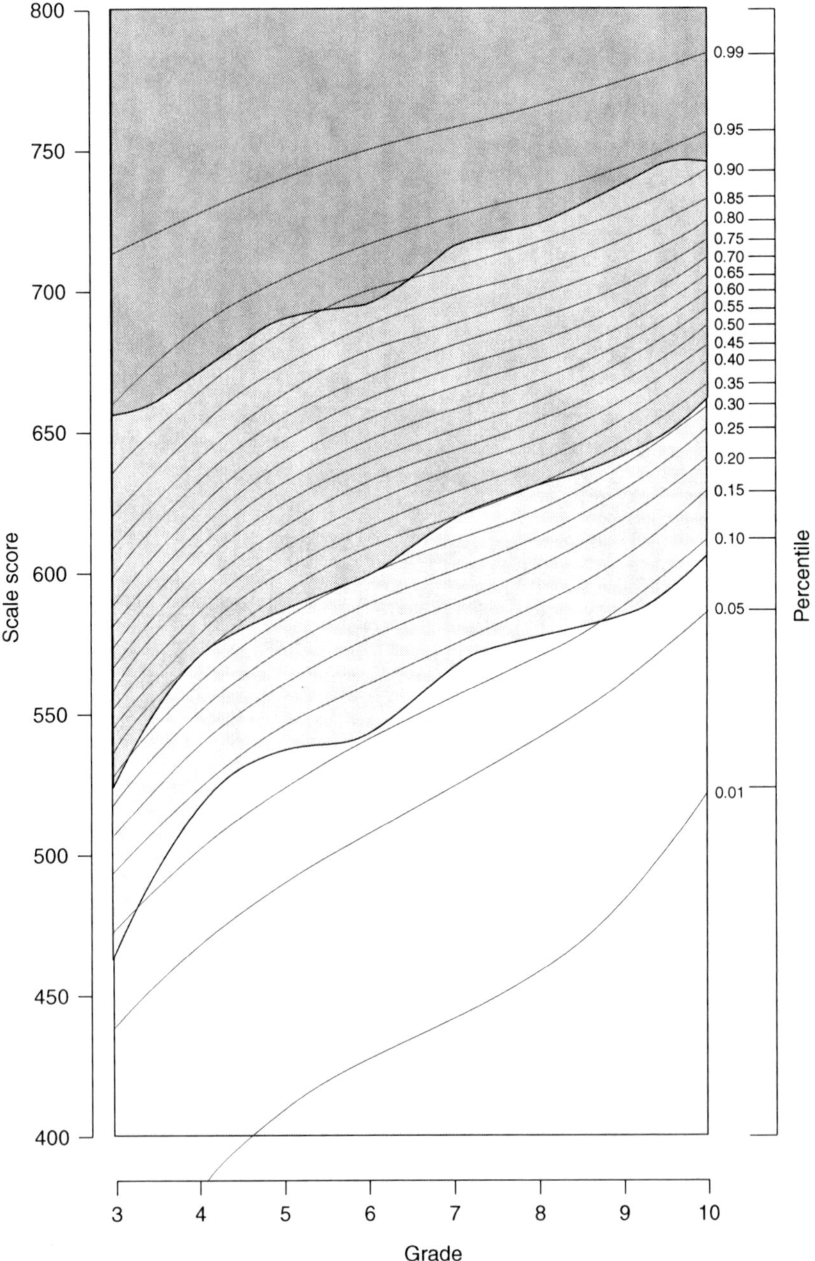

Figure 8.2 Unconditional Reference Growth Chart for Cross-Sectional State Reading Scores, Grades 3 to 10, 2005.

current reference percentiles. It is important to note that once performance levels are set, they provide a foundational basis for making absolute (as opposed to relative) determinations of achievement and effectiveness.

Although Figures 8.1 and 8.2 take advantage of an existing vertical scale to construct the picture, such a scale is not a requirement for the quantile regression techniques employed to establish normative achievement and growth curves. Reference achievement charts, because they are based upon the estimation of percentile curves across grades, do not require a vertical scale. This is also the case with the conditional percentile analyses considered later, where prior student scores and other demographic variables are used as conditioning variables for screening or prediction purposes.

Achievement Growth Reference Charts

Whereas achievement reference charts are appropriate for a normative understanding of single measurements taken on an individual, they are inappropriate for making judgments about the adequacy of the rate of growth over time (Cole, 1994, p. 2,478). Parents and doctors are accustomed to assuming that a two-year old at the twentieth percentile is growing normally if the child stays at roughly the twentieth percentile in a subsequent year. Similarly they might also expect their two-year old to be at the twentieth percentile in weight. Strictly speaking, however, these intuitive expectations or predictions are not accurate, which would be important if parents were to be held accountable for inches gained from age two to age three. Because measurements from one grade to the next are not perfectly correlated, growth predictions must take account of the phenomenon known as regression to the mean. Although some two-year olds at the twentieth percentile will fall to the fifteenth or tenth percentile the next year, the vast majority will be well above the twentieth percentile at age three—a phenomenon that pediatricians call "catch-up" growth. Importantly, normative growth for children at the ninetieth percentile in height and for students achieving at the ninetieth percentile in mathematics would place them well below the ninetieth percentile the next year. A student at the ninetieth percentile would have to grow at a significantly faster rate than other ninetieth percentile students to stay at the ninetieth percentile.

With longitudinal data, like that presently available from state assessment programs, it is possible to extend the techniques used for reference achievement charts and produce reference achievement growth charts appropriate for scrutinizing individual growth from one grade to the next. To do so it is necessary to derive student-specific longitudinal percentiles, which I call student growth percentiles. That is, by conditioning upon prior achievement, the derivation of student growth percentiles enables a normative understanding of growth rates associated with the starting point of individual subjects. Such analyses have numerous potential benefits including:

- for diagnostic purposes, a distribution of potential outcomes for each starting point is derived and individuals with extreme values compared to this distribution can be flagged for further screening;
- for accountability systems, it is possible to quantify rigorously "average," "above average," and "below average" growth; for example, one can define seventy-fifth percentile growth for each child, which can then be used as a hypothetical growth target;
- such analyses can assist practitioners and policymakers in setting attainable individual achievement goals that are based upon performance standard criteria. These goals can then be related to aggregate level systemic improvement initiatives embedded within state accountability plans.

Figure 8.3 provides an illustration, using grades 6 and 7 reading data, of the range of possible outcomes—the conditional grade 7 distributions—associated with four different grade 6 initial achievement scenarios. To aid in interpretation, grade 6 performance-level cut points are superimposed to show the distribution's relationship to absolute performance levels. For a given grade 6 and grade 7 reading score, the student growth percentile is defined as the percentile associated with the student's grade 7 score in the distribution derived from their grade 6 score. For example, in Figure 8.3, a grade 7 scale score of 550 resides at approximately the fiftieth percentile of the distribution associated with a grade 6 scale score of 500 (at the tenth achievement percentile). Thus, fiftieth percentile growth for a student scoring 500 in grade 6 reading would result in a score of 550 in grade 7. The same conditional density indicates that the threshold between unsatisfactory and partially proficient is at approximately the seventieth percentile of sixth graders with a reading score of 500. Thus, seventieth percentile growth would be needed for a student with a grade 6 scale score of 500 to move out of the unsatisfactory category. Equivalently, based on current resources and instructional practices, only three in ten such students would be expected to make such a transition given their prior student growth and achievement.

The conditional distributions associated with the grade 7 reading scores in Figure 8.3 provide data on individuals appropriate for both individual screening and prediction and goal setting purposes. In pediatrics, for example, infants and children with inferior growth percentiles are selected for further tests to determine if inferior growth is a symptom of a larger problem. In a similar fashion, children with low growth percentiles could be flagged for further review to determine whether their low rate of achievement growth coincides with teacher and other observational data on the child. Based upon the results of such review, remedial interventions can be implemented in an attempt to correct the problem.

Figure 8.4 depicts three years of achievement data and associated growth

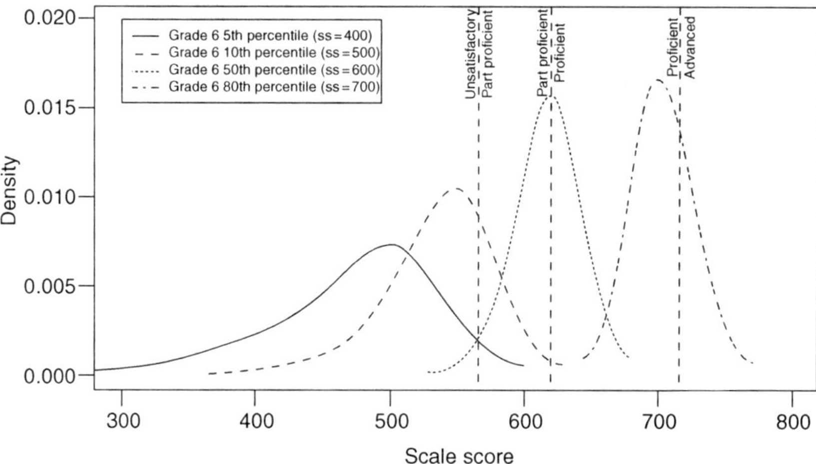

Figure 8.3 Four Conditional Distributions Giving Ranges of Possible Outcomes Based Upon Grades 6 and 7 Reading Data.

percentiles for a hypothetical student. As in Figures 8.1 and 8.2, the shaded regions represent the four reported performance levels. The student's grade 3, 2003, achievement—in the middle of the vertical rectangle—was well within the lowest performance level (more than one conditional standard error of measurement below the threshold for partially proficient as indicated by the box surrounding the achievement score). The grade 4 achievement for this student was similarly poor. The twentieth percentile growth rate suggests that, compared to similar students, this student grew at a rate exceeded by 80% of similar students. Merely reporting unsatisfactory performance or numeric scores in 2003 and 2004 masks this. However, deficient growth becomes readily apparent when the student's growth rate is reported normatively. Between grades 4, 2004, and 5, 2005, the student moved out of the lowest performance level by demonstrating ninety-nine percentile growth—a rate of growth exceeding almost all similar students.

In addition to evaluating the adequacy of individual growth rates, conditional distributions can also be used to set challenging but reasonable goals for students at every possible starting point. Referring once again to Figure 8.3, the conditional distribution associated with the grade 6 scale score of 400 demonstrates that such individuals are "expected" to score approximately 450 in grade 7, using the median of the distribution as a measure of expectation. Using the conditional density, one could provide confidence intervals associated with such students' outcomes as well. Examining the distribution further, students whose scores fell below 350 in grade 7 are in the tail of the distribution and are demonstrating what might be termed "below average" growth—that is, growth associated with the lowest percentiles of the conditional distribution. Conversely, those students scoring 500 in grade 7 appear to be demonstrating "seventy-fifth percentile" growth. This "above average growth rate" based upon the conditional density associated with an individual student's score could form the basis for ambitious goal setting. It is important to note, however, by observing the grade 7 performance-level cuts superimposed on the scale, that there is little chance for someone scoring 400 in grade 6 to move out of the lowest performance category. Thus, single year growth expectations requiring individuals to make that much growth are highly unrealistic.

Normative examinations of student growth using student growth percentiles provide a flexible and transparent means to assess student growth (i.e., description) and to establish future achievement targets for students that are both challenging and reasonable (i.e., prescription). There has been a glaring lack of clarity in current discussions of accountability and growth. I believe that the techniques and representations introduced thus far have the capacity to clarify these discussions and to enable more realistic and productive conversations about educational quality defined in terms of student growth.

Discussion

NCLB mandates universal proficiency by 2014. This is currently implemented in state accountability systems as requiring incremental increases in the percentage of students at or above proficient leading to 100% proficiency by 2014. Despite criticism that the goal is unreachable (Popham, 2004), even partial realization requires that: (1) the achievement levels of students

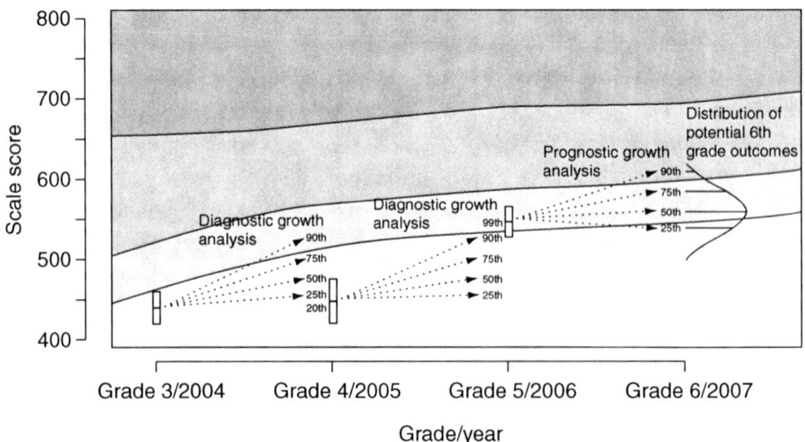

Figure 8.4 Individual Reference Growth Chart with Annual Student Growth Percentiles.

entering the education system must increase, or (2) the education system must become more effective in order to sustain the performance levels envisioned by NCLB. It is likely the second requirement that underlies accountability systems focused on improving school quality: it is expected that educational achievement will improve over time (cell A2 in Table 8.1) if educational effectiveness increases from its current level (cell E2 in Table 8.1).

Using reference achievement charts to operationalize this transformation of the education system is instructive. Universal proficiency implies that all the percentile curves in Figures 8.1 and 8.2 will shift upward and eventually be located entirely within the performance-level regions associated with proficient or better performance. The incremental increases in percent proficient currently embedded in accountability systems, if attained, will result in the gradual upward movement of the achievement chart percentile curves into the proficient and above regions. The more that current percentile curves lay outside of the proficient regions, however, the greater the task of achieving universal proficiency.

Closer examination of the math achievement chart reveals that it is not enough for the percentile curves just to move up without a commensurate increase in their rate of change (i.e., the steepness of the curve). This rate of change reflects achievement growth and is a proxy for the mandated degree of increase in educational effectiveness. If policymakers wish to build accountability systems around achievement growth, then it is imperative to understand the distinction between individual growth and system-level effectiveness. It is not uncommon to hear phrases such as "student growth," "school growth," or "district growth" used without serious consideration of what, for example, "school growth" means. Does school growth refer to the aggregate growth rate of students in a given school, or does it refer to changes (i.e., aggregate-level change) in effectiveness at the school level? The two represent fundamentally different, but related, concepts—each of which provides information about the quality of the education system. In essence, individual growth is a function of system-level effectiveness. Where policy is concerned with increasing education effectiveness, how effectiveness trickles down to expectations for individual student growth has not been well articulated.

Student growth percentiles quantify the levels of student growth that can be expected given the current levels of system effectiveness. That is, the growth percentiles derived from the conditional distributions express what is, as opposed to what should be. An example of a conditional distribution is depicted in Figure 8.4 in grade 6/2007. In a more effective system, the conditional distributions would be shifted upwards by some amount depending upon the magnitude of increase in educational quality. How large of a shift can be expected? Linn (2003) has put forward the notion of an existence proof in setting accountability system goals. He argued that ambitious achievement or growth targets should be set based upon realizable targets.

This requires the use of normative data such as student growth percentiles to inform accountability targets. The norm, or fiftieth percentile, does not automatically become the target. Rather, the full range of the normative distribution of growth rates helps to say what is possible and to clarify how likely it is that ambitious growth rates can be attained.

Using student growth percentiles, one could define individual target growth rates to be at, for example, the seventy-fifth percentile of growth rates. Setting ambitious growth rate targets explicitly, such as the seventy-fifth percentile of the original distribution, makes it possible to say what is expected in terms of increased effectiveness of the system. In other words, expected (i.e., average) growth in a more effective system would coincide with what is currently seventy-fifth percentile growth. Based upon this envisioned shift in the distributions, it is also possible to calculate what changes would result for increases in percentages of students at the different performance levels. If school achievement targets are set in a manner consistent with realizable individual student growth outcomes, it is possible nonetheless to demonstrate that such targets would result in truly impressive increases in the percentage of students reaching proficiency.

Recent flexibility in federal accountability requirements has given states the opportunity to augment their current status-based accountability systems with growth analysis techniques. However, when Secretary of Education Spellings announced a growth model pilot program in November 2005, proposal guidelines stipulated that models submitted for consideration must maintain NCLB's 2014 universal proficiency mandate. Unfortunately, the rush to modify the criteria by which AYP for schools is determined has led states to put forward models that fail to address significant shortcomings of the accountability mandates of the original legislation (Dunn and Taylor, 2007).

Normatively situating student growth avoids many of the traps imposed by current models by separating the description of growth—the student growth percentile—from the question of how much growth is enough. Distinguishing what a current year's growth is and deciding what it *should* be is not the same. The question of what a current year's growth is can be addressed statistically; the question of what a current year's growth *should* be, however, can't be answered solely by statistical means. For example, it might be that fiftieth percentile growth should be the expectation for the current year's growth for a given starting point. If such growth is deemed inadequate, however, then higher growth percentiles could be designated as the criterion for meeting the desired "year's growth." Clearly, the most obvious criteria to use in determining what a year's growth should be are to consider individual student growth toward performance standard attainment.

Consistent with the desire to qualify student growth relative to performance-level attainment, the most popular model submitted by states for accountability purposes under the growth model pilot program is the "growth toward a standard model," which use prior student achievement scores to make projections about whether students are on track to be proficient within a given allotment of time (usually three years). Such analyses are attractive from a policymaking perspective because they combine analyses of growth based upon scale scores with the performance standards on which accountability systems rest. The models implicitly define what a year's growth should be based upon adequate growth toward the proficiency standard in a given time frame. However, the models lack any context for judging whether such a standard is attainable. For example, does reaching proficiency in three years require a growth exceeding the eightieth percentile of growth for students starting at a similar level of proficiency? If so, is it reasonable to expect such performance knowing that, based upon prior data, 80 out of 100 students will not meet the declared growth targets? Establishing growth percentile targets using performance standards requires explicit consideration of the likelihood of meeting such criteria. This is Linn's existence proof (Linn, 2003) employed at the individual level.

Although the growth-toward-a-standard conceptualization used in current pilot programs begins with individual student growth, because what a year's growth should be is ill-defined, the aggregate school results derived from such models fail to provide a valid measure of school effectiveness and do not correct for the fundamental flaws in AYP. For a given school, the models yield a percentage of students projected to be proficient. However, this percentage confounds the present achievement level of students at the school with the school's effectiveness. Specifically, high achieving schools will have to make less growth to meet AYP-determined growth targets and therefore will be declared effective based on the entering characteristics of their students (Dunn & Taylor, 2007). Student growth percentiles offer a context in which to establish challenging, realistic, and easy to understand year's growth goals. Debates will ensue about whether uniform or non-uniform student growth percentile goals should be established. Such debates form the basis of productive discussions concerning the interface between student growth and its relationship to education quality.

Acknowledgments

The author is grateful to Steve Ponisciak, Lloyd Bond, Lorrie Shepard, and Katherine Ryan for providing careful reviews and constructive suggestions for improving the technical quality and readability of the chapter and to Andrea Solarz for editorial assistance.

Notes

1. A measure's inclusion in a cell merely suggests its intended purpose. It does not imply all such measures are equally valid.

2. The use of prior information or covariates to assess effect subtly weaves a causal web that is not well grounded. Lord's paradox (1967) and its resolution by Holland and Rubin (1983) demonstrate the limits of using prior data to attribute and quantify causal effects. See Briggs and Wiley in this edition.

References

Ballou, D., Sanders, W., & Wright, P. (2004). Controlling for student background in value-added assessment for teachers. *Journal of Educational and Behavioral Statistics*, 29 (1), 37–65.

Braun, H. I. (2005). *Using student progress to evaluate teachers: A primer on value-added models* (Policy Information Perspective). Princeton, NJ: Educational Testing Service.

Carlson, D. (2001). Focusing state educational accountability systems: Four methods for judging school quality and progress. Unpublished manuscript. Online, available at: http://www.nciea.org/publications/Dale020402.pdf (accessed June 25, 2007).

Cole, T. J. (1988). Fitting smoothed centile curves to reference data. *Journal of the Royal Statistical Society, Series A—General*, 151 (3), 385–418.

Cole, T. J. (1994). Growth charts for both cross-sectional and longitudinal data. *Statistics in Medicine*, 13, 2,477–2,492.

Cole, T. J. & Green, P. J. (1992). Smoothing reference centile curves: The LMS method and penalized likelihood. *Statistics in Medicine*, 11, 1,305–1,319.

Dunn, J. L. & Taylor, M. A. (2007, April). Modeling growth: Purposes and consequences of using various models. Paper presented at the annual meeting of the National Council on Measurement in Education, Chicago, IL.

Edley, C. (2006, April 10). Educational "opportunity" is the highest civil rights priority: So, what should researchers and lawyers do about it? [Video of speech with slides]. Invited address presented at the annual meeting of the American Educational Research Association, San Francisco, CA. Online, available at: http://www.cmcgc.com/Media/WMP/260407/63_011_files/Default.htm#nopreload=-1 (accessed June 1, 2007).

Holland, P. W. & Rubin, D. B. (1983). On Lord's paradox. In H. Wainer and S. Messick (Eds.), *Principles of modern psychological measurement* (pp. 3–25). Hillsdale, NJ: Lawrence Erlbaum Associates.

Linn, R. L. (2003, July). *Accountability: Responsibility and reasonable expectations* (CSE Report 601). Los Angeles, CA: Center for the Study of Evaluation, CRESST.

Linn, R. L., Baker, E. L., & Betebenner, D. W. (2002). Accountability systems: Implications of requirements of the No Child Left Behind Act of 2001. *Educational Researcher*, 31 (6), 3–16.

Lord, F. M. (1967). A paradox in the interpretation of group comparisons. *Psychological Bulletin*, 68 (5), 304–305.

Popham, J. (2004, May 26). Shaping up the "No Child" act: Is edge-softening enough? *Education Week*, 38 (23), 40.

Quetelet, L. A. J. (1871). *Anthropometrie*. Brussels: C. Muquardt.

Raudenbush, S. W. (2004). What are value-added models estimating and what does this imply for statistical practice? *Journal of Educational and Behavioral Statistics*, 29 (1), 121–129.

Rubin, D. B., Stuart, E. A., & Zanutto, E. L. (2004). A potential outcomes view of value-added assessment in education. *Journal of Educational and Behavioral Statistics*, 29 (1), 103–116.

Sanders, W. L., Saxton, A. M., & Horn, S. P. (1997). The Tennessee value-added assessment system: A quantitative outcomes-based approach to educational assessment. In J. Millman (Ed.), *Grading teachers, grading schools: Is student achievement a valid evaluation measure?* (pp. 137–162). Thousand Oaks, CA: Corwin Press, Inc.

Wei, Y. & He, X. (2006). Conditional growth charts. *Annals of Statistics*, 34 (5), 2,069–2,097.

Wei, Y., Pere, A., Koenker, R., & He, X. (2006). Quantile regression methods for reference growth charts. *Statistics in Medicine*, 25, 1, 369–1,382.

9
Causes and Effects

Derek C. Briggs and Edward W. Wiley

Educational accountability systems and causal inferences are inextricably linked. This is because all accountability systems provide both some measure of the current status of student academic achievement, and the extent to which this status is changing each year. At the same time, students within schools are constantly being exposed to what we might think of as "educational treatments." Examples of such treatments might be the curricular choices or teaching strategies taken within classrooms, or administrative policies invoked to regulate student behavior. In a broader sense, most accountability systems appear to conceptualize teachers and schools themselves as educational treatments to be evaluated. Once stakeholders are given systematic information about student achievement, it is a natural tendency to speculate about the causal role that one or more of these educational treatments has played in producing achievement levels and changes in these levels over time. It is equally natural to speculate about *how* educational treatments may have managed to increase (or decrease) student achievement. The problem, of course, is that the act of speculating is subjective and open to debate. Even in the context of a controlled laboratory setting, making valid causal inferences is difficult, and clearly educational settings are far from controlled. From a policy standpoint we must recognize that to some extent, causal inferences about changes in student achievement will necessarily involve a mixture of speculation and science. The aim of this chapter is to help distinguish between the two, and to describe some approaches that help shift the causal inferences drawn from educational accountability systems toward a basis with greater reliance on science than on speculation.

Our framework for this chapter is based upon the idea that a causal inference, often expressed using the symbolic expression X → Y, can be separated into three elements: the *attribution* that it is in fact X (and not, say, Z) that is causing Y, the *estimation* of the effect of X on Y, and the *explanation* of how X is causing Y. It can be useful conceptually to recast these three elements in terms of different types of causal questions (Holland, 2004) that might be generated and addressed as part of accountability systems:

1. *Causal attribution*: what educational treatment(s) caused an observed change in student achievement?
2. *Causal estimation*: what is the magnitude of the effect of an educational treatment on student achievement?
3. *Causal explanation*: what is the mechanism by which one or more educational treatments lead to an observed effect on student achievement?

Although implicit or explicit answers to these three questions are typically present in every causal inference, in our view educational policy decisions and actions hinge primarily upon efforts to answer questions of causal estimation. Unlike causal attribution or explanations, estimating a causal effect is something for which we have a large body of statistical and research design theory available to guide practice. Given the combination of a well-designed experiment and associated statistical model, it becomes possible to support statements about a numeric value that represents the causal effect of an educational treatment on student achievement. The combination of study design and statistical analysis can also be used to rule out alternative explanations for the estimated effect. Once estimated, a causal effect can be used to support a subsequent causal attribution to an educational treatment, which in turn can lead to more informed investigations about the practice through which the treatment in producing the observed effect.

There are two fundamental steps to estimating a causal effect with a valid interpretation using the data generated by an accountability system. A first step is to conceptualize a frame of reference for the interpretation of the effect. For example, if students are the units of analysis, then the impact of some educational treatment on student achievement must be interpreted relative to the achievement outcome that *would have been observed* had students *not* been assigned to the treatment. Hence the frame of reference for an estimated effect is always the *counterfactual* outcome from a rival educational treatment, where the latter is quite frequently conceptualized in terms of "business as usual." However, defining this counterfactual situation is not straightforward in educational contexts, and because a counterfactual is not something that can be directly observed, it can only be approximated. This is done in practice by substituting the observed outcome for a different group of students not exposed to the treatment of interest as the counterfactual outcome of the students exposed to the treatment. This different group of students represents what is commonly known as a "control group." When the control group has been selected through random assignment, estimating a causal effect is relatively straightforward. Unfortunately, in educational contexts, even when a control group has been carefully established, students are seldom assigned to it at random. The upshot of this is that, absent any statistical adjustments, a causal effect that is estimated on the basis of comparing the observed achievement outcomes of treatment and control groups will be biased—that is, the estimated value of the causal effect will tend to over- or underestimate the true value. A second step needed to estimate a causal effect is to adjust for bias in the estimated effect. The ability of any accountability system to support causal estimation will depend upon the way that the system provides the information and analyses such that these two steps necessary for causal estimation can be taken.

A point of emphasis in this chapter is that while the steps above are related (e.g., if the control group has been ideally established, there will be no need to adjust for bias), they should be distinguished conceptually. Our view, which is consonant with that expressed by Rubin, Stuart, & Zannato (2004) and Raudenbush (2004b) when discussing educational accountability, is that too much focus is often placed upon statistical solutions to bias in estimated causal effects (step 2) when the more daunting problem is that the causal effect being estimated has an ambiguous interpretation because insufficient thought has been given to how the control group has been defined (step 1).

This chapter now focuses in turn upon the way that educational accountability systems in the United States are, or can be, used to address each of the three types of causal questions we have introduced above. Accountability systems readily lend themselves to causal attribution because any quantification of student academic achievement invariably leads to comparisons with other students and schools. As we illustrate first, when such comparisons are favorable, there is a natural inclination to attribute praise; when such comparisons are not favorable, there is a natural inclination to attribute blame. Yet, student achievement outcomes are likely to be influenced by many different causes; hence, even when one or more causal attributions are plausible, they can only be evaluated substantively by estimating and interpreting the size of the effect associated with a hypothesized cause. We then reach the heart of this chapter; in it we introduce what is known as the *potential outcomes model* for causal inference. We use fundamental concepts from the potential outcomes model to evaluate two approaches for estimating causal effects that could be taken using the information available within state accountability systems. The first approach involves the use of a school comparability index; the second approach involves the use of value-added assessment. Third, we move from questions of causal estimation to questions of causal explanation. The latter is typically of greatest interest to the educational research community, and can only be addressed through sustained and intensive long-term programs of research through a combination of qualitative and quantitative research methods. We conclude by summarizing some general principles for making causal inferences on the basis of data from educational accountability systems.

Making Causal Attributions

It is typically assumed that the test scores that form the basis for state accountability systems are valid descriptive measures of what students know and can do in a given subject area.[1] When aggregate test score performance at the school level is presented to the public, explicit causal inferences are rarely made. Yet, as the passages below illustrate, the slope from description to causal attribution is a slippery one.

> An impressive 87% of Alabama's 1,364 public schools met state standards in reading and math, according to the latest progress reports of test results released Monday. In all, 1,194 schools met standards this year in reading and math, up from 725 schools, or 53%, of the total a year ago. The jumps are remarkable considering that two years ago seven in 10 public schools failed their first attempt to meet tougher standards driven by the No Child Left Behind law. [State School Superintendent Joe] *Morton credited the improvement in test results over the past two years to lots of things—the impact of the Alabama Reading Initiative in improving the teaching of reading, a similar effort in math and science instruction, and the plain hard work of teachers.* But, he said there is more. "I can tell you there is an atmosphere in Alabama schools today that is very different, an atmosphere and culture of learning and a belief that all children can learn," he said. "…I think that philosophy permeates schools now like never before. I think it's a total cultural shift."
>
> (Dean, 2006, p. A5, italics added)

> With the act requiring all children to be proficient or advanced by 2014, state Education Secretary Gerald Zahorchak said, "Pennsylvania remains on track statewide toward our 2014 NCLB requirements." Last year, 80.6% of schools and 89.8% of districts met AYP [adequate yearly progress] or made progress. "*This is progress and progress made due to the classroom teachers and support staff at every level, including the teachers as well as district staff and community members*," said Dr. Zahorchak. He also credited state investments in early childhood programs and tutoring pushed by Gov. Ed Rendell as well as high expectations and the spotlight created by the standards.
>
> (Chute, 2006, p. A1, italics added)

> Recently released test scores for the latest Illinois Standards Achievement Test, or ISAT, show improvement in the Alton School District over scores taken in 2003. The test is given each April to third- through eighth-graders at all Illinois public schools. Alton officials said that in 2003, white third-graders performed 31 percentage points better on the

> math section of the ISAT than minority, or black, students. In 2006, that gap narrowed by 16 percentage points, but white students in general still performed better on the test. "School districts across the nation search for consistent ways to close achievement gaps between white and black students," Assistant Superintendent Don Lindsey said in a statement. *"Our ISAT data is indicative of our district's success in closing the gap over the past four years." Alton school administrators say teachers are the primary reason students—and not just minority students—are doing better.*
>
> (Lucchesi, 2006, italics added)

In all three of these excerpts from newspaper reports, some outcome based on the test scores within a state accountability system has been observed: more public schools have met state academic performance standards, more schools and districts have made adequate yearly progress (AYP), and the white–black achievement gap has narrowed. In each case, the outcome represents a change from what had been previously observed, and constitutes a noteworthy "effect" (which we define rather loosely at this point). It is natural to attribute such effects to one or more possible educational treatments: newly implemented curricula, tutoring, improved teaching, and the like. In these examples, the attributions are all positive ones as they dole out praise and credit to the presumed causal agents. Of course, when the outcomes can be interpreted as negative effects, causal attributions often take on a different tone:

> "Every year more and more schools will not make adequate yearly progress because the bar keeps going higher, higher and higher," said Joan Raymond, superintendent of the South Bend Community School Corp. "Two years ago 57% of our students were expected to pass (the ISTEP exam). Now it's in the 60s, and by the year 2014, it will be 100%. *I can tell you right now," Raymond said, "that as long as there are children who are in financial need, who don't speak English as a first language, who are handicapped in some way, we're not going to make it."*
>
> (Wanbaugh, 2006, p. A1, italics added)

> [State Education Commissioner Richard P.] Mills also stressed that money alone was not enough. "You can see in those three school districts—Buffalo, Rochester and Syracuse—big drops in performance that occur right after the fourth grade, and it would lead me to ask what is the quality of the math program after the fourth grade?" he said. *Mr. Mills added that schools should review their programs, provide better training for teachers and scrutinize student test data to understand where weaknesses lie. He said the state would closely review the requirements for teacher training and would also enforce rules that teachers who earned*

> *their licenses since 1998 must attend at least 175 hours of training to remain certified.*
>
> (Herszenhorn, 2006, p. B3, italics added)

Paul Holland (2004) has remarked that "careless comparisons lead to casual causal inferences." Indeed, the problem with causal attributions that are byproducts of the test score information provided by accountability systems is that they are very difficult to defend against alternative attributions. For example, the test scores of students may increase or decrease for reasons that have nothing to do with changes in teaching practices. And, because there will usually be many causes of changes in test performance, the importance of one cause relative to another will almost always be unclear.

Estimating Causal Effects

In making causal attributions, we start with an observed effect and speculate about a plausible cause. In causal estimation, we start with a hypothesized cause and then formally estimate the effect of that cause. Two examples of causal estimation in the context of the data provided by an accountability system might be as follows:

1. What is the effect of implementing a mandatory study hall period during high school on tenth grade student performance on a state-mandated reading test?
2. What is the effect of a school on the gains of its students on a state-mandated reading test from ninth to tenth grade?

Both questions have a similar structure, and both can be answered in terms of one or more numeric values. There are also some apparent differences between the two questions in terms of the educational treatment that represents the "cause" (a study hall versus a school), and the variable that represents the outcome (tenth grade test scores versus test score gains from ninth to tenth grade). For each question we would need to consider the two steps to estimating a causal effect that we have previously identified: (1) establishing the right control group, and (2) adjusting for bias in the estimated effect. The potential outcomes model provides a framework for conceptualizing this process.

Conceptualizing Causal Effects with the Potential Outcomes Model

In what follows, we illustrate the principles of the potential outcomes model[2] using the hypothetical study hall scenario from example 1 above. We begin by defining three key elements of the model: the units of analysis, the specific educational treatment (or treatments) that some or all of these units have received, and the response outcome of interest. In this case, we assume that the students enrolled in a particular school are the units of analysis, the single educational treatment is attending a study hall period, and the response outcome is a score on a standardized reading test. The crux of the potential outcome model is the concept that for each student, there is more than one outcome that we could observe: the test score if the student is required to attend study hall (i.e., cause #1), and the test score if the student is not required to attend study hall (i.e., cause #2). If both of these potential outcomes could actually be observed, it would be easy enough to calculate the *unit-level causal effect* of study hall as the difference in test scores for each student. The unit-level causal effect indicates the amount by which any given student's reading score increases (or decreases) because he or she attended study hall. Given *N* students, a one-number summary of the *average causal effect* of study hall could be readily computed by summing all the unit-level causal effects and then dividing by *N*. This number indicates the average amount by which the typical student's reading score would increase (or decrease) because he or she was required to attend study hall.

The fundamental problem of causal inference is that neither a unit level nor an average causal effect can be directly computed, because for any student only one potential outcome can eventually be observed. A statistical solution to this problem is to think of the average causal effect of study hall as an unknown population parameter about which we would like to make inferences. Because the average causal effect is based upon the difference between the averages of our two potential outcomes—both of which are also unknown—we can take a familiar approach in inferential statistics: a random sample is taken from a defined population, a sample statistic is computed, and that statistic is compared to some hypothesized population parameter. In this case, if there are *N* students in a school, and two potential outcomes per student, the population consists of the 2**N* potential outcomes. From this population we will take two samples of students. Sample 1 receives the mandatory study hall and sample 2 does not. We can estimate an average causal effect for study hall as the difference in average test scores for these two samples, and then compare this to some hypothesized value (i.e., a null hypothesis of no treatment effect).

The critical distinction in this example between the average causal effect—which cannot be directly observed and is, therefore, an unknown parameter—and the average causal effect that is estimated, is somewhat subtle. The former is based upon a comparison of the averages of two different *potential* outcomes for the *same* group of students (i.e., sample size in each group = N); in the latter we are comparing two different *observed* outcomes for two *different* groups of students (i.e., sample size in each group < N). From the perspective of statistical inference, the key issue is whether we are able to get an unbiased estimate of the average causal effect. This depends upon the way that the two student samples in our hypothetical example have been selected.

The counterfactual of interest here is the average test score outcome for the students in sample 1 had they not attended study hall. When students have been selected into samples 1 and 2 (i.e., treatment and control groups) at random by the researcher, the average test score outcome for those students in sample 2 who do not attend study hall will generally be a good approximation for this counterfactual.

When students are non-randomly assigned to treatment and control groups (as is the case in the observational study designs typical of educational research), this is likely to introduce some bias into our estimated causal effect. For example, suppose the students selected for the control group in sample 2 tended to have higher grade point averages than those students selected for the treatment group in sample 1. Given that prior academic achievement is positively correlated with subsequent test performance, we would expect that the average test score observed for the control group overestimates the average test score (i.e., the counterfactual outcome) that would have been observed had students in the treatment group not attended study hall. If this were the case and no other statistical adjustments were made, the average causal effect for study hall would be underestimated (i.e., biased downwards).

Note that the interpretation of an estimated causal effect under the potential outcomes model depends almost entirely upon how well the average outcome for units exposed to some control condition approximates the average counterfactual outcome for units exposed to the treatment condition. This is what we mean when we say that establishing the right control group is the first step in causal estimation. For our example above, this raises an interesting question: if study hall is the experience a student receives in the treatment, is the counterfactual outcome based upon the experience students would have had if they were instead sent home from school one period early? Or, is it based upon the experience students would have had if additional time had instead been allotted for test coaching during existing English classes? The relative interpretation of our estimated causal effect will depend upon which "alternate cause" defines the counterfactual of interest. Carefully evaluating (and if necessary, adjusting for) the match between counterfactual and control group is the second step to causal estimation. If a study hall has been implemented at the school level, it will not be possible to assign students randomly within the same school to a control condition that matches whatever counterfactual scenario is of interest to the school. Instead, a control group of students would have to be selected either from past students or from students attending different schools. To mitigate selection bias, either a strategy would need to be used to match students purposely in study halls to a comparable control group before estimating a causal effect, or some statistical procedure would need to be used to adjust for preexisting differences in the two groups of students after the fact. We now consider how each of these strategies can be employed on the basis of the information being made available in contemporary accountability systems.

Estimating the Effect of Study Hall on Reading Achievement Using the School Comparability Index

One example of an operational accountability system that provides the kind of information a school could use to select an appropriate control group for the study hall example is California's "School Characteristics Index" (SCI; Technical Design Group of the Advisory Committee for the Public Schools Accountability Act of 1999, 2000). The SCI was created in response to a legislative mandate (the California Public School Accountability Act) that required any school ranking system to include a comparison to schools with similar characteristics. Under California law, each school receives a measure of absolute performance (known as the "Academic Performance Index" or API) as well as a measure meant to reflect its academic performance relative to schools facing similar challenges. Technical details of the SCI can be found on the California Department of Education website.[3] In short, school demographic characteristics (e.g., mobility rates), teacher quality measures (e.g., credential status), and operational characteristics (e.g., average class size) are used to calculate the SCI as a means of establishing for each school a unique comparison group of 100 schools. A school's "similar schools rank"—its API decile ranking relative to the API scores of only those 100 schools in its unique comparison group—provides a measure of that school's performance relative to those schools most comparable to it.

California's SCI is used as a complement to its absolute performance measures as part of the state accountability system; however, by providing a basis for comparison it could also be used to estimate the effects of a school-level educational treatment. Consider the following hypothetical case. South Pasadena High School (SPHS) in California has implemented a mandatory study hall period as of the 2007–2008 school year. After a few years with the study hall in place, Ms. Ramirez, the principal of SPHS, would like to evaluate whether this intervention has had an effect on achievement as measured by the API. Assume in what follows that California's accountability system includes data that would help Ms. Ramirez identify all high schools in the state that have or have not implemented a mandatory study hall. (We return to consider the plausibility of this assumption in our discussion at the end of this chapter.)

Ms. Ramirez could look to the SCI as a means of choosing an appropriate control group. Doing so would help identify a sizeable comparison group of California high schools similar to SPHS in terms of student characteristics, teacher experience, and operational characteristics. The SCI can be used to help schools select an appropriate control group (the first step in causal estimation), and this in turn might help schools adjust for the bias introduced by non-random assignment of students to treatments (the second step in causal estimation). However, while this is a good adjustment to make, it is relatively crude. To the extent that there are systematic differences between SPHS and its comparison schools not captured by the SCI (for example, preexisting differences in academic achievement), the estimated effect may still be biased, hindering an objective evaluation of the study hall intervention.

Estimating the Effects of Schools Using a Value-Added Assessment Approach

In the second example we posed at the outset of this part of the chapter, the educational treatment appears to be the school itself, and the outcome of interest is now a change in test scores. This is probably the most common causal question that is posed (at least implicitly) under a state accountability system, and it merits closer inspection relative to the potential outcomes model. Our specific focus here is on the statistical approach that underlies what is known as value-added assessment (VAA), and how this approach might work in conjunction with the two steps to causal estimation. First, it is important to understand the rationale for taking a VAA approach.

Policymakers intuitively understand the "Beverly Hills" problem: school test scores tend to be strongly correlated with the average wealth of the families in a given community. Therefore, status measures of student achievement at one point in time may reveal little about the quality of teaching and learning going on in schools and classrooms. To hold schools accountable, policymakers would prefer to measure the contribution each school makes to changes in student achievement. This would be the "value added" by a school.[4] Value-added assessment has become increasingly popular in the context of accountability systems because it offers the potential to estimate the effect of a specific school on student achievement independent of the influences of race, socioeconomic status, and other contextual factors. Currently, the most widely used program is the Educational Value-Added Assessment System (EVAAS; SAS Corporation, n.d.). Some form of the EVAAS has been implemented (or is being considered for implementation) in over 300 school districts in 21 states. The statistical models that underlie VAA approaches such as the EVAAS are complex and incorporate techniques that, in theory, adjust for such factors as preexisting differences in the demographic and academic characteristics of students and the influence of previous schooling on test score growth (Ballou, Sanders, & Wright, 2004; McCaffrey, Lockwood, Koretz, & Hamilton, 2003; Sanders, Saxton, & Horn, 1997; Thum, 2003).

A necessary condition for the use of VAA to estimate school effects is the availability of longitudinal data on a collection of schools with student test scores that have been linked over time. A statistical model can then be used to estimate the average score increment each school has contributed to the achievement of its students in a current year over and above the achievement that had been observed for students in prior years. These "increments" are not interpretable as causal effects in and of themselves. For this we must establish—for each school—a control group of students to represent the average test score increment that would have been observed had students not attended the school being viewed as the educational treatment. In the EVAAS, this outcome is represented by the full sample of students across the collection of schools being analyzed. As a result, value-added school effects are estimated and interpreted relative to the average score gain contributed by all schools under analysis. For example, if the average test score gain for the students in all schools from ninth to tenth grade is 50 points, a very good school might have an effect of ten because their students gained an average of 60 points, and a poor school might have an effect of minus ten because their students averaged only a 40 point gain. A negative effect does not mean that students lost achievement, only that they did not gain as much as the average student in that grade.

It is easy to see why taking a VAA approach appears to be an improvement over the more implicit and speculative approaches that may be used to drive causal inferences about school effectiveness. An example of the latter can be taken from the accountability context of the 2001 reauthorization of the Elementary and Secondary Education Act, "No Child Left Behind" (NCLB). NCLB attached high stakes to schools making progress toward accountability targets and required every state to set its own standards for measuring AYP. This was accomplished within each state by first deciding upon the test score required for students to be classified as "proficient" in a given subject and then by deciding on a progress trajectory that would lead to 100% proficiency classification in 2014. The law specified that the baseline for percent proficient be set at the level earned by the twentieth percentile of schools in 2002. In Figure 9.1, the bold solid line shows the AYP targets set in Colorado for high school mathematics. In 2002, the percent of students reaching proficiency in mathematics at the twentieth percentile of schools was 47%; therefore, the baseline was set at 47% proficient. Colorado's AYP targets increase every three years; hence the stair-step graph leading to 100% proficiency in 2014.

As we have already argued, causal inferences about school effectiveness in accountability contexts such as NCLB are naturally driven by causal attribution. Yet these sorts of inferences, made primarily on the basis of comparisons between a school's performance status and AYP progress targets, can become nonsensical once we take the trouble to conceptualize them as estimated causal effects. In Figure 9.1, the dashed line is an example of a low performing school that is making substantial gains of 5% per year from 2002 to 2014. Yet for each year, one could theoretically estimate the "effect" of the school on student performance under NCLB as consistently negative because the performance status of this school is below the AYP target line in each year. In contrast, the plain solid line illustrates an initially high performing school that

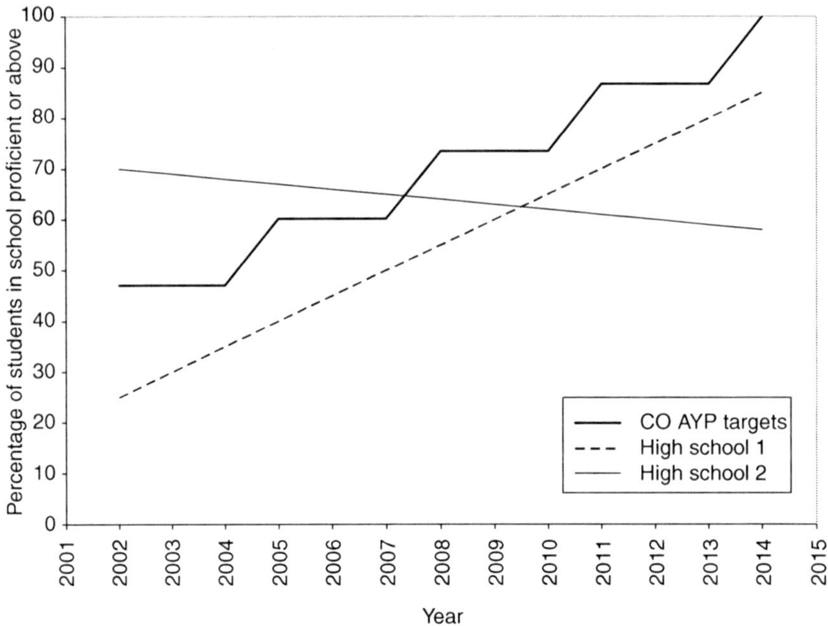

Figure 9.1 Estimating Causal Effects on the Basis of Status and Growth Under NCLB.

is not making progress, yet because its performance status is above the AYP target until the 2008 school year, the annual school effect could be estimated as positive up until 2009. From the perspective of the two steps of causal estimation we have been describing, the problem with such causal effects should be apparent: (1) the match between the control outcome (the AYP target for each school in each year) and the counterfactual outcome of interest is unclear, and (2) no attempt is being made to adjust for probable bias in the estimated effect.

Applying a VAA approach would change our interpretation of school effects with respect to both steps of causal estimation. First, each estimated school effect would be relative to a control group outcome based upon the average progress that students across all schools in an accountability system actually make. In this sense, the control outcome is one that is norm-referenced rather than criterion-referenced, and this might be viewed as a safeguard against unrealistic or implausible expectations for school progress. By contrast, the set of AYP targets presented in Figure 9.1 provide a criterion-referenced control outcome that represents expectations for the average progress that all schools *should* make. Unfortunately, there is no guarantee that the latter will also represent the average progress that all schools *could* make, and this represents an obvious and well-understood disconnect between the requirements for AYP under the NCLB policy and what Bob

Linn has described as "reasonable expectations" (Linn, 2003). Second, a VAA approach would adjust for preexisting differences among schools by estimating annual effects as a function of the *change* in student achievement from year to year. Because of this, the annual effects estimated for the school showing positive growth over time in Figure 9.1 would be higher than those estimated for the school showing negative growth over time. This would be the case even before the year 2009, when the initially low performing school surpasses the other in terms of both growth and status.

Of course, the examples of growth trajectories displayed in Figure 9.1 are both hypothetical and extreme. A key question for policymakers is the extent to which empirical estimates of school effects based solely upon current year achievement status differ considerably from those estimated on the basis of growth in achievement. Using nationally representative longitudinal data for students in elementary, middle and high school levels, Raudenbush (2004a) examined the correlation between school effect estimates based upon status and growth for different academic subjects. The resulting values ranged from extremes of 0.0 to 0.9, with moderate positive values between 0.3 and 0.7 being most typical. Raudenbush makes a compelling case to support the contention that causal inferences based solely upon comparisons of status are "scientifically indefensible" by examining the annual achievement trajectories of students from low- and high-poverty schools. These trajectories are for the most part parallel. In other words, although low-poverty schools had student achievement at higher levels than high-poverty schools in any given year, the average growth in achievement across years was about the same. It seems clear that when the data from accountability systems are being used to estimate school effects, then VAA approaches that adjust for preexisting differences in student achievement using longitudinal data are an improvement over approaches that do not make any adjustments.

There are however, some considerable limitations to what a VAA such as the EVAAS can accomplish as a tool for estimating causal effects. To begin with, the interpretation of value-added school effects that are estimated using the EVAAS is somewhat ambiguous. A control group outcome based upon the normative progress of all schools may not be very meaningful as a representation of the counterfactual outcome of interest: the test performance of students had they attended a specific different school (i.e., a school in geographic proximity to the treatment school). We may not be very interested in the experience of students at the "average" school but at a different school that students could have plausibly attended. A related problem with the causal interpretation of a value-added effect is that the definition of a school as an educational treatment is at best vague, a point that has been illustrated clearly by both Rubin et al. (2004) and Raudenbush (2004b) in their evaluations of VAA relative to the potential outcomes model. Raudenbush and Willms (1995) have distinguished what they call type A and type B school effects. For a type A school effect, the treatment consists of a combination both of school context (e.g., social environment) and school practice (e.g., teaching, choice of curriculum). For a type B school effect, the treatment consists solely of school practice. Raudenbush (2004b) points out that though type A effects are probably of greatest interest to parents, type B effects are of greatest interest to policymakers. While Raudenbush suggests that models such as the EVAAS may provide good estimates of type A effects, he is pessimistic about the prospects for estimating type B effects because there are no good ways to separate school context and practice.

Braun (2005) describes what he terms the "fundamental concern" about the statistical models used for VAA: whether value-added systems can in fact reliably estimate the effect of a particular school on student learning, given that students are not randomly assigned to schools. To illustrate Braun's concern, we summarize the results of an empirical analysis in which different specifications of the EVAAS were applied to estimate annual school effects. The data consist of the longitudinal reading test scores for a cohort of students that was in grade 4 in 2001 and in grade 8 in 2005. This cohort, taken from a mid-sized state west of the Mississippi, includes 17,839 students that attended 191 elementary schools (K-5) and 65 middle schools (6–8). The two specifications of the EVAAS we present here differ in terms of assumptions made about the cumulative persistence of schools effects. In most applications of the EVAAS, it is assumed that the effect of a school on student achievement in earlier grades persists undiminished into future grades. However, this assumption can be relaxed to allow for the possibility, intuitively plausible, that school effects decay over time (McCaffrey, Lockwood, Koretz, Louis, & Hamilton, 2004; Lockwood, McCaffrey, Mariano, & Setodji, 2007).

Different school effects for grades 5 through 8 were estimated using each specification of the EVAAS. The correlations of these estimated effects for grades 5 through 8 were 0.58, 0.67, 0.85, and 0.95. For grades 5 and 6 in particular, it appears that many schools with positive or negative effects under

Table 9.1 Cross-Tabulation of School Effects in EVAAS Model Specifications with Different Assumptions about Cumulative Persistence

	Complete persistence not assumed			
	Effect	–	*0*	+
Complete persistence assumed	–	13	6	1
	0	34	82	31
	+	0	8	16

Note
Indicates that the estimated school effect would be flagged as likely to be negative, 0 indicates the estimated school effect could not be reasonably distinguished from zero, and ± indicates that the estimated school effect would be flagged as likely to be positive.

one specification do not appear to have effects that can be distinguished from "0" under another. This point is demonstrated in Table 9.1. The rows and columns of this table display the estimated value-added school effects from grade 5 in three categories: negative, zero, or positive. The classification of schools across the rows is based upon estimates for the specification of the EVAAS in which complete persistence is assumed. The classifications across columns are based upon the specification in which this assumption is relaxed. Where a school is classified depends principally upon the precision with which school effects are being estimated. The more precisely school effects are being estimated, the more likely we can distinguish schools as having positive or negative effects. If the two models resulted in the same classifications, we would expect to see all schools along the diagonal cells of the table—clearly this is not the case. Under the traditional specification of the EVAAS, 23% (44 out 191 elementary schools) can be classified as having either positive or negative effects. Under the specification of the EVAAS in which school effects are not assumed to persist undiminished, there is a dramatic increase in our ability to distinguish schools: 50% of the schools can now be classified as having either positive or negative effects. This demonstrates that the way statistical models such as the EVAAS are specified can have important ramifications for the ability of these models to reliably estimate school effects.

There are a number of other technical issues that have yet to be resolved with respect to how statistical models for VAA should be specified. These include:

- whether to model multiple subjects (e.g., math, reading, and writing) through a single *multivariate* model or separate *univariate* models;
- whether to *include* or *exclude* statistical controls for the demographic characteristics of students and schools;
- whether to model individual achievement growth *parametrically* or *nonparametrically.*

Until threats to the validity of the estimates derived from the many different types of VAA modeling approaches are better understood,[5] VAA-based estimates do not appear suitable as the primary basis for high-stakes estimates of school effects.

Explaining Causal Effects

Questions about causal explanation within an accountability system are quite different from those of causal estimation. The aim of causal estimation—to obtain a valid estimate for the magnitude of a causal effect—is fundamentally quite modest; though as we have pointed out, accomplishing this in educational settings can be challenging. Yet, an estimated causal effect in and of itself is unlikely to provide much insight about *how* a given cause leads to an observed effect. As one example, if we were to find that a curricular intervention led to a positive effect on reading achievement, this opens the door to a host of new questions about the way in which the new curricular approach facilitates students learning. These questions might range from those that would explore student, classroom, and school-level variables that interact with the curricular intervention, to those that explore the effect of the intervention from a cognitive perspective. As another example, Cohen, Raudenbush, and Ball (2003) make the case that estimating the causal effect of school resources on student achievement should be viewed as only a first step in the development of a broader model of causal explanation that takes into account the moderating role of classroom instructional environments. In other words, while experimental designs and statistical modeling are a necessity to answer questions of causal estimation, they will typically be poorly suited to provide comprehensive answers to questions of causal explanation in the absence of a deep understanding of the classroom and school context in which learning takes place. These sorts of deep understandings require ongoing research programs that involve classroom observations and interviews with students, teachers, and school administrators.

A recent example in which causally explanative research questions have been combined with the estimation of causal effects can be found in a research project initiated by the RAND Corporation. In one study, McCaffrey, Rubin, Stuart, and Zannato (2006) estimated the effect of incorporating a value-added assessment program into Pennsylvania's statewide educational accountability system. McCaffrey et al. began by addressing a question of causal estimation: the achievement outcomes of students in school districts that had begun to report the results from using the value-added methodology were compared with the outcomes in similar districts that were not using the value-added methodology. In addition to this, qualitative information was gathered about *how* value-added results were being used by the schools to affect teaching and learning. In a related study, Stecher and Hamilton (2006) surveyed and interviewed teachers and administrators from a random sample of schools in three states (California, Georgia, and Pennsylvania) to find out how and the extent to which the results from state-mandated tests were being used to influence classroom instruction.

A second example of research exploring questions of causal explanation is the *California Best Practices Study* (*CBPS*), a three-year collaborative effort of Springboard Schools (formerly the Bay Area School Reform Collaborative), Just For The Kids—California, and the National Center for Educational Accountability (Springboard Schools, 2005, 2007a). Using California API data, the *CBPS* identified schools that were "high performing" relative to what would have been expected given their student demographics. Note that this identification is implicitly based upon finding schools with positive school effects, where the effect is estimated as the difference in observed performance and a counterfactual (the performance that was expected). These schools were matched with a control group of demographically similar but less successful schools to determine practices that contributed to school success. Such practices were explored via intensive site visits and interviews covering areas such as instructional and curricular goals, leadership, use of data, and self-monitoring. By uncovering practices that distinguish "high performing" schools from their less successful (but demographically comparable) counterparts, the *CBPS* approaches the causal explanation of mechanisms that led to identification of schools as "high performing." As the *CBPS* sponsors note, the study "does not offer conclusive causal analysis of how these disproportionately high performing sites reached these levels of achievement" (Springboard Schools, 2007b). Nonetheless, the *California Best Practices Study* provides an excellent example of how causal estimation can be used to support subsequent explorations of causal explanation.

Discussion

It is common to think of causal inference in terms of some cause, X, having an effect on some outcome, Y, as in X → Y. In this chapter we have broken this inferential process into three distinct elements: causal attribution, causal estimation, and causal explanation. To a great extent, answers to all three of these questions are necessary to establish the causal inference X → Y. In the context of educational accountability systems, causal inferences are most intuitively (and in our view erroneously) supported by making causal attributions; that is, by asserting the most important cause or causes after observing some perceived effect. The obvious candidates for causal attribution when student achievement changes are observed tend to be associated changes in educational practice or specific teachers or schools. Causal attributions are inherently speculative, and without establishing the magnitude of the effect associated with a specific cause through causal estimation, will be difficult to support. Causal estimation differs from causal attribution in answering questions about the effect of a given cause rather than the cause of a given effect. Valid answers to such questions require at least intuitive understanding of the foundations of the potential outcomes model, which helps to clarify explicitly the two key steps to estimating valid causal effects: (1) establishing the right control group and (2) adjusting for bias in the estimated effect. Finally, we have presented a third element of causal inference in which the focus is on explaining the mechanism through which one or more causes leads to one or more effects. Causal explanation is potentially the most important question that the information from an accountability system can be used to address, but while it hinges upon an underlying understanding of causal effects, it also requires long-term programs of research that employ both quantitative analyses and qualitative explorations.

From the perspective of supporting causal inferences, educational accountability systems have two very useful features that can facilitate efforts to estimate the causal effects of educational treatments. First, to the extent that information about schools and the characteristics of their students is made publicly available in a centralized location (e.g., California's School Characteristics Index), the task of establishing proper control groups becomes more manageable. Second, the availability of longitudinal data on the academic performance of students and schools can be used to attempt to adjust statistically for the bias in estimated effects due to nonequivalent groups of students and schools (using, for example, value-added assessment approaches).

Both of these useful features also have some clear limitations. The first limitation is the difficulty of distinguishing school context from school practice. In our study hall example, it would do SPHS's principal Ms. Ramirez no good to find a comparable group of schools on the basis of contextual indicators using the SCI if no information is available to distinguish those schools that had implemented a study hall from those schools that had not. This difficulty also hinders the causal interpretation of value-added estimates of school effects. A related limitation is the ability of VAA statistical models to estimate reliable causal effects, particularly when schools are defined as the educational treatment of interest. These models are far better suited for estimating the effects of treatments that can be conceptualized as policy interventions. In our view, the value-added estimates of school effects that can be presently derived from the information in educational accountability systems are unlikely to be robust enough to support *high-stakes* causal inferences about school quality in educational settings.

Estimates of causal effects are best used in conjunction with other accountability indicators, and long-term programs of research exploring causal explanation. For example, the estimates of school effects using VAA methodology could form the basis for subsequent investigations of best practice using the approach taken by the *CBPS*. These investigations might lead to the identification of school practices that are hypothesized to bring about higher student achievement. Once identified, a new study could be conducted to estimate the effect associated with the identified practice (rather than the effect of a particular school) on student achievement. In this example, causal inference is an iterative and ongoing process of scientific investigation, cycling from the estimation of a causal effect, to the explanation of that effect, to the attribution of a new cause, to the estimation of a new effect, and so on. It is in this sense that an emphasis on causal estimation can go a long way in moving the basis of causal inferences from speculation to science.

Acknowledgments

The authors thank Henry Braun and Pete Goldschmidt for reviewing an earlier draft of this chapter. Special thanks to Lorrie Shepard for her constructive edits and suggestions.

Notes

1. This assumption of test validity is typically considered a precondition for making generalizable causal inferences (cf., Shadish, Cook, & Campbell, 2002). This topic is beyond the scope of this chapter; for a further discussion of test validity in accountability systems see Koretz (this volume).
2. This is also sometimes referred to as "Rubin's Causal Model" or the "Neyman–Rubin Causal Model." The seminal reference for this is Holland (1986). For more recent presentations see Rubin (2005) and Stuart (2007).
3. Online, available at: http://www.cde.ca.gov/ta/ac/ap/ (accessed December 13, 2006).
4. The use of VAA approaches has been as prevalent—if not more prevalent—in the context of estimating teacher effects. For consistency we focus on estimating school effects throughout; however, most of the same points will apply when VAA is being used to evaluate teachers instead of schools.
5. See, for example, the Spring 2004 issue of the *Journal of Educational and Behavioral Statistics* and two books (Lissitz, 2005, 2006) that summarize the presentations given at two conferences devoted to the topic of value-added assessment.

References

Ballou, D., Sanders, W., & Wright, P. (2004). Controlling for student background in value-added assessment of teachers. *Journal of Educational and Behavioral Statistics*, 29 (1), 37–65.

Braun, H. (2005, September). *Using student progress to evaluate teachers: A primer on value-added models* [Policy Information Perspective]. Princeton, NJ: Educational Testing Service.

Chute, E. (2006, August 4). Schools on track to meet standards. *Pittsburgh Post-Gazette*, p. A1.

Cohen, D., Raudenbush, S., & Ball, D. (2003). Resources, instruction, and research. *Educational Evaluation and Policy Analysis*, 25 (2), 119–142.

Dean, C. (2006, August 8). 87% of state schools meet progress standards. *Birmingham News*, p.A5.

Herszenhorn, D. (2006, October 12). Scores on state math tests dip with districts' income. *New York Times*, p. B3.

Holland, P. W. (1986). Statistics and causal inference (with discussion and rejoinder). *Journal of the American Statistical Association*, 81 (396), 945–970.

Holland, P. W. (2004, April). Evidence for causal inference in education research. Paper presented at the American Educational Research Association Presidential Invited Session on Inference, Evidence and Scientific Research, San Diego, CA.

Linn, R. (2003). Accountability: Responsibility and reasonable expectations. *Educational Researcher*, 32 (7), 3–13.

Lissitz, R. (2005). *Value added models in education: Theory and applications.* Maple Grove, MN: JAM Press.

Lissitz, R. (2006). *Longitudinal and value added models of student performance.* Maple Grove, MN: JAM Press.

Lockwood, J. R., McCaffrey, D. F., Mariano, L. T., & Setodji, C. (2007). Bayesian methods for scalable value-added assessment. *Journal of Educational and Behavioral Statistics*, 32 (2), 125–150.

Lucchesi, N. (2006, November 18). Achievement gap narrows. *Telegraph.* Online, available at: http://www.thetelegraph.com/ (accessed November 24, 2006).

McCaffrey, D., Lockwood, J. R., Koretz, D. M., & Hamilton, L. S. (2003). *Evaluating value-added models for teacher accountability* (Report MG-158). Santa Monica, CA: RAND Corporation.

McCaffrey, D., Rubin, D., Stuart, A., & Zannato, E. (2006, April). Design and implementation of case-control matching to estimate the effects of value-added assessment. Paper presented at the annual meeting of the American Educational Research Association, San Francisco, CA.

McCaffrey, D. F., Lockwood, J. R., Koretz, D., Louis, T. A., & Hamilton, L. (2004). Models for value-added modeling of teacher effects. *Journal of Educational and Behavioral Statistics*, 29 (1), 67–101.

No Child Left Behind Act of 2001, Pub. L. No. 107–110, 115 Stat. 1425 (2002). Online, available at: http://www.ed.gov/legislation/ESEA02/ (accessed July 22, 2007).

Raudenbush, S. W. (2004a). Schooling, statistics, and poverty: Can we measure school improvement? Paper presented at the William H. Angoff Memorial Lecture Series, Princeton, NJ. Online, available at: http://www.ets.org/Media/Education_Topics/pdf/angoff9.pdf (accessed November 16, 2006).

Raudenbush, S. (2004b). What are value-added models estimating and what does this imply for statistical practice? *Journal of Educational and Behavioral Statistics*, 29 (1), 121–129.

Raudenbush, S. & Willms, J. D. (1995). The estimation of school effects. *Journal of Educational and Behavioral Statistics*, 20 (4), 307–335.

Rubin, D. B. (2005). Causal inference using potential outcomes: Design, modeling, decisions. *Journal of the American Statistical Association*, 100 (469), 322–331.

Rubin, D., Stuart, A., & Zannato, E. (2004). A potential outcome view of value-added assessment in education. *Journal of Educational and Behavioral Statistics*, 29 (1), 103–116.

Sanders, W. L., Saxton, A. M., & Horn, S. P. (1997). The Tennessee value-added assessment system, a quantitative, outcomes-based approach to educational measurement. In Jason Millman (Ed.), *Grading teachers, grading schools: Is student achievement a valid evaluation measure?* (pp. 137–162). Thousand Oaks, CA: Corwin Press.

SAS Corporation (n.d.). *Schooling Effectiveness, SAS® EVAAS® for K-12.* Online, available at: http://www.sas.com/govedu/edu/services/effectiveness.html (accessed January 4, 2006).

Shadish, W., Cook, T., & D. Campbell. (2002). *Experimental and quasi-experimental designs for generalized causal inference.* Boston, CA: Houghton-Mifflin.

Springboard Schools (2005). *Challenged schools, remarkable results: Three lessons from California's highest achieving high schools.* San Francisco, CA: Springboard Schools.

Springboard Schools (2007a). *Balancing act: Best practices in the middle grades.* San Francisco, CA: Springboard Schools.

Springboard Schools (2007b). *California best practices study.* Online, available at: http://www.springboardschools.org/research/best_practices.html (accessed August 9, 2007).

Stecher, B. & Hamilton, L. (2006, April). Using test-score data in the classroom. (RAND Working Paper). Presented at the annual meeting of the National Council for Measurement in Education, San Francisco, CA.

Stuart, E. (2007). Estimating causal effects using school-level data sets. *Educational Researcher*, 36 (4), 187–198.

Technical Design Group of the Advisory Committee for the Public Schools Accountability Act of 1999 (2000, April). *Construction of California's 1999 school characteristics index and similar schools ranks* (PSAA Technical Report 00–1). Sacramento, CA: California Department of Education, Office of Policy and Evaluation. Online, available at: http://www.cde.ca.gov/ta/ac/ap/documents/tdgreport0400.pdf (accessed December 15, 2007).

Thum, Y. M. (2003). Measuring progress toward a goal: Estimating teacher productivity using a multivariate multilevel model for value-added analysis. *Sociological Methods and Research*, 32 (2), 153–207.

Wanbaugh, M. (2006, August 28). Schools feeling the bite of No Child Left Behind. *South Bend Tribune*, p. A1.

10
Fairness Issues and Educational Accountability

Katherine E. Ryan

Today, the role of high-stakes assessments in educational accountability is challenging long and enduring understandings about the function and character of testing in society. In essence, test-based accountability is now seen as a powerful policy lever used to steer school improvement (Linn, this volume). Although there were precursors in the 1980s and 1990s, it was the passage of No Child Left Behind (NCLB, 2002) legislation that institutionalized a reliance on standardized test score performance or test-based accountability as a key mechanism for improving student achievement.

At the outset I acknowledge that the goal of NCLB performance-based educational accountability is praiseworthy—to improve teaching and learning for all students. In this chapter, I examine fairness issues in relationship to high-stakes assessments and test-based accountability. I begin with a brief overview of accountability in the global context and in a democratic society (e.g., identifying inequities). After addressing the changing context of educational testing (high-stakes assessments and educational accountability), I discuss the implications of increasing stakes to the tests themselves and fairness concerns (measurement validity issues). Next, I examine fairness and test-based accountability by reviewing evidence concerning (a) how test results are used in educational accountability, (b) equity issues in opportunity to learn, and (c) consequences (e.g., do students learn more?). I close by proposing that an educational accountability model emphasizing *high standards* and *high quality educational conditions for all* are essential to formulating educational accountability that improves student learning and ensures educational equity.

Educational Testing Context Changes

The current preoccupation with educational accountability in the United States is part of a larger social transformation, known as New Public Management (NPM), that continues to intensify nationally and globally. This set of initiatives, which has resulted in significant changes in modern life, is characterized by a regulatory style that makes individuals and organizations accountable through auditable performance standards (Biesta, 2004; Power,

1997). These standards are intended to improve internal performance and to make these improvements externally confirmable and public.

The U.S. educational accountability context illustrates this kind of change, particularly since the passage of the No Child Left Behind Act of 2001 (NCLB, 2002). NCLB essentially legislates an educational accountability by which individuals and organizations are *evaluated* against auditable performance standards. By law, statewide learning standards are proposed with statewide tests administered to see if students are meeting the standards. In addition to tests, there are other auditing mechanisms (e.g., indicators such as attendance and teacher quality).

There is no argument here—educational accountability is a fundamental right of citizens in a democratic society serving the public interest. Importantly, educational equity is a critical public interest that is promoted by educational accountability. Test scores and other performance indicators are an efficient way to identify educational inequalities within and across school achievement comparisons (Rizvi, 1990). It is not possible to identify lagging performance generally or achievement gaps between groups without them.

However, today tests are not just being used to identify and describe achievement differences among student subgroups (e.g., race, ethnicity). As Brennan (2006) states, "It certainly appears that a testing revolution is underway in the country that is based on the nearly unchallenged belief, with very little supporting evidence, that high-stakes testing can and will lead to improved education" (p. 9). As noted by McDonnell (this volume), the critics who oppose the accelerated use of tests and intensified consequences have a very limited voice compared to the dominant belief system. The role of NCLB high-stakes testing shifts testing from its traditional role of achievement description, placement, and selection to holding students, teachers, and schools accountable for educational improvement.

When test results are used for potentially serious consequences like grade promotion, certification, or school closings, the assessment is characterized as *high stakes* (Madaus, 1988). As noted by Kane (2002), "... it is their consequences that insert the *high stakes*" (p. 31). High-stakes assessment consequences impact students, teachers, and schools. Although the goal of standards-based accountability is to improve teaching and learning for all, particular groups of students, teachers, and schools (e.g., low income) may be disproportionately affected by the unintended negative consequences.

The test score meanings or interpretations for students in different groups have been a challenging and compelling area of debate and research within the measurement community, the public, and the media for the past several decades. That measurement professionals, the public at large, and the media are sometimes in conflict about the test score meanings for different groups has further complicated this issue. However, this tension has also contributed in positive ways to the substantive and empirical study of assessment fairness.

I now provide a brief summary of assessment fairness issues related to bias in standardized assessments illustrating this tension, and I consider the implications for high-stakes assessments.

Fairness and Standardized Assessments

The notion that tests should be equitable for all students—free from bias to the extent possible—is a cardinal principle in educational measurement theory and practice today. For the purposes of this chapter, bias is defined as construct-irrelevant[1] elements (e.g., lack of clarity in instructions) in assessments or assessment process that lead to systematically higher or lower scores for identifiable groups of students (e.g., low income) (American Educational Research Association, American Psychological Association, and National Council of Educational Measurement (AERA), 1999; Camilli, 2006).

Assessment Fairness Perspectives

Although simply stated here, assessment fairness has been especially challenging to define. There are many definitions, sometimes competing, that highlight important concerns about assessment fairness. For example, there are *four* distinct perspectives on fairness presented in the *Standards for Educational and Psychological Testing* (AERA, 1999), with a caveat that there are many additional views that could be identified: (1) absence of bias, (2) equitable treatment for all examinees, (3) equality of testing outcomes for test-taking subgroups, and (4) equal opportunity to learn. There is broad agreement regarding the first two fairness perspectives—that tests should be as free from bias as possible and equitable for all test takers during the testing process (e.g., standardized testing procedures and comparable score use). The third perspective, equality of testing outcomes for all groups, essentially means no group differences in test score averages or no achievement gaps. Although the general public and members of the media often interpret score differences as evidence of bias, from a technical perspective, test score differences among groups are not considered to be evidence of bias. At the same time, however, the fourth perspective, opportunity to learn, is considered to be especially relevant in the educational accountability context. The *Test Standards* (AERA, 1999) emphasize that when decisions about student promotion are involved, evidence that students had the opportunity to learn the tested content and skills is required. If students did not have the opportunity to learn, the assumption that students failed to learn would be incorrect. Thus, rewards and sanctions based on accountability have the potential to create inequities. Nevertheless, the complexities involved with opportunity to learn and assessment fairness are significant (e.g., defining opportunity to learn). I discuss these issues at length later in the chapter.

Assessment Comparability and Assessment Fairness

Defining assessment fairness, developing quantitative methods and logical analysis to study these issues, and conducting empirical investigations of assessment fairness have been a primary concern and focus of study in the educational measurement community since the 1970s (Berk, 1982; Camilli & Shepard, 1994). While I agree in principle with Brennan (2006) who suggests that there is no "gold standard" with respect to assessment fairness, I find the work of Willingham and Cole (1997) and Cole and Zieky (2001) to be reasonable and representative of the consensus view of fairness in the measurement literature. Willingham and Cole (1997) present a definition for test fairness that is grounded within the notion of validity, the foundational concept of test theory. Conceptualizing test fairness as a feature of test validity, they suggest that test fairness is defined as comparability in assessment for all individuals and groups. Further, they propose three criteria for assessing test fairness that follow from the notion of comparability. These criteria include "comparable opportunities for examinees to demonstrate relative proficiency, comparable exercises and scores, and comparable treatment of examinees in test interpretation and use" (p. 11).

Assessment Fairness Origins

Historically, bias in tests was identified as an issue at the start of the twentieth century and perhaps earlier (Camilli & Shepard, 1994). In 1910, Binet examined whether some items measured family background instead of mental capacity (Binet & Simon, 1916/1973). In the 1950s, Eells, Davis, Havighurst, Herrick, and Tyler (1951) investigated the extent to which the substantial differences in test performance between groups (e.g., different gender or ethnic groups) could be test artifacts and what might be attributed to genuine performance differences. In the 1970s, these concerns intensified in response to the Civil Rights movement and Jensen's (1969) article arguing that group IQ differences (African American and white) were genetically based (Camilli & Shepard, 1994). Over the past 35 years, two lines of work have characterized assessment fairness in educational measurement: models of fair use in selection and item fairness models (Cole & Zieky, 2001).

Prediction and Selection

Both legal and social requirements for fairness in test use resulted in substantial research in studying test bias in relationship to external performance criteria. According to the equal prediction model, a test is considered unfair or biased if it either systematically underpredicts or overpredicts the criterion (assumed to be unbiased) in the selection for a particular group (e.g., African American compared to white) (Cleary, 1968). Unfairness in the testing process would occur if prediction is too low for members of a particular subgroup. Logically, it followed that tests like the Scholastic Assessment Test (SAT) were unfair if they predicted lower college performance for subgroups (e.g., African Americans) than those groups actually achieved.

Detecting underprediction proved to be challenging, in part because of technical issues. For example, the equal prediction model and others (Cole, 1973; Linn, 1973) assume that there is a reliable and valid criterion that is also unbiased, which is rare or possibly does not exist (Linn, 1984). In addition, prediction models usually do not include other factors that are important to successful performance. There is also the problem that ordinary measurement error can make a test look unbiased—even appear to overpredict for African Americans—when the underlying relationship between test and criterion is in fact biased.

The fair test use in selection literature reflects some of the enduring issues in assessment fairness research. First, trying to define fairness is very difficult. Further, technical solutions alone are not enough to address assessment fairness issues (ibid.). Ultimately, there is a question about whether in meeting social goals, individuals with higher test scores should be rejected while individuals with lower test scores should be accepted. Values, whether explicitly or implicitly defined, are embedded in the technical solutions.

Item Fairness

The study of item fairness has yielded important changes in testing practices. There has been important theoretical and empirical work in this area that has led to the inclusion of what are now routine procedures designed to improve item fairness and, in turn, overall test fairness. Moreover, this work pointed to several important conceptual distinctions that have led to a deeper and more rigorous understanding of subgroup performance differences.

Like fairness in selection, the origins of examining item performance differences in achievement are based on what were considered to be bias issues. Early contributions introduced new statistical methods for detecting bias in items (e.g., Linn, Levine, Wardrop, & Hastings, 1981) as a means of identifying particular item types that may be systematically biased for particular groups. For example, Linn and Harnish (1981) found math word problems to be differentially difficult for African American students unless the story problems incorporate material involving money. This finding turned out to be an early illustration of multidimensionality. Whether multidimensionality is a form of bias depended on whether the secondary dimensions or skills were defined as part of the construct measured.

As the notion of what bias meant shifted throughout the late 1970s and 1980s, the more neutral term "differential item functioning" (DIF) was proposed for the statistical techniques used as initial flags (Holland & Thayer, 1986). Differential item functioning refers to items that do not function the same for comparable members of different groups; it is a statistical finding.

Whether DIF is evidence of bias depends on the interpretation and judgment of the construct-related evidence that is available (Angoff, 1993; Shealy & Stout, 1993). Judgmental reviews, which also include examinations for offensive material, are used in conjunction with statistical findings to determine item fairness (Bond, 1993; Shepard, 1982).

Note again in this brief discussion on item fairness, there is continuing ambivalence about determining whether an item is fair or not, which reflects the larger issues characterizing assessment fairness. The technical tools can sometimes be helpful in finding troublesome items. However, they are not adequate for resolving the central question: when are group differences real and when do the differences reflect some bias or irrelevant source of difficulty in the item?

Sources of Assessment Bias

WHAT IS MEASURED

For the most part, standardized multiple-choice test scores in reading, math, and science are the key components for statewide and NCLB accountability decisions. Obviously, using only multiple-choice items for high-stakes testing is a significant constraint that limits what content is represented. Further, while subgroup test score differences are a longstanding concern, this is a central issue in test-based accountability with the now routine reporting of subgroup performance for accountability purposes. Given the educational experiences for some student subgroups (e.g., children living in poverty), it has been widely acknowledged that these differences are likely valid and do not represent unfairness (Bond, 1987; Cole & Zieky, 2001). That these differences might be moderated to some extent through choices in the test design process has, however, been a topic of discussion (Bond, 1987; Cole & Zieky, 2001). Recent work has found that some portion of group differences can sometimes be moderated based on item selection even while maintaining significant constraints on test quality relating to item type, difficulty, and discrimination (Stocking et al., 2002).

HOW IT IS MEASURED

Perhaps the most critical feature of high-stakes testing and educational accountability is the change in context from a low-stakes to a high-stakes environment for students, teachers, and schools. To date, there is little work comparing the measurement characteristics for tests administered under high-stakes conditions to tests administered under low-stakes conditions for the population of test takers overall and by subgroup (Brennan, 2006). Such analysis would include, at a minimum, an inspection of the descriptive statistics, reliability estimates, test-taker response processes, and internal structure of the test overall and by different groups. In additional to general measurement characteristics, the technical work addressing item fairness like DIF under low stakes and high stakes may be different.

TEST ANXIETY AND MOTIVATION

Student responses to the change in the test context from low to high stakes have not been studied. There is an underlying assumption by policymakers that changing assessments from a low-stakes to high-stakes context will have a similar motivating power for all students to the same degree and in the same direction (Clarke, Abrams, & Madaus, 2001). However, evidence of stereotype threat and how it is induced by the intended purpose of the assessment suggests that high-stakes pressure could have different effects on members of various groups (Steele, 1997).

There are also concerns that test anxiety may influence high-stakes test taking processes (Haldyna & Downing, 2004). Although previous studies established that there were no group (e.g., whites and African Americans) differences in test anxiety effects on test performance (Crocker, Schmitt, & Tang, 1988), this question has not been studied within the test-based accountability context. There are two studies that suggest that the relationship between test anxiety and achievement may vary by context (Helmke, 1988), and that high-stakes situations can contribute to test anxiety (Zohar, 1998).

SPECIAL POPULATIONS NEEDS

In addition to other context changes, a more diverse population is being tested under accountability mandates. These newly included students increase the number of groups that are relevant when considering fairness issues: low income, special education, English language learners (ELL), gender, and students identified by race or ethnicity.

The increase in the number of subgroups that must be considered under accountability mandate is creating challenges for test publishers in constructing assessments that meet technical standards (Harris, 2006). For example, ELL students and students with disabilities may have limited fluency in English or learning disabilities that prevent them from showing what they know and can do. They may thus require testing accommodations, which generally refers to "any action taken in response to a determination that an individual's disability [or limited English proficiency] require a departure from established testing protocol" (AERA, 1999, p. 101). Accommodations are implemented so students can demonstrate their knowledge and skills. Although there is research on accommodations in testing, the research on assessment fairness is primarily focused on comparing students' scores under standard and accommodated conditions illustrating that there are performance differences. There is no conclusive evidence whether test score interpretations with accommodations are more valid (Koenig & Bachman, 2004).

Building Better Assessments

As I noted, there are sources of assessment bias that continue to be a concern, such as the over-reliance on multiple-choice assessments. These kinds of issues are exacerbated when test results have consequences for students, teachers, and schools. I briefly discuss some remedies to address these fairness concerns below.

UNIVERSAL DESIGN

Universal design, a concept that comes out of work in architecture, is a possible solution for addressing accommodation complexities (Wilson & Bertenthal, 2005). This notion, that buildings should be designed from the beginning to be accessible to the entire population, when adapted to the educational measurement context, calls for developing assessments so that individuals will not need accommodations. For example, assessments would be developed without time constraints so no extended-time accommodations (e.g., increased testing time) would be required. Incorporating universal design as the basis for assessment design will involve significant technical work, but it holds promise for moderating group achievement test score differences.

MULTIPLE MEASURES

There are longstanding concerns about the extent to which a test composed of a single item type is an adequate measure of what all students know and can do (Baker, 2003; Cole & Zieky, 2001; Heubert & Hauser, 1999). The notion of making decisions about students based on a single test score was addressed in the *Standards for Educational and Psychological Testing* (Standard 13.7; AERA, 1999). Using multiple measures is especially relevant for assessing individual student performance and for NCLB high-stakes accountability involving teachers, schools, and districts (Henderson-Montero, Julian, & Yen, 2003).

Multiple measures, or providing additional ways for students to show what they know and can do, are defined in a variety of ways. These include, for example, varying the following: assessment form (e.g., performance assessment, portfolios), assessment task type (e.g., constructed response, selected response), assessments in different content areas (mathematics, social studies), different types of assessment information (e.g., standards-based, norm-referenced, classroom assessments) (Baker, 2003). Non-cognitive measures such as school attendance, drop out, and truancy rates are other potential measures. Multiple measures are useful for addressing score inflation (Koretz & Hamilton, 2006) and as part of an accountability system. Although there is agreement that multiple measures are crucial, there are significant tensions in considering these issues—broadening construct representation while increasing costs and decreasing reliability that are difficult to disentangle (Cole & Zieky, 2001).

Thus far, I have addressed technical fairness issues (e.g., bias) related to the test itself. I will now discuss accountability uses of test results and accountability consequences.

Fairness and Test-Based Accountability

The passage of the No Child Left Behind Act was aimed at addressing the achievement gaps for subgroups (e.g., low income, Hispanic, African American). This legislation is intended to provide opportunities to learn by focusing national attention on: (a) achievement for all, including students with greatest needs; (b) closing the achievement "gaps"; (c) providing challenging content for all students; and (d) providing all students with qualified teachers. The extent to which these goals are met is operationalized by the level of student performance relative to state targets for demonstrating annual yearly progress (AYP).[2] By requiring states to report assessment information by subgroup (e.g., low income), information about differences in learning among different groups of students, schools, and districts is highlighted.

This kind of test-based accountability, what I call the *high standards for all* model, is based on the notion that by incorporating challenging educational standards, assessments, and sanctions or rewards, students will be motivated to learn more, teachers' instruction will improve, and educational organizations will become more effective (Baker & Linn, 2004; Lane & Stone, 2002). In considering fairness issues, there is an important distinction between using assessment results for high-stakes purposes involving school-level decisions and those involving individual-level decisions (American Educational Research Association, 2000). For example, NCLB requires that a school's quality—a decision about schools—be judged based on the percentage of its students who reach proficiency targets. In addition, however, many states have raised test score stakes for individual students (e.g., denial of high school diploma)—a decision about individuals.

In essence, this test-based educational accountability purports to improve achievement *and* ensure equity by holding students, teachers, and schools to high educational standards. Further, there are no other assessments or information about individuals, schools, and districts that are considered when making a judgment about school quality based on AYP. Critics claim there are negative effects that actually exacerbate existing inequalities (e.g., Kim & Sunderman, 2005; Orfield & Kornhaber, 2001). Under what circumstances is this test-based accountability model unfair? Below, I look at evidence that is central to fairness and test-based accountability regarding how test results are used in educational accountability systems, opportunity to learn, and educational consequences.

Fairness and Educational Accountability Approaches

Essentially, there are two approaches to designing educational accountability systems. One approach, the *current status* approach, attempts to compare all students to the same standard (Linn, this volume); the Illinois AYP example presented earlier is an illustration of this approach. The other approach, based on a *growth* model, should in principle lead to greater fairness because it takes initial student status into account (Linn, this volume).

NCLB accountability, based on the *current status accountability* or school percent proficient approach, has *high standards for all* as the explicit commitment to equity. Although the notion of "high standards" is appealing, this approach poses particular problems for high-poverty schools with large minority populations (Kim & Sunderman, 2005; Linn, this volume; Raudenbush, 2004). For example, findings from a simulation by Raudenbush (2004) and a study by Kim and Sunderman (2005) show that the current status accountability approach identifies high-poverty schools as more frequently failing to meet AYP due to a combination of low achievement and sampling error.

The *matched longitudinal growth model* addresses many of these issues given that low-income, high-minority enrollment schools have similar gains to low-poverty schools (Raudenbush, 2004). By taking prior achievement into account, the longitudinal growth approach is likely to be fairer to students and schools (Linn, this volume). However, there are also concerns that longitudinal growth models will lower expectations because implicitly lower targets are set for students who start with lower prior achievement.

In addition to the overall educational accountability approaches, there are other educational accountability system elements that raise fairness concerns. NCLB accountability incorporates multiple hurdles where students must meet performance targets in each subject area to make AYP. Similarly, schools must meet multiple targets, and as the number of disaggregated subgroups increases, it becomes more difficult for schools with heterogeneous populations to meet AYP targets (Sunderman & Kim, 2005; Linn, this volume). In contrast, some statewide accountability systems use a compensatory notion that involves calculating an academic index across multiple subject areas. This allows high performance in one area (e.g., reading) to offset lower gain in another area (e.g., science). Kim and Sunderman (2005) provided an example comparing Virginia's compensatory model and the NCLB multiple-hurdles approach. Potential unfairness was evident for the 352 schools that met state standards but did not make AYP because these schools were more likely to have a larger percentage of low-income and minority student.

Based on the evidence I examined about how tests are used in NCLB test-based accountability, the causal claims that one school is more effective than another based on standardized test scores cannot be justified (Linn, this volume; Raudenbush, 2004). In the academic community and the public at large, there is sentiment to "fix" NCLB test-based accountability (e.g., Darling-Hammond, 2007; Linn, 2007). Linn (2007) provides several suggestions about how NCLB test-based accountability may be improved. These include to (1) set achievable goals that can be met with sufficient effort, (2) define the term *proficient* achievement so there is some kind of common meaning (e.g., median achievement in a base year), (3) combine *growth* and *status* approaches for determining AYP, and (4) incorporate the compensatory notion and partial credit instead of multiple hurdles in setting AYP criteria.

Incorporating Linn's proposals would improve NCLB accountability. However, these kinds of technical solutions (e.g., incorporating growth and status approaches for AYP) do not address whether test-based accountability provides equitable learning opportunities or is a sufficient treatment for improving student learning. In the next section I provide a broad overview of issues related to opportunity to learn and the implications for test-based accountability fairness issues.

Fairness and Opportunity to Learn

The degree to which the interpretation of assessments is fair is linked to whether students had the opportunity to learn (OTL) both the knowledge and skills assessed. In particular, attention to OTL is a critical feature in improving education overall and in addressing equity issues (Black & William, 1998; Massell, Kirst, & Hoppe, 1997). When students have *not* had the opportunity to learn the material tested, the assessment results cannot be interpreted as the same outcome for students who *have* had the opportunity to learn (Wilson & Bertenthal, 2005). OTL is a critical fairness concern in high-stakes testing when test performance has individual- and school-level consequences.

However, determining whether students had the opportunity to learn the content and skills is difficult. Both defining and assessing opportunity to learn is challenging (AERA, 1999). As the stakes increase (e.g., high school graduation or promotion), there is more attention paid to collecting this kind of information through questionnaires, interviews, logs, and the like. These instruments have typically covered such topics as content, instruction, and instructional resources assessing the enacted curriculum (Brewer & Stacz, 1996; Porter, 1991).

However, the enacted curriculum and the notion of resources in the test-based accountability context is complex. Educational resources can be significantly entangled and impede efforts to provide the necessary curriculum and instruction so learning can occur. Resource issues can be further distinguished as quality of education, educators, and school finances—elaborating what "instructional resources" are (Darling-Hammond, 2006; Ryan, 2002; Wilson & Bertenthal, 2005).

QUALITY OF EDUCATION AND EDUCATORS

Quality of education includes advanced courses offered at middle school and high school and Advanced Placement (AP) courses that are important for improved performance on statewide assessments (Sunderman & Kim, 2005; Wilson & Mertenthal, 2005). These issues are also related to teacher qualifications. Students have higher standardized test scores when their teachers are certified in the area they teach (e.g., certified math teachers teaching math) (Darling-Hammond, 2006).

Test-based accountability may be inadvertently contributing to equity issues and access to quality teachers. Teachers with expertise may choose to teach in higher performing schools to avoid the pressure to attain adequate yearly progress and other negative consequences that could occur (Wilson & Bertenthal, 2005). There is evidence that lower performing districts having less access to qualified teachers (Darling-Hammond, 2006; Sunderman & Kim, 2005; Turek, 2005), and that districts with less qualified teachers often serve low-income students. Further, schools identified as needing the most improvement have been shown to have the least qualified teachers (Sunderman & Kim, 2005). In contrast, there is evidence that better schools hire more qualified teachers (Clotfelter, Ladd, Vigdor, & Diaz, 2004).

SCHOOL FINANCES

The district or state economic base is also a significant concern. When subgroups of students do *not* meet educational standards, the extent to which there is adequate funding to provide the instruction these students need to meet standards becomes an issue. Low-income students and districts can be at a disadvantage in states like Illinois where the school resources are not equally distributed across the state. The question becomes whether subgroups of students (e.g., low-income) receive similar curriculum and instruction funded at similar levels in comparison to other subgroups of students (e.g., middle or high income).

Under these kinds of circumstances, interpreting low student achievement as a lack of opportunity to learn is plausible. Limited resources provided by schools and districts for instruction and a lack of highly qualified teachers means that students have not had the opportunity to learn, and this lack of opportunity to learn is accurately captured in low test scores. The same kind of problem exists for holding teachers accountable for low student achievement when students' initial status is low and there are minimal school and district instructional resources and support for improving student learning. The accountability model becomes unfair, then, if students or teachers are accountable for outcomes they cannot control given a lack of resources.

Educational Accountability Consequences

The question remains whether *high standards for all* test-based accountability leads to educational consequences that are beneficial while avoiding negative side effects (Heubert & Hauser, 1999). Examining consequences involves specifying how these kinds of systems are supposed to improve student learning and studying the evidence that these systems are functioning as intended (i.e., are students learning more?) (Linn, 1993; Shepard, 1997). Below I briefly examine the available empirical evidence investigating test-based accountability consequences. I focus on particular groups of students, teachers, and schools (e.g., low achieving, students who are often low income) to see if they are affected negatively (e.g., drop-out rates increase) or positively (students learn more) by test-based accountability.

Results from studies examining the relationship between high-stakes high school exit exams and the drop-out rates vary (Amrein & Berliner, 2002; Jacob, 2001). However, in a more recent empirical investigation, researchers studying exit exams and General Education Degree (GED) rates from 1975 to 2002 found that more difficult state high school exams are related to lower high school completion rates (Warren, Jenkins, & Kulick, 2006). Further, the magnitude of this relationship increases for states with higher poverty rates and a more ethnically and racially diverse population (Warren et al., 2006).

Studies examining test-based accountability post-NCLB are inconclusive. The recent findings from the Center on Educational Policy (2007) exemplify some of the complexities with research examining whether (a) student learning has increased, and (b) the achievement gap has decreased since the passage of NCLB. The findings are a "qualified" yes, although the positive findings cannot be directly attributed to NCLB because there is no basis for comparison. Test scores increased in several states accompanied by a decrease in the achievement gap (CEP, 2007). However, the study results are not confirmed by the National Assessment of Educational Progress (NAEP), which functions, to an extent, as an audit test. That is, states that reported increased achievement on their own state assessments did not necessarily have corresponding increases on NAEP (Lee, 2006). NAEP shows a small narrowing of the achievement gap that began prior to NCLB. There is evidence from a Chicago public schools study, for example, that lower achieving students, likely to be African American or Hispanic, did not make gains after NCLB or other test-based reforms were initiated (Neal & Whitmore Schanzenback, 2007).

To date, the available empirical findings about educational accountability consequences and fairness are limited. There are theoretical resources (specifying the validity argument), wide-ranging methods, and sophisticated analytic strategies (e.g., hierarchical linear modeling) for studying educational accountability consequences (e.g., Lane & Stone, 2002). However, the modest propositions (e.g., high-stakes tests based on high standards will motivate educational actors) that form a theory of action underlying the *high standards for all* educational accountability is limited. A coherent program for improving student learning precedes a coherent research program for evaluating test-based accountability consequences.

Looking Forward: Educational Accountability and Fairness

Educational science resources are underutilized and have much to offer in the study of fairness and educational accountability. As I have highlighted in this chapter, making the judgment that one school is more effective than another based on standardized test scores cannot be justified given the current accountability reporting requirements (Linn, this volume; Raudenbush, 2004). Further, evidence suggests that there are potential fairness issues with *high standards for all* educational accountability (e.g., inequality in access to qualified teachers). Nevertheless, test score results and other information from test-based accountability systems are a signal: low test scores within a school, district, or group (e.g., females or low-income students) *do* indicate a problem.

Building Better Educational Accountability

The *high standards for all* educational accountability model is based primarily on test score information that locates low achievement in students and schools. Although perhaps not intended, there is an implicit model that makes students and schools the causal agents with achievement as the outcome. Drawing on Cohen, Raudenbush, and Lowenberg Ball (2003), I propose an educational accountability model based on *high standards and conditions for all.* This broadened framework locates key causal agents (e.g., instructional practices) and moderators (e.g., resource access and use) in the instruction process with student achievement as the outcome. By reconceptualizing the notion of resources and the role of resources in improving student learning, the questions become "What instructional approach, aimed at what instructional goals, is sufficient to insure that students achieve these goals (e.g., closing the achievement gap)?" and "What resources are required to implement this instructional approach?" (p. 134).

ACCESS TO RESOURCES

What is required? Information and assessments of human and fiscal resources, instructional practices, and organizational characteristics are critical to a complete and accurate assessment of school quality and student achievement. Perhaps community resources should also be part of this framework. Conceptualizing school quality in a broader framework sets the stage for more formative information. Often curriculum, instruction, and systemic issues (e.g., unequal distribution of financial and human resources in schools, lowered expectation of student performance related to social class) are salient concerns. AYP does not target these kinds of issues. In principle, this kind of information can be used to describe or monitor school reform and even provide some explanation about successes.

Although creating a school process indicator system appears attractive

(Porter, 1991), there are challenges to conceptualizing and implementing a system incorporating the assessment of resources, instruction, and organizational characteristics. Currently, relationships among resources, instruction, and school organizational characteristics are not well understood. For example, the role of resources as inputs has been studied extensively with disappointing results. Most studies suggest a modest relationship between resources and student achievement at best after taking student background characteristics into account (e.g., Coleman et al., 1966; Hedges, Laine, & Greenwald, 1994). Thus, an increase in resources does not necessarily increase capacity.

RESOURCE USE AND DEPLOYMENT

What accounts for this counter-intuitive finding? Both *resource access* and knowledge about *resource use* and *how resources are deployed* are essential to improving schools and student learning. Drawing from several lines of research (e.g., effective schools, instructional processes, and resource use, etc.) Cohen et al. (2003) propose resources need to be "reconsidered." That is, traditional resource access (fiscal resources, teacher qualifications) are necessary but not sufficient for improving student learning. Further, they propose how resources are used in instructional practices, organizational arrangements, and teachers' and students' engagement with academic content and the like are also critical. Instead of serving as a causal agent, within this model resources are designated as moderators of instruction (e.g., practices, organizational arrangements). Educational accountability based on this framework emphasizes high standards for all *and* makes the "conditions under which students are educated" equally important (Noguera, 2007, para. 3).

Acknowledgments

The author acknowledges with much thanks constructive criticisms of an earlier draft from Greg Camilli, Gail L. Sunderman, and Lorrie Shepard. Responsibility for the final product, of course, remains with the author.

Notes

1. Construct irrelevant variance is a psychological or situational factor affecting test performance that is irrelevant to what is intended to be measured (Messick, 1995).
2. For instance, in Illinois, annual yearly progress is the (a) percent of reading and math scores that meet or exceed standards, compared to the annual state targets, and (b) the participation rate of students in taking the state tests, which must meet or exceed 95%.

References

American Educational Research Association, American Psychological Association, and National Council on Measurement in Education. (1999). *Standards for educational and psychological testing.* Washington, DC: American Educational Research Association.

American Evaluation Research Association. (2000, July). *AERA position statement on high stakes testing in pre K-12 education.* Online, available at: http://www.aera.net/policyandprograms/?id=378 (accessed April 1, 2007).

Amrein, A. L. & Berliner, D. C. (2002). High-stakes testing, uncertainty, and student learning. *Education Policy Analysis Archives*, 10 (8). Online, available at: http://epaa.asu.edu/epaa/v10n18 (accessed May 5, 2007).

Angoff, W. H. (1993). Perspectives on differential item functioning methodology. In P. W. Holland & H. Wainer (Eds.), *Differential item functioning* (pp. 3–24). Hillsdale, NJ: Lawrence Erlbaum.

Baker, E. L. (2003). Multiple measures: Toward tiered systems. *Educational Measurement: Issues and Practice*, 22 (2), 13–17.

Baker, E. L. & Linn, R. L. (2004). Validity issues for accountability systems. In S. H. Fuhrman & R. F. Elmore (Eds.), *Redesigning accountability systems for education* (pp. 47–72). New York: Teachers College Press.

Berk, R. A. (1982). *Handbook for detecting biased test items*. Baltimore, MD: Johns Hopkins University Press.

Biesta, G. J. (2004). Education, accountability, and the ethical demand: Can the democratic potential of accountability be regained? *Educational Theory*, 54 (3), 233–250.

Binet, A. & Simon, T. (1973). *The development of intelligence in children* (Classics in Psychology). New York: Arno.

Black, P. & William, D. (1998). Inside the black box: Raising standards through classroom assessment. *Phi Delta Kappan*, 80 (2), 139–148.

Bond, L. (1987). The golden rule settlement: A minority perspective. *Educational Measurement: Issues and Practice*, 6 (2), 18–20.

Bond, L. (1993). Comments on the O'Neill and McPeek paper. In P. W. Holland & H. Wainer (Eds.), *Differential item functioning* (pp. 277–280). Hillsdale, NJ: Lawrence Erlbaum.

Brennan, R. L. (2006). Perspectives on the evolution of educational measurement. In R. L. Brennan (Ed.), *Educational measurement* (4th ed., pp. 1–16). New York: American Council on Education and Praeger.

Brewer, D. J. & Stacz, C. (1996). *Enhancing opportunity to learn measures in NCES data*. Santa Monica, CA: Rand Corp.

Camilli, G. (2006). Test fairness. In R. L. Brennan (Ed.), *Educational measurement* (4th ed., pp. 221–256). New York: American Council on Education and Praeger.

Camilli, G. & Shepard, L. A. (1994). *Methods for identifying biased test items*. Thousand Oaks, CA: Sage.

Center on Educational Policy (2007). *Answering the question that matters most: Has student achievement increased since No Child Left Behind?* Washington, DC: Center on Educational Policy.

Clarke, M., Abrams, L., & Madaus, G. (2001). The effects of and implications of high-stakes achievement tests for adolescence. In T. C. Urdan & F. Pajares (Eds.), *Adolescence and education: General issues in the education of adolescents* (pp. 2, 101–102, 230). Greenwich, CT: Information Age Publishing.

Cleary, T. A. (1968). Test bias: Prediction of grades of negro and white students in integrated colleges. *Journal of Educational Measurement*, 2 (2), 115–124.

Clotfelter, C T., Ladd, H. F., Vigdor, J. L., & Diaz, R. A. (2004). Do school accountability systems make it more difficult for low performing schools to attract and retain high quality teachers? *Journal of Policy Analysis and Management*, 23 (2), 251–271.

Cohen, D. K., Raudenbush, S. W., & Loewenberg Ball, D. (2003). Resources, instruction, and research. *Educational Evaluation and Policy Analysis*, 25 (2), 119–142.

Cole, N. S. (1973). Bias in selection. *Journal of Educational Measurement*, 10 (4), 237–255.

Cole, N. S. & Zieky, M. J. (2001). The new faces of fairness. *Journal of Educational Measurement*, 38 (4), 369–382.

Coleman, J., Campbell, E., Hobsen, C., McPartland, J., Mood, A., Weinfeld, F. et al. (1966). *Equality of educational opportunity survey*. Washington, DC: U.S. Government Printing Office.

Crocker, L., Schmitt, A., & Tang, L. (1988). Test anxiety and standardized achievement test performance in the middle school years. *Measurement and Evaluation in Counseling and Development*, 20 (4), 49–57.

Darling-Hammond, L. (2006). *Standards, assessments, and educational policy: In pursuit of genuine accountability (updated)* (Rep. No. PIC-ANG8). The eighth annual William H. Angoff Memorial Lecture. Princeton, NJ: Educational Testing Service.

Darling-Hammond, L. (2007, May 21). Evaluating "No Child Left Behind." *Nation*. Online, available at: http://www.thenation.com/doc/20070521/darling-hammond (accessed May 21, 2007).

Eells, K., Davis, A., Havighurst, R. J., Herrick, V. E., & Tyler, R. W. (1951). *Intelligence and cultural differences*. Chicago, IL: University of Chicago Press.

Haladyna, T. M. & Downing, S. M. (2004). Construct-irrelevant variance in high-stakes testing. *Educational Measurement: Issues and Practices*, 23 (1), 17–27.

Harris, W. T. (2006). The challenges of meeting the standards: A perspective from the test publishing community. *Educational Measurement: Issues and Practice*. 25 (3), 42–45.

Hedges, L. V., Laine, R. D., & Greenwald, R. (1994). Does money matter? A meta-analysis of studies of the effects of differential school inputs on student outcomes (An exchange: Part I). *Educational Researcher*, 23 (3), 5–14.

Helmke, A. (1988). The role of classroom context factors for the achievement impairing effect of test anxiety. *Anxiety Research*, 1 (1), 37–52.

Henderson-Montero, D., Julian, M. W., & Yen, W. (2003). Multiple measures: Alternative design and analysis models. *Educational Measurement: Issues and Practice*, 22 (2), 7–12.

Heubert, J. P. & Hauser, R. M. (Eds.). (1999). *High stakes: Testing for tracking, promotion, and graduation*. Washington, DC: National Academies Press.

Holland, P. W. & Thayer, D. T. (1986). *Differential item performance and the Mantel-Haenszel procedure* (Research Report No 86–31). Princeton, NJ: Educational Testing Service.

Jacob, B. A. (2001). Getting tough? The impact of high school graduation exams. *Educational Evaluation and Policy Analysis*, 23 (2), 99–121.

Jensen, A. R. (1969). How much can we boost I.Q. and scholastic achievement? *Harvard Educational Review*, 39, 1–123.

Kane, M. T. (2002). Validating high-stakes testing programs. *Educational Measurement: Issues and Practice*, 21 (2), 5–17.

Kim, J. S. & Sunderman, G. L. (2005). Measuring academic proficiency under the No Child Left Behind Act: Implications for educational equality. *Educational Researcher*, 34 (8), 3–13.

Koenig, J. A. & Bachman, L. F. (Eds.). (2004). *Keeping score for all: The effects of inclusion and accommodation policies on large-scale assessments*. Washington, DC: National Academies Press.

Koretz, D. & Hamilton, L. S. (2006). Testing for accountability in K-12. In R. L. Brennan (Ed.), *Educational measurement* (4th ed., pp. 579–622). New York: American Council on Education and Praeger.

Lane, S. & Stone, C. A. (2002). Strategies for examining the consequences of assessment and accountability programs. *Educational Measurement: Issues and Practice*, 21 (1), 23–30.

Lee, J. (2006). *Tracking achievement gaps and assessing the impact of NCLB on the gaps*. Cambridge, MA: Civil Rights Project at Harvard University.

Linn, R. L. (1973). Fair test use in selection. *Review of Educational Research*, 43 (2), 139–164.

Linn, R. L. (1984). Selection bias: Multiple meanings. *Journal of Educational Measurement*, 21, 33–47.

Linn, R. L. (1993). Educational assessment: Expanded expectations and challenges. *Educational Evaluation and Policy Analysis*, 15 (1), 1–16.

Linn, R. L. (2007, April). Needed modifications of NCLB. Paper presented at the annual meeting of the National Council of Educational Measurement, Chicago, IL.

Linn, R. L. & Harnisch, D. (1981). Interactions between item content and group membership on achievement test items. *Journal of Educational Measurement*, 18 (2), 108–118.

Linn, R. L., Levine, M. V., Hastings, C. N., & Wardrop, J. L. (1981). Item bias in a test of reading comprehension. *Applied Psychological Measurement*, 5 (3), 159–173.

Madaus, G. F. (1988). The distortion of teaching and testing: High-stakes testing and instruction. *Peabody Journal of Education*, 65 (3), 29–46.

Massell, D., Kirst, M., & Hoppe, M. (1997). *Persistence and change: Standards-based reform in nine states*. Brunswick, NJ: Consortium for Policy Research in Education.

Messick, S. (1995). Validity of psychological assessment: Validation of inferences from persons, responses and performances as scientific inquiry into score meaning. *American Psychologist*, 50 (9), 741–749.

Neal, D. & Whitmore Schanzenbach, D. (2007). *Left behind by design: Proficiency counts and test-based accountability.* Chicago, IL: National Bureau of Economic Research.

No Child Left Behind Act of 2001, Pub L. No. 107–110, 115 Stat. 1425 (2002).

Noguera, P. (2007, May 21). Responses to Darling-Hammond. *Nation.* Online, available at: http://www.thenation.com/doc/20070521/nogueracobbmeier (accessed May 21, 2007).

Orfield, G. & Kornhaber, M. (2001). *Raising standards or raising barriers? Inequality and high stakes testing in public education.* Washington, DC: Brookings Institute.

Porter, A. (1991). Creating a system of school process indicators. *Educational Evaluation and Policy Analysis*, 13 (1), 13–29.

Power, M. (1997). *The audit society.* New York: Oxford Press.

Raudenbush, S. W. (2004). What are value-added models estimating and what does this imply for statistical practice? *Journal of Educational and Behavioral Statistics*, 1 (29), 121–129.

Rizvi, F. (1990). Horizontal accountability. In J. Chapman (Ed.), *School-based decision-making and management* (pp. 299–324). Basingstoke: Falmer Press.

Ryan, K. E. (2002). Shaping educational accountability systems. *American Journal of Evaluation*, 23 (4), 453–468.

Ryan, K. E. (2008). Performance measurement and educational accountability: The U.S. case. In P. Julnes, F. Berry, M. Aristigueta, & K. Yang, (Eds.), *Practice-based performance management: An international handbook* (pp. 213–232). Thousand Oaks, CA: Sage.

Shealy, R. & Stout, W. (1993). An item response theory model for test bias and differential test functioning. In P. Holland & H. Wainer (Eds.), *Differential item functioning* (pp. 197–240). Hillsdale, NJ: Lawrence Erlbaum.

Shepard, L. A. (1982). Definitions of bias. In R. A. Berk (Ed.), *Handbook for detecting test bias items* (pp. 2–35). Baltimore, MD: Johns Hopkins University Press.

Shepard, L. A. (1997). The centrality of test use and consequences for test validity. *Educational Measurement: Issues and Practice*, 16 (2), 4–30.

Steele, C. M. (1997). A threat in the air: How stereotypes shape intellectual identity and performance. *American Psychologist*, 52 (6), 613–629.

Stocking, M., Lawrence, I., Feignebaum, M., Jirele, T., Lewis, C., & Van Essen, T. (2002). An empirical investigation of impact moderation in test construction. *Journal of Educational Measurement*, 39 (3), 235–252.

Sunderman, G. L. & Kim, J. (2005). *Teacher quality: Equalizing educational opportunities and outcomes.* Cambridge, MA: Civil Rights Project at Harvard University.

Turek, P. W. (2005). Psychology and Washington research in the high-stakes era: Achievement, resources, and No Child Left Behind. *Psychological Science*, 16 (6), 419–425.

Warren, J. R., Jenkins, K. N., & Kulick, R. B. (2006). High school exit examinations and the state-level completion and GED rates, 1975–2002, *Educational Evaluation and Policy Analysis*, 28 (2), 131–152.

Willingham, W. W. & Cole, N. S. (1997). *Gender and fair assessment.* Mahwah, NJ: Erlbaum.

Wilson, M. R. & Bertenthal, M. W. (Eds.). (2005). *Systems for state science assessment.* Washington, DC: National Academies Press.

Zohar, D. (1998). An additive model of test anxiety: Role of exam specific expectations. *Journal of Educational Psychology*, 90 (2), 330–340.

Part III
Educational Accountability Effects

11

Accountability and Assessment

Is Public Interest in K-12 Education Being Served?

Joan L. Herman

The reauthorization of the No Child Left Behind Act of 2001 (NCLB) makes this a good time to consider whether and how current accountability serves the public interest and whether and how it can do so better. In this chapter, I explore these issues in the context of the current literature on the effects of accountability in K-12 education. I'll first consider the meaning of "public interest" and share a model of how accountability and assessment may operate in the public interest by benefiting student learning. I then consider how well the model fits available evidence by examining whether and how accountability assessment influences students' learning opportunities and the relationship between accountability and learning. I end with conclusions about how well accountability currently serves the public interest and recommendations for improvements.

The Meaning of Public Interest

What is the public interest? Although policy debates, politicians, the media, and public groups often evoke it, public interest is a slippery concept to define. Reich (1988) speaks of transcendent ideas and concerns for the good of society, rather than self-interest, that motivate political action. Moyers (2007) notes that the proposition that each of us has the right to "life, liberty, and the pursuit of happiness" is the foundation of this country and that this proposition carries with it the imperative that members of society have "obligations to each other, mutually and through their government, to ensure that conditions exist enabling every person to have the opportunity for success in life." But as Hochschild and Scovronick (2003) have observed, in the context of public schooling, the proposition blends both collective and individual responsibilities, and contains inherent conflicts between policies designed for the good of *all* students and those designed to enable individuals to succeed, particularly the privileged of society.

Different perspectives on what constitutes the public interest and the policies that can promote it grow out of differing ideals and the conflicts among them, varying definitions of basic societal goals such as liberty and equality, and different analyses of the sources of problems and obstacles (Stone, 2001). What constitutes the public interest is an interaction between the facts as one sees them and one's values. For example, some see the success of schools overseen by the Department of Defense (e.g., on military bases) as support for integration, high academic expectations, shared decisionmaking, and investment in professional development for educators; others see it as ratifying their ideas about the importance of home culture and discipline.

Whose and how many individuals' interests need to be served and how a policy should be designed to address the public interest remain open questions. To what end? Is an action that serves some but hurts none in the public interest? What of policies that serve the many, but hurt the few? Although these may be unanswerable questions, they reflect tensions that must be balanced in any discussion of whether and how current accountability and assessment systems may serve the public interest to benefit (or not) the education and learning of K-12 students.

Do current accountability systems serve all students? If action in the public interest means addressing needs that would otherwise be left unmet, then accountability in the public interest must benefit students who traditionally have been underserved—economically disadvantaged students, English learners, and diverse students of color. Yet, if all students are to be served, then the system also needs to benefit—or at least not harm—students who have traditionally been higher achieving. Furthermore, accountability that promotes attention to the short-term, bottom line of student performance must yield long-term benefits for student learning and for public education.

The concept of public interest also brings with it a basic concern with social ends and goals. If we are an accountable society, for what aspects of student learning should we and education be held? Recent commissions have *again* raised questions about whether schools are sufficiently preparing students for creative thinking and problem solving and in science and technology for this country to keep its competitive edge (Friedman, 2005; Partnership for 21st Century Skills, 2002). Further, in the rush to reach consensus on the meaning of proficiency in reading and math, we have sometimes neglected to focus on the goals of schooling (Ramaley, 2005) and to have settled for standards that fail to articulate clearly the academic knowledge and skills that students need for future success (Wilson & Berenthal, 2005). Democracy carries with it the responsibility to create citizens who recognize and serve the public good and not only their own interests (Parker, 2003). The public, too, wants schools that promote self-discipline and social responsibility (Mathews, 2006). But, schools currently seem overwhelmed by the need to raise test scores and meet academic mandates, and public interest goals seem to be beyond current official standards and expectations for schooling.

The Role of Accountability in Serving the Public Interest: a General Model

The *Merriam-Webster Collegiate Dictionary* (n.d.) defines accountability as "the quality or state of being accountable, *especially*: an obligation or willingness to accept responsibility or to account for one's actions." In current educational contexts, the concept carries with it the idea that individuals, organizations, and the community are not only responsible for their actions, but must answer for their performance to an outside authority that, in turn, may impose a penalty for failure. In the simplest sense, students come to school to learn and schools and the educators within them exist to teach and to promote learning. Because tests show which students and what schools are meeting or exceeding standards and those that are not, students and teachers who are falling short should be held accountable for their failure (and less frequently, those who succeed beyond expectations should be rewarded for their success).

Spurred in part by the No Child Left Behind Act of 2001, and the Goals 2000: Educate America Act (1994) that preceded it, all states except Iowa have agreed on standards for student learning and have created assessments that make explicit what the standards mean. Pressured by fear of sanctions—and less often by the possibility of rewards—teachers are motivated to teach and students to learn the expected standards and to use the information from the assessment to improve their efforts, even as those same assessment results reveal who has succeeded in meeting targets and who has not. The assessment system thus serves both as a performance measurement system that provides feedback, and as a motivational system that serves a number of social, political, or symbolic purposes. These purposes, which stimulate all levels of the education system to focus on achieving the NCLB goals for adequate yearly progress (AYP), include: establishing the target for reform efforts; communicating to educators, administrators, and parents what is expected; insisting on high expectations for all students; and providing incentives and sanctions.

Figure 11.1 shows one view of how accountability is supposed to work: the accountability system establishes goals and creates incentives for action. That action must improve students' opportunity to learn—termed OTL in Figure 11.1—that is, what and how well students are taught in classrooms, through supplemental services and programs, and through specially targeted in- and out-of-school activities and interventions. And these improvements in OTL, in turn, are necessary precursors to improvements in students' learning, as indicated by performance on state tests and other indicators of students' progress toward standards.

Feedback from the assessments serves to improve learning opportunities for students in terms of targeting instruction on areas of need and evaluating and refining educational programs, materials, and strategies. Because NCLB requires that every subgroup of students within the school attain established adequate yearly progress targets, all students must be provided with effective learning opportunities, including whatever augmented programs and special services traditionally low-achieving students (i.e., children of poverty, English learners, and student with disabilities) may need to attain success.

However, improving student learning is not simply a measurement or management problem. Professional responsibility and capacity must drive the actual improvement (Darling-Hammond, 2006). In fact, recent research on the power of formative classroom assessment shows not only the value of ongoing assessment relative to accountability assessment, but also supports the benefits of reflective, professional practice (Black & Wiliam, 1998).

Although Figure 11.1 focuses the impact of accountability on OTL, the underlying theory of action assumes that the federal government, states, districts, and schools will be accountable for assuring that appropriate expertise and resources, policies, and practices are available at all levels of the educational system, and that these will be coordinated and integrated to support teaching and learning. Moreover, policymakers and actors at these levels are expected to improve their schools by using the feedback from state assessments to gauge strengths and weaknesses; identify students, schools, and classrooms that may need special help; and be strategic in taking action and coordinating available resources to improve student performance (e.g., through professional development, instructional materials, mentoring, or technical assistance).

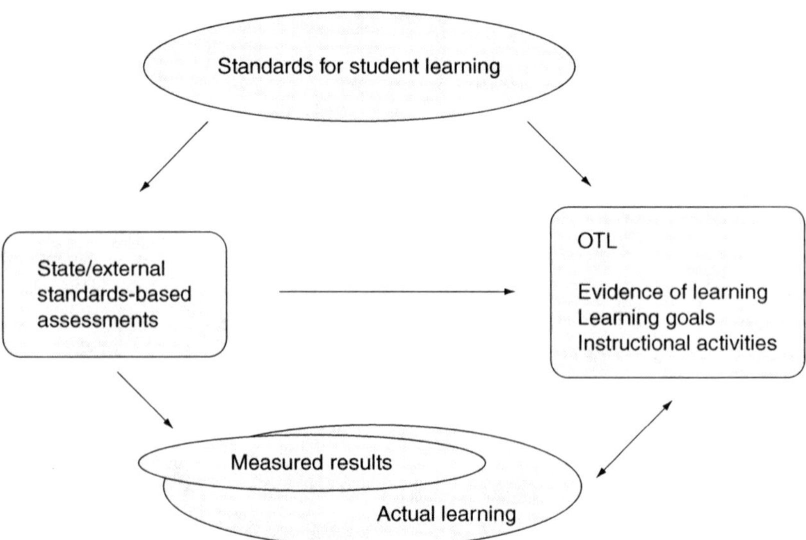

Figure 11.1 Accountability Model.

This simplified theory provides a starting point for examining whether and how accountability is serving the public interest. Despite intractable problems in attributing causality and the innumerable factors in state and local policy and practice that have an influence, I ask: what is the evidence that accountability and assessment are improving students' opportunities to learn? Is there evidence that accountability is promoting student learning and attainment of standards and, if so, for whom?

Effects of Accountability on Learning Opportunities

Relying largely on surveys, interviews, and observational data from teachers and school administrators, research over the last decade has shown a consistent picture of the effects of state-level accountability testing on curriculum and teaching. An extensive review of studies conducted in 14 different states is provided in Herman (2004). Summaries of key findings are provided here, along with illustrative citations.

State Assessments Focus Instruction

Research and practical experience show that teachers and principals indeed pay attention to what is tested and adapt their curriculum and teaching accordingly (Stecher, Barron, Chun, & Ross, 2000). Principals, with or without the involvement of their staff, analyze test results and develop school plans to concentrate on areas where test results show a need for improvement. Research shows that almost all principals also take action to assure that teachers engage their students in direct test preparation. Teachers consistently report that state tests have a substantial effect on the content they teach and how they assess student learning.

Teachers Model What is Assessed

When states developed performance assessments in the early 1990s, many classroom teachers revised their instruction and classroom assessment accordingly. Teachers scrambled to replace their own multiple-choice tests with the same types of open-ended items or extended writing questions that state tests had begun to use. In the mid 1990s, when states largely moved back to multiple-choice and short answer formats, teachers also reverted to multiple choice, vocabulary lists, and the like. More recently, Hamilton et al. (2007), in examining the effects of NCLB in California, Georgia, and Pennsylvania, found that more mathematics teachers in Pennsylvania, as compared to the other two states, reporting using open-ended tests in their classrooms, a result the researchers attributed to the use of open-ended items on Pennsylvania's math assessment. In other words: change the test and instruction follows.

Schools Focus on the Test Rather Than the Standards

At least initially, educators have paid more attention to what is tested and how it is tested, rather than to the underlying standards that the tests are supposed to represent. Teachers in Washington, for example, reported that their instruction tended to be more like Washington's state assessment than the Washington state standards (Stecher & Borko, 2001). When Washington and Kentucky tested different topics in different years, researchers found that teachers provided more time on particular subjects in the years they were tested than in those they were not (Stecher & Barron, 1999; Stecher et al., 2000). If math was tested in fifth grade but not language arts, teachers spent more time on math and less on language arts than did fourth grade teachers, where language arts was tested.

What is Not Tested Becomes Invisible

As a corollary, focusing on the test rather than the standards also means that what does not get tested tends to get less attention or may be ignored all together (Koretz, Mitchell, Barron, & Stecher, 1996). This seems true both within and across subjects. For example, if extended math problems are not included on the math test, instructional time may go to computation or other problem types that are on the test. Similarly, as more time goes to the tested subjects—typically reading, language arts, and mathematics—this time must come from other areas of the curriculum.

Curriculum and Instruction are Aligned

Across the board, districts and schools have made efforts to align curriculum and instruction with standards. This is particularly true for schools failing to meet their targets that are identified as under performing. For example, the national evaluation of Title I accountability systems and school improvement efforts (Shields et al., 2004) found that 80% of the sampled schools were actively working to align their curricula with standards and assessment, and many were also implementing new curricula in reading and language arts and mathematics. Similarly, Consortium for Policy Research in Education's study of designated underperforming high schools uniformly shows the schools concentrating on aligning curriculum and instruction with assessments—through revisions in their regular curriculum, through the addition of new courses, test preparation, and remedial and extra-school tutoring (Gross & Goertz, 2005).

More Attention to Assessment and Student Data

Shields et al. (2004) also found that 85% of schools reported using student achievement data to target their instruction, echoing other studies that similarly report schools using data to identify students who need special help and increasingly using interim or benchmark testing throughout the year to monitor student progress (Center on Education Policy (CEP), 2006; Hamilton et al., 2007). Because these assessments tend to mimic the content and format of state assessments, they encourage teachers to keep their eyes firmly on student progress—especially as it relates to the knowledge and skills that will be tested—and correspondingly may increase the narrowing of curriculum to focus on what is tested rather than on underlying standards. At the same time, districts have become more prescriptive about how and what teachers are supposed to teach, have moved to common instructional materials, and have created pacing guides that detail what is to be covered and when (even prescribing what textbook pages teachers should be covering on any given day).

Growing Attention to Formative Assessment

Even so, formative assessment, the use of classroom assessment to inform ongoing teaching (Wiliam, 2006) shows growing popularity. Black and Wiliam's (1998) landmark review showed the potential power of formative assessment, and educators have increasingly recognized that they need ongoing information about student learning if they are to be accountable for results. Yet, available evidence suggests that the rhetoric surpasses the reality of formative assessment use: all teachers are increasingly talking the talk (Hamilton et al., 2007; Herman & Yamashiro, 2001), but the studies looking at practice more closely highlight the challenges of developing teachers' capacities to engage in valid, formative practice (Gearhart et al., 2006).

At-Risk Students Face Curricular Distortions

There is also growing evidence that curriculum options are grossly narrowing for low-scoring students and underperforming schools. The requirements for annual yearly progress are leading schools increasingly to concentrate on reading and mathematics to the exclusion of all other subjects and, at the secondary level, low performing students are being pulled from other academic and elective courses to get double doses of reading or math or both (CEP, 2006; Gross and Goertz, 2005). At the extreme, there are anecdotes as well about schools using "triage" strategies to focus on what they consider "pushables" and "slippables" (relative to reaching proficiency) and virtually ignoring both students in greatest educational need and overriding issues of improving instructional quality (Booher-Jennings, 2006). Such distortions provide counter evidence to the claim that current accountability is improving instruction for low performing students and are worrisome as well in the context of a Gates Foundation survey indicating that students do not drop out of school primarily because they cannot do the work or pass their courses, but because they are bored by school (Bridgeland, DiIulio, & Morison, 2006).

Across school levels and types of schools, research suggests that accountability testing does serve to motivate attention and action and that the action so motivated serves to change the alignment of curriculum and instruction with standards and assessment and to change students' opportunities to learn. In some cases, changes in curriculum are schoolwide, and in other cases they are specialized courses or services for students identified as at risk. But do these changes in instruction and opportunities to learn represent real *improvements* that actually benefit learning for students, and particularly students who are most at risk? Or, do they in fact impoverish learning opportunities, as critics have charged, relegating students to a narrow curriculum of test preparation that is devoid of complex thinking and problem solving and devoid of learning in the arts and sciences, as previous evidence suggests (National Research Council, 2003; Pellegrino, 2006). Koretz (2005) has conceptualized a number of ways in which schools and teachers respond to the alignment challenge, ways that differ dramatically in terms of their potential to improve student learning (in contrast to inflating their test scores), including: changes in the allocation of time (do more of the same), meaningful alignment of instruction (do something different in curriculum and instruction), substantive and non-substantive coaching or test preparation, and cheating. Available evidence shows more attention to changes in the allocation of time and attention to test preparation than to changes in the quality or effectiveness of instruction.

Ultimately, the proof of whether accountability actually improves students' opportunities to learn may lie in student performance. We turn now to this body of evidence, including studies conducted prior to the passage of NCLB in 2001 when there was more diversity in state accountability systems, and post passage.

Effects of Accountability on Performance Prior to NCLB

Several studies have used data from the National Assessment of Educational Progress to study the effects of accountability on student performance. Generally, their results have been positive. For example, Grissmer and Flanagan (2001) hypothesized that accountability reforms might be responsible for the rapid growth, relative to other states, found for North Carolina and Texas for the period 1990 to 1996. Similarly, Carnoy and Loeb (2004) observed a relationship between the strength of a state's accountability system (its consequences for schools) and gains in the percentage of students scoring at least "basic" on National Assessment of Educational Progress (NAEP) mathematics assessments 1996 to 2000, but saw no relationship in retention or survival rates. A similar relationship was observed in the percentage of white and African American students scoring at least "proficient" at eighth grade. Fourth grade effects were less clear in that only African American students showed significant gains at the basic level.

Student Accountability: Ending Social Promotion

In terms of effects of consequences for students, research on the Chicago Public Schools "end to social promotion" policies represents one of the most extended and thorough studies. The authors were careful to note that the social promotion reform occurred simultaneously with new accountability programs for the lowest achieving district schools and that the effects of the two programs could not be disentangled. Overall, Roderick, Nagaoka, and Allensworth (2005) concluded that the 1996 reforms were associated with improvements in performance in the middle grades that extended into high school. However, there were no effects in the early grades—perhaps an area where student motivation would not otherwise be problematic, Details of the findings showed that some students near the cut-off worked harder and escaped retention, so the threat of retention helped them. More problematic, however, the study found that low-achieving students who were retained because of the reform did not benefit educationally during the retained year, experienced lower achievement gains in the sixth grade than students with similar test scores who were promoted, leaving them at higher risk of dropping out. In short, the most vulnerable students did not benefit from this student-level accountability reform.

Student Accountability: High School Exit Exams

Today's high school exit exams revisit some of these same patterns and echo issues that emerged in response to the minimum competency exams of the late 1970s and 1980s. Then, as now, results have shown initial high failure rates that decline over time, with large disparities in performance for poor and minority students, students with disabilities, and English learners (CEP, 2005, 2006; Heubert, 2004). California represents a current example: one year before the graduation test requirement went into effect, an estimated 78% of the class of 2006 had passed the state's High School Exit examination, leaving nearly 100,000 who had not. By the time of graduation in June 2006, an estimated 40,173 students still did not meet the requirement (California Department of Education, July 2006).

As with the effects of retention, a number of studies have suggested a troubling relationship between high school exit exams (or their precursors) and students dropping out of school. For example, research by Bishop (2005) looking across states showed that high school enrollment and completion rates generally were lower for economically disadvantaged and low ability students in states that had such tests compared to states without such tests. These studies, however, have also found positive effects on subsequent educational success: eighth graders in states with high school exit exams were more likely to go to college and to graduate from college and, controlling for high school graduation, more likely to earn more than their peers in other states.

Different Effects for Different Kinds of Tests

Moreover, there also is evidence that the effects of high school exit exams may be different for different types of tests. Bishop (2005) shared empirical data from a variety of sources to argue that rigorous, course-based exit examinations, such as those used in Europe and introduced in North Carolina and New York, benefit student achievement (as assessed by NAEP) substantially more so than more typical minimum competency tests, and these positive effects are achieved without any increase in drop-out rates. Similarly, Darling-Hammond, Rustique-Forrester, Pecheone, and Andree (2005) used evidence from NAEP to show that while states that use a single exit exam for high school graduation show higher drop-out rates, particularly for African American and Latino students, students with disabilities, and English learners, those states that use a multiple measures approach and consider a variety of student work in making graduation decisions have tended to maintain high achievement and high graduation rates. Thus, the nature of the accountability and assessment system apparently matters.

Performance Effects Since the Passage of NCLB

What of more recent effects of accountability? *Education Week* released ten years of *Quality Counts* data in 2006, which has monitored state progress in adopting core elements of standards-based reform, including establishing academic standards, aligning assessment with those standards, implementing accountability measures, and providing supports for improving teacher quality (Swanson, 2006). *Quality Counts* indicators show increases since 1997 in the implementation of policies in all of these areas across states, although the trajectories of individual states vary considerably (Swanson, 2006).

National trends on NAEP document a similarly positive trajectory over a similar time period, showing definite if modest increases from 2000 to 2005 in mathematics at grades 4 and 8 and some improvement for grade 4 reading; grade 8 reading, however, shows a decline. Further, although there has been some reduction in the achievement gap during the ten-year period, substantial differences persist, and there has been little or no reduction since NCLB (Lee, 2006).

Looking at the relationship between states' standards-based policy implementation and their progress on NAEP, *Quality Counts* shows a consistently positive—though again, modest—relationship for policies related to academic content standards, aligned assessment, and accountability measures, particularly for mathematics. Oddly, however, the implementation of policies related to teacher quality correlated negatively with performance.

In order to take a closer look at what assessment and accountability system characteristics might be related to state performance, we used available data to validate existing quality indicators and to identify states that were over and under performing based on NAEP results. While recognizing the multitude of variables and system levels that could influence student learning, we speculated that if accountability is supposed to be a strong intervention, the quality of standards and assessments and the nature of the accountability system might make a difference for student performance. States that communicate strong expectations with clear standards and back them up with rigorous assessments of high technical quality that include multiple measures and in turn can provide accurate feedback, we thought, might do better than states whose systems lack these features. At the same time, we thought that we might be able to find differences in the assessment and accountability systems of states that showed exceptional performance on NAEP, compared to those that did not. Beyond the obvious caveats related to any analysis, we encountered a number of conundrums.

What States are Achieving Well?

A first challenge was to identify over- and underperforming states using NAEP as the common comparable measure across states. We reasoned that such classifications should be based on both the status and progress of student performance. We thus identified states whose performance, controlling for socioeconomic status (SES), was better than expected across two recent NAEP administrations (2001 and 2003) in reading or math or both across both fourth and eighth grades (drawn from School Matters, 2005). Massachusetts and New York stood out uniquely from this analysis as outperforming states with similar SES in reading at grades 4 and 8 and math at grade 8—that is, for three of the four NAEP assessments. South Carolina, Kansas, and Minnesota showed better than expected performance in mathematics for both grades 4 and 8, and Kentucky for reading in grades 4 and 8.

However, in moving to the identification of states whose *improvements* in performance were outstanding relative to other states (defined as states showing at least one standard deviation above the mean state gain from 2001 to 2003), the consistent performers were generally different. Massachusetts was the exception, showing exceptional improvement[1] for three of four possible assessments—reading at grade 4 and math at grades 4 and 8. Six additional states achieved better than average on three of four assessments. Of these, Pennsylvania and Washington showed consistent improvement in reading (i.e., at both grades 4 and 8), and Arkansas, New Jersey, Ohio, and Texas in math. Idaho showed consistent improvement at grade 4 in both reading and math.

Using the Trial Urban District Assessment as another proxy for how traditionally lower achieving, poor, and minority students are doing, results showed greater improvement in mathematics than in reading, with eight of the ten participating districts showing a statistically significant increase from 2003 to 2005 in grade 4 mathematics (Rampey, Lutkus, & Dion, 2005).

Boston, Houston, Los Angeles, and San Diego also showed a significant increase in eighth grade mathematics, with Los Angeles showing significant increases across all four assessments. Mirroring weaker performance trends in reading nationally, only Atlanta showed consistent increases from 2002 to 2003 and 2005 in reading, while New York showed consistent increases at fourth grade. It is interesting to note that the two districts that performed highest relative to their peers, Charlotte and Austin, were the only two that did not show any significant increase over the period. Because both Charlotte and Austin are in states that implemented strong accountability systems early, one might suspect that this lack of improvement reflects a topping out of what can be accomplished with traditional accountability methods without dramatic changes in teaching and learning practices. But then, what explains Houston? And as noted above, Boston—which showed positive gains—has been operating under Massachusetts' longstanding and stable accountability system.

The two sets of NAEP analyses—status relative to SES and improvement in scores—uniquely identify Massachusetts as a high performer, but the state assessment results for the same period show more modest improvements relative to other states, and as one compares state assessment and NAEP results in other states, the patterns (or lack thereof) are puzzling. Moreover, *Quality Counts* ranks Massachusetts as number 49 in the achievement gap on NAEP between students who do and do not qualify for the federal free lunch program, even as results also show that the state is making progress in closing the gap. It is also interesting to note that Massachusetts started in 1997 as the highest ranked amongst the 50 states in their implementation of standards-based reform and has maintained its position over the years. Could it be that consistency in policy is a contributing factor, even as we know that relative wealth and early childhood indicators also contribute?

Further, although there is limited consistency in which states are identified as high performers on NAEP across SES and improvement analyses, there is more consistency in the under performers. However, as we see next, it is difficult to differentiate these states based on features or qualities of their assessment or accountability systems.

Differentiating System Characteristics Using Available Indicators

If we believe that assessment and accountability ought to have benefits for student learning, then it stands to reason that the quality of the assessment and accountability system ought to matter. However, it is difficult to get a handle on quality, given the limited depth and validity of existing indicators. *Quality Counts* data show more surface similarities than deep differences in current state systems. For example, virtually all states combine multiple-choice testing with an extended assessment of language arts (writing). Two-thirds also include open-ended items on their assessments; and half the states include extended responses in subjects in addition to language arts. Most states claim they have developed customized tests relative to their standards, and almost all claim that they've done alignment studies. Of course, these are required under NCLB. But, evidence from these alignment studies shows uneven quality, with some states showing major imbalances between standards and assessment and most disproportionately focusing on lower-level skills relative to thinking and problem solving (e.g., Webb, 1999).

Studies commissioned by the Fordham Foundation show a more varied picture of the quality of standards and assessment systems across states (Cross, Rebarber, Torres, & Finn, 2004; Finn, Petrelli, & Julian, 2006; Stotsky & Finn, 2005). For example, Finn et al. (2006) reviewed state standards in English language arts, mathematics, history, and science for clarity in communicating learning expectations, academic rigor, and attention to fundamental knowledge in the discipline. Summarizing ratings across subjects and review criteria using an A to F grading scale, the researchers gave states, on average, a C-minus, although a few states were highly rated. Because they used somewhat different criteria, it perhaps is not surprising that we found only modest relationships between the Fordham and *Quality Counts* ratings—0.49 for ratings of standards in mathematics and 0.39 for ratings in English, based on analyses of states' standards in 2005.

To determine the quality of state tests, the Fordham study reviewed available documents and technical reports. Rating state assessments in terms of their content, alignment of standards and assessment, academic rigor, and technical trustworthiness, the study found significant room for improvement, starting with the lack of availability of materials from which state tests can be described and evaluated (Cross et al., 2004).

Effects of Accountability on Special Populations

We have noted above glimmerings that accountability is having an impact both nationally and within states on low SES students—students who qualify for free lunch and in general students served by large urban school districts. What of other special populations? The research base examining effects on students with disabilities and on English language learners is scanty. What we do know is that the validity and comparability of the state assessment results for these groups is suspect and thus it is hard to get a handle on the status and progress of their performance. The logic of using state assessment results to support the improvement of learning for these groups also is weak, given that the assessment results may well lack integrity. Nonetheless, advocates for these groups generally see the inclusion of special populations in state accountability systems as a plus because it has made the educational needs of these students visible, and has mandated expectations and plans for progress in mainstream contexts that were too often without them. At the same time, proponents worry about accountability targets that are unrealistic and fear backlash when the performance of English learners and/or students with disabilities subgroups deter schools and districts from meeting AYP targets.

What of the impact of accountability on other segments of the student population—the traditionally higher performing students, or the gifted, or the average student? From a measurement perspective, we know that it is difficult for a single test of limited duration to differentiate or motivate students at all points on the achievement spectrum. High ability students may be engaged with Advanced Placement and college entry exams, as well as in honors classes and gifted programs, which serves to motivate attention to their learning needs. But there is no obvious accountability mechanism for the "average student" who may have made it just over the proficient level. There is little research on this issue, but one might speculate that current federal accountability requirements do little to spur attention to the learning of these students although they represent the majority of students.

Effects on Teachers

Although a thorough treatment of the effects on teachers is beyond the scope of this chapter, it is worth noting a growing literature that is cause for concern. Research shows the strong relationship between student learning and the quality of teachers (Carey, 2004; Haycock, 1998; Sanders & Rivers, 1996) and the quality of interactions between teachers and students. Yet, any number of survey studies have suggested that teachers believe that current accountability models are focusing schools too much on state tests and not pushing schools in educationally productive directions. This includes concerns that have been raised earlier about curricular distortion, neglect of complex thinking, and a focus on test format and test preparation rather than on effective pedagogy (Hoffman, Assaf, & Paris, 2001; Jones & Egley, 2004; Pedulla et al., 2003). These studies similarly raise questions about whether accountability is increasing student learning (rather than simply inflating scores on state tests) and about the potential negative effects of accountability on teacher morale and motivation.

Concerns about accountability effects on teacher morale and motivation in the current NCLB context are bolstered by both theory and empirical evidence. Expectancy theory (Vroom, 1964) suggests that motivation is a function of one's perceived probability of success (expectancy), connection of success and reward (instrumentality), and value of obtaining goals (valence). In other words, people are motivated by things that are desirable, that they know how to do, and that they feel capable of achieving. Yet, much has been written about the feasibility of even most effective schools achieving NCLB annual yearly progress goals and closing the achievement gap (Linn, 2003; Rothstein, 2006). Research further shows that schools serving low performing students and students of color are least likely to be able to achieve these goals and have been the first to be subject to increasingly severe sanctions (Kim & Sunderman, 2005). Expectation theory would anticipate severe negative effects on motivation (and subsequent retention) in these settings where there is a low expectation of success. Indeed, the theory is supported by empirical evidence from a North Carolina study documenting the negative effects of strong accountability systems on low performing schools' ability to retain teachers in general, and quality teachers in particular (Clotfelter, Ladd, Vigdor, & Diaz, 2004).

Further, if ultimately it is professional accountability—that is, teachers' day-to-day commitment to effective practice and their ongoing motivation and sense of pedagogical responsibility—that is most important in advancing student learning, then one must question the relationship between professional accountability and unrealistic bureaucratic accountability requirements.

Summary and Conclusions

Returning to the question of whether accountability is serving the public interest: trite but true, the answer is complicated. Available evidence suggests that the theory of action underlying accountability is generally working.

Support for Theory of Action

Accountability systems make public expectations and motivate educators and students to pay attention to learning and performance: schools are changing what they are doing, they are focusing teaching and learning, and aligning curriculum and instruction with standards—or at least those that are tested. They are working to use data better to refine their programs and to identify students who are falling behind; districts and schools are trying to expand available opportunities so that students will get the extra help they need to catch up. Administrators and teachers are paying better attention to and making plans to respond to and engage *all* their students, particularly traditionally low-achieving, identifiable subgroups. Moreover, as we look to NAEP results as an external indicator of performance effects, we find a modest relationship between strength and duration of accountability systems and improvement in student performance, and we find some improvements in NAEP performance for economically poor students and perhaps some small movement in closing of the achievement gap.

Danger Spots

Admittedly, these effects are quite modest compared to the challenge of helping all children reach their potential, and it must be acknowledged that there are dangers here for our most vulnerable children; for example, those neediest students who got left behind in Chicago's promotion program and who were at greater risk of dropping out, students who do not pass high school exit exams required for diplomas and are more likely to drop out, and the lowest ability students who may be ignored as schools work to move students closer to the proficiency level over the line.

That accountability is changing what gets taught is clear from the research, but how much the change represents real improvement in students' opportunity to learn is moot. Research suggests a narrowing of the curriculum to focus on what is tested on state assessments, as well as what is included in standards, tends to overrepresent lower-level skills to the detriment of attention to higher-level thinking and complex applications. In responding to current accountability systems, then, teachers may be less likely to engage students, and particularly low performing and minority children, in meaningful problem-solving and reasoning activities, or to build the skills that students will need for success in the twenty-first century. Teachers echo this concern, believing that accountability is moving education in the wrong direction. At the same time, unrealistic accountability targets may be discouraging the best teachers from teaching in schools with high proportions of academically needy students. The potential combination of a meager curriculum and lesser quality teachers in the long run could increase rather than decrease the real achievement gap.

Yet, even against these dangers, perhaps modest positive effects for most students, and particularly for traditionally under-achieving students, should be viewed as an important accomplishment, even as we work to make the system work better for the most vulnerable and work to guard against unintended curriculum effects. It is sad but true that expecting something of all students, even if it is only what is tested, may in fact be an improvement for some. We can and should do better.

Toward Better Accountability Systems for the Public Interest

Accountability systems are most apt to serve the public interest when they are designed to maximize benefits and minimize negative effects. To maximize the benefits, this review suggests the importance of assuring that:

- Standards clearly communicate realistic expectations and represent the knowledge and skills that students will need for future success. One of the reasons that schools may teach to the test is that it is the only concrete guidance they have about learning expectations. Standards must provide a solid foundation for assessment, instruction, and accountability systems and focus on meaningful learning. They must be rigorous and address fundamental knowledge and skills in each discipline.
- Accountability systems reflect the full depth and breadth of standards and encourage good educational practice. Clearly, on demand annual state tests of limited duration cannot measure all that is important for students to know and be able to do. Measurement

theory and policy analysis suggests the value of multiple measures (American Educational Research Association, American Psychological Association, and National Council on Measurement in Education, 1999; Darling-Hammond et al., 2005). Assessments, or simply accountability requirements that students be engaged students in meaningful problem solving and reasoning tasks, could help to ameliorate current imbalances. Rather than simply mimicking state tests, benchmark assessments could be used to expand the depth and breadth of standards coverage and could be embedded in meaningful curriculum activities.
- Performance expectations are suitably high yet attainable. Grossly unrealistic performance expectations that carry sanctions are counter-productive to good teaching and learning. They discourage teacher motivation and encourage testing to the test. Linn (2003) has suggested using the trajectories of the fastest improving schools as a starting point for setting reasonable targets. Accountability models that credit schools for improvement in student performance at each level of the proficiency continuum (e.g., from below basic to basic, from proficient to advanced), could help assure that schools do not ignore their lowest achieving or average students.

Yet, even with the most optimal system, there are limits to what accountability alone can accomplish. Accountability systems can provide motivation, evidence, and a target for action, but effective action depends on educators' capacity. If educators already knew how to respond to the needs of their most challenging or all of their students, they would be doing so. Available evidence cited here suggests that educators are trying, but without dramatic success. Without continued investment in capacity building and resources to improve teaching and learning, there can be little closing of the achievement gap.

Even so, there is only so much that public schools can do to close an achievement gap that grows out of greater social and historical inequities. As Richard Rothstein (2006) has observed:

> If as a society we choose to preserve big social class differences, we must necessarily also accept substantial gaps between the achievement of lower-class and middle-class children. Closing those gaps requires not only better schools, although those are certainly needed, but also reform in the social and economic institutions that prepare children to learn in different ways. It will not be cheap.
>
> (p. 1)

So, is accountability serving the public interest? I say yes—though it's not a resounding success, and clearly we can do better. We need more safeguards in the system to guard against the potentially deadening effects of accountability and to stimulate the empowerment and efficacy it can bring when we as educators make a difference. We need to continue to ask: are our systems in the public interest? For whom are they working, and for whom not? How do we know? How can we optimize? Research and development and capacity building must continue. But at the same time, we need to be honest about what accountability systems can and cannot accomplish in helping all children to succeed.

Acknowledgments

The author is grateful to Suzanne Lane and Sheila Baron for their very thoughtful reviews and helpful suggestions for improving the technical quality and readability of the chapter and to Rachel Montgomery for editorial assistance.

Note

1. Exceptional improvement was defined as a z-score equal to or greater than 1.0, compared to the 50 states, plus DC sample.

References

American Educational Research Association, American Psychological Association, and National Council on Measurement in Education. (1999). *Standards for educational and psychological testing.* Washington, DC: American Educational Research Association.

Bishop, J. (2005). High school exit exams: When do learning effects generalize? In J. Herman & E. Haertel (Eds.), *Uses and misuses of data in accountability testing* (Yearbook of the National Society for the Study of Education) (pp. 260–288). Malden, MA: Blackwell.

Black, P. & Wiliam, D. (1998, March). Assessment and classroom learning. *Assessment in Education,* 45 (1), 7–74.

Booher-Jennings, J. (2006). Rationing education in an era of accountability. *Phi Delta Kappen,* 87 (10), 756–761.

Bridgeland, J., DiIulio, J., & Morison, K. (2006). *The silent epidemic.* Seattle, WA: Gates Foundation.

California Department of Education. (July, 2006). *California high school exit exam reports.* Online, available at: cahsee.cde.ca.gov/reports.asp (accessed January 7, 2007).

Carey, K. (2004). The real value of teachers. *Thinking K-16,* 8 (1), 3–32.

Carnoy, M. & Loeb, S. (2004). Does external accountability affect student outcomes? A cross-state analysis. In S. H. Fuhrman & R. F. Elmore (Eds.), *Redesigning accountability systems for education.* New York: Teachers College Press.

Center on Education Policy. (2005). *State high school exit exams: States try harder but gaps persist.* Washington, DC: CEP.

Center on Education Policy. (2006). *Year 4 of the No Child Left Behind Act.* Washington, DC: CEP.

Clotfelter, C., Ladd, H., Vigdor, J., & Diaz, R. (2004). Do school accountability systems make it more difficult for low performing schools to attract and retain high quality teachers? *Journal of Policy Analysis and Management,* 23 (2), 251–271.

Cross, R., Rebarber, T., Torres, J., & Finn, C. (2004). *Grading the system: The guide to state standards, tests and accountability policies.* Washington, DC: Thomas B. Fordham Foundation.

Darling-Hammond, L. (2006). No Child Left Behind and high school reform. *Harvard Educational Review,* 76 (4), 642–667.

Darling-Hammond, L., Rustique-Forrester, E., Pecheone, R., & Andree, A. (2005). *Multiple measures approaches to graduation.* Palo Alto, CA: School Redesign Network, Stanford University.

Finn, C., Petrilli, M., & Julian, L. (2006, July 26). *The state of state standards.* Washington, DC: Fordham Foundation.

Friedman, T. (2005). *The world is flat.* New York: Farrar, Straus & Giroux.

Gearhart, M., Nagashima, S., Pfotenhauer, J., Clark, S., Schwab, S., Vendlinski, T., et al. (2006). Developing expertise with classroom assessment in K-12 science. *Educational Assessment,* 11 (3&4), 237–263.

Goals 2000: Educate America Act, Pub. L.103–227, 108 Stat. 125 (1994).

Grissmer, D. & Flanagan, A. (2001). *The role of federal resources in closing the achievement gaps of minority and disadvantaged students* (RAND Publication No. DRU-2501-Edu.). Santa Monica, CA: RAND. Online, available at: http://stinet.dtic.mil/cgi-bin/GetTRDOC?AD=ADA389089&Location=U2&doc=GetTRDoc.pdf/ (accessed February 20, 2008).

Gross, B. & Goertz, M. E. (Eds.). (2005). *Holding high hopes: How high schools respond to state accountability policies* (CPRE Research Report Series No. RR-056). Philadelphia, PA: University of Pennsylvania, Consortium for Policy Research in Education.

Hamilton, S., Stecher, B., Marsh, J. A., Sloan McCombs, J., Robyn, A., Russell, J., et al. (2007). *Standards-based accountability under No Child Left Behind: Experiences of teachers and administrators in three states.* Santa Monica, CA: RAND.

Haycock, K. (1998). *Good teaching matters.* Washington, DC: Education Trust.

Herman, J. L. (2004). The effects of testing on instruction. In S. Fuhrman & R. Elmore (Eds.), *Redesigning accountability* (pp 141–166). New York: Teachers College Press.

Herman, J. & Yamashiro, K. (2001) *Exploring data use and school performance in urban public schools.* Los Angeles, CA: University of California, National Center for Research on Evaluation, Standards, and Student Testing.

Heubert, J. P. (2004). High stakes testing in a changing environment: Disparate impact, opportunity to learn and current legal protections. In S. Fuhrman & E. Elmore, (Eds.), *Redesigning accountability systems for education.* New York: Teachers College Press.

Hochschild, J. & Scovronick, N. (2003). *The American dream and the public schools.* Oxford: Oxford University Press.

Hoffman, J. V., Assaf, L. C., & Paris, S. G. (2001). High-stakes testing in reading: Today in Texas, tomorrow? *Reading Teacher,* 54 (5), 482–492.

Jones, B. D. & Egley, R. J. (2004, August 9). Voices from the frontlines: Teachers' perceptions of high stakes tests. *Educational Policy Analysis Archives,* 12 (39). Online, available at: http://epaa.asu.edu/epaa/v12n39 (accessed March 24, 2007).

Kim, J. & Sunderman, G. (2005). Measuring academic proficiency under the No Child Left Behind Act: Implications for educational equity. *Educational Researcher,* 34 (8), 3–13.

Koretz, D. (2005). Alignment, high stakes, and the inflation of test scores. In J. Herman & E. Haertel (Eds.), *Uses and misuses of data in accountability testing* (Yearbook of the National Society for the Study of Education) (pp. 99–118). Malden, MA: Blackwell.

Koretz, D., Mitchell, K. J., Barron, S., & Stecher, B. M. (1996). *Perceived effects of the Maryland State Assessment Program* (CSE Technical Report No. 406). Los Angeles, CA: National Center for Research on Evaluation, Standards, and Student Testing, University of California.

Lee, J. (2006). *Tracking achievement gaps and assessing the impact of No Child Left Behind on the gaps: An in-depth look into national and state reading and math outcome trends.* Cambridge, MA: Harvard Civil Rights Project.

Linn, R. L. (2003). Accountability: Responsibility and reasonable expectations. *Educational Researcher,* 32 (7), 3–13.

Mathews, D. (2006). *Reclaiming public education by reclaiming our democracy.* New York: Kettering Foundation Press.

Merriam-Webster's online dictionary. Online, available at: http://www.m-w.com/cgi-bin/dictionary?va=accountability (accessed March 28, 2006).

Moyers, B. (2007, January 22) For America's sake. *Nation.* Online, available at: www.thenation.com/doc/20070122/moyers (accessed December 6, 2006).

National Research Council. (2003). *Assessment in support of instruction and learning: Bridging the gap between large-scale and classroom assessment.* Washington, DC: National Academies Press.

No Child Left Behind Act of 2001, Pub. L.107–110, 115 Stat.1425 (2002).

Parker, W. C. (2003). *Teaching democracy: Unity and diversity in public life.* New York: Teachers College Press.

Partnership for 21st Century Learning. (2007, July 23). *Framework for 21st century learning.* Online, available at: http://www.21stcenturyskills.org/documents/frameworkflyer_072307.pdf (accessed February 13, 2008).

Partnership for 21st Century Skills. (2002). *Learning for the 21st Century.* Online, available at: http://www.21stcenturyskills.org/index.php?option=com_content&task=view&id=29&itid=21 (accessed February 13, 2008).

Pedulla, J., Abrams, G., Madaus, G., Russell, M., Ramos, M., & Miao, J. (2003). *Perceived effects of state mandated testing programs on teaching and learning.* Boston, MA: National Board on Educational Testing and Public Policy, Boston College.

Pellegrino, J. (2006, November). Rethinking and redesigning curriculum, instruction, and assessment: What contemporary research and theory suggest. Paper commissioned by the National Center on Education and the Economy for the New Commission on the Skills of the American Workforce. Online, available at: http://www.skillscommission.org/pdf/commissioned_papers/Rethinking%20and%20Redesigning.pdf (accessed March 24, 2007).

Ramaley, J. D., 2005. Goals for Learning and assessment. In J. Herman & E. Haertel (Eds.), *Uses and misuses of data in accountability testing* (Yearbook of the National Society for the Study of Education) (pp. 55–77). Malden, MA: Blackwell.

Rampey, B. D., Lutkus, A. D., & Dion, G. (2005). *The nation's report card: Trial urban district assessment, mathematics 2006* (NCES 2006–457r). Washington, DC: U.S. Government Printing Office.

Reich, R. (1988). *Introduction in the power of public ideas.* Cambridge, MA: Ballinger.

Roderick, M., Nagaoka, J., & Allensworth, E. (2005). Is the glass half full or mostly empty? Ending social promotion in Chicago. In J. Herman & E. Haertel (Eds.), *Uses and misuses of data in accountability testing* (Yearbook of the National Society for the Study of Education) (pp. 223–259). Malden, MA: Blackwell.

Rothstein, R. (2006). *Reforms that could help narrow the achievement gap* (WestEd Policy Perspectives). San Francisco, CA: WestEd.

Sanders, W. L. & Rivers, J. C. (1996, November). *Cumulative and residual effects of teachers on future student academic achievement* (Research Progress Report). Knoxville, TN: University of Tennessee Value-Added Research and Assessment Center.

School Matters. (2005, December). *Leveling the playing field: Identifying outperforming and underperforming states on the NAEP in demographic context.* Online, available at: http://www.schoolmatters.com/pdf/naep_comparative_state_performance_2005_schoolmatters.pdf (accessed March 24, 2006).

Shields, P., Esch, C., Lash, A., Padilla, C., Woodworth, K., LaGuardia, K., et al. (2004). *Evaluation of Title I accountability systems and school improvement: First year findings.* Washington, DC: U.S. Department of Education.

Stecher, B. M. & Barron, S. L. (1999). *Quandrennial milepost accountability testing in Kentucky* (CRESST Report 505). Los Angeles, CA: University of California, National Center for Research on Evaluation, Standards, and Student Testing.

Stecher, B. M. & Borko, H. (2002). *Combining surveys and case studies to examine standards-based educational reform* (CRESST Report 565). Los Angeles, CA: University of California, National Center for Research on Evaluation, Standards, and Student Testing.

Stecher, B. M., Barron, S. L., Chun, T., & Ross, K. (2000). *The effects of the Washington state education reform on schools and classroom* (CRESST Report 525). Los Angeles, CA: University of California, National Center for Research on Evaluation, Standards, and Student Testing.

Stone, D. (2001). *Policy paradox and political reason.* New York: W.W. Norton and Company.

Stotsky, S. & Finn, C. E. (2005). *The state of English standards 2005.* Washington, DC: Thomas Fordham Foundation.

Swanson, C. (2006). *Making the connection: A decade of standards-based reform and achievement* [online only]. *Education Week,* 25 (17). Online, available at: http://www.edweek.org/media/ew/qc/2006/MakingtheConnection.pdf (accessed March 24, 2006).

Vroom, V. H. (1964). *Work and motivation.* New York: John Wiley & Sons.
Webb, N. L. (1999). *Alignment of science and mathematics standards and assessments in four states* (Research Monograph No. 18). Madison, WI: University of Wisconsin, Wisconsin Center for Education Research.
Wiliam, D. (2006). Formative assessment: Getting the focus right. *Educational Assessment,* 11 (3&4), 283–287.
Wilson, M. & Berenthal, M. (Eds.). (2005). *Systems for state science assessment.* Washington, DC: National Academies Press.

12
A View from the Teacher Trenches
Accountability and the Betrayal of the Standards Vision

Bella Rosenberg[1]

Why would so many of America's teachers be heartsick over the No Child Left Behind Act (NCLB) (Johnson, Arumi, & Ott, 2006)? Why would teachers, who have consistently supported high standards (Peter D. Hart Research Associates and the Winston Group (Peter D. Hart & Winston), 2007; Johnson & Duffett, 2004; Peter D. Hart Research Associates (Peter D. Hart), 1999), be so negative about a law that its bipartisan proponents consider the crowning achievement of the standards movement?

To many politicians and influential education-reform seekers across the political spectrum, the answer is obvious: teachers hate accountability (*Diane Piché* vs. *Mike Petrelli* vs. *Joel Packer on No Child Left Behind* (Piché), 2007; Moe, 2003; Navarette, 2007; Toppo, 2004). According to this view, "we know how to educate poor and minority children of all kinds ... to high levels" (Commission on Chapter 1, 1992, p. 3). But, most teachers don't do "what works," either because they are lazy, resistant to reform, infected with the hard or soft bigotry of low expectations, controlled by their retrograde unions, or all of the above. Teachers thus need a muscular accountability system to force them to shape up and do "what works" (Bush, 2000; Commission on Chapter 1, 1992, pp. 3, 7; see Edley as discussed in Koretz, 2006; see also Margaret Spellings' comments in Sanchez, 2006). With the passage of NCLB, they got it.

Indeed, NCLB champions view teachers with such suspicion, if not downright contempt, that some of them hail educators' criticisms of the law as further proof of NCLB's fundamental soundness. "Vive la resistance!" exults the executive director of the Citizens Commission on Civil Rights. NCLB is doing exactly what it was intended to do:

> It is making the education establishment uncomfortable, pushing the adults in the system to work harder and smarter and to confront their own racism and other biases.... In fact, there are some of us who view much of the resistance as a sign that the law really is working!
>
> (Piché, 2007, Vive la resistance! section)

Even those who now concede that the law's universal proficiency goal is unrealistic nonetheless insist that schools must continue to be held accountable for achieving it lest teachers and other educators slack off (Gordon, 2006; see also Edley as discussed in Koretz, 2006; and George Miller's comments in Sanchez, 2006).

Is it true that teachers oppose accountability? They certainly don't like NCLB's regimen. They have also chafed under other less stringent federal, state, or local systems that use an inappropriate measure for judging a school's effectiveness. NCLB has reified that measure, a measure that does not track individual students' yearly progress during school and cannot distinguish between in-school and other contributions to their performance, and thereby fails to discriminate validly or reliably between effective and ineffective schools (Barton, 2005, 2006; Herman & Haertel, 2005; Koretz, 2002; Linn, 2000, 2003a; Linn, Baker, & Betebenner, 2002). As this suggests, teachers, like most people, condition their support for accountability on the system's fairness—and to teachers, NCLB's system represented a new zenith of unfairness (Peter D. Hart & Winston, 2007; Johnson, Arumi, & Ott, 2006). For, not only did it reify a misleading method of judging school effectiveness, it also set virtually every public school, irrespective of its productivity, on a course to failure[2] (Kane & Staiger, 2002; Kane, Staiger, & Geppert, 2001; Linn 2003a; Nelson & Rosenberg, 2005; Rosenberg, 2004; Rothstein, Jacobsen, & Wilder, 2006).

As the following account of the standards movement suggests, the disconnect between the views of NCLB champions and teachers who support standards is more profound than simple patch-ups of the law or additional funding would repair. For if the law's champions see NCLB as the crowning achievement of the standards movement, teachers experience it as the ultimate betrayal of the visionary concept of standards-based reform that had inspired their support and hard work. Indeed, by inscribing into federal law the scientifically baseless proposition that "bad" schools are *the* root cause of low achievement and achievement gaps and, conversely, that "good" ones are *the* cure-all for these problems, NCLB secured a national victory for the view that schools and their teachers are the chief culprit in America's shameful, ongoing story of leaving children behind (Gamoran & Long, 2006; Heckman, 2006; Jencks & Phillips, 1998; Mosteller & Moynihan, 1972; Rothstein, 2004; Shonkoff & Phillips, 2000). Ironically, not only is that view rejected by science and aggrieved by teachers, it also fails to command the support of parents and the public (Johnson & Duffett, 2004; Johnson et al., 2006; Rose & Gallup, 2006, Tables 8 and 9).

The First Wave of the Standards Movement: Do More, Do Better

A Nation at Risk, the 1983 report of the National Commission on Excellence in Education (NCEE) (1983) convened by the U.S. Department of Education, is widely credited with initiating the contemporary standards movement. In words that riveted the public's attention, the Commission declared that:

> the educational foundations of our society are presently being eroded by a rising tide of mediocrity that threatens our very future as a Nation and a people ... [because] our society and its educational institutions seem to have lost sight of the basic purposes of schooling, and of the high expectations and disciplined effort needed to attain them.
>
> (pp. 5–6)

The Commission called for increasing and strengthening academic course requirements for high school graduation and laid out general content standards in Five New Basics—English, math, science, social studies, and computer science—to drive its proposal. It also called for high schools to have "programs requiring rigorous effort in subjects that advance students' personal, educational, and occupational goals, such as the fine and performing arts and vocational education" (p. 26), and noted that curriculum in the preceding grades should "be specifically designed to provide a sound base" for the Five New Basics, as well as for studying a foreign language and the arts (pp. 26–27). It also recommended adopting more rigorous standards for student academic performance (and discipline), revising textbooks and curriculum to reflect the new standards and evaluating their effectiveness, as well as increasing the school day or year or making more effective use of the existing time.

The Commission further called for having students take achievement tests at major transition points between levels of schooling in order to "(a) certify the student's credentials; (b) identify the need for remedial intervention; and (c) identify the opportunity for advanced or accelerated work." These new tests "should be administered as part of a nationwide (but not federal) system of State and local standardized tests ... [that] should include other diagnostic procedures that assist teachers and students to evaluate student progress" (p. 28).

Although the Commission linked students taking the Five New Basics and achievement exams to high school graduation, it recognized that "the variety of student aspirations, abilities, and preparation" made a one-size-fits-all approach to education neither realistic nor desirable. It declared "that everyone can learn, everyone is born with an *urge* to learn which can be nurtured, that a solid high school education is within the reach of virtually all," but it did not advocate a single performance standard for all students and called instead for a "common expectation: We must demand the best effort and performance from all students, whether they are gifted or less able, affluent or disadvantaged, whether destined for college, the farm, or industry"(p. 24).

This is clearly not because the Commission sanctioned differences in educational outcomes that are based on class, race, and ethnicity. Rather, it understood that egalitarian ideals and quests for excellence must still contend with the scientific laws of *individual* differences. As Daniel Koretz points out, "Most of the variation in the entire population arises from the huge variation in scores *within* groups, not from the differences *between* groups" (2006, p. 18).

Many critics, however, read *A Nation at Risk* as valuing excellence over equity. Similarly, the report's recommendations on improving teacher evaluation and compensation were widely interpreted as a simple embrace of traditional merit pay. What the Commission actually called for was increasing teacher salaries and making them "professionally competitive, market-sensitive and performance-based." It also recommended tying "salary, promotion, tenure, and retention decisions" to "an effective evaluation system that includes peer review so that superior teachers can be rewarded, average ones encouraged, and poor ones either improved or terminated" (NCEE, 1983, p. 30). The Commission did not further clarify what it meant by "performance-based."

The National Education Association (NEA), the larger of the two teacher unions, was mostly negative toward *A Nation at Risk* (Cross, 2004, p. 80), which it saw as an attack on public education, deficient on equity, and in favor of traditional merit pay. The smaller, more urban-based American Federation of Teachers (AFT), which was then under the leadership of Albert Shanker, had similar concerns. But, the AFT had long deplored declining standards. Moreover, it had not expected that a report coming out of the administration of President Ronald Reagan, whose election neither union had supported, would argue for investing more in educating disadvantaged students. And, it certainly didn't expect it to ignore the President's favorite anti-public education and anti-union hobby horses and instead point the nation toward a direction that was more compatible with AFT's views. Convinced that *A Nation at Risk* held more promise than risk for public education and for AFT members and their students—whose schools did not typically experience official concern for either excellence or equity—the AFT passed a largely favorable resolution about the report at its 1983 convention (American Federation of Teachers, 1983; Shanker, 1997a).

The standards movement the report unleashed has had extraordinary holding power. Present day controversies notwithstanding, teachers do not want to turn back the clock on standards (Johnson et al., 2006). This is rather remarkable because, starting in 1983, teachers' support for the movement has been sorely tested by policymakers' implementation of reform.

For example, the typical state response to the Commission's call for more rigorous high school graduation requirements was to increase seat time and neglect the recommendations about content standards. Similarly, its call for new achievement tests largely prompted more states to adopt the kind of curriculum-neutral, minimum competency tests that 37 of them were already using. The report's proposals for improving teacher quality (NCEE, 1983, pp. 30–31) were more often followed by colleges raising requirements for entering pre-service programs than by improving program quality and by states' adoption of alternative certification programs whose standards were often lower than those governing regular teacher licensure. More states also adopted entry-level teacher tests, which the Commission had not directly recommended, the NEA opposed, and the AFT supported while criticizing their low quality. Teacher career ladders were implemented, often without the input from teachers as the report had advised, and—as some had predicted—traditional merit pay came back into fashion (Airasian, 1987; Firestone, Fuhrman, & Kirst, 1989; Kohut & Wright, 1984).

The Commission had put some academic content and other meat into its brief report on the need to do more and better. Policymakers instead issued reams of new process regulations that gave schools little substantive guidance about what was expected of them. Yet, in 1986, with the ink barely dry on new education reform laws, the nation's governors, backed by the business community, announced that it was *Time for Results* and for greater accountability (National Governors Association, 1986).

Standardized tests, which had been developed and used to make judgments about students (typically along with teacher-made tests and other criteria), were now pressed into the service of school and, sometimes, district accountability. At first, sanctions typically involved public shaming and being required to develop improvement plans. By the late 1980s, however, school restructuring, which had been associated with giving teachers more voice in their schools' improvement efforts, was rapidly assuming the punishing face of reconstitution (Bowers, 1989; Klauke, 1989; Ornstein, 1988).

Because the trigger for academic accountability was low student achievement, accountability was in effect confined to high-poverty districts or schools—urban ones in particular. This mainly affected AFT members, who viewed it as a mixed blessing. On the one hand, they knew that some of their schools were truly dysfunctional, that most of them were under-resourced, and that all of them could use help to improve. They also understood that states' new educational investments had been conditioned on greater accountability. On the other hand, they resented—as later, most teachers would—a form of accountability that made most of their schools appear to be failing, whether they were or not (AFT, 1992; Public Agenda, 2003).

Then, as now, accountability systems that were publicly purported to be measuring school or student progress were instead comparing the achievement of different students in the same grade or grades over time and also failing to account for the level at which students started. Then, as now, these systems disguised the fact that the outcomes they reported were not only the result of that year's instruction but also of students' prior in- and out-of-school educational experiences. And then, as now, they could not distinguish between low-*achieving* schools that were truly low *performing* and low-achieving schools that, because of the substantial progress their students had made, were actually high performers (Barton, 2006; Linn, 2003a; Raudenbush, 2004).

The system, however, was politically self-reinforcing. Rising test scores meant that the accountability model was working, while falling scores meant that the stakes needed to be raised. For the most part, scores rose but fell well below reformers' expectations. Achievement still wasn't good enough (Cross, 2004, p. 80). Fair enough; but what did this mean?

Standards-Based Systemic Reform: What Students Should Know and Be Able to Do

Starting in the late 1980s, the standards movement turned to giving more shape and substance to the demand for higher expectations. To some, the key impediment to improved achievement was teachers' presumably low expectations of their students. Shanker, however, saw the problem in larger, more systemic terms: "Sure everybody can improve. But the problems we have are not … in our efforts or in our intentions or our expectations. The problem is in the way this whole school system is organized" (Shanker, 1997d, p. 67).

Marshall Smith and Jennifer O'Day's seminal article on systemic education reform (1991) pointed to America's highly decentralized, loosely coupled system of public education. Controlled by a broad, uncoordinated, and often competing and fad-inspired array of public and non-governmental actors, schools had never been given a clear, coherent, or consistent base of goals and were therefore ill-equipped to respond effectively to a national call to raise expectations. There was wide variation among and even within states in official expectations for schools, which in any case were rarely clear guides for instruction. There was similar variation in curriculum, even among and within schools in the same districts. In short, there was little that was systematic about the public education "system," except for its systemic inequities. Absent clearly defined expectations, there inevitably would be little common understanding of what doing better meant.

Like *A Nation at* Risk, these newer calls for systemic, standards-based reform did not, as Karen Seashore Louis (1998, p. 21) observed, blame teachers for America's educational "mediocrity." Rather, teachers "were seen as victims of a fragmented social vision about the goals of education." Indeed, to its main architects, standards-based reform and professionalizing teaching were inextricably linked (Louis, 1998; Shanker, 1985).

Echoing *A Nation at Risk*, proponents argued that the first step in systemic reform was to establish rich academic content standards for what students should know and be able to do, so that the meaning of higher expectations would be clear to schools, as well as to parents and the public. Next came developing curriculum frameworks and adopting new textbooks based on those standards—which were also meant to drive professional development and inform teacher preparation—followed by new assessments that were aligned with the new standards and curriculum frameworks. Moreover, because teaching and learning to higher standards would be challenging work, teachers and students should be given time and support to tackle these new demands (AFT, 1992; Smith & O'Day, 1991).

This staged and aligned implementation of reform was central to the standards vision. It was also profoundly important to AFT teachers, who knew either directly or indirectly that disadvantaged students were the chief victims of the nation's "fragmented social vision about the goals of education" (Louis, 1998, p. 21). When the AFT leadership translated this reform model into a Convention resolution, it passed overwhelmingly. As the background paper, which was voted on with the resolution, unequivocably stated:

> If new assessments, no matter how good they are, precede the production and dissemination of standards and are a substitute for high-quality curriculum and staff development, then students and teachers will continue to be mystified about what's expected of them, and the result will be widespread failure. We do not need another thermometer to tell us how sick we are; we need a system that helps us get well.
>
> (AFT, 1992, p. 19)

The degree to which this vision of reform resonated with AFT teachers cannot be overemphasized. Of course, they were also anxious. Although AFT polls revealed that the majority of its teachers, including a sizeable percentage of those in non-urban districts, believed that standards in their schools were too low, many worried that students who were challenged even by the basics would struggle even more with higher standards. They also knew that the kind of professional development they typically had been getting would be of no help.

Understandably, they were also anxious about school accountability. The 1988 reauthorization of the Elementary and Secondary Education Act (ESEA) had featured the adoption of an unprecedented requirement that states define some outcome measure for Title 1 schools and identify those in which "students were not achieving as expected" (Cross, 2004, p. 88). States typically used a low-level outcome standard and a status measure in complying with the federal requirement, but the law also stimulated more states to adopt their own and largely tougher accountability systems (Bowers, 1989; Pipho, 1987). As Chris Pipho of the Education Commission of the States wryly observed, "Turning the media spotlight on a host of outcome variables without alerting everyone concerned to the differences at the starting gate will undoubtedly cause some problems at the local level" (Pipho, 1987, p. 22).

"America leads the world in idiotic and counterproductive accountability practices," the AFT charged. They are "educationally bankrupt and politically driven" and "corrupt the very accountability" they seek. Still, accountability was necessary, it said, because

> if there is no accountability—and therefore no incentives—for students, schools, and officials to improve their performance, it is doubtful that we will see results from a new system of standards and assessments because not enough people will pay attention.

But, "recognizing the need for accountability is easier than figuring out a responsible course of action. There are no defensible models of school accountability in this nation [and] little or no agreement over how to do this productively" (AFT, 1992, pp. 19–20).

In response to a Florida teacher merit pay proposal in the late 1980s, the AFT had proposed a merit schools plan that featured schools rather than individual teachers competing for rewards based on student outcomes. Recognizing that the prevailing accountability model would typically favor advantaged schools, the AFT called for grouping schools by their students' poverty level and determining their academic progress from their start points. The state adopted this plan but soon dropped it despite teacher support and a favorable evaluation (Lawther, Lange, & Winston, 1990). In 1988, South Carolina Governor Caroll Campbell, Jr., included grouping schools by their students' poverty status in his plan to exempt high-achieving school districts from almost all state regulations (Bowers, 1989). Although a few states later moved toward accounting for different starting points, the snapshot model of accountability continued to reign.

Yet, AFT teachers embraced the standards vision, despite their misgivings. For one, they believed that it held great promise for securing the future of public education, which was increasingly besieged by privatization advocates. Second, they believed that the vision offered up more decent accountability terms than anything they had previously experienced because it contained a logically staged and aligned order of standards-based reforms that also emphasized helping rather than punishing teachers and their students (AFT, 1992).

AFT teachers also knew that the standards movement was an opportunity to revive the nation's moribund equity agenda (Shanker, 1997a, 1997b). The union had always understood that equalizing educational opportunity required more than school reform. As it noted in 1992, "higher standards and better assessments will not spontaneously produce higher achievement." That requires making sure that children are ready for school and "working equally hard at overcoming America's appalling level of childhood poverty." It was time, the union insisted, for politicians and the public "to cease acting as though the cries of despair from our poor districts were mere noise and teachers' advocacy on behalf of their students were mere self-interest." If America wanted world class public schools, then it needed to understand that its "competitors' success with their systems of standards and assessments cannot be separated from their exemplary records of supporting children and families, providing adequate and roughly equal resources for their schools, and treating teachers like professionals" (AFT, 1992, p. 18).[3]

Of course, teachers were not so naïve as to believe that social policy would be harnessed to education reform just because of their union's say-so. But in 1989, the nation's governors, under the leadership of President George H. W. Bush, had convened the first National Education Summit in American history, which resulted in an equally unprecedented agreement to set national education goals and, in 1990, the fulfillment of that pact (Cross, 2004, Ch. 6). The goals were novel in another way: they recognized that producing higher achievement required more than education reform.

Although the goals were intended to be strictly outcomes based, what emerged after intense negotiations between the White House and the National Governors Association (then under the leadership of Governor Bill Clinton) were short, outcomes-focused statements followed by objectives—indicators or measures—that sometimes strayed into input territory (Cross, 2004, Ch. 6).

The first goal, school readiness by the year 2000, was conceptually agreed to at the Summit by both political parties, but negotiations over the objectives were particularly heated. What emerged cast a bright political light on bedrock components of improving student achievement. The goal's objectives were to reduce the number of low-birthweight babies through "enhanced prenatal health systems" and ensure that children received "the nutrition, physical activity experiences, and health care needed to arrive at school with healthy minds and bodies, and to maintain the mental alertness necessary to be prepared to learn." Acknowledging parents as their children's first teachers, the objectives said they "will have access to the training and support parents need" and also committed to all children having "access to high-quality and developmentally appropriate preschool programs" (National Education Goals Panel (NEGP), n.d.).

Goal 6, which committed to "adult literacy and lifelong learning," also seemed to recognize that fostering parent success paid off in their children's education. So did Goal 8 on parent participation, which Congress added in 1994 when it enacted the goals. Its objectives called on states to assist every school to promote partnerships that would improve parent involvement, at home and in the school, in fostering "the social, emotional, and academic growth of children." Goal 7 called for safe, disciplined, and alcohol- and drug-free schools, which also gave teachers hope that help was on the way because its objectives enjoined "parents, businesses, governmental and community organizations" to work together with schools on these problems.

Goal 4, which Congress also added in 1994, spoke to teachers' need for help with teaching to higher standards. The goal stated that "the Nation's teaching force will have access to programs for the continued improvement of their professional skills and the opportunity to acquire the knowledge and skills needed to instruct and prepare all American students for the next century."

Of course, since their overall objective was to improve student achievement and close gaps, the National Education Goals also set academic outcome goals. Today, memory of those goals is chiefly confined to Goal 5, which expected American students to become first in the world in math and science achievement by the year 2000. Now, as in 1990, that goal provokes headshakes over its delusional and deluding ambition (Cross, 2004, p. 97), which is ironic since it is more attainable than NCLB's goal (Rothstein et al., 2006, World class standards section). It is therefore worth revisiting[4] Goal 3, which stated that "all students will leave grades 4, 8, and 12 having demonstrated competency over challenging subject matter including English, mathematics, science, foreign languages, civics and government, economics, arts, history, and geography" (NEGP, n.d.).

With the major exception of its broad curriculum reach, which makes NCLB's narrow focus on reading and math look like a case of the soft bigotry of low expectations, Goal 3 looks similar to NCLB's goal. But, this similarity is deceiving. In contrast to NCLB's definition of excellence and equity as universal student attainment of a cut point for proficiency set on a test, the first of Goal 3's six indicators set a higher but more achievable standard: "The academic performance of all students at the elementary and secondary level will increase significantly *in each quartile, and the distribution of minority students in each quartile will more closely reflect the student population as a whole*" (emphasis added).

Put another way, Goal 3's performance standard simultaneously reflected egalitarian ideals, science, and common experience: it recognized that because of *individual* differences, there will always be a distribution of achievement; the challenge was to raise both its floor and ceiling—and everything in between—while also eradicating illegitimate *group* distinctions, such as those based on class, race, and ethnicity. Indeed, one consequence of NCLB's lower standard is that, despite its praiseworthy requirement to disaggregate test scores, it obscures the full range of achievement gaps between disadvantaged and other students (Linn, 2003b; Barton, 2005; Nelson & Rosenberg, 2005). Ironically, too, although the law was sold and is defended on the basis of research that identified beat-the-odds schools—many of which later failed under NCLB—those studies used far lower standards for "effectiveness" than were set in NCLB, as well as a measurement system that, like NCLB's, did not reveal students' academic starting points (Harris, 2007; Nelson & Rosenberg, 2005; Rothstein, 2004, pp. 61–85).

Of course, NCLB did not pioneer a system that both fails to meet standards for educational accountability (Baker, Linn, Herman, & Koretz, 2002; Barton, 2006) and is at odds with best practices in other sectors, including business (Stecher & Kirby, 2004; Rothstein et al., 2006, A return to norm-referenced reporting section). Rather, its achievement was to exacerbate severely the unfairness and unintended consequences of an inappropriate model of school accountability that a bipartisan group of state and federal policymakers and other influential reformers had steadily freighted with additional purposes as they steered the standards movement through the 1990s (Barton, 2006; Cross, 2004, Ch. 6; Linn et al., 2002).

Teachers' first major experience of the corruption of the standards vision came with the near universal failure to implement the rationally staged and aligned set of reforms that vision had detailed (Barton, 2005, 2006; Cross, 2004, p. 113; Resnick & Zurawsky, 2005). Instead of first developing content standards, most states drove reform by administering either existing or new tests to determine if schools and students were meeting higher performance standards that had not been articulated to them. When content standards—for better or for worse—eventually were adopted, they were typically useless as guides for instruction and were rarely accompanied by new curriculum frameworks or relevant professional development (AFT, 1995, 1999, 2001; Marzano & Kendall, 1998). Moreover, although reformers heard plenty about the need to rethink the prevailing accountability model and about the danger of a single performance standard, most of them simply ignored it (Koretz, 2002; Linn, 1991; Rosenberg, 1992; Rothman, 1990; Shanker, 1997c, 1997e).

Still, state and local test scores often increased, either because of better instruction, or more narrow, test-driven teaching, or some combination (Linn, 1991). In any case, teachers got more blame than credit, even when scores on the no-stakes National Assessment of Educational Progress (NAEP) increased (Grissmer, Flanagan, Kawata, & Williamson, 2000; National Center for Education Statistics, 2005). This is because in 1991, when NAEP's governing board began reporting results on the basis of what students *should* be able to do and used a very challenging—and much debunked—standard for proficient performance, many influential critics of public education started to use the low percentage of proficient students that the board's method yielded to persuade the public that the nation's schools were hopelessly broken (Pellegrino, Jones, & Mitchell, 1998; Shepard, Glaser, Linn, & Bohrnstedt, 1993; U.S. General Accounting Office, 1993).

Though feeling increasingly scapegoated, teachers were also gratified by other key outcomes of the standards movement. Among these was a sharper focus on the academic mission of schools, more support for struggling students, and improvements in the quality of professional development. Indeed, when teachers say—to this day—that they want to stay the course with high standards, it is not only because they believe in them, but because they have seen higher standards improve teaching and learning. And, although they do not think that this accomplishment is good enough or reaches far enough across the curriculum, they strongly believe that the chief reason for these shortcomings is the failure of the standards movement to be more faithful to a vision of reform that saw beyond the schoolhouse door (Peter D. Hart, 1999; Peter D. Hart & Winston, 2007; Johnson & Duffet, 2004; Johnson et al., 2006; Public Agenda, 2003).

In 1999, when Congress began work on the reauthorization of the Elementary and Secondary Education Act, it had a different view of what wasn't good enough. The 1994 amendments to ESEA had called on states to develop procedures for determining "adequate yearly progress,"[5] and the states had been slow to do so (Barton, 2006, p. 7; Cross, 2004, p. 124). The outcome of this anger at the states was the bipartisan passage of NCLB, which operationalized an aspirational goal, grafted it onto an inappropriate method of measuring "progress" toward its attainment, and created an amalgam that would inexorably make almost all schools appear to be failing. Even worse for the nation's prospects for achieving both equity and excellence, NCLB repealed the National Education Goals, the only unified federal statement that had recognized that improving student achievement requires *both* school improvement and social policies that attack disadvantage at its roots.

The road to hell is paved with good intentions. When reformers spin noble fantasies, require schools to fulfill them, and then subject those schools to contempt and punishment when they don't create utopia practically overnight, then teachers and other practitioners are bound to cry unfair. Moreover, when reformers sweep the role of poverty and class completely off the table and illogically cast schools and educators as both the chief culprit and cure-all for achievement gaps, they are not serving their stated aim of securing a bright future for America's vulnerable youngsters. Rather, they are fostering the perpetuation of a dystopia that generations of these children have already had to endure. And that's worse than unfair, it's tragic.

Acknowledgments

The author thanks Paul Barton, Richard Kahlenberg, Lorrie Shepherd, and Andrea Solarz for their helpful comments on an earlier draft.

Notes

1. Unless otherwise supported by more general evidence, my discussion of the standards movement reflects the experiences and views of teachers represented by the American Federation of Teachers (AFT), where I worked from 1983–2005. I assisted AFT President Albert Shanker, a leader in the standards movement, from 1983 until 1997, the year of his death. References to teachers in my discussion of No Child Left Behind (NCLB) pertain to teachers in general.
2. If NCLB's 100% proficiency goal continues to drive its accountability system, then shifting to a growth model (whether a true one or not), as many have urged, would be unlikely to reduce the incidence of school "failure."

3. The AFT opposed opportunity-to-learn standards when they were introduced in the 1994 federal Goals 2000 bill, even though its 1992 Convention Resolution supported them. The AFT had good reason to believe that this proposal was intended to forestall development of new content standards and assessments. If politicians, business leaders, and the public didn't see swift action on raising standards, the union thought, they would turn more readily to supporting school privatization. The decision to oppose the Goals 2000 opportunity-to-learn standards was a much-debated and wrenching one within the AFT.
4. The failure to mention Goal 2, which calls for increasing the "graduation rate to at least 90%" (NEGP, n.d.), is not to slight its importance; rather, since Goal 2 links to Goal 3, which includes high school graduation, Goal 2 is encompassed by the Goal 3 discussion.
5. The goal of achieving 100% student proficiency in challenging subject matter was first adopted in the 1994 reauthorization of ESEA. Although efforts were made to operationalize that aspirational goal with a formula for holding schools accountable for making "adequate yearly progress" (AYP) toward the goal, they failed. Instead, the law deferred to the states to define AYP. The AFT, then still under Shanker's leadership, opposed the pre-NCLB attempt to install this NCLB-like accountability system in federal law.

References

Airasian, P. (1987). State mandated testing and educational reform: Context and consequences. *American Journal of Education*, 95 (3), 393.

American Federation of Teachers. (1983, July). *Resolutions and proceedings of the 1983 AFT Convention (educational issues).* (Available from the AFT Archives at the Walter P. Reuther Library, 5401 Cass Ave., Detroit, MI 48202).

American Federation of Teachers. (1992). *Background paper for 1992 AFT convention resolution, "National education standards and assessments."* (Available from the AFT Archives at the Walter P. Reuther Library, 5401 Cass Ave., Detroit, MI 48202).

American Federation of Teachers. (1995). *Making standards matter 1995: A fifty-state progress report on efforts to raise academic standards.* Washington, DC: AFT.

American Federation of Teachers. (1999). Making standards matter 1999: An update on state activity. *Educational Issues Policy Brief*, 11, 1–12.

American Federation of Teachers. (2001). *Making standards matter 2001: A fifty-state report on efforts to implement a standards-based system* (Item No. 39–0262). Washington: AFT.

Baker, E. L., Linn, R. L., Herman, J. L., & Koretz, D. (2002). *Standards for educational accountability systems* (Policy Brief 5). Los Angeles, CA: National Center for Research on Evaluation, Standards, and Student Testing.

Barton, P. (2005, January). *Unfinished business: More measured approaches in standards-based reform.* Princeton, NJ: Educational Testing Service.

Barton, P. (2006). *"Failing" or "succeeding" schools: How can we tell?* (Item No. 39–0468). Washington, DC: AFT.

Bowers, B. (1989). *State-enforced accountability of local school district* (ERIC digest series number EA 36). Eugene, OR: ERIC Clearinghouse on Educational Management. (ERIC Document Reproduction Service No. ED309556).

Bush, G. W. (2000, July 10). George W. Bush's Speech to the NAACP [Transcript of speech]. *eMediaMillWorks.* Online, available at: http://www.washingtonpost.com/wp-srv/onpolitics/elections/bushtext071000.htm (accessed September 30, 2007).

Commission on Chapter 1. (1992). *Making schools work for children in poverty: A new framework prepared by the Commission on Chapter 1.* Washington, DC: Council of Chief State School Officers (ERIC Document Reproduction Service No. ED373120).

Cross, C. (2004). *Political education: National policy comes of age.* New York: Teachers College Press.

Dianne Piché v. *Mike Petrilli* v. *Joel Packer on No Child Left Behind.* (2007, February 5). Edspresso.com. Online, available at: http://www.edspresso.com/2007/02/february_59_dianne_piche_vs_mi.htm (accessed September 30, 2007).

Firestone, W., Fuhrman, S., & Kirst, M. (1989). *The progress of reform: An appraisal of state education initiatives.* New Brunswick, NJ: Center for Policy Research in Education.

Gamoran, A. & Long, D. (2006, December). *Equality of educational opportunity: A 40-year retrospective* (WCER Working Paper No. 2006–9). Madison, WI: Wisconsin Center for Education Research.

Gordon, R. (2006). Robert Gordon replies. In *Point counterpoint: Should we repair "No Child Left Behind" or trade it in? (A conversation between Robert Gordon and Richard Rothstein)* (pp. 20–22). Washington, DC: Economic Policy Institute.

Grissmer, D., Flanagan, A., Kawata, J., & Williamson, S. (2000). *Improving student achievement: What state NAEP test scores tell us* (Document No. MR-924-EDU). Santa Monica, CA: RAND.

Harris, D. (2007). High flying schools, student disadvantage and the logic of NCLB. *American Journal of Education*, 113 (3), 367–394.

Heckman, J. (2006, June). Skill formation and the economics of investing in disadvantaged children. *Science*, 312 (5782), 1,900–1,902.

Herman, J. & Haertel, E. (Eds.). (2005). *Uses and misuses of data for educational accountability and improvement.* Chicago, IL: National Society for the Study of Education.

Jencks, C. & Phillips, M. (Eds.). (1998). *The black–white test score gap.* Washington, DC: Brookings Institution Press.

Johnson, J. & Duffett, A. (2004). *An assessment of survey data on attitudes about teaching, including the views of parents, administrators, teachers and the general public.* New York: Public Agenda. Online, available at: http://www.publicagenda.com/research/pdfs/attitudes_about_teaching.pdf (accessed September 30, 2007).

Johnson, J., Arumi, A., & Ott, A. (2006). *Is support for standards and testing fading?* (Reality check 2006: Issue no 3). New York: Public Agenda.

Kane, T. J. & Staiger, D. O. (2002). *Volatility in school test scores: Implications for test-based accountability systems* (Brookings Papers on Education Policy). Washington, DC: Brookings Institution.

Kane, T. J., Staiger, D. O., & Geppert, J. (2001). *Assessing the definition of "adequate yearly progress" in the House and Senate education bills* (Working paper) (ERIC Document Reproduction Service No. ED474881).

Klauke, A. (1989). *Restructuring the schools* (ERIC Digest Series Number EA 37). Eugene, OR: ERIC Clearinghouse on Educational Management (ERIC Document Reproduction Service No. ED309563). Online, available at: http://www.eric.edu.gov (accessed September 30, 2007).

Kohut, S. & Wright, J. (1984). Merit pay movement 1980s style. *Educational Horizons*, 62 (2), 52–54.

Koretz, D. (2002). Limitations in the use of achievement tests as measures of educators' productivity. *Journal of Human Resources*, 37 (4), 752–777.

Koretz, D. (2006, October 10). The pending reauthorization of NCLB: An opportunity to rethink the basic strategy. Invited paper for the November 16, 2006, Civil Rights Project/Earl Warren Institute Roundtable Discussion on the Reauthorization of NCLB, Washington, DC. Unpublished draft.

Lawther, W., Lange, R., & Winston, D. (1990). *Evaluation of the merit schools program: Final report.* Orlando, FL: University of Central Florida (ERIC Document Reproduction Service No. ED324803).

Linn, R. L. (1991, April) (Chair). Effects of high-stakes educational testing on instruction and achievement. Symposium conducted at the annual meeting of the American Educational Research Association and the National Council on Measurement in Education, Chicago, IL.

Linn, R. L. (2000). Assessment and accountability. *Educational Researcher*, 29 (2), 4–16.

Linn, R. L. (2003a). Accountability: Responsibility and reasonable expectations. *Educational Researcher*, 32 (7), 3–13.

Linn, R. L. (2003b). Performance standards: Utility for different uses of assessments. *Education Policy Analysis Archives*, 11 (31). Online, available at: http://epaa.asu.edu/apaa/v11n31/ (accessed February 18, 2007).

Linn, R. L., Baker, E. L., & Betebenner, D. W. (2002). Accountability systems: Implications of requirements of the No Child Left Behind Act of 2001. *Educational Researcher*, 31 (6), 3–16.

Louis, K. S. (1998). "A light feeling of chaos": Educational reform and policy in the United States. *Daedalus*, 127, 13–40.
Marzano, R. & Kendall, J. (1998). *Awash in a sea of standards.* Aurora, CO: Mid-Continent Regional Education Lab.
Moe, T. (2003). Politics, control, and the future of school accountability. In M. R. West & P. E. Peterson (Eds.), *No Child Left Behind? The politics and practice of school accountability* (pp. 80–102). Washington, DC: Brookings Institution.
Mosteller, F. & Moynihan, D. (Eds.). (1972). *On equality of educational opportunity: Papers deriving from the Harvard University faculty seminar on the Coleman report.* New York: Random House.
National Center for Education Statistics. (2005). *NAEP 2004 trends in academic progress: Three decades of student performance in reading and mathematics.* U.S. Dept. of Education, Institute of Education Sciences. Washington, DC: U.S. Government Printing Office.
National Commission on Excellence in Education. (1983, April). *A nation at risk: The imperative for educational reform.* Washington, DC: U.S. Government Printing Office.
National Education Goals Panel. (n.d.). *Building a nation of learners: Complete information for all goals.* Online, available at: http://govinfo.library.unt.edu/negp/page3–1.htm (accessed October 1, 2007).
National Governors Association. (1986, August). *Time for results.* Washington, DC: National Governors Association.
Navarette, R. (2007, July 11). Democrats step on NCLB running into teachers' arms. *The San Diego Union-Tribune.* Online, available at: http://www.realclearpolitics.com/articles/2007/07/democrats_step_on_nclb_running.html (accessed September 30, 2007).
Nelson, F. H. & Rosenberg, B. (2005). *What's wrong with NCLB's AYP formula? A summary of internal and external research findings.* Online, available at: http://www.aft.org/topics/nclb/downloads/AYPresearch.pdf (accessed September 30, 2007).
Ornstein, A. (1988). The evolving accountability movement. *Peabody Journal of Education*, 65 (3), 12–20.
Pellegrino, J., Jones, L., & Mitchell, K. (Eds.). (1998). *Grading the nation's report card: Evaluating NAEP and transforming the assessment of educational progress.* Washington, DC: National Academy Press.
Peter D. Hart Research Associates. (1999, August–September). *Standards-based education reform: Teachers' and principals' perspectives.* Online, available at: http://www.shankerinstitute.org/Downloads/R5571–2.pdf (accessed September 30, 2007).
Peter D. Hart Research Associates, Inc., and The Winston Group. (2007, June). *Standards, accountability and flexibility: Americans speak on No Child Left Behind reauthorization.* Princeton, NJ: Educational Testing Service. Online, available at: http://www.ets.org/Media/Education_Topics/pdf/5884_Key_Findings.pdf (accessed September 30, 2007).
Pipho, C. (1987). Education indicators—the accountability tool of the 80s. *Education Week*, VI (18), 22.
Public Agenda. (2003, June 4). *America's teachers—don't make us scapegoats* [Press release]. Online, available at: http://www.publicagenda.org/press/press_release_detail.cfm?list=53 (accessed October 1, 2007).
Raudenbush, S. (2004). *Schooling, statistics, and poverty: Can we measure school improvement?* Princeton, NJ: Educational Testing Service.
Resnick, L. & Zurawsky, C. (2005). Getting back on course: Fixing standards-based reform and accountability. *American Educator*, 29 (1), 8–46.
Rose, L. & Gallup, A. (2006). *38th Annual Phi Delta Kappa/Gallup poll of the public's attitudes toward the public schools.* Bloomington, IN: Phi Delta Kappa International. Online, available at: http://www.pdkintl.org/kappan/k0609pol.htm (accessed September 30, 2007).
Rosenberg, B. (1992). Supplemental statement of Bella Rosenberg. In Commission on Chapter 1. *Making schools work for children in poverty: A new framework prepared by the Commission on Chapter 1* (pp. 98–99). Washington, DC: Council of Chief State School Officers (ERIC Document Reproduction Service No. ED373120).
Rosenberg, B. (2004, May). *What's proficient? The No Child Left Behind Act and the many meanings of proficiency.* Washington, DC: American Federation of Teachers. Online, available

at: http://www.aft.org/pubs-reports/downloads/teachers/WhatsProficient.pdf (accessed September 30, 2007).

Rothman, R. (1990, January 31). *NAEP plan to set performance goals questioned. Education Week.*

Rothstein, R. (2004). *Class and schools: Using social, economic, and educational reform to close the black–white achievement gap.* Washington, DC: Economic Policy Institute and Teachers College, Columbia University.

Rothstein, R., Jacobsen, R., & Wilder, T. (2006, November). "Proficiency for all"—an oxymoron. Paper prepared for Examining America's commitment to closing achievement gaps: NCLB and its alternatives. Symposium sponsored by the Campaign for Educational Equity, New York.

Sanchez, C. (Reporter). (2006, January 8). No Child Left Behind fails to close achievement gap. *Weekend Edition Sunday* [Radio broadcast]. Washington, DC: National Public Radio.

Shanker, A. (1985). The making of a profession. *American Educator,* 9 (3), 10–17, 46, 48.

Shanker, A. (1997a). A nation at risk (Convention proceedings, Los Angeles, CA/July 1983). *American Educator,* Spring/Summer (Special issue), 63–64.

Shanker. A. (1997b). Excellence and equity (From remarks to the NYSUT Representative Assembly, New York City, March, 1982). *American Educator.* Spring/Summer (Special issue), 63.

Shanker, A. (1997c). How business can motivate students (Where we stand/March 5, 1989). *American Educator,* Spring/Summer (Special issue), 70–71.

Shanker, A. (1997d). It's the system that's not working (Convention proceedings, San Francisco, CA/July, 1988). *American Educator,* Spring/Summer (Special issue), 66–67.

Shanker, A. (1997e). Single standard versus multiple standards (From "Education reform—What's not being said" *Daedalus,* Fall 1995). *American Educator,* Spring/Summer (Special issue), 79–80.

Shepard, L., Glaser, R., Linn, R., & Bohrnstedt, G. (1993). Setting performance standards for student achievement. A report of the National Academy of Education panel on the evaluation of the NAEP trial state assessment: An evaluation of the 1992 achievement levels. Stanford, CA: Stanford University and National Academy of Education.

Shonkoff, J. & Phillips, D. (Eds.). (2000). *From neurons to neighborhoods: The science of early childhood development.* Washington, DC: National Academy Press.

Smith, M. S. & O'Day, J. (1991). Systemic school reform. In S. H. Fuhrman & B. Malen (Eds.), *The politics of curriculum and testing* (Politics of Education Association Yearbook, 1990) (pp. 233–267). London: Taylor & Francis.

Stecher, B. & Kirby, S. (Eds.). (2004). *Organizational improvement and accountability: Lessons for education from other sectors* (Document No. MG-136-WFHF). Santa Monica, CA: RAND.

Toppo, G. (2004, February 23). Education chief calls teachers union "terrorist organization." *USA Today.* Online, available at: http://www.usatoday.com/news/washington/2004–02–23-paige-remarks_x.htm (accessed September 30, 2007).

U.S. General Accounting Office. (1993). *Educational achievement standards: NAGB's approach yields misleading interpretations* (GAO Publication No. GAO/PEMD-93–12). Washington, DC: U.S. Government Printing Office (ERIC Document Reproduction Service No. ED35926).

13

Data for School Improvement and Educational Accountability

Reliability and Validity in Practice

M. David Miller

No Child Left Behind (NCLB) and the current state of accountability clearly have a strong emphasis on reporting the outcomes of schooling. However, as pointed out by Linn (2007), "a major shortcoming of current accountability systems for purposes of making valid inferences about school quality is due to severe limitations on the data that are generally included in systems" (p. 28). Current accountability systems, as required to meet state and federal mandates, provide valid and reliable data on school outcomes as well as information on student demographics including gender, race and ethnicity, indicators of economic disadvantage, disability status, and English language proficiency. However, current accountability systems are often narrow in scope and do not provide the breadth that educators might want from a more comprehensive data system that includes full representations of achievement in reading and mathematics. For example, mathematics at the high school level should include scores for arithmetic, algebra, geometry, measurement, and data analysis and probability to provide a broader sampling of content. It would also include more complete measures of achievement in writing, social studies, and science, as well as achievement-related variables such as attitudes toward reading, persistence in solving problems, self-efficacy in each achievement area, and the like.

Although some progress has been made toward focusing on student outcomes rather than the prior historical emphasis on school resources, it is clear that there are many other indicators that can be used to judge the quality of schools. Student achievement provides a valuable indicator of school performance, but judgments about school quality are stronger when they are based on multiple indicators in conjunction with student achievement. These indicators can include a combination of student achievement, prior achievement and backgrounds of students, school organization, and instructional processes. The need for increased data of several types to define successful and unsuccessful schools is a clear concern of states and the directors of their accountability systems. However, perhaps the strongest push is for accountability assessments to provide more information through the reporting of "diagnostic" results that can help teachers and schools improve teaching and learning. At the opening address of the 2006 Council of Chief State School Officers (CCSSO) Policy Forum, Executive Director Gene Wilhoit (2006) emphasized the need for robust and comprehensive systems that provide diagnostic data to be used in instructional decisionmaking:

> The growing consensus is that in the era of standards based reform, a major missing piece of the puzzle is data. Every state must quickly develop a robust system of student data and information that allows us not only to report on assessment data for state and NCLB accountability purposes, but to use those data for diagnostic and instructional decision making.
>
> (p. 6)

In this chapter, I examine the reliability and validity of accountability systems as they currently exist to serve the dual functions of school accountability and student diagnosis. In addition, alternatives to current data systems that would provide additional data for school improvement are discussed.

Accountability Systems and Multiple Uses

The No Child Left Behind Act (2001) clearly requires some uses for accountability systems that emphasize accountability at the school, district, and state levels. Such data may be used and reported at the group level without much concern about individual student scores. Data are reported by content area and for subpopulations (e.g., race, ethnicity, disability) by grade level. The emphasis has been on aggregate data; student-level accountability has not been required by NCLB. In contrast, state and district-level uses of the data in many states have included student-level accountability, including grade to grade promotion or retention, graduation, and course credit (e.g., Florida has a third grade retention and a high school graduation requirement). In addition, some states (e.g., Florida) are using the accountability system in their merit pay plans for teachers.

Many states also feel pressure from the field to provide diagnostic information that would allow schools and teachers to focus instruction in a way that leads to school improvement. In particular, states are being pushed to move from scores for accountability purposes (e.g., total reading or mathematics scores) to subscores that reflect specific content areas (e.g., algebraic thinking), and from subscores to content objectives that are linked to more detailed elements in state content standards (e.g., can solve quadratic equations).

This type of content-specific information can be used for individual student diagnostic information or program evaluation information. For example, an individual student diagnostic test indicates when an individual student can decode words well but is having trouble with reading comprehension beyond the literal level. Program evaluation information might tell when the students as a whole are having more difficulty with statistics and probability items than with geometry. Often the desire for this level of specificity results in the reporting of subscores from the assessments with minimal psychometric data on the quality of the subscores and their potential use. Although extensive psychometric work has been done to examine the accountability functions of the assessments and the broad scores used for accountability, far less psychometric data are available on the quality of the subscores or objectives that are used for purposes other than accountability.

Although NCLB requires evidence for the validity and reliability of the assessments and the accountability system, the required validity and reliability are limited to the federally mandated uses of the accountability system. Validity and reliability are based on particular uses or interpretations of assessments (American Educational Research Association, American Psychological Association, and National Council on Measurement in Education (AERA), 1999; Haertel, 2006; Kane, 2006; Messick, 1989) and different uses of the same assessment may require different evidence for validity and reliability. The more fine-grained the use of results, the greater the requirement that each subpart of the test be reliable and valid.

Multiple uses of the test would require potentially different evidence for reliability and validity than what is required for the aggregate scores used to define adequate yearly progress. It may not be reasonable to expect the same tests to be used for additional purposes, particularly with regard to diagnostic information that may be needed for school improvement. That is, a test built to measure school or higher-level achievement may not provide enough information at the student level to provide reliable and valid diagnostic information. Because reliability is a function of test length, and subscores and objective scores have substantially fewer items than the total scores used for accountability, a substantially longer test would clearly be required to meet the dual goals of accountability and student diagnosis.

School Versus Student Use of Assessments

NCLB requires reporting of group-level data to make decisions about schools, districts, and states. Assessment at the group level has potential advantages over assessment at the individual level because content coverage can be greatly enhanced if all students are not required to respond to all of the items. For example, a matrix sampling design, such as that used with the National Assessment of Educational Progress, would include samples of students answering different samples of items. The potential advantages of matrix sampling include shorter testing times and less testing burden on students. This is especially useful for constructed-response items where extended time is needed for even a single item. In addition, the coverage of content can be broader at the group level even with sacrifices in coverage at the individual level. Finally, scores will be more reliable at the group level.

However, designing an accountability system at the group level may yield scores at the individual level that are difficult to use or interpret (Mazzeo, Lazar, & Zieky, 2006). First, with matrix sampling designs, the content on any single form of the test may be underrepresented, leading to decreased validity for the interpretation of individual scores. Second, the multiple forms may not provide comparable scores across individuals. Third, one intent of sampling items is to reduce the length of testing time for individuals; reduced testing time is accomplished by reducing the length of the test, which in turn results in reduced reliability and validity at the individual level.

Diagnostic Results in an Accountability System

It is a common practice in accountability systems to report subscores, but the usefulness of these scores for diagnostic purposes has not been established. The primary purpose of NCLB assessments has been for accountability at the level of the total score (i.e., reading or mathematics). Thus, the development of the tests and the initial validity and reliability studies are based on the total score. The need for diagnostic information to inform learning and school improvement often leads to reporting of subscores (e.g., algebra, geometry, measurement) that are not the focal point of the development, validation, and reliability analyses. The implications of reporting subscores intended to inform learning are discussed below with regard to reliability, defined as the consistency of the measurement, and validity, which refers to the adequacy of evidence marshaled to support the interpretation and use of the measurement.

Reliability

Ferrara and DeMauro (2006) examined reliability reported in technical reports for state assessments across multiple content areas in 12 states. They found that the predominant method of reporting reliability was internal consistency, which reflects the degree to which a set of items measures the same construct. Most assessments had internal consistency estimates above 0.85 (some into the low to mid 0.90s), although some shorter tests reported lower reliability estimates. They concluded that the total tests were "highly reliable (i.e., internally consistent), homogeneous tests" (p. 609).

Florida also reported subscore results based on content focus areas in reading, mathematics, and science in their state assessment (see Table 13.1 for the content focus areas for reading, mathematics, and science). The content focus areas are the same across grade levels but objectives vary across grades. As can be seen, the number of subscores is relatively small (four or five) which helps Florida maintain the reliability of the information reported.

The total score for many assessments, including Florida's, are based on latent trait modeling, which assumes unidimensionality (i.e., that the test measures a single trait). This assumption, combined with the practice of

Table 13.1 Florida Content Focus Clusters

Content (scores)	*Content focus cluster for subscore reporting (subscores)*
Reading	Words and phrases in context Main idea, plot, and purpose Comparisons and cause/effect Reference and research
Mathematics	Number sense, concepts, and operations Measurement Geometry and spatial sense Algebraic thinking Data analysis and probability
Science	Physical and chemical sciences Earth and space sciences Life and environmental sciences Scientific thinking

removing items during field tests that would not fit the model, suggest that a single trait is being measured for the total score. As a result, the reliability of the subscores can be approximated with the Spearman-Brown formula.[1] Table 13.2 shows projected subscore reliabilities when the overall reliability is equal to 0.85, 0.90, and 0.95—consistent with data reported by Ferrara and DeMauro (2006).

In Table 13.2, the subscores show a broad range of reliabilities; as can be seen, the subscore reliabilities are reasonable only when the internal consistency is 0.95 or when the reliability is 0.90 and the number of subscores is small. When the total score reliability is 0.85, the reliability of the subscores is below 0.70, even when the number of subscores is limited to three.

Content focus clusters that typically define the subtest scores are fairly broad and would probably not provide good diagnostic information to guide individual student learning. Instead, teachers would need reliable information at a more fine-grained level (i.e., the content objective level). For example, the main idea, plot, and purpose cluster at the fourth grade level includes five clusters: chronological order, details/facts, author's purpose, character

Table 13.2 Spearman-Brown Projected Subscore Reliabilities*

	Internal consistency for total score		
Number of subscores	*0.85*	*0.90*	*0.95*
3	0.65	0.75	0.86
4	0.59	0.69	0.83
5	0.53	0.64	0.79

Note
*All values in the table assume that the total number of items for the assessment is constant.

Table 13.3 Spearman-Brown Projected Objective Reliabilities*

	Internal consistency for total score		
Number of objectives	*0.85*	*0.90*	*0.95*
15	0.27	0.38	0.56
25	0.18	0.26	0.43
40	0.12	0.18	0.32

Note
*All values in the table assume that the total number of items for the assessment is constant and the same as in Table 13.2.

development, and plot development. In reading, the fourth grade number of objectives ranges from two for reference and research to six for comparisons and cause/effect. The range of objectives per content area cluster is larger in mathematics (three to 11) and science (seven to 11). The number of objectives ranges from approximately 15 to 40 within reading, mathematics, and science across grade levels. Table 13.3 shows the projected reliabilities at the content objective level when there are 15, 25, or 40 objectives.

Even with a total score reliability of 0.95, the projected range of reliabilities for the content objectives would be 0.56 for 15 objectives and 0.32 for 40 objectives. This projection assumes that all items have the same properties as the initial test. In practice, the reliabilities for the objectives would range around the projected values, but regardless, the reliabilities would not be sufficient under any condition to make instructional decisions at the objective level.

Similarly, using the Spearman-Brown formula, projections of test length to achieve sufficient reliability can be calculated. If the total score internal consistency is in the range of 0.85 to 0.95, the length of the test would need to be substantially increased to have projected reliabilities for the objectives at 0.70. Table 13.4 shows the projected increase in test length that would be needed for each objective to have a reliability of 0.70.

With only 15 objectives, the length of the total test would need to be almost

Table 13.4 Spearman-Brown Projected Magnitude Increases in Test Length for Objective Reliabilities = 0.70

	*Initial internal consistency for total score**		
Number of objectives	*0.85*	*0.90*	*0.95*
15	6.31	3.81	1.83
25	10.63	6.64	3.09
40	17.11	10.63	4.96

Note
*Internal consistency is for the total score with the current assessment; it would increase with the increases in test length projected in the table.

doubled (a factor of 1.83) when the internal consistency of the total score is 0.95. At the other extreme, a test that has a reliability of 0.85 with 40 objectives would need to increase in length by a factor of 17.11. That means that if the original state test takes one hour to complete, more than 17 hours of test-taking time would be needed to establish reliable information for 40 objectives.

The results for Florida are not atypical. The state assessment was developed with a focus on having reliable and valid total scores for accountability purposes, not for student diagnostic purposes. Yet, subscores based on content focus clusters are reported because schools want information about student learning to be able to make changes that will lead to school improvement. The projected reliabilities for the subscores exceed 0.70 only when the total score reliability is 0.95 and when the total score reliability is 0.90 and only three clusters are used. The results are even worse at the content objective levels, which are based on still fewer items. In other words, subtest scores and objectives are often reported and used even though they can't support reliable inferences at the student level.

The contrast between the content area subscores and the objectives should trigger serious discussion among policymakers and educators about the level at which scores should be reported and their usefulness for instruction and learning. If there are too few subscores, the system will not be useful for school improvement because it yields information that is too global to guide instruction. On the other hand, if there are too many subscores, it will overly burden an accountability system that already requires substantial testing time. In fact, once-per-year tests can never be fully diagnostic and the best they can do is to report a limited number of subtests.

Of course, the reliability of subscores for *program evaluation* purposes would be higher than diagnostic information at the student level. Thus, subscores could be used to provide diagnostic information about class or school level areas needing greater instructional emphasis. However, as Mazzeo et al. (2006) point out, even when tests are developed for group-score interpretations, the length of the test would need to be increased substantially to report reliable subscores:

> Group-score assessments must be designed and reviewed at the level of total item pools rather than at the level of the individual test forms, because the entire pool of items is the unit on which reported results are based. Pool design is influenced both by content coverage demands and by subscale reporting goals. If subscores are reported, the item pool must be rich enough in each subscale domain to support such reporting. Even if relatively few skills are measured, the need to represent different types of stimuli, as in the measurement of reading, will increase the number of items required in the pool.
>
> (p. 684)

Thus, even program evaluation use of subscores requires careful planning during test development and careful use.

Validity

A test is valid to the degree that it measures what it is intended to measure, whether intelligence, feelings and attitudes, or skills and abilities. Validity is based on evidence (e.g., scores on a test accurately predict academic performance) and theory (e.g., the items tap into an underlying construct that is theorized to be associated with a particular behavior or outcome) that support its proposed uses (AERA, 1999). When more than one use for a test is proposed—for example, for accountability purposes, program evaluation, and for student-level diagnostic feedback—different evidence might be needed to establish the test's validity for different uses.

Diagnostic testing should include many of the same elements that are now a standard part of validation of accountability programs. Although accountability programs vary in the types and amount of validation evidence provided, examples of validation evidence can be found that covers the full range of evidence outlined in the *Standards for Educational and Psychological Testing* (AERA, 1999). This evidence includes analysis of (a) the content and its relationship to state content standards; (b) the response processes that reflect the construct; (c) the relationships among items and the construct; (d) the relationships with other variables, including other tests and instructional practices; and (e) the intended and unintended consequences of test use. Each of these is also important to diagnostic testing, but the specific studies for diagnostic testing and accountability differ. Thus, the costs of validation increase with the number of uses and for the most part, these types of studies have not been undertaken to support the use of accountability tests for diagnostic purposes. In fact, limitations of test development make it virtually impossible to meet minimum standards for content representation for multiple purposes such as accountability and student diagnosis.

Test Development

Test development for accountability programs includes a strong emphasis on content. The same content would be relevant to diagnostic testing except that the sampling of content would vary substantially at different levels of score reports. For accountability purposes, content is sampled from the broadly defined content area and reflects the breadth of the state content standards. Any individual form may contain different objectives depending on the test development guidelines, the number of objectives, and the number of items. This results in tests that may have very few items for any specific content objective. Furthermore, with multiple forms there is little equivalence across forms at the objective level. Even with a single form used per administration, the sample of items per objective is often limited due to restrictions in test length. For example, the *Florida Comprehensive Assessment Test* in grade 3 mathematics has 36 objectives and 40 score points. Because the intent of the assessment is to represent broadly the state content standards, and the blueprint calls for each objective to be represented on the test, there is no attempt to sample a representative set of items for any given objective. In fact, no objective has more than two items. Consequently, there is very weak or no sampling of content at the objective level and the content at the objective level needed for diagnostic purposes is underrepresented.

Aside from the small number of items at the objective level, test development methods focused on the total test score can systematically create validity problems for estimates of the objectives (or even subscores). Test development at the total score level can lead to (a) selecting items from a limited range of content within an objective, and (b) dropping items that do not contribute to the overall internal consistency of the total score. Each of these issues can lead to construct underrepresentation when interpreting diagnostic information. First, selection of items is typically based on multiple criteria. Although content should be central to the selection of items, statistical and other criteria will also be used. That is, items might be selected to fill gaps in the information function (the underlying statistical model guiding test development) or to match a blueprint requirement for different item formats (i.e., performance based versus multiple choice). Because some objectives will be more amenable to creating difficult items or to creating open-ended extended-response items, the distribution across the information function will intentionally select items from an objective that meet the needs of the total test rather than being representative of the objective. As a result, an item may be developed to improve the properties of the total test score while creating a bias in the estimate of the objective due to the limited selection of items from the objective. Given that the items are not broadly representative of the objective, this leads to a biased estimate of achievement on the objective.

In addition to the selection of items that may not be representative of the objectives, statistics may systematically remove some items that would contribute to the interpretation of an objective. If an objective measures in part a different skill from the other objectives (i.e., a second dimension), an item that clearly defines the second dimension is more likely to be eliminated at field testing based on item discriminations or other statistical criteria. Thus, only items that are more strongly related to the total test score are retained, removing items that may be critical to defining a particular objective.

Other Indicators of School Quality

Although the reliability and validity of current accountability systems are not adequate for using the systems as tools to provide diagnostic information on students, it is also clear that a more comprehensive accountability system is needed to enable studies that track the effects of program or policy changes.

Central to this argument is the need to expand data collection to include indicators of school organization, instructional processes, and teacher and student background. Such indicators would inform schools and teachers about the context within which learning needs to occur. The National Center for Education Statistics (2007) has compiled a list of indicators from the 2000 to 2007 editions of *The Conditions of Education*. Table 13.5 summarizes the indicators that might be used to measure school quality.

At the elementary and secondary school levels, the indicators were broadly classified as (a) participation in education, (b) learner outcomes, (c) student effort and educational progress, and (d) the context of education. The current state of accountability systems emphasizes the learner outcomes with minimal data from the other areas. However, the other areas provide a foundation for understanding the learning environment and the prior knowledge and experiences that students bring to the classroom. This type of data is crucial to understanding the reasons for success or failure on the educational outcomes (Linn, 2007; Raudenbush, 2004).

The indicator of participation in education includes enrollment in different types of schools and in early intervention programs. An accountability system should include the educational background of students, which would include prior schools enrolled in as well as early childhood programs such as Head Start, nursery school, and prekindergarten. This indicator shows the scope and access that students have for programs in education prior to their current setting.

The student effort and educational progress indicator area includes

Table 13.5 Indicators of School Quality

Indicator area	*Type of information*	*Examples of indicators*
Participation in education	What educational opportunities have the students participated in prior to the current school?	• Participation in early childhood education programs • Prekindergarten
Learner outcomes	What are the levels of academic achievement and other educational outcomes?	• Achievement tests • Employment after high school
Student effort and educational progress	What progress do students make through the educational system?	• Student aspirations • Drop out and retention • Graduation and transition to college
Context of education	What is the school experience for students?	• Learning opportunities • Coursetaking and standards • Special programs • Teachers

student attitudes and aspirations, student effort, and elementary and secondary school persistence and progress. Student effort shows the extent of participation once a student has entered a program. The leading indicator for effort is student absenteeism; other indicators of effort include homework and prior performance (e.g., test scores and grades). Persistence and progress variables monitor grade retention, drop out, and graduation. This set of indicators has an increased importance when there are state policies governing individual accountability in the form of grade retention or graduation.

Finally, the indicators for the context of education category provide a broad understanding of the school experience. They include:

- coursetaking and standards—the courses being taken by students and the standards of performance that students are expected to meet for course credit;
- learning opportunities—the content and expectations of student learning and the processes of instruction, including grouping and methods of instruction;
- special programs—special programs for students with special needs;
- teachers—the characteristics of teachers, including educational background and years of teaching experience; and,
- school characteristics and climate—school environment and organization, including principal characteristics, parents' attitudes, and perceptions of school's social and learning environment.

Conclusion

As pointed out in the National Research Council report on *Knowing What Students Know* (Pellegrino, Chudowsky, & Glaser, 2001),

> it is essential to recognize that one type of assessment does not fit all [purposes]. Often a single assessment is used for multiple purposes; in general, however, the more purposes a single assessment aims to serve, the more each purpose will be compromised.
>
> (p. 2)

Thus, the multiple purposes of accountability, student diagnosis, and program evaluation require compromises in test development and usage. The high stakes of accountability limit the amount of compromise that states are willing to make for a test to serve multiple purposes. In addition, the reliability and validity requirements of diagnosis and accountability would result in essentially different tests. Consequently, accountability tests hold little promise for providing reliable and valid student-level diagnostic information and limited promise for providing effective information for program evaluation.

Instead, a technically and substantively sound accountability system should look to provide the best possible information for school improvement. The current accountability demands have often precluded many of the important functions of testing and have created a narrow focus on the educational system that does not maximize the use of data for school improvement. Some of the important functions of testing that are lost in the strong accountability emphasis include the use of tests for early warning and diagnostic assessment. Schools would benefit from early warning and formative assessments that could be given early in the academic calendar with tests that are specifically built to be valid and reliable for that specific use. It is clear that one test cannot serve both accountability and diagnosis functions equally well.

In addition, schools must continue to look at other indicators such as those outlined previously from *The Conditions of Education* to understand the effects of schooling. Current achievement needs to be understood in the context of prior achievement and educational experiences, student effort and persistence, curriculum and instructional processes, and school organization.

Acknowledgments

The author thanks H. D. Hoover and John C. Poggio for reviewing earlier drafts of this chapter and providing constructive suggestions.

Note

1. Spearman-Brown assumes that tests are parallel to the original tests. Changing the length of the test and using items that are not parallel to the original test could result in higher or lower reliabilities.

References

American Educational Research Association, American Psychological Association, and National Council on Measurement in Education. (1999). *Standards for educational and psychological testing*. Washington, DC: American Educational Research Association.

Ferrara, S. & DeMauro (2006). Standardized assessment of individual achievement in K-12. In R. L. Brennan (Ed.), *Educational measurement* (4th ed., pp. 579–622). Westport, CT: American Council on Education and Praeger.

Haertel, E. H. (2006). Reliability. In R. L. Brennan (Ed.), *Educational measurement* (4th ed., pp. 65–110). Westport, CT: American Council on Education and Praeger.

Kane, M. T. (2006). Validity. In R. L. Brennan (Ed.), *Educational measurement* (4th ed., pp. 17–64). Westport, CT: American Council on Education and Praeger.

Koretz, D. M. & Hamilton, L. S. (2006). Testing for accountability in K-12. In R. L. Brennan (Ed.), *Educational measurement* (4th ed., pp. 531–578). Westport, CT: American Council on Education and Praeger.

Linn, R. L. (2007, January). Educational accountability systems. Paper presented at the annual conference of the National Center for Research on Evaluation, Standards and Student Testing, Los Angeles, CA.

Mazzeo, J., Lazer, S., & Zieky, M. J. (2006). Monitoring educational progress with group-score assessments. In R. L. Brennan (Ed.), *Educational measurement* (4th ed., pp. 681–700). Westport, CT: American Council on Education and Praeger.

Messick, S. (1989). Validity. In R. L. Linn (Ed.), *Educational measurement* (3rd ed., pp. 13–103). New York: American Council on Education and Macmillan.

National Center for Education Statistics (2007). *The Conditions of Education.* Online, available at: http://nces.ed.gov/programs/coe/list/index.asp (accessed February 18, 2007).

No Child Left Behind Act of 2001, Pub. L. No. 107–110, 115 Stat. 1425 (2002).

Pellegrino, J., Chudowsky, N., & Glaser, R. (Eds.). (2001). *Knowing what students know: The science and design of educational assessment.* Washington, DC: National Academy Press.

Raudenbush, S. W. (2004). Schooling, statistics, and poverty: Can we measure school improvement? The ninth annual William H. Angoff Memorial Lecture. Princeton, NJ: Educational Testing Service.

Wilhoit, G. (2006, November 17). The vision and role of CCSSO in the 21st century. Opening address to the Council of Chief State School Officers Annual Policy Forum. Online, available at: http://www.ccsso.org/content/pdfs/2006_APF_Gene%20Wilhoit.pdf (accessed November 17, 2006).

14
Enhanced Assessment for School Accountability and Student Achievement

Stephen B. Dunbar

For several generations now, efforts to improve student achievement in the United States have been tied in some way to test scores (Koretz & Hamilton, 2006). Large-scale testing programs at the state level have varied in purpose and design, but they share the view that test scores should have a central role in monitoring and evaluating student learning. The prominent position of tests in current efforts to improve education has made instrument quality a critical concern. The purpose of this chapter is to describe contextual factors in assessment programs that have direct effects on the quality of measures used for accountability and to consider ways in which accountability systems can provide for enhanced assessments of student learning.

If learning and assessment could be reduced to a counting exercise, then educational accountability would be a simple matter: enumerate the measurable objectives of the curriculum in each grade, design a test with a sufficient number of questions for each objective, and count how many questions each student can answer. Educators and measurement specialists argue vociferously that assessment is a much more complex, nuanced enterprise than this, yet at their core, the assessment models for many if not most accountability tests are consistent with this caricature of the process. Add to this Linn's (this volume) bare-bones validation argument for a finding that a given school has met its adequate yearly progress (AYP) target, which does not presume that meeting AYP means that a school is more effective than schools not meeting AYP, then indeed, as he observes, "validation of the [AYP] claim is rather straightforward" (p. 16).

A critical shortcoming of this view of learning and assessment becomes obvious as soon as a school superintendent tries to determine why the elementary schools in her district made AYP and the middle schools did not. A causal explanation for different results in different types of schools, as Linn notes, "is much more difficult to justify from the information provided by the NCLB [No Child Left Behind] accountability system" than the factual statement of results. Competing explanations are likely to exist in every case. One of the arguments of this chapter is that any accountability test—no matter how comprehensive its content coverage, how rich and cognitively complex its questions, and how psychometrically sound its design and implementation—cannot by itself be used to explain why one school made AYP and another did not, nor why one school improved and another did not. In Linn's descriptive accountability system, however, improvements to assessment design can lead to more comprehensive descriptions of student achievement and a stronger foundation for arguments about how to improve teaching and learning for schools, classrooms, and individual students.

Contrasts in Assessment Design

Although NCLB initiated the nation's most comprehensive data collection activity in support of education, its scope is nonetheless far more limited than the decennial census, which has been called "the federal government's largest and most complex peacetime operation" (Citro, Cork, & Norwood, 2004). To the general public, the U.S. Census is a straightforward—albeit mammoth—count of the entire population for the constitutional purpose of reapportioning seats in the House of Representatives. In 2000, every household received a short seven-item questionnaire about basic population characteristics and housing to gather the information needed for reapportionment. In addition to these population data, however, a sample of households received a longer questionnaire with 45 items used to estimate population characteristics not essential to reapportionment, but nonetheless of social or political importance. Only the constitutionally mandated count for reapportionment is a true census of the population. The additional information, however—although collected from only a sample of individuals—can be used to enrich our understanding of the U.S. population in ways that would not be possible based on the "head count" data alone. As with the U.S. Census, testing programs in American schools also include census-based as well as sample-based assessments, and each type of assessment generates information that is useful for different purposes. These approaches are described in more detail below.

Census Testing

With the possible exceptions of the National Assessment of Educational Progress (NAEP) and special studies of national and international scope (e.g., National Assessment of Adult Literacy, Programme for International Student Assessment), most testing programs in American schools are census programs; that is, *all students* in the population take the *same test* and receive individual score reports. Individual scores are aggregated into classroom, school, district, and state averages. Census testing permits multiple levels of analysis, inference, and decisionmaking. Census designs also make intuitive sense to policymakers and the public who might find alternative sampling approaches incomplete, inconclusive, or simply confusing. By federal law, NCLB testing is census testing.

Census designs have many advantages. They remove statistical uncertainty associated with the performance of aggregate groups because entire populations and subpopulations are assessed and because all students answer all test questions. Many school administrators would also argue that testing all students in a building on a common schedule is far less disruptive than pulling a sample of students out of classrooms to participate in programs like NAEP. Testing large numbers of students also reduces the per-pupil costs associated with hand scoring open-ended questions because the up-front costs of developing rubrics and training readers are covered by large student volume. Of course, NCLB is predicated on the overriding principle that all students should be assessed on exactly the same content standards and grade-level expectations—in practice, the same items—and only census testing guarantees that is the case.

Sampling Models for Testing

Long before NCLB went into effect, sampling approaches to student assessment were used in states such as North Carolina and Illinois to monitor student performance and curriculum coverage and, in cases where national norms were available, to provide a national benchmark for general achievement levels in the state. Simple random sampling of students within schools would generate estimates of school, district, region, and state performance levels as well as permit disaggregation of results by subgroups relevant to state or local district policy. States such as California took sampling a step further, borrowing the concept of matrix sampling from NAEP to increase the content coverage of the assessment at the state level and obtain estimates of performance disaggregated by content strands and curriculum objectives.

Sampling designs can estimate performance with respect to a broader content domain per unit of testing time because items can be matrix sampled across cells of the student sampling design (Bock & Mislevy, 1988). For example, a given state's content standards in reading may include specifications based on the type of passage to be read (e.g., fiction, literary nonfiction, informational text, poetry) as well as cognitive processes related to comprehension or depth of knowledge (e.g., understanding facts, making inferences, drawing conclusions, evaluating points of view). Cells of these content and process specifications can be sampled across multiple test forms administered to students within classrooms in a spiraled fashion rather than be exhaustively represented in a single long test form administered to all students. A sampling design for an assessment thus could require that fewer students be tested with less testing time for each student, without sacrificing inferences to the student population or the universe of content. When individual scores are required, Bock and Mislevy's duplex design provides an example of how test forms can be designed structurally to allow for individual scores (the hallmark of census testing) as well as reliable inferences about specific content strands for classrooms, schools, or districts within a state (the goal of matrix sampling) without excessive amounts of testing time. However, current laws would have to be substantially modified before such approaches could be considered as alternatives to census-based testing for accountability, because in a duplex design students receive a sampling of items, not all the items in the domain.

The benefits of sampling designs accrue in settings like NAEP, whose purposes are simply to monitor national achievement trends over time and to provide the nation with periodic information about what students know and can do in specific subjects (cf., Pellegrino, Jones, & Mitchell, 1999). A periodic assessment like the NAEP that does not seek to evaluate specific students or programs can readily tolerate incomplete population data across wide domains of content and cognitive processes.

In principle, sampling designs used in test forms assembly could yield *school-level* inferences required for AYP determinations and at the same time increase the content coverage of accountability systems without a concomitant increase in testing time for individual students. However, sampling designs introduce complications in testing programs such as needing multiple spiraled forms and the concomitant increased development, processing, and scoring costs. In addition, they present individuals with test forms matched differentially to specific grade-level expectations; instead the match is made at the school level. This feature represents a fundamental inconsistency with a basic tenet of federal law, that all individuals be measured against the same content standards and expectations.

Regardless of what type of assessment design is used—whether a census or sampling approach—contextual factors relevant to the quality of assessment programs stem from the purpose and use of test results. In state and federal accountability systems, test scores have become the sole basis for judgments of school quality and, indirectly, the identification of non-proficient students in a school's AYP determinations. Positioned in this way, tests bear the entire burden of proof for the accuracy and integrity of conclusions and decisions based on them. It perhaps comes as no surprise, then—only one year after the full implementation of assessments in all grades mandated by NCLB—that concerns for the quality of measures have come into national focus.

Test Quality and Development Practices

Professional standards for educational tests are guided in large part by psychometric principles related to test validity and reliability and by technical aspects of test development and assembly related to comparability of multiple forms (American Educational Research Association, American Psychological Association, and National Council on Measurement in Education (AERA), 1999). The *Standards for Educational and Psychological Testing* explicitly recognize that best practice in test development is defined by the assessment context.

Components of the process are organized into stages based on (1) the purpose of testing, (2) the writing and evaluation of test specifications, (3) the development and field testing of items and scoring procedures, and (4) the assembly and evaluation of the test itself. Schmeiser and Welch (2006) add to these stages the development of item banks for assembly of future test forms and the specification of quality control measures as a mechanism to monitor and ensure the success of the test development process. Setting performance standards for NCLB reporting could also be considered a stage in the development process as it constitutes an integral part of scoring for accountability purposes.

States must adhere to the process outlined in the *Test Standards* (AERA, 1999) in order to satisfy federal guidelines for technical adequacy of NCLB assessment programs. They usually do so with the assistance of one or more contractors, typically test publishers or consortia of professionals who deliver educational materials and services. Determining the purpose of testing, developing content standards and test specifications, and setting of performance standards are typically one-time aspects of the test development process. Their successful execution sets the stage for—but does not guarantee—quality. Writing and revising items, field testing and scoring, test assembly, and printing and distribution are recurring activities that are critical to the quality of an assessment program.

To consider the possibilities for enhanced assessments it is helpful to understand more fully the implications of the recurring aspects of test development for states. With high-stakes uses of accountability tests, most states introduce new test items (if not entirely new test forms) each year. Consumable test booklets create annual costs for test materials and also require that the infrastructure for test form assembly and the production schedule for editorial and publication services—including bias and sensitivity reviews of new test materials, which takes up to six-months in many commercial testing contexts—must remain active on a year-round basis. To develop and maintain item pools for future secure test forms, states must work with contractors to devise field testing designs and schedule additional time for field tests. When field testing is incorporated into the operational assessment, states must construct multiple test booklets and randomly assign them at the student level to obtain the data needed for future test assembly.

By and large, states have marshaled the human and financial resources necessary to meet the initial demands of annual census testing for high-stakes accountability purposes (although not without significant scheduling, delivery, and scoring problems in the day-to-day operation of statewide programs). But that is only to say that states have used the four-year start-up window established by federal law to put test-based accountability systems in place. Continued internal and external monitoring of such systems for quality control and maintaining timely delivery of new test forms, processing and scoring systems, and reporting mechanisms involves significant recurring costs and human resources. The recurring costs for programs customized to state specifications are in marked contrast to the costs states and school districts might have formerly associated with the use of off-the-shelf tests in low-stakes applications.

States now engaged in best practices for the development of accountability tests are preparing materials today for tests that might be administered two or three years from now. The high-stakes environment of NCLB testing, as well as federal regulations for technical adequacy, require states to maintain high standards in the test development process. It is reasonable, however, to ask what is feasible in this context if a future goal of accountability testing is the enhancement of the tests themselves.

Enhanced Assessments for Accountability

Federal regulations that govern the review and evaluation of the tests that states use to measure reading, math, and science achievement reflect a simple validity claim laid out by Linn (this volume): tests are adequate for measuring AYP only to the extent that they are aligned to content standards. Standards and procedures for test development play a critical role in defining the domain of potential test-based inferences. However, a validity argument (Kane, 2006) goes beyond test development standards and procedures to pose questions about the fidelity of test materials to the uses of results.

The complexity of using assessments for multiple purposes, coupled with the sheer magnitude of NCLB testing programs in the U.S. and its territories, produce significant challenges for developing and producing materials for accountability testing. Recent calls for enhancements to accountability tests (e.g., U.S. Department of Education, 2007) recognize the importance of instrument quality; however, "instrument quality" is a slippery term in measurement and evaluation. The same instrument may represent an acceptable level of quality in one context and not in another depending on how information from the instrument is used (e.g., Shepard, 1997).

The term "enhanced assessment" has entered the discourse on testing for accountability because of the realization that using tests for student or school accountability leads to irreversible consequences not easily justified solely on the basis of existing tests. The Institute for Education Sciences recently announced a grant competition to support enhancements to state accountability tests, to include (1) improvements to test reliability and validity, (2) multiple measures of academic achievement from multiple sources, (3) ability to track individual student progress over time, and (4) new or improved methods of assessment that incorporate performance- and technology-based tasks (U.S. Department of Education, 2007). Implicit in the federal priorities for enhanced assessment is the idea that multifaceted approaches are important to ensure that instruments used for accountability provide the full range of *descriptive* information to support varied inferences from them. Enhancement in this context perhaps means greater breadth in both content coverage and measurement method.

Improvements to Reliability and Validity

Enhancements to reliability and validity that are focused on instrumentation rather than interpretation and use have been the subject of great debate since the advent of large-scale standardized achievement tests (Office of Technology Assessment, 1992). In developing standards-based assessments for federal accountability, states have specified major strands of content in reading, mathematics, and science as well as detailed grade-level expectations (GLEs) to ensure they can document each child's test performance in terms of grade-appropriate criteria. Some have argued the net effect of detailed GLEs is to reduce learning and assessment to the counting caricature described previously. Fewer primary (and perhaps more global) standards might instead encourage teachers to emphasize conceptual understanding in math and science, for example, and to engender learning that might better transfer to novel tasks students encounter in and out of school (Baker, this volume; Commission on Instructionally Supportive Assessment, 2001).

Focusing item development and test assembly on major content strands as opposed to GLEs would add considerable flexibility to the test development process for NCLB programs. Although aligning test content to highly specific GLEs creates highly comparable test forms, it tends to encourage item development practices known as cloning. An example of cloning is given in Table 14.1.

After a particular GLE is translated into aligned test items, item writers may choose to generate many nearly identical versions of those particular representations of the GLE, as shown in Table 14.1, unnecessarily (and perhaps unwittingly) narrowing the domain coverage within a general content strand. In the case of this example, not only is the GLE delimited by the fact that the items simply require dividing a whole number in half, but the syntax becomes a shell that can be directly taught, which can reduce the generalizability of math achievement gains and, as Koretz (this volume) argues, be a source of test score inflation. Conceptualizing content domains and even grade-level expectations broadly frees item writers to use more imaginative contexts and

Table 14.1 Two Items for a Common Grade-Level Expectation in Grade 3 Mathematics

Grade-level expectation: solve single-step word problems involving whole numbers	
Item in base form	*Item in new form*
During student council elections, Carla received 52 votes. This was twice as many as Jackson received. How many votes did Jackson receive?	The town of Bergen planted 28 trees on Arbor Day last year. This was twice as many as the town of Castile planted. How many trees did Castile plant?

approaches to measuring skills. To the extent that this increases the variety of specific test content included in items across test forms (i.e., domain sampling), it argues for potential enhancement of the validity and generalizability of interpretations based on the assessment.

Multiple Measures from Multiple Sources

A cornerstone of any validity argument is the principle that evidence from multiple indicators of a construct should converge on a particular interpretation of assessment results (Messick, 1989; Kane, 2006). A corollary to this principle is guidance that even test developers advocate: that important educational decisions should not be made on the basis of a single test score (Hoover et al., 2003). It thus goes without saying that using multiple measures from multiple sources would enhance an assessment system.

The information derived from multiple measures itself can be used in many ways depending on whether it is incorporated directly into AYP determinations or is seen as part of validating them. As noted by Linn (this volume), AYP is a multiple-hurdle concept, and multiple measures themselves will do little to change that fact unless data sources independent of the NCLB assessment can be used to moderate AYP determinations. Suppose, for example, that a community high school failed to make AYP because of a single subgroup's test performance, but in that same subgroup the percent of students pursuing higher education exceeded the AYP target for percent proficient. Under current law, the AYP determination would stand despite the argument that the percentage pursuing higher education calls into question the proficiency cut-off score and the validity of the NCLB assessment results. For this type of collateral information to affect AYP determinations, the additional measure would have to become part of an index used for AYP.

In general, the use of multiple measures as enhancements to NCLB assessments might best be viewed as a way to expand the assessment domain given state content standards. As part of an accountability system, multiple data sources open an array of possibilities for expanded definitions of school quality. Exactly how they might contribute to all-or-nothing decisions like AYP is not immediately apparent, however, and the mere presence of multiple measures may not guarantee greater validity in the use of assessment information within the accountability system.

Tracking Student Progress

Many policymakers have recognized a potential flaw in the original NCLB design that compares grade-level cohorts of students year after year against AYP targets rather than matched longitudinal records of individual students. Designing an accountability system around student growth has intuitive appeal, and basing AYP decisions on grade cohorts has obvious limitations, especially for small schools. The pilot growth model program recently instituted by the Institute for Education Sciences (U.S. Department of Education, 2007) is a step in the direction of added flexibility, but one can reasonably ask in what sense tracking individual student progress represents enhancement of NCLB assessments.

As was discussed in the context of multiple measures, growth can be thought of as an alternate data source, with its integration with assessment instruments and AYP decisions being an issue of assessment design and policies on accountability. An emphasis on student growth could have a considerable effect on content standards, requiring that they be reviewed for the existence of a developmental sequence of test content across grade levels (defined as vertical articulation by Lissitz & Huynh, 2003) so that inferences about growth reflect an underlying dimension or continuum of student learning over time. Components of the test development process such as item writing and test assembly might be influenced by whether or not particular kinds of tasks showed evidence of growth during field testing. Certain models for measuring growth and tracking student progress over time also place psychometric demands on the vertical scaling of test results (Kolen & Brennan, 2004).

Performance- and Technology-Based Assessment

The development of tasks to include on a test that bear close resemblance to real world behavior—what Lindquist (1951) termed the "criterion situation" that good assessment tasks should emulate—has long been a goal in test development. The performance assessment movement of the 1990s was successful in focusing attention on the desirability of authentic performances represented in test scores, but administrative and financial constraints of large-scale testing programs, as well as the shackles of high stakes, dealt a serious blow to the performance assessment movement. For the most part, today's accountability tests pay lip service to performance assessment through relatively small numbers of short-answer items and extended-response tasks (e.g., on-demand writing) that can be efficiently scored during the processing window available for timely reporting of AYP results.

The promise of technology-based solutions to the large-scale implementation problems encountered with performance tasks is embedded in the definition of Mislevy's model for evidence-centered design (Mislevy, Almond, & Lukas, 2003). He argues that not only the instrument itself but also the inference structure it must support and the delivery and reporting system it uses should be considered an integral whole as opposed to separate components of an assessment program. Computer-based testing provides an obvious vehicle for integrating a test with its delivery, scoring, and reporting system. One can even imagine electronic reports feeding directly into AYP calculations at the school, district, and state levels. In many NCLB programs, test administration, scoring, and reporting test results and AYP calculations back to schools are separate activities. A bigger question for technology-based enhancements is the extent to which computer-based testing or other technology solutions allows for the development of new item types that more closely resemble criterion situations or have greater fidelity to actual student performance than short-answer and other constructed-response items currently being used in accountability tests.

Assessment System Enhancements for Description and Inference

Linn (this volume) argues that "accountability system results can have value without making causal inferences about school quality solely from the results of student achievement measures and demographic characteristics" (p. 21). The U.S. Census provides both descriptive information in the basic count that can be used for reapportionment decisions, and estimates for an array of other characteristics that are flexible and change with social and political imperatives of the time. Causal inferences about social phenomena are enabled by census data, but they do not follow directly from having complete data on a population. More often they are (partially) supported only from secondary analyses that exploit the full array of descriptive measures included in the information system. Secondary analyses of this sort remain observational studies. Moreover, the inferences themselves lie *outside* the data system that accounts for facts about the U.S. population.

The census analogy for educational accountability is relevant to Linn's call for a descriptive accountability system, one rich in information and populated with multiple indicators of relevant educational and social constructs. A census approach to accountability in education would augment complete data on student achievement with additional indicators of, for example, school quality, student background variables, school curriculum and instructional practices, student mobility, teacher quality, and community support for education. In contrast, current AYP reports in the states are void of context, and as such encourage endless speculation as to why some schools are deemed successful and others in need of improvement.

Ironically, the sanctions, penalties, and stigmata riding on AYP results together burden the quality and completeness of assessment data generated by NCLB. Initiatives by the U.S. Department of Education to enhance NCLB assessments point to a critical need for improvements in instrumentation. But the criteria that define truly enhanced assessments, interestingly enough, are not specific to instrumentation but instead argue, however subtly, for flexibility in the regulations that govern AYP determinations, such as use of multiple measures or models of student growth.

If the most important inferences about educational progress, such as *why* achievement increased in one school but not another, are beyond the assessments used in accountability programs, then enhancements will need to reach beyond current assessments to result in lasting improvements in teaching and learning nationwide. The challenge of better tests may actually be a challenge not just of instrumentation but of larger design and reporting issues in the development of accountability systems that ultimately are used for multiple and varied purposes in improving education.

Acknowledgments

The author gratefully acknowledges the comments and suggestions of Robert Mislevy, Delwyn Harnish, and the editors on the outline and earlier versions of this chapter.

References

American Educational Research Association, American Psychological Association, and National Council on Measurement in Education. (1999). *Standards for educational and psychological testing.* Washington, DC: American Educational Research Association.

Bock, R. D. & Mislevy, R. J. (1988). Comprehensive educational assessment for the states: The Duplex design. *Educational Evaluation and Policy Analysis,* 10 (2), 89–105.

Citro, C. F., Cork, D. L., & Norwood, J. L. (Eds.). (2004). *The 2000 census: Counting under adversity.* Washington, DC: National Academies Press.

Commission on Instructionally Supportive Assessment. (2001). *Building tests to support instruction and accountability: A guide for policymakers.* Online, available at: http://www.nea.org/accountability/buildingtests.html (accessed September 30, 2007).

Hoover, H. D., Dunbar, S. B., & Frisbie, D. A. (2003). *Iowa tests of basic skills: Interpretive guide for teachers and counselors, Levels 9–14.* Itasca, IL: Riverside.

Kane, M. T. (2006). Validation. In R. L. Brennan (Ed.), *Educational measurement* (4th ed., pp. 17–64). Westport, CT: American Council on Education/Praeger.

Kolen, M. J. & Brennan, R. L. (2004). *Test equating, scaling, and linking: Methods and practices* (2nd ed.). New York: Springer-Verlag.

Koretz, D. M. & Hamilton, L. S. (2006). Testing for accountability in K-12. In R. L. Brennan (Ed.), *Educational measurement* (4th ed., pp. 531–578). Westport, CT: American Council on Education/Praeger.

Lindquist, E. F. (1951). Preliminary considerations in objective test construction. In E. F. Lindquist (Ed.), *Educational measurement* (1st ed., pp. 119–158). Washington, DC: American Council on Education.

Lissitz, R. W. & Huynh, H. (2003). Vertical equating for state assessments: Issues and solutions in determination of adequate yearly progress and school accountability. *Practical Assessment, Research and Evaluation,* 8 (10), 1–10.

Messick, S. (1989). Validity. In R. L. Linn (Ed.), *Educational measurement* (3rd ed., pp. 13–103). New York: American Council on Education/Macmillan.

Mislevy, R. J., Almond, R. G., & Lukas, J. F. (2003). *A brief introduction to evidence-centered design* (RR-03–16). Princeton, NJ: Educational Testing Service.

Office of Technology Assessment (1992). *Testing in American schools: Asking the right questions.* Washington, DC: United States Congress.

Pellegrino, J. W., Jones, L. R., & Mitchell, K. J. (Eds.). (1999). *Grading the nation's report card: Evaluating and transforming the assessment of educational progress.* Washington, DC: National Academy Press.

Schmeiser, C. B. & Welch, C. J. (2006). Test development. In R. L. Brennan (Ed.), *Educational measurement* (4th ed., pp. 307–353). Westport, CT: American Council on Education/Praeger.

Shepard, L. (1997). The centrality of test use and consequences for test validity. *Educational Measurement: Issues and Practice,* 16 (2), 5–8, 13, 24.

U.S. Department of Education (2007). Office of Elementary and Secondary Education; overview information; enhanced assessment instruments. *Federal Register,* 72 (70), 18,462–18,466.

Part IV
Future Directions for Educational Accountability

15
Learning and Assessment in an Accountability Context

Eva L. Baker

Assessment, the determination of students' capability and learning through performance, is at the heart of educational endeavors, from personal growth to forming policy. Can assessment be more tightly linked to research on learning? Where is there clear integration of research on learning and assessment? Although both learning and assessment have a prodigious research literature, and scholarship in one may often proceed without reference to the other, we can find syntheses, analyses, and research over the years that connect them. The publications *Knowing What Students Know* (Pellegrino, Chudowsky, & Glaser, 2001), *How People Learn* (Donovan, Bransford, & Pellegrino, 1999), and Shepard (2000) show the importance of integrating learning research in instruction and assessment design and illustrate the deep roots of both in the psychological literature (Cronbach & Suppes, 1969). These roots can be seen in research-based instructional programs (for instance, those from R&D centers in Pittsburgh and Wisconsin) in the 1960s and 1970s (see Baker, 1973; Lumsdaine & Glaser, 1960), which incorporated research on feedback, learner control, practice, scaffolding, and sequencing. These early systems translated into practice the best research available at the time. New instructional systems required new ways to assess performance, emphasizing the importance of bounded domains of learning rather than broader surveys of general content knowledge. This need led to the emergence of objectives-based or criterion-referenced tests, presaging today's standards-based tests (see Glaser, 1963; Hively, Patterson, & Page, 1968).

Over the next several decades, the burgeoning area of cognitive research on learning generated knowledge in five areas of continuing relevance to assessment design: (a) the explorations of cognitive processes and mental models focusing on the internal rather than observable processes underlying learning (see Rumelhart & Norman, 1985); (b) the social construction of learning, which depends upon social and cognitive interactions in particular contexts (see Greeno, Collins, & Resnick, 1996; Vygotsky, 1962; Wenger, 1987); (c) robust differences between expert and novice performance (see Chi, Glaser, & Farr, 1988; Ericsson & Simon, 1984); (d) students' ability to manage their own learning, developing self-regulation, and metacognitive skills (see

Boekaerts, Pintrich, & Zeidner, 2000); and, (e) interactions between the learner's general aptitude and instructional experiences in order to optimize instruction for different students (Cronbach & Snow, 1977).

Educational research also explored methods for systematically integrating learning and assessment in reading, writing, and mathematics (Bereiter & Scardamalia, 1987; Campione & Brown, 1990; Treisman, 1990). The common lesson learned by researchers was that instructional effects were best obtained with tests relevant to a specified set of skills and knowledge (this was anticipated by Glaser, 1963). In a far different venue, training in the U.S. military also incorporated learning research (see Price, 2007). Task analysis, a technique to parse jobs and skill sets into discrete tasks for instruction, was based on information processing requirements (Gagné, 1985). Similarly, cognitive task analysis (Means & Gott, 1988) obtained detailed descriptions of cognitive and content requirements by asking questions of learners as they progressed through target tasks.

Large-Scale Assessment and Learning

At its outset in 1969, the National Assessment of Educational Progress (NAEP) was intended to measure current instructional effects as well as to model innovative testing methods (Wirtz & Lapointe, 1982). In fact, early administrations of NAEP employed the use of complex, contextualized test problems as suggested by learning researchers. Similarly, beginning in 1974, the Bay Area Writing Project influenced states and districts to assess students' writing production in large-scale testing (Jago, 2003). Before that time, writing ability usually was assessed by proxy with multiple-choice questions like "Of the five sentences above, which sentence is incorrect?" In the late 1970s, studies comparing written composition in other countries (Baker, 1982; Purves & Takala, 1982) exposed U.S. educators to assessments that emphasized content understanding as well as expression, and gave the examinees help—in the form of ideas, quotes, poems, and other prompts—within the assessment task. Clearly, students were expected to learn during the assessment administration. In the 1980s, NAEP began again to use actual student-generated writing to assess student proficiency in composition.

Large-scale assessment and research were affected by two important events that connected learning and assessment: the report by the National Council of Teachers of Mathematics (1989) that showed model math standards and complex open-ended assessment tasks embedded in day-to-day problems, and the use of performance assessment in the United Kingdom (Burstall, 1986; Nuttall, 1991). Drawing upon approaches from cognitive psychology, both called for learners to demonstrate subject matter competency by generating answers to sets of multi-stepped, open-ended tasks drawn from out-of-school life. In some cases, a portfolio of such tasks was developed over time (Herman, Gearhart, & Baker, 1993). Tasks included projects, reports, performances, and solving problems, with proficiency to be rated by trained teachers. The authenticity of these assessments and related motivating effects led some to argue that they be substituted for, or used in addition to, multiple-choice, standardized tests (Newmann, 1991).

Influential educational researchers (e.g., Darling-Hammond, 2000; Gardner, 1992; Resnick & Resnick, 1992) developed performance assessments that were widely used. Similar assessments were innovatively used in some states (Connecticut, California, New York, and Kansas), and Kentucky's wholesale adoption of performance tests was carefully studied (Gong & Reidy, 1996; Hambleton et al., 1995). Policy discussions at the national level led to federal funding for such assessments (Improving America's Schools Act of 1994; National Council on Education Standards and Testing, 1992; National Education Goals Panel, 1993). Assessment research blossomed with studies focused on the design, context of use, scoring, teacher professional development, and validity of performance assessments.

At the same time, psychometricians refined methods of analysis to improve the technical quality of performance assessments (see Cronbach, Linn, Brennan, & Haertel, 1997; Mislevy, Almond, & Steinberg, 1998; Tatsuoka, 1995). The validity of these tests was studied in terms of both measurement accuracy and the consequences of decisions based on the assessment (American Educational Research Association, American Psychological Association, & National Council on Measurement in Education (AERA), 1999; Messick, 1989). The *Standards for Educational and Psychological Testing* also emphasized the role of underlying models of cognition in designing assessments (AERA, 1999, pp. 37–48). At that moment, it appeared that assessment design would integrate with learning research based on a century of scholarship.

Yet today, at least in the U.S., it is difficult to find examples of the large-scale use of educational performance assessments. With the exception of measures of oral and written language ability, performance assessment survives mainly in business, in the military, in higher education, and as a tool for formative assessment in classrooms. The explanations for the rapid fall from favor of performance assessments include problems of feasibility, cost, technical quality, and conceptual sloppiness, which resulted in a loss of public credibility.

As the No Child Left Behind Act of 2001 (NCLB, 2002) ramped up testing requirements to include annual census testing of all children at many grade levels, the still fragile, time-consuming, and relatively expensive performance-based assessments were largely excluded from accountability tests. Correlations between selected-response tests and learning-focused performance assessments were used to argue speciously for the briefer, less costly standardized multiple-choice test formats. Although NCLB measures were labeled "standards-based tests or assessments" and they used criterion-referenced interpretations of performance (such as "basic" or "proficient"), the influence of learning-based research in test design involving extended performance simply slipped away.

Under the Radar—Links of Learning and Assessment

Outside of policy strictures, the linkage of learning and assessment nonetheless continues in three R&D areas. The first area is intelligent tutoring systems (ITS), which are based on the early work of programmed instruction and computer programming (Chi & VanLehn, 2007; Koedinger & Anderson, 1998). Using artificial intelligence to adapt to each student's learning models, they rely both on explicit learning domains and on data that continuously update student progress, usually on open-ended tasks. In education, ITS research has had more impact on research than the tutors themselves, and has been applied more widely in innovative approaches to test design (e.g., Baker, Chung, & Delacruz, 2008; Mislevy 1996).

A second place where learning research comes together with assessment is in the area of formative assessment in classrooms. Drawing on much of the same research base as ITS, formative assessment focuses on how teachers use student work or test data to improve subsequent performance. Assessments are used to help teachers first identify areas where students falter, and then to provide feedback and encourage learning. Performance-based assessment survives in classrooms in some formative assessment practices. Research on learning and assessment in this context has been conducted by Black and Wiliam (1998), Hunt and Minstrell (1994), among many others. Successful formative assessment depends on the quality and accuracy of findings, the sensitivity of the end-of-year assessment of learning outcomes, and the deftness of instructional revisions (see Linn, Baker, & Dunbar, 1991).

However logical, high quality formative assessment is difficult to find in practice. To be successful, teachers must have the capacity to interpret performance reports and student work, to encourage learning with guidance or intervention, and to detect, when needed, deeper reasons for student difficulty. Even with these skills, teachers must possess adequate time to address different students' needs as well as a repertoire of options to stimulate instructional engagement. Unfortunately, they may have neither, and consequently, formative assessment can devolve into superficial practices focused exclusively on raising test scores rather than on assuring more robust learning.

The third area where learning research and assessment come together is in the design of assessments themselves. I will try to illustrate how a set of newly developed, stand-alone assessments—not necessarily integrated within a specific curriculum or on a technologically sophisticated instructional platform—can incorporate research on learning. As a preview, I believe that learning research must be used in the design of assessment if real learning is to be sustained as opposed merely to improving temporary performance on a particular set of test items. The assumption here is not new: test design will drive teaching if test or assessment results can result in sanctions.

Although accountability is extensively treated elsewhere in this volume, the thrust of my argument depends upon questioning the adequacy of many measures currently used in accountability systems. Does educational accountability work as it is framed in the NCLB legislation? Opinions vary from somewhat to not at all (Choi, 2006; Fuller & Wright, 2007; Jennings & Rentner, 2006). Are tests used in accountability good enough? Recent California state score reports suggest that any progress is leveling off (Dang, 2007). These results conform to predictions in prior studies of accountability-based tests (see, notably, Koretz, Linn, Dunbar, & Shepard, 1991). There are two related explanations for the leveling-off phenomenon. The first is that only limited benefits occur when students practice test-like exercises. The second is that the tests now used for accountability are not designed to detect systematic growth in complex learning domains. The second explanation draws us to the topic of my major concern: better assessments.

What Future Educational Requirements Should Influence Assessment Design?

Putting aside concern for this year's accountability system for the moment, let's turn our attention to what the educational future holds. If expectations for performance are to change, then measures must anticipate new learning goals. There are numerous analyses of what will be required of students in order for them to succeed in the future (see, for example, the National Center on Education and the Economy, 2007). All of these reports synthesize data on demographics, school performance, international comparisons, and potential work and life options. Most analyses note the accelerating rate of change, global competition, uncertainty, and the need to develop more sophisticated problem-solving, decision-making, and collaborative skills. They also suggest that flexibility and the ability to search for and apply relevant new knowledge will be key competencies. In other words, students must be prepared to face and succeed in new contexts. Education for future requirements thus must go beyond performance on the examination of the moment and must argue against marshalling all resources to improve short-term test scores. In addition to learning that represents mastery of important content standards, students (and their teachers) must be able to identify the features of any new setting and to figure out how to apply, adapt, or invent solutions relevant to unforeseen expectations. From a psychological view, students will need to be confident in their abilities and be able to transfer their learning and activate their cognitive resources; that is, to apply and combine knowledge acquired under one set of conditions to other settings (Bassock & Holyoak, 1989; Bransford & Schwartz, 1999).

If one believes that assessments can be designed to foster and measure students' ability to transfer and generalize learning to complex settings, and that assessments of this sort can supplement or substitute for existing tests, then we have a strategy for moving our educational system to focus on change. Even if the accountability system remains committed exclusively to existing standards and instruction, it may be possible to address future demands through the mechanisms of formative assessment and supplemental outcome measurement.

How is Research on Learning Relevant to Test Design?

How does research on learning that emphasizes adaptation and knowledge transfer get incorporated into the design and use of assessments? There is disagreement about the best answer. For example, in *Knowing What Students Know* (Pellegrino et al., 2001), the great preponderance of research has been conducted to address specific content topics. For example, if we know that an electrical system is configured as pattern A, we can teach students to solve similar problems; or with research evidence that algebra strategy "y" is best learned through procedure "p," then we have a learning model that can be incorporated in the problem–solution of that algebra task. Research on learning of this sort is termed "domain-specific" research, as it applies to a particular set of topics, skills, or content domains. One would not extrapolate from such findings in mathematics, for example, and use a similar approach to teach history or English literature; they would not be appropriate. The details offered by domain-specific approaches apply narrowly to content and strategies in the particular area. Their specificity makes them powerful.

At the other end of the continuum is learning research that gives "domain-independent" findings. This label does not mean that the findings apply to no content at all, such as general critical thinking expertise, but rather that the learned cognitive models or strategies apply to more than one topic or subject matter area. For example, it has been shown that experts consolidate specific knowledge into principles, a finding that applies in a wide variety of subject areas. Consider an example that is in the middle of the domain-independent/-domain-dependent continuum. In written composition and in social psychology, there are rules guiding effective persuasion. One rule, *refute negative arguments*, could be applied across a wide number of content areas in essays or arguments, for instance, "avoiding transfats," "arguing for a consumer role in pharmaceutical development," or "considering ideal savings plans for middle-aged couples." This rule, from research in social psychology, is reusable in different topics, even though the specifics of each argument would be embedded in dietary science, pharmaceutical content, or equity and cash sequestering plans. The approach we have taken, called model-based assessment (MBA), incorporates the full continuum of domain-specific and domain-independent learning research. To the extent that learning research findings from a variety of fields can apply, then the models may be serviceable across topics or subjects. As a result, the cost for creating additional assessments in relevant domains has been shown to be reduced (Baker et al., 1996). There are also principles and strategies unique to subject matter that experts apply (e.g., in biology, procedures for calculating genetic dominance). MBA considers the whole range of performance and its potential utility for transfer to other domains. We expect that the exact balance between domain-independent and domain-specific knowledge research will vary with the goals of learning. In every test or task there is some aspect that can be explicitly evoked from student background knowledge or existing schemas. In fact, a premise of our current version of MBA is that a major function of assessment practice is to illuminate and support students' learning, a holdover from the performance assessment days. Student learning is not only directed to external accountability measures like state assessments; it should be robust over variations in setting and constraints, enabling students to generalize and transfer learning beyond the limited form of their standards-based test. For systems that have a formative purpose, MBA must also reliably identify weaknesses at the conceptual or skill level rather than the item level. Although MBA procedures apply to the design process that precedes the actual test administration, our interests and research also address the consequences of particular assessment results and how to improve less-than-acceptable performance. In professional development, topics include the ways in which instruction might occur, options, feedback methods, and developing students' skills to manage their own learning. It should be underscored that the instructional decisions made by teachers should be related intimately to the model underlying the design of the assessments rather than to the assessment items alone.

Learning and Model-Based Assessment

The three major components of the Center for Research on Evaluation, Standards, and Student Testing (CRESST) assessment model are (a) the range of cognitive demands of the tasks or test, (b) a detailed representation of the knowledge map that shows content relations of the subject matter to be learned and tested, and (c) criteria to judge student performance that are derived from appropriate expert performance. The first element requires that cognitive demands be identified along the continuum of those unique to a subject matter or topic and those that apply across topics or even between disciplines. One source for information about cognitive demands is the learning literature that contrasts expert and novice performance, which shows regular patterns for experts in different fields, as well as domain-specific strategies used by experts within a discipline. We have looked at expertise in comprehension, problem solving, communication, teamwork, and learning to learn. At the domain-independent end of the continuum, experts in many fields approach problems by trying to see their deep structure (what is really wanted) rather than the superficial nature of the question (Chi et al., 1988).

Experts search for patterns—called schema—that might match their constraints for a solution. These schema represent dominant principles or big ideas in a subject matter that organize the content-specific minutia. Schema allow problems or other tasks to be solved more quickly using less working (short-term) memory (see Kalyuga, 2006; Sweller, 1999).

Our assessments both measure and support initial learning and its application to new settings. Although experts themselves are usually unaware of the ways they solve problems because the process is familiar and automatic, learners can be taught to regulate and be aware of their own learning processes (Bjork, deWinstanley, & Storm, 2007). We ask students to explain aloud or in writing why they have answered problems as they have, to think about their learning processes, and at the same time, to deepen their understanding. The combination of research from expert performance and learning to learn (or metacognition) is at the heart of our test designs.

The second major element of our work is the detailed representation of the content domain as an ontology, network, or map. Ontologies present both the content elements to be learned and their hierarchical or lateral relationships (Chung, Delacruz, Dionne, & Bewley, 2003b). An ontology presents elements and structure of domain-specific knowledge, including relevant declarative, procedural, and strategic knowledge. It is used to guide assessment design and instructional practice. Ontologies in this form have their original source in computer science (Miller, 1995). Examples of areas in which CRESST researchers have most recently created ontological maps include mathematics, high school biology, college-level engineering, the force and motion topics in middle school physics, and procedural skills in marksmanship.

When a resulting assessment is to be used for formative purposes, the ontology is also used to guide learning for students and teachers. Key nodes may be identified through test performance, by using cognitive task analysis, or by inspecting the frequency with which major network nodes are linked to other nodes in the graphic ontology. Attention to these well-connected nodes is likely to assist the learner having difficulty.

The third part of MBA uses scoring schemes derived from comparing the performance of experts and novices on the tasks of interest; that is, scoring schemes and cut scores are developed in part from the analysis of the empirical performance of individuals of known greater expertise than the target learners. A sequential arrangement of these performance levels by degree of expertise can help develop scoring schemes for solutions.

We continue to explore the use of computer technology to support assessment design and to improve feasibility and lower costs. Savings are achieved by reusing strategies, related templates, or scoring schemes and referencing them to the extant or updated knowledge map. The notion of reusable learning objects (Merrill, 2000; Wiley, 2000) or content objects (Tobias & Fletcher, 2000) is simply extended to test design (Baker, 2003). Feasibility also involves attention to time constraints for development and often intractable limits on classroom time available for administration.

We have used MBA as a conceptual and practical guide to generate multipurpose assessment tasks (for outcomes and for formative use), to create scoring protocols, and to offer appropriate validity interpretations. We have designed and scaled-up assessments and relevant professional development for teachers and instructors in various subjects, including literature, engineering, mathematics, humanities, history, and problem solving (Baker & Mayer, 1999; Baker et al., 1996; Chung, Shel, & Kaiser, 2006). Our largest efforts involved examining 350,000 students over a three-year period (Chung, Niemi, & Bewley, 2003a). Components of our model have been empirically tested to determine whether they contribute to hypothesized relationships among variables (e.g., score differences between instructed and uninstructed students). We have observed an equity benefit on high school exit examinations for our tests compared with more typically designed tests (Goldschmidt & Martínez-Fernández, 2007). The findings showed that performance on MBA assessments was a better predictor of exit exam scores for an underserved minority group.

Learning Research in POWERSOURCE©—a Current Example of Model-Based Assessment

The POWERSOURCE©[1] (Baker, Herman, & Linn, 2004) system, which is intended to be used as a formative assessment system for pre-algebra and algebra in grades 6, 7, and 8, uses MBA as its structure. An explicit integrated learning model is included in its design. The model draws from previously described research literature on expertise as well as research on schema development, working memory, and transfer. To facilitate rapid learning and to support its application to new areas, we have added research on schema development (Marshall, 1995), focusing the assessment on a handful of "big ideas" recurring in pre-algebra in the sixth, seventh, and eighth grades. These big ideas relate to schemas related to the core understandings needed for success in algebra. In order to make developing schemas efficient, we are using the idea of "worked examples" (Mayer, 2003; Sweller, 1999). Worked examples provide a type of backward chaining for learners, allowing them to see at the beginning of learning (or testing) what a finished product looks like. Research by both Sweller and Mayer and their many associates has demonstrated that use of these examples at the outset of learning (or testing) improves performance and speed of learning. Effects, they hypothesize, occur because worked examples reduce the "cognitive load" on working memory. They argue that it is more efficient to store a complete example in memory than to store separately the set of individual steps needed for a solution. Chi (2000), among others, also proposes this general approach to schema development. When students encounter problems or situations with properties similar to those learned, they will identify the problem type, pattern, or principles that underlie its solution, access the worked example, and adapt their previously learned schema to the new problem. Sweller and his colleagues (Paas, Renkl, & Sweller, 2003), for example, have found that the use of worked examples influences transfer.

Although worked examples have been used in general to improve instruction, they form the basis for some of our assessment templates guiding task design. Here, students are given partially worked examples and asked to complete an increasing number of steps. We also ask students to explain in writing *why* they solved a problem in a particular way. Research on the power of explanation as a means to deeper understanding is extensive (see Chi & VanLehn, 1991). On practical grounds, our previous CRESST studies reassure us that explanation skills can be reliably scored and that their quality predicts deeper understanding of content (Baker, 1994). Students are given POWERSOURCE© tasks 12 times a year, a schedule of spaced practice that is supported by literature in learning research (Rohrer & Pashler, 2007).

In POWERSOURCE©, we are developing performance aids based on learning research for teacher and student use, to include the knowledge map and worked examples as well as a website intended to support formative assessment and instruction. The website has a large number of very short, but pointed, bits of instruction. These are one- to two-minute reminders, directed to either common errors, recall of principles and patterns, or missing prior knowledge, for students to use when they encounter difficulties. Linked by a data management system, the website can provide just-in-time help to improve learning.

Although the major focus of POWERSOURCE© is student learning, any assessment system must include teacher learning as well. We use strategies to assist teachers to become more expert in math content and pedagogy. Teachers see worked examples as a way to expand their existing repertoire, and they also provide a tactful way of approaching their potential gaps in domain knowledge or pedagogy. Task performance aids are structured so that they remind students (and teachers) of where they are in the ontology, show with relevant worked examples which big ideas, principles, or patterns (schemas) are in play, and give guidance for constructing and evaluating student explanations. Using a randomized experimental design, the POWERSOURCE© system is now being evaluated over a period of three years to determine the best use of performance aids in regular grade 6 to 8 classrooms (National Center for Research on Evaluation, Standards, and Student Testing, 2007). We expect that POWERSOURCE© students will show improved growth on their state assessment as well as on transfer examinations drawn from national and international tests on the same topics. Transfer of learning, not surprisingly, is our primary goal.

Summary

Knowledge gained from research on learning can transform assessments used in accountability. This transformation serves the growing need for students to apply their learning and adapt to change. Model-based assessment (as illustrated by the use of the POWERSOURCE© system) presents only one approach to integrating learning research and assessment design toward those ends. It grows out of a long and important corpus of educational and psychological research, one we know will yield continued insights.

It is also our hope that our research on POWERSOURCE© and similar systems will stimulate commercial producers to incorporate learning research in the design of their tests and to emphasize transfer of learning in their outcome measures. We and others must continue to explore ways that research on learning and assessment can work both to expedite and to deepen learning so that students may meet today's expectations and tomorrow's challenges.

Acknowledgments

My sincere thanks to Scott Marion and Lorrie Shepard for their review comments.

Note

1. The POWERSOURCE© is copyrighted by the Regents of the University of California. The work reported herein was supported under the Educational Research and Development Centers Program, PR/Award Number R305B960002 and Award Number R305A050004, as administered by the Institute of Education Sciences, U.S. Department of Education. The findings and opinions expressed in this report do not reflect the positions or policies of the National Center for Education Research, the Institute of Education Sciences, or the U.S. Department of Education.

References

American Educational Research Association, American Psychological Association, and National Council on Measurement in Education. (1999). *Standards for educational and psychological testing.* Washington, DC: American Educational Research Association.

Baker, E. L. (1973). The technology of instructional development. In R. M. W. Travers (Ed.), *Second handbook of research on teaching* (pp. 245–285). Chicago, IL: Rand McNally.

Baker, E. L. (1982). Writing prompts: Integrating assessment and teaching. In A. Purves & S. Takala (Eds.), *An international perspective on the evaluation of written composition* (pp. 33–46). Oxford: Pergamon Press.

Baker, E. L. (1994). Learning-based assessments of history understanding [Special Issue]. *Educational Psychologist,* 29 (2), 97–106.

Baker, E. L. (2003, April). Templates, objects, and assessment models: We're not in Kansas anymore. Presentation at the annual meeting of the American Educational Research Association, Chicago, IL.

Baker, E. L. & Mayer, R. E. (1999). Computer-based assessment of problem solving. *Computers in Human Behavior,* 15 (3/4), 269–282.

Baker, E. L., Chung, G. K. W. K., & Delacruz, G. C. (2008). Design and validation of technology-based performance assessments. In J. M. Spector, M. D. Merrill, J. J. G. van Merriënboer, & M. P. Driscoll (Eds.), *Handbook of research on educational communications and technology* (3rd ed., pp. 595–604). Mahwah, NJ: Erlbaum.

Baker, E. L., Herman, J. L., & Linn, R. L. (2004, November). *Center for Research on Evaluation, Standards, and Student Testing. RFA Goal: One–assessment, standards, and accountability* (Proposal submitted to the U.S. Department of Education, Institute of Education Sciences). Los Angeles, CA: University of California, National Center for Research on Evaluation, Standards, and Student Testing (CRESST).

Baker, E. L., Niemi, D., Herl, H., Aguirre-Muñoz, Z., Staley, L., & Linn, R. L. (1996). *Report on the content area performance assessments (CAPA): A collaboration among the Hawaii Department of Education, the Center for Research on Evaluation, Standards, and Student Testing (CRESST) and the teachers and children of Hawaii* (Final Deliverable). Los Angeles, CA: University of California, National Center for Research on Evaluation, Standards, and Student Testing.

Bassok, M. & Holyoak, K. J. (1989). Transfer of domain-specific problem solving procedures. *Journal of Experimental Psychology: Learning, Memory, and Cognition*, 16, 522–533.

Bereiter, C. & Scardamalia, M. (1987). *The psychology of written composition.* Hillsdale, NJ: Erlbaum.

Bjork, E. L., deWinstanley, P. A., & Storm, B. C. (2007). Learning how to learn: Can experiencing the outcome of different encoding strategies enhance subsequent encoding? *Psychonomic Bulletin and Review*, 14 (2), 207–211.

Black, P. & Wiliam, D. (1998). Assessment and classroom learning. *Assessment in Education: Principles, Policy and Practice*, 5 (1), 7–73.

Boekaerts, M., Pintrich, P. R., & Zeidner, M. (Eds.). (2000). *Handbook of self-regulation.* San Diego, CA: Academic Press.

Bransford, J. D. & Schwartz, D. L. (1999). Rethinking transfer: A simple proposal with multiple implications. In A. Iran-Nejad & P. D. Pearson (Eds.), *Review of research in education* (Vol. 24, pp. 61–100). Washington, DC: American Educational Research Association.

Burstall, C. (1986). Innovative forms of assessment: A United Kingdom perspective. *Educational Measurement: Issues and Practice*, 5 (1), 17–22.

Campione, J. C. & Brown, A. L. (1990). Guided learning and transfer: Implications for approaches to assessment. In N. Frederiksen, R. Glaser, A. Lesgold, & M. G. Shafto (Eds.), *Diagnostic monitoring of skill and knowledge acquisition* (pp. 141–172). Hillsdale, NJ: Erlbaum.

Chi, M. T. H. (2000). Self-explaining: The dual processes of generating inference and repairing mental models. In R. Glaser (Ed.), *Advances in instruction psychology* (Vol. 5, pp. 161–238). Mahwah, NJ: Erlbaum.

Chi, M. T. H. & VanLehn, K. (1991). The content of physics self-explanations. *Journal of the Learning Sciences*, 1 (1), 69–106.

Chi, M. T. H. & VanLehn, K. (2007). Domain-specific and domain-independent interactive behaviors in Andes. In R. Luckin, K. R. Koedinger, & J. Greer (Eds.), *Artificial intelligence in education* (pp. 548–550). Amsterdam, Netherlands: IOS Press.

Chi, M. T. H., Glaser, R. & Farr, M. (Eds.). (1988). *The nature of expertise.* Hillsdale, NJ: Erlbaum.

Choi, K. (2006, April). A new value-added model with an educational gap parameter capturing the distribution of student growth using multi-site multiple-cohort longitudinal data. Paper presented at the annual meeting of the American Educational Research Association, San Francisco, CA.

Chung, G. K. W. K., Niemi, D., & Bewley, W. L. (2003a, April). Assessment applications of ontologies. Paper presented at the annual meeting of the American Educational Research Association, Chicago, IL.

Chung, G. K. W. K., Shel, T. C., & Kaiser, W. J. (2006). An exploratory study of a novel online formative assessment and instructional tool to promote students' circuit problem solving. *Journal of Technology, Learning, and Assessment*, 5 (6). Online, available at: http://escholarship.bc.edu/jtla/vol5/6/ (accessed August 20, 2007).

Chung, G. K. W. K., Delacruz, G. C., Dionne, G. B., & Bewley, W. L. (2003b). Linking assessment and instruction using ontologies. *Proceedings of the I/ITSEC*, 25, 1,811–1,822.

Cronbach, L. J. & Snow, R. E. (1977). *Aptitudes and instructional methods.* New York: Halsted Press.

Cronbach, L. J. & Suppes, P. (Eds.). (1969). *Research for tomorrow's schools: Disciplined inquiry for education*. Stanford, CA/New York: National Academy of Education, Committee on Educational Research/Macmillan.

Cronbach, L. J., Linn, R. L., Brennan, R. L, & Haertel, E. H. (1997). Generalizability analysis for performance assessments of student achievement or school effectiveness. *Educational and Psychological Measurement*, 57, 373–399.

Dang, S. (2007, August 15). Math, English STAR test results flat. *Alameda Times Star*. Online, available at: http://www.insidebayarea.com (accessed August 20, 2007).

Darling-Hammond, L. (2000). Teacher quality and student achievement: A review of state policy evidence. *Education Policy Analysis Archives*, 8 (1). Online, available at: http://epaa.asu.edu/epaa/v8n1/ (accessed August 21, 2007).

Donovan, M. S., Bransford, J. D., & Pellegrino, J. W. (Eds.). (1999). *How people learn: Bridging research and practice*. Washington, DC: National Academy Press.

Ericsson, K. A. & Simon, H. A. (1984). *Protocol analysis: Verbal reports as data*. Cambridge, MA: MIT Press.

Fuller, B. & Wright, J. (2007). Parallel play—Preschool and K-12 finance reform in New Jersey and Texas (Working Paper 07–3). Berkeley, CA: University of California, Policy Analysis for California Education.

Gagné, R. M. (1985). *The conditions of learning and theory of instruction* (4th ed.). New York: Holt, Rinehart and Winston.

Gardner, H. (1992). Assessment in context: The alternative to standardized testing. In B. R. Gifford & M. C. O'Connor (Eds.), *Future assessments: Changing views of aptitude, achievement, and instruction* (pp. 77–119). Boston, MA: Kluwer.

Glaser, R. (1963). Instructional technology and the measurement of learning outcomes: Some questions. *American Psychologist*, 18 (8), 519–521.

Goldschmidt, P. & Martínez-Fernández, J.-F. (2007). Relationships among measures as empirical evidence of validity: Multiple indicators of achievement and incorporating school context. *Educational Assessment*, 12 (3/4), 239–266.

Gong, B. & Reidy, E. (1996). Assessment and accountability in Kentucky's school reform. In J. N. Baron & D. P. Wolf (Eds.), *Performance-based student assessment: Challenges and possibilities* (Ninety-fifth Yearbook of the National Society for the Study of Education, Part 1) (pp. 215–233). Chicago, IL: National Society for the Study of Education (distributed by the University of Chicago Press).

Greeno, J., Collins, A., & Resnick, L. (1996). Cognition and learning. In D. Berliner & R. Calfee (Eds.), *Handbook of educational psychology*. New York: Simon & Schuster Macmillan.

Hambleton, R., Jager, R., Koretz, D., Linn, R., Millman, J., & Phillips, S. (1995). *Review of the measurement quality of the Kentucky instructional results information system, 1991–1994*. Frankfort, KY: Office of Education Accountability, Kentucky General Assembly.

Herman, J. L., Gearhart, M., & Baker, E. L. (1993). Assessing writing portfolios: Issues in the validity and meaning of scores. *Educational Assessment*, 1 (3), 201–224.

Hively, W., Patterson, H. L., & Page, S. H. (1968). A "universe-defined" system of arithmetic achievement tests. *Journal of Educational Measurement*, 5 (4), 275–290.

Hunt, E. & Minstrell, J. (1994). A cognitive approach to the teaching of physics. In K. McGilly (Ed.), *Classroom lessons: Integrating cognitive theory and classroom practice* (pp. 51–74). Cambridge, MA: MIT Press.

Improving America's Schools Act of 1994, Pub. L. No. 103–382, 108 Stat. 3518 (1994).

Jago, C. (2003). The national writing project: A best idea from James Gray. *Voices from the Middle*, 10 (4), 31–32.

Jennings, J. & Rentner, D. S. (2006). Ten big effects of the No Child Left Behind Act on public schools. *Phi Delta Kappan*, 88 (2), 110–113.

Kalyuga, S. (2006). Rapid cognitive assessment of learners' knowledge structures. *Learning and Instruction*, 16 (1), 1–11.

Koedinger, K. R. & Anderson, J. R. (1998). Illustrating principled design: The early evolution of a cognitive tutor for algebra symbolization. *Interactive Learning Environments*, 5 (2), 161–180.

Koretz, D., Linn, R. L., Dunbar, S. B., & Shepard, L. A. (1991, April). The effects of high-stakes testing on achievement: Preliminary findings about generalization across tests. Paper presented at the annual meeting of the American Educational Research Association, Chicago, IL.

Linn, R. L., Baker, E. L., & Dunbar, S. B. (1991). Complex, performance-based assessment: Expectations and validation criteria. *Educational Researcher*, 20 (8), 15–21.

Lumsdaine, A. A. & Glaser, R. (Eds.). (1960). *Teaching machines and programmed learning: A source book*. Washington, DC: National Education Association of the United States.

Marshall, S. P. (1995). *Schemas in problem-solving*. New York: Cambridge University Press.

Mayer, R. E. (2003). *Learning and instruction*. Upper Saddle River, NJ: Merrill Prentice Hall.

Means, B. & Gott, S. P. (1988). Cognitive task analysis as a basis for tutor development: Articulating abstract knowledge representations. In J. Psotka, L. D. Massey, & S. A. Mutter (Eds.), *Intelligent tutoring systems: Lessons learned* (pp. 35–57). Hillsdale, NJ: Erlbaum.

Merrill, M. D. (2000). Knowledge objects and mental-models. In D. A. Wiley (Ed.), *The instructional use of learning objects* [online version]. Online, available at: http://www.reusability.org/read/chapters/merrill.doc (accessed August 23, 2007).

Messick, S. (1989). Validity. In R. L. Linn (Ed.), *Educational measurement* (3rd ed., pp. 13–103). New York: Macmillan.

Miller, G. A. (1995, November). WordNet: A lexical database for English. *Communications of the ACM*, 38 (11), 39–41.

Mislevy, R. J. (1996). Test theory reconceived. *Journal of Educational Measurement*, 33 (4), 379–416.

Mislevy, R. J., Almond, R. G., & Steinberg, L. S. (1998). *A note on knowledge-based model construction in educational assessment* (CSE Tech. Rep. No. 480). Los Angeles, CA: University of California, National Center for Research on Evaluation, Standards, and Student Testing (CRESST).

National Center for Research on Evaluation, Standards, and Student Testing (CRESST). (2007). *The development and impact of POWERSOURCE©: Progress report year 2* (Deliverable to IES). Los Angeles, CA: University of California, CRESST.

National Center on Education and the Economy (U.S.). New Commission on the Skills of the American Workforce. (2007). *Tough choices or tough times: The report of the New Commission on the Skills of the American Workforce*. San Francisco, CA: John Wiley.

National Council of Teachers of Mathematics. (1989). *Curriculum and evaluation standards for school mathematics*. Reston, VA: National Council of Teachers of Mathematics.

National Council on Education Standards and Testing. (1992). *Raising standards for American education*. Washington, DC: U.S. Government Printing Office (ERIC Document Reproduction Service No. ED338721).

National Education Goals Panel. (1993). *The national education goals report: Building a nation of learners. Volume one: The national report*. Washington, DC: U.S. Government Printing Office.

Newmann, F. M. (1991). Linking restructuring to authentic student achievement. *Phi Delta Kappan*, 72 (6), 458–463.

No Child Left Behind Act of 2001, Pub. L. No. 107–110, 115 Stat. 1425 (2002).

Nuttall, D. L. (1991). *Assessment in England*. London: Centre for Educational Research, London School of Economics and Political Science.

Paas, F., Renkl, A., & Sweller, J. (2003). Cognitive load theory and instructional design: Recent developments. *Educational Psychologist*, 38 (1), 1–4.

Pellegrino, J., Chudowsky, N., & Glaser, R. (Eds.). (2001) *Knowing what students know: The science and design of educational assessment*. Washington, DC: National Academy Press.

Price, H. B. (2007). Demilitarizing what the Pentagon knows about developing young people: A new paradigm for educating students who are struggling in school and in life (CCF Working Paper). Washington, DC: Brookings Institution, Center on Children and Families. Online, available at: http://www.brookings.edu/views/papers/price200705.htm (accessed August 23, 2007).

Purves, A. & Takala, S. (1982). *An international perspective on the evaluation of written composition*. Oxford: Pergamon Press.

Resnick, L. B. & Resnick, D. P. (1992). Assessing the thinking curriculum: New tools for educational reform. In B. G. Giford & M. C. O'Conner (Eds.), *Changing assessments: Alternative*

views of aptitude, achievement and instruction (pp. 37–75). Boston, MA: Kluwer Academic Publishers.
Rohrer, D. & Pashler, H. (2007). Increasing retention without increasing study time. *Current Directions in Psychological Science*, 16 (4), 183–186.
Rumelhart, D. E. & Norman, D. A. (1985). Analogical processes in learning. In J. R. Anderson (Ed.), *Cognitive skills and their acquisition* (pp. 335–359). Hillsdale, NJ: Erlbaum.
Shepard, L. A. (2000, October). The role of assessment in a learning culture. *Educational Researcher*, 29 (7), 4–14.
Sweller, J. (1999). *Instructional design in technical areas*. Camberwell, Australia: ACER Press.
Tatsuoka, K. K. (1995). Architecture of knowledge structures and cognitive diagnosis: A statistical pattern recognition and classification approach. In P. D. Nichols, S. F. Chipman, & R. L. Brennan (Eds.), *Cognitively diagnostic assessment* (pp. 327–359). Hillsdale, NJ: Erlbaum.
Tobias, S. & Fletcher, D. (Eds.). (2000). *Training and retraining: A handbook for business, industry, government and the military*. New York: Macmillan.
Treisman, P. U. (1990). Teaching mathematics to a changing population: The Professional Development Program at the University of California, Berkeley. Part I. A study of the mathematics performance of black students at the University of California, Berkeley. In N. Fisher, H. Keynes, & P. Wagreich (Eds.), *Mathematicians and education reform* (pp. 33–46). Washington, DC: American Mathematical Society.
Vygotsky, L. S. (1962). *Thought and language*. New York: Wiley.
Wenger, E. (1987). *Artificial intelligence and tutoring systems: Computational and cognitive approaches to the communication of knowledge*. Los Altos, CA: Morgan Kaufmann.
Wiley, D. A. (Ed.). (2000). *The instructional use of learning objects* [Online version]. Online, available at: http://www.reusability.org/read/ (accessed August 23, 2007).
Wirtz, W. & Lapointe, A. (1982). *Measuring the quality of education: A report on assessing educational progress*. Washington, DC: Wirtz and Lapointe.

16

Future Directions for Educational Accountability

Notes for a Political Economy of Measurement

Michael J. Feuer

For laypersons who innocently wander into the murky terrain of educational accountability and pose outwardly simple questions such as "how are our schools doing?" the professional research community's response often sounds like it was scripted by that great American philosopher, Casey Stengel. New Yorkers in particular may remember with affection how the legendary Yankee baseball manager could lapse into endlessly labyrinthian answers to seemingly straightforward questions. Asked by Senator Estes Kefauver (Democrat, Tennessee) about antitrust law and baseball, Casey took the Senators in attendance at a 1958 hearing on an extended autobiographical tour, including side trips along the scenic byways of the philosophy of sport, syntheses of his accumulated erudition on capitalism and white collar crime, opinions about the essence of performance measurement drawn from his 48 years in baseball, and pronouncements on the comparative virtues of life in the USA, Europe, and South America—but in 45 minutes never quite answered the original question. (Mickey Mantle was up next, and when asked the same question brought the house down: "my views are about the same as Casey's.") (Baseball Almanac, n.d.).

Why are responses to seemingly simple questions about educational performance frequently so dense? The answer lies partly in a paradox of measurement: the simplicity of test scores—higher numbers usually are better than lower ones—masks complex psychological and statistical theories upon which those scores are based. There is virtue in parsimony, which is one reason test scores offer such an attractive abbreviation of complex phenomena like teaching and learning. But the fact that scores are just that, abbreviations or estimates, is often forgotten, as is the possibility that the way scores are reported and used can distort their accuracy. Measurement experts who are aware of this dilemma tend to be humble about the precision of scores and typically exercise caution when explaining their meaning; interpreting simple-looking test results turns out to be a fairly complicated matter.

In this chapter I focus on one cause of the measurement paradox: behavioral responses to testing by teachers and students can compromise the validity and meaning of scores and undermine their uses in accountability. If conventional psychometrics is largely about the measurement of behavior, my interest here is with the *behavior of measures*: how is their validity affected by their application? This is not a new question in the educational measurement literature (see, e.g., the discussion of score inflation, an effect of what I refer to as behavioral responses to testing, in Linn's chapter in this volume; Koretz, 2002, and this volume; Messick, 1988; Shepard, 2002). But, I approach it here from a different angle.

I focus on the intended and unintended consequences of test-based accountability and borrow from selected themes in political economy: incomplete information, market imperfections, measurement errors, the presence of "externalities," limits to human information-processing capacity, and the effects of opportunism on rational self-interest seeking. *If political economy is largely about the measurement of externalities, my interest here is in the externalities of measurement.* My argument ends with two conclusions: I propose (but do not prove) a theorem that states that there is no accountability system that can optimally satisfy a plausible set of acceptable conditions. Though perhaps depressing on the surface (yes, economics is still a dismal science...), my second conclusion is more optimistic: *reasonable* goals for educational accountability, including rational uses of standardized tests, are both feasible and desirable. This chapter is meant as a first set of notes for what may eventually become more formal theory. I introduce assumptions, terms, and explanations of selected concepts in political economy, and offer extensions and analogies to education generally and test-based accountability specifically. I argue for a "procedurally rational" approach to educational accountability, including suggestions for the policy and research agenda.

Accountability: Politics and Markets

Democracy thrives on public accountability. Because resources for public goods and services are collected through a taxation system that requires "mutually acceptable coercion" (Olson, 1965) and are allocated through the politics of the budgetary process (e.g., Wildavsky, 1974), the sustainability of public goods such as education, clean air, defense, and transportation hinges on evidence that public money is spent efficiently and equitably. A core principle of tax policy is enshrined in our Declaration of Independence: government derives its powers from the consent of the governed. This tenet prescribes an implicit—and increasingly explicit—compact regarding the collection and allocation of public funds.

Electoral politics provides a first line of defense against coercive taxation and spending sprees that violate public preferences and ethical norms, but the ballot box alone is an inadequate disciplining mechanism—political authority systems have "strong thumbs but no fingers" (Lindblom, 1977). Eventually, the stewards of public funds who behave badly are (we hope) thrown out of office, suggesting a powerful, albeit delayed, incentive apparatus. Even while in power, though, they are held accountable for performance through a variety of formal and informal devices. Formal mechanisms include legislative hearings, regulations that circumscribe behavior *ex ante*, and disclosure of spending records and other performance-related data *ex post*. Probably the most important informal mechanism is a strong and independent press, the disciplining power of which is based on the fact that disclosure of information is itself a tool of accountability because it affects behavior even without formal rewards and sanctions.

Markets, unlike political systems, theoretically run on the unregulated transactions between atomistic buyers and sellers. Accountability is assumed through a different mechanism than in political or bureaucratic systems, but still depends heavily on information about performance and quality (e.g., Baumol & Blackman, 1991; Varian, 1999; Nordhaus & Samuelson, 1985). Price is a proxy for value, and quality is assured via incentives to maintain market share and maximize profit: *caveat emptor* and *caveat venditor* are symmetric forces that keep markets alive. Absent explicit rules regarding quality and price of goods and services, collective welfare is assumed to be maximized through incentives that govern the behavior of producers and consumers (this is a much abridged version of competition theory; see, e.g., Smith, 1776).

Advanced market economies, however, do not rely solely on implicit modes of accountability for perhaps obvious reasons: information is imperfect and sometimes intentionally distorted, economic actors may stretch the limits of ethical behavior in pursuit of self-interest, private behavior has both intended and unintended consequences (externalities), and society is too risk averse to rely completely on tacit or *ex post* regulatory schemes. Thus, *ex ante* enforcement of securities laws (e.g., mandatory filing of annual reports), regulation and restraint of economic behavior that can otherwise produce negative externalities (e.g., limits on toxic emissions), and requirements for labeling of product ingredients and known side effects of approved drugs, are examples of accountability mechanisms that characterize modern regulated capitalism (e.g., Williamson, 1985).

Economic theory exalts markets, but is anxious about their viability. Proponents of market solutions often forget that the literature of market *failure* is as rich—and at least as compelling—as the literature of competitive equilibrium (e.g., Arrow, 1974). In the modern economy the management of externalities has evolved well beyond the stage of relying exclusively on stringent *ex ante* regulations, and instead relies on innovations based on assumptions about individual and organizational incentives and responses. Environmental economics, for example, suggests that taxing polluting firms is more efficient and has better social effects than setting limits to production (e.g., Portney & Stavins, 2000; Coase, 1988).

Education as a Public Good

Educational accountability in its various modes is part of the broader family of arrangements designed to instill discipline in the quality and provision of public goods. Test-based accountability may appear to be a relatively recent addition to the toolkit of educational policy and governance (e.g., Levin, 1974), but in fact its roots can be found in common school reforms of the early nineteenth century that reflected legal and philosophical principles of the new Republic—in particular, notions of diffused governance and "checks and balances" (Feuer, 2006; Kaestle, 1983; Office of Technology Assessment (OTA), 1992; Tyack, 1974).

From the earliest applications of uniform written examinations *circa* 1840, standardized testing has been viewed as an objective antidote to authoritarian and discriminatory instincts and as an apparatus of the so-called meritocracy. But as part of the broader family of mental measures, educational tests (especially those in standardized and multiple-choice formats) have always been suspected of bias and have been held at least partially responsible for the perpetuation of educational and socioeconomic inequalities (Cronbach, 1975). An unresolved dilemma regarding educational tests is whether the measurement of individual and group differences inadvertently (or purposely) perpetuates those differences.

In political economy terms, testing is a technology (e.g., Madaus, 2001) and its benefits need to be weighed against its potential hazards: narrowing of the curriculum, misleading and inflated scores, excessive rote memorization of basic facts at the expense of deeper learning, reduction of educational goals to low minimum standards, and the misuse of student assessments in comparing the quality of schools (e.g., Koretz, 1992, 2005; OTA, 1992; Shepard, 2002). These negative effects are analogous to externalities or unintended negative effects of other technologies. I will argue later for greater consideration of lessons learned from policy treatments of other externalities, such as environmental protection, and how they might apply to reducing the negative consequences of test-based accountability (see also Heubert & Hauser, 1999).

The notion that test use has consequences is, of course, not new (e.g., Messick, 1988), but recasting it as a problem of externalities is. In a sense, test scores serve a purpose similar to quantitative measures and rankings that inform and guide consumer product markets. The problem is that test scores are a much weaker proxy for underlying academic knowledge and capacity than, say, miles-per-gallon is as an indicator of fuel efficiency of automobiles. Although test precision has improved thanks to a century of rigorous psychometric research, it is still the case that scores are estimates; they are imperfect measures of complex underlying constructs such as student learning or teacher and school quality. Whether the general public understands the inherent limitations on the validity and reliability of scores is a serious matter; indeed, as psychometric science has advanced and the reporting of scores has become more quantitatively rich, so too has the mistaken impression grown that scores are accurate scientific measures analogous to, say, the chemical composition of fluids or the physics of planetary motion. From the standpoint of the professional measurement community, which certainly does understand the bounds of precision, *scores are only useful as indicators to inform or guide decisionmaking*. Hence, the profession issues strong admonitions about relying on any one measure, especially for decisions that have significant consequences; whether those warnings are sufficiently heeded is another matter.

The nearly insatiable public appetite for quantitative evidence of school quality, the steady demand for accurate and fair disclosure of student and teacher performance, and the availability of relatively inexpensive mass-produced tests have all contributed to the rising concerns over growth of test-based accountability. Market instincts (self-interest seeking) of test producers coupled with the technical naïveté of government officials combine to produce an oversupply of tests with questionable psychometric properties and misleading score reports; yet, there is currently no governmental agency authorized to set and enforce standards on either the testing industry or the public testing bureaucracy. Some would argue that governments (national, state, local) have been largely responsible for the increased reliance on testing and standards, fueled largely by politicians' incentives to "get tough" about school reform. Yet, there has been little more than rhetoric about "holding the accountability system ... accountable."

Behavioral Responses to Accountability

At root, formal systems of accountability are necessary because individuals and organizations are tempted to distort information, shirk responsibility, under perform, and skew behavior toward their own self-interest and away from the public good. As the satirist Ambrose Bierce defined it almost a century ago, "accountability is the mother of caution" (Bierce, 1911). Utopian fantasies may be inspirational and soothing, but empirical evidence of human frailty is strong enough to suggest that the rise of accountability is not accidental. Rather, it is the invention of an advanced civilization keen on self-preservation. As I suggested earlier, market systems thrive on incentives and self-interest seeking; but they collapse without collective discipline (for arguments to the contrary, however, see, e.g., Friedman, 2002 and Hayek, 1944/2001).

It follows that systems designed to curb the negative effects of opportunism and manipulation may themselves be vulnerable to manipulation. The tax system, for example, is a highly complex legal architecture of accountability. Through its requirements for disclosure of detailed economic data, it holds individuals and businesses accountable. But the tax system, which not only raises needed public revenues but has grown into an increasingly complex machinery to keep economic transactions reasonably honest, is itself vulnerable to behavioral impulses that necessitate its existence in the first place. (Were it not for opportunistic self-interest seeking there would be no need for a mandatory system of taxation, as citizens would contribute voluntarily to the public welfare.)

Efforts to evade or undermine accountability systems are pervasive. In the case of taxation, we have a robust industry of accountants and lawyers whose livelihoods depend on helping clients pursue self-interest via tolerable manipulations of the law. Other examples abound: strategically incomplete disclosure of toxic emissions data by polluting companies, illegibly small print on drug labels, and concealing of data by tobacco companies are all too familiar. However, we have the Internal Revenue Service (IRS) and other government agencies to monitor this sort of behavior and enforce compliance with accountability rules. And it doesn't stop there: we have public authorities devoted to curbing the overzealous instincts of other public authorities charged with holding individuals and organizations in society accountable!

Efforts to circumvent (or "game") accountability systems reflect a capacity for advanced rational judgment and strategic behavior to increase the chances for personal gain. Insurance markets provide an example of an accountability system vulnerable to opportunistic distortion. An essential ingredient of insurance is the disclosure of objective and accurate indicators of risk, without which there can be no rational basis for setting prices (premiums) efficiently and fairly. But, cost-conscious people have incentives to conceal or misreport information selectively. Masking certain aspects of one's driving behavior, for example, seems like a rational and easy way to lower one's premiums. But, such behavior distorts the efficient and equitable operation of a free insurance market, and may ultimately lead to government-mandated rules and higher premiums for everyone (see, e.g., Williamson, 1975, for a lucid explanation of "adverse selection"). Once again, and contrary to narrow economic teaching about markets, individual self-interest does not always yield socially acceptable (let alone optimal) outcomes (e.g., Hardin, 1968; Schelling, 1978, 2006).

Games and Educational Accountability

There is ample evidence that educational accountability systems are vulnerable to gaming and strategic manipulation, but there has been little effort to compare the degree of fragility to other accountability systems. Manipulation ranging from possibly acceptable coaching to outright cheating (Koretz, 2002, 2005, and this volume; Linn, this volume) is predictable (especially because it has already been documented). *As government-mandated accountability testing increases, so then does the need to hold the accountability system accountable.* At present, however, there is no monitoring and enforcement agency with authority analogous to the IRS and other federal regulatory bodies; and to date there has been inadequate attention on the part of the policy research community to the design of regulatory mechanisms that would be more effective than reliance on self-imposed codes of ethics or repeated exhortations about "appropriate test use."

Scores on large-scale standardized tests are relatively weak proxies for the underlying constructs they measure compared, say, to the measured particulates in the air as a proxy for air quality. It follows that both the danger of manipulation and the size of the externalities may be greater for testing than for other accountability systems. Further, strategic gaming of test performance creates more complex externalities: not only does it hinder genuine improvement of teaching and learning (the putative purpose of the accountability system), but it undermines the long-term validity of the measures. Both the educational system and the accountability system are at risk, and the risks increase as the stakes associated with test results rise.

Intended and Unintended Behavioral Response

Accountability systems do more than account. The underlying theory of action in many accountability systems is that provision of information about behavior can have both direct and indirect effects. Direct effects come about through legal or other formal actions taken as a result of the information that is collected and reported. Indirect influences come about through the credible threat that certain information will be disclosed and possibly become the basis for decisions with important consequences. Chess players know that a threat is often more powerful than its execution (O. Feuer, personal communication, n.d.).

In most cases, accountability systems operate through an implicit coupling of both types of effects. Consider again the tax system: income data reported to the IRS can be the basis for formal audits, but it is also the *threat* of audit that influences both the underlying behavior and how it is reported (e.g., accurate reporting of permissible deductions taken for charitable contributions or other purposes). Another example of an accountability system with both direct and indirect effects is the measurement of driving speed on highways and local roads. Radar detection of speeding (never entrusted to voluntary disclosure, for obvious reasons) can lead to legal punitive action; but posted *warnings* of detection, even if the detection does not lead directly to action by the police, are intended to curb speeding *ex ante.* Gaming behavior vis-à-vis speed detection provides fresh insights about the efficacy of certain accountability mechanisms generally as well as in education specifically (Lazear, 2006).

All accountability measures are proxies, or estimates, of broader underlying behaviors of interest. For example, summary data on corporate performance in the form of price/earnings ratios provide approximations to the more complex totality of business transactions; detected speed of drivers is an indicator, a proxy intended to capture and signal in abridged form the complex combination of behaviors that add up to "safe" driving.

The strength (validity) of proxy or indicator measures and their immunity to gaming behavior are inversely related to their separation or distance from the underlying behavior of interest (the size of the externality, on the other hand, is directly related to the weakness of the proxy). For example, if the phenomenon of interest is defined as "likelihood of being a hazard on the road," then clearly measured speed provides a stronger signal than other physical attributes of the car or driver, such as the number of strange bumper stickers, even if the latter might vaguely be correlated with driving habits. *Signal-to-noise ratio* is not commonly mentioned in such discussions, but is a critical determinant of the quality and efficacy of accountability systems. Further, there is an inherent tradeoff between the complexity and validity of measures and their costs: the closer a proxy measure comes to representing authentically the underlying domain of which it is an estimate, the more expensive it is (currently, at least) to design, field test, and validate. The ideal indicator system would provide accurate proxy information at minimal cost.

Accountability measures are typically chosen with respect to objective criteria: for example, driving speed is interesting because of known technological relationships between a vehicle's speed and a driver's ability to control it under varying conditions. Accountability *standards*, too, are based at least in part on objective criteria: speed limits on local roads presumably are determined as a function of measurable relations between speed and danger. But such standards are also a function of behavioral norms; that is, empirical evidence about the performance of samples of drivers and the effects of speed on driver control and other variables. Pure "criterion-related" indicators—those without any underlying "norm-referencing"—are rare, especially when the phenomenon of interest defies simple definition and precise measurement.

In theory there are arguments for differential performance standard. For example, if it is known that certain cars can be driven at higher speeds because of technological improvements in stability, it would be plausible to imagine a system of differential speed limits for old and new cars. However, in practice, implementing such a system would incur high transaction costs and would appear to be unfair. A final observation about standards: setting standards in accountability systems requires sensitivity to their behavioral objectives and consequences. High standards reflect ambitious goals, but if set too high or out of reach they can be demoralizing and counterproductive.

Test Scores and Behavior

Well-designed and validated educational tests can provide useful proxy measures for underlying cognitive and behavioral phenomena of interest. Even large-scale and mass-produced standardized multiple-choice tests, often unfairly demonized by critics of testing, can yield valid and reliable indicators of achievement, and are not necessarily limited to trivial basic skills (e.g., OTA, 1992). But, scores on such tests need to be understood in terms of their limited purposes and as imperfect estimates of complex phenomena. For this and other reasons, professional testing norms caution against the use of any single measure to draw broad and significant inferences (e.g., American Educational Research Association, American Psychological Association, and National Council for Measurement in Education, 1999).

Tests that provide stronger and more complex measures of cognitive functioning are typically more expensive than tests of more limited domains (Pellegrino, Chudowsky, & Glaser, 2001). Economic constraints create incentives for multiple uses of existing testing technologies, although most tests are designed to provide only specific data and to support specific types of inferences. "Test misuse," which usually refers to the use of test scores to support inferences and decisions that go beyond those for which the test has been designed and validated, is an unfortunate but predictable consequence of the pursuit of economic efficiency. Dual and multi-use technologies have obvious appeal, a point often overlooked by critics of test policy. (It is futile to expect accountability systems to produce information that is hermetically shielded from unintended uses.)

Bad News: Impossibility

Implicit in my discussion is a set of goals for educational testing that may be mutually incompatible. Specifically, here is a list of conditions, or characteristics, of an optimal test-based accountability system:

- *domain robustness*: authentic criterion-based representations of complex cognitive functioning based on efficient domain sampling;
- *recursive stability:* immunity of scores to opportunistic behavioral responses and degradation of validity;
- *causal neutrality*: description of population differences without risk of implied attribution of cause and/or implied acceptance of lower standards or expectations for students traditionally at risk;
- *policy precision*: incentives for improved performance in desired domains without unintended degradation of performance in other domains;
- *instrument selectivity*: use of tests solely for the purposes for which they were designed and validated;

- *diagnostic generality*: measures of aggregate performance (or growth) based on population sampling that yield valid inferences for high-stakes individual-level decisions;
- *minimal burden*: comprehensive information based on multiple measures within constraints on budget and testing time; and,
- *rational exuberance*: standards set high enough to motivate public commitment to improvement without risk of cyclical disappointment and erosion of morale.

Can these conditions be met? My tentative answer, in the form of an impossibility theorem, is "no": *There is no test-based accountability system that maximizes the preceding conditions simultaneously.*

Good News: Procedural Rationality

Impossibility theorems (e.g., Arrow, 1963) are to political economy what perfect vacuums are to physics. By defining extremes they invite consideration of conditions that fall short of the extremes, and they call attention to the need for policy responses in an imperfect world. In this spirit, my assertion of the impossibility of designing an educational accountability system that can satisfy a minimal set of conditions should not be taken as a prima facie case for abandoning test-based accountability. Rather, I hope it generates a more moderate set of expectations and a way to reframe the accountability debate in terms of realistic options.

My baseline assumptions are: (i) accountability is inevitable, (ii) testing can produce social benefits and negative externalities, and (iii) no accountability system will be perfect. Therefore, the goal should be to find *reasonably good* accountability policies—rather than be perpetually disappointed by the failure to find *optimal* ones. This approach applies the notion of "procedural rationality" (Feuer, 2006; Simon, 1976).

What lessons from the analysis and management of analogous externality situations can be imported to educational accountability? To begin, we need better measures of both the magnitude and distribution of the externalities associated with test-based accountability. What we currently know—that undesired behaviors can result from distorted or perverse incentives associated with high-stakes testing—is necessary, but not sufficient as a basis for policy without at least several additional pieces of information. Are the costs (negative consequences) of the testing always greater than the benefits (e.g., Hartigan & Wigdor, 1989)? Are certain groups of students or teachers necessarily disproportionately harmed by the externalities? The same logic holds for specific aspects of testing, for example the problem of test score linkage and equivalency and the quest for a single scale upon which to order results from multiple tests (Feuer, Holland, Green, Bertenthal, & Hemphill, 1999).

Similarly, we need reliable measures of the counterfactual: what would be the magnitude and distribution of externalities associated with the *elimination* of testing as a tool of accountability?

Finally, we need to become more rigorous in modeling the possibility of unintended *positive* consequences; that is, the possibility that some externalities might be welcome. We know that some policies (not related to accountability) yield what might be called "pleasant surprises," and we should keep our minds open to the possibility that even test-based accountability might produce some unanticipated good. This requires a nontrivial temperamental shift, especially given the penchant of social scientists to focus on program flaws, imperfections, and the tragedy of unintended negative consequences (Hirschmann, 1991).

It is important to note that these suggestions all involve more measurement, which is likely to suffer from many of the imperfections inherent in the measurement system that we are trying to remedy in the first place. It would be disingenuous to suggest, suddenly, that measures of the magnitude, distribution, and potential benefit of externalities of accountability are more accurate than the measures in testing that are the source of the externalities. The idea is not, however, to seek perfect or optimal measures of the externalities, but rather to find reasonably good ones that provide at least some basis for improved decisions and correction of at least some of the error (this is the essence of the "procedurally rational" approach).

To cope with externalities, modern democracies use a combination of upstream and downstream strategies. Upstream here has two meanings: first, it denotes *ex ante* specification of allowable externalities (e.g., acceptable toxic emission levels from industrial plants or carbon dioxide rules for new cars). Second, it denotes innovative forms of production that are designed to reduce, if not eliminate, externalities in the first place. An example of upstream policy is the establishment of the Corporation for Public Broadcasting (CPB), intended as an innovative organizational remedy for the increasingly commercial and arguably low quality programming of mainstream television. Similarly, public–private partnerships for urban housing rehabilitation, community-based environmental protection, and funding of the fine arts can be viewed as efforts to establish upstream alternatives preferable to pure commercial systems at least from the standpoint of predictable externalities. The meaning of downstream is essentially *ex post*; that is, the implementation of policies to correct externalities or compensate victims after the fact or both. The most obvious downstream strategy to deal with unintended negative consequences of private behavior is tort law and the complex apparatus of litigation, which theoretically enables compensation to victims of production externalities of various sorts.

The future of educational accountability would be more pleasant to anticipate if resources were made available to design and experiment with innovative policies aimed at reducing unwanted externalities and promoting desired positive ones. In the upstream category I recommend the establishment of a Corporation for Public Accountability (CPA) modeled loosely after the CPB; its mandate would be to produce useful tests—and other accountability instruments—without the usual pressures of market share and profit maximization. Its board would consist of experts and stakeholders, its staff would include public-minded testmakers and evaluators, and its products would be made available competitively to states and localities seeking alternatives to cheap off-the-shelf tests of questionable quality. The CPA would become for educational (and presumably other) testing what CPB has become for television: a source for alternative programming based on combined public and private inputs.

Downstream strategies are more difficult to contemplate. For example, because negative effects of testing are not equitably distributed, it would be tempting to compensate individuals who shoulder a disproportionate part of the error burden. But such a strategy has obvious complexities that may make it impossible to enact. A conversation about how we might better identify and possibly compensate unintended victims of accountability could be informative as part of a broader conversation about lessons from other strategies for dealing with externalities. Models from political economy of environmental protection, energy, food and drug labeling, business accounting, and so forth, will most likely not be directly applicable but are worth considering.

One of the most important improvements to the future of educational accountability would come from the recognition by policymakers that tests are not the only instrument appropriate for answering the public's legitimate concerns about the quality of teaching, the relevance of the curriculum, the extent to which schools prepare young people for productive futures, and the risks of unmonitored schools. Lessons from other sectors—and other countries—would be worth learning, even if they are not instantly and wholly importable. For example, the externality associated with the risk of nuclear energy is not, thankfully, controlled by pure market forces and *ex post* measurement of radiation and adjudication of responsibility, nor by periodic evaluations based on statistical samples of radioactive output. On-site inspections, certification of employees based on knowledge and personality traits, and other active (*ex ante*) approaches that do not rely exclusively on proxy estimates of performance and output are very much part of the system. Surely these models are not perfect, but they do represent a more procedurally rational effort to collect, analyze, and act upon complex and incomplete data as a means toward achieving important social outcomes.

Finally, a word about rhetoric: regardless of what measures are used and how information about performance is gathered, more care should be taken in the articulation of goals and the interpretation of evidence. Lofty statements may be needed to jolt an otherwise complacent public into concerted action; the example of *A Nation at Risk* (Commission on Excellence in Education, 1983) stands out for its long-term influence on the political psyche of school reform. On the other hand, education reform requires a steady hand and delayed gratification; setting expectations that exceed even the most optimistic estimates of the capacity of the system to improve may do more harm than good in the long run. As I have argued (Feuer, 2006), policymakers and researchers need a compact about their respective rhetoric; and although knowing where to set the dial between complacency and exuberance is no trivial matter, it is worthy of our attention as we face a future of imperfect but continuing educational accountability.

Acknowledgments

The author acknowledges with much thanks constructive criticisms of an earlier draft from participants in the CRESST conference, and from Lorrie Shepard, Bob Mislevy, and Katherine Ryan for superb editorial and substantive suggestions. Responsibility for the final product, of course, remains with me. The opinions in this chapter are the author's solely, and do not necessarily represent the positions of the National Research Council, the National Academy of Sciences, or its constituent boards.

References

American Educational Research Association, American Psychological Association, and National Council for Measurement in Education. (1999). *The standards for educational and psychological testing*, Washington, DC: American Educational Research Association.

Arrow, K. J. (1963). *Social choice and individual values*, New York: Wiley.

Arrow, K. J. (1974). Organization and information. In K. J. Arrow (Ed.), *The limits of organization* (pp. 33–43). New York: Norton.

Baseball Almanac. (n.d.). *Casey Stengel testimony: July 8, 1958 Senate anti-trust and monopoly subcommittee hearing*. Online, available at: http://www.baseball-almanac.com/quotes/casey_stengel_senate_testimony.shtml (accessed February 18, 2008).

Baumol, W. J. & Blackman, S. A. (1991). *Perfect markets and easy virtue: Business ethics and the invisible hand*, Cambridge, MA: Blackwell.

Bierce, A. (1911). *The devil's dictionary*. Online, available at: http://www.thedevilsdictionary.com/ (accessed February 18, 2008).

Coase, R. (1988). *The firm, the market, and the law*, Chicago, IL: University of Chicago Press.

Commission on Excellence in Education. (1983). *A nation at risk*, Washington, DC: U.S. Government Printing Office.

Cronbach, L. (1975). Five decades of public controversy over mental testing. *American Psychologist*, 30, 1–14.

Feuer, M. J. (2006). *Moderating the debate: Rationality and the promise of American education*. Cambridge, MA: Harvard Education Press.

Feuer, M. J., Holland, P. W., Green, B. F., Bertenthal, M. W., & Hemphill, F. C. (Eds.). (1999). *Uncommon measures: Equivalence and linkage among educational tests*. Washington, DC: National Academy Press.

Friedman, M. (2002). *Capitalism and freedom*. Chicago, IL: University of Chicago Press.

Hardin, G. (1968). The tragedy of the commons. *Science*, 162, 1,243–1,248.

Hartigan, J. & Wigdor, A. (Eds.). (1989). *Fairness in employment testing: Validity generalization, minority issues, and the General Aptitude Test Battery*. Washington, DC: National Academy Press.

Hayek, F. A. von. (2001). *The road to serfdom* (Routledge Classics). London: Routledge.
Heubert, J. P. & Hauser, R. M. (Eds.). (1999). *High stakes: Testing for tracking, promotion, and graduation.* Washington, DC: National Academy Press.
Hirschmann, A. (1991). *The rhetoric of reaction.* Cambridge, MA: Harvard University Press.
Kaestle, C. (1983). *Pillars of the republic: Common schools and American society, 1780–1860.* New York: Hill and Wang.
Koretz, D. (1992). What happened to test scores, and why? *Educational Measures: Issues and Practice*, 11 (4), 7–11.
Koretz, D. (2002). Limitations in the use of achievement tests as measures of educators' productivity. *Journal of Human Resources*, 37 (4), 752–777.
Koretz, D. (2005). Alignment, high stakes, and the inflation of test scores. In J. Herman and E. Haertel (Eds.), *Uses and misuses of data in accountability testing* (Yearbook of the National Society for the Study of Education) (pp. 99–118). Malden, MA: Blackwell.
Lazear, E. P. (2006). Speeding, tax fraud, and teaching to the test. *Quarterly Journal of Economics*, 121 (3), 1,029–1,061.
Levin, H. (1974). A conceptual framework for accountability in education. *School Review*, 82 (3), 363–391.
Lindblom, C. E. (1977). *Politics and markets: The world's political economic systems.* New York: Basic Books.
Madaus, G. (2001). Educational testing as a technology. *National Board on Educational Testing and Public Policy Statements*, 2 (1), 1–11. Online, available at: http://www.bc.edu/research/nbetpp/statements/NB_V2N1.pdf. (accessed February 18, 2008).
Messick, S. (1988). The once and future issues of validity: Assessing the meaning and consequences of measurement. In H. Braun & H. Wainer (Eds.), *Test validity* (pp. 33–45). Hillsdale, NJ: Lawrence Erlbaum Associates.
Nordhaus, W. & Samuelson, P. (1985). *Economics.* New York: McGraw-Hill.
Office of Technology Assessment. (1992). *Testing in American schools: Asking the right questions.* Washington, DC: U.S. Government Printing Office.
Olson, M. (1965). *The logic of collective action.* Cambridge, MA: Harvard University Press.
Pellegrino, J. W., Chudowsky, N., & Glaser, R. (Eds.). (2001). *Knowing what students know: The science and design of educational assessment.* Washington, DC: National Academy Press.
Portney, P. & Stavins, R. (2000). *Public policies for environmental protection* (2nd ed.). Washington, DC: RFF Press.
Schelling, T. C. (1978). *Micromotives and macrobehavior.* New York: Norton.
Schelling, T. C. (2006). *Strategies of commitment and other essays.* Cambridge, MA: Harvard University Press.
Shepard, L. A. (2002). Standardized tests and high-stakes assessment. In J. Guthrie (Ed.), *Encyclopedia of education* (Vol. 6, 2nd ed., pp. 2,533–2,537). New York: Macmillan Reference.
Simon, H. (1976). From substantive to procedural rationality. In S. J. Latsis (Ed.), *Method and appraisal in economics.* Cambridge: Cambridge University Press.
Smith, A. (1776). *An inquiry into the nature and causes of the wealth of nations.* Online, available at: http://www.adamsmith.org/smith/won-index.htm (accessed February 14, 2008).
Tyack, D. B. (1974). *The one best system: A history of American urban education.* Cambridge, MA: Harvard University Press.
Varian, H. R. (1999). *Intermediate microeconomics: A modern approach.* New York: W. W. Norton & Co.
Wildavsky, A. (1974). *The politics of the budgetary process.* Boston, MA: Little, Brown.
Williamson, O. E. (1975). *Markets and hierarchies: Analysis and antitrust implications.* New York: Free Press.
Williamson, O. E. (1985). *The economic institutions of capitalism: Firms, markets, relational contracting.* New York: Free Press.

Index

Printed in the United States
140754LV00002B/39/P

9 780805 864700